International Financial Markets and Institutions

Arvind K. Jain

Kolb Publishing Company
6395 Gunpark Dr., Suite N, Boulder, CO 80301
(303) 530-7778   FAX (303) 530-7773

For

Andrea, Bachay, Chipi, Gitanjali, Gitu, and Karen

Printed in the United States of America.

Library of Congress Catalog Card Number 94–76278

ISBN: 1–878975–44–7

K
KOLB
Kolb Publishing Company
6395 Gunpark Dr., Suite N, Boulder, CO 80301
(303) 530-7778   FAX (303) 530-7773

International Financial Markets and Institutions

Preface

Those studying international business are confronted with a unique problem: every scholar knows that international business is very different from domestic business, yet the scholarship in this field cannot lay a proprietary claim to a body of theoretical constructs. Although a large part of what we study as international business relies upon the foundations of one of the functional areas of management, most of the interesting and lasting work is interdisciplinary in nature, relying upon theories that have originated in a number of different fields.

Teachers in this field face a similar dilemma. On the one hand they must approach various aspects of international business from the perspective of one of the functional areas of management, and on the other hand, they must go beyond the confines of this functional area to discuss the working of international business in all its manifestations. The task of teaching international business is often made more complex than necessary because existing texts in this field fall in one of two categories, neither of which can satisfy a teacher who wants to give students a grasp of the theoretical principles underlying the material.

The first category consists of books written by experts in the functional area, and international extensions of the area are often relegated to the last two chapters of the book. Few are surprised when the end of the semester becomes more hectic than some had thought and the "international" chapters find themselves becoming "optional." The second category consists of books written for stand alone courses on the international extensions of one of the areas of management. While providing rich details of the international markets, these books sometimes fail to provide appropriate theoretical foundations for the discussions. Students who wish not to specialize in international business, but still want to understand how internationalization of business makes their operations more complex, have the difficult task of choosing between the two opposite approaches to the study of this material.

This book tries to bridge the gap between these two approaches. It presents the complexities as well as the economic principles of international financial markets for students who recognize that international markets are an integral part of financial markets in general, and not merely an appendage that can be used or not. It treating the international markets as part of the global capital markets, the book does not create a conceptual difference between domestic and international markets. Different segments of the financial markets are seen as responding to the same fundamental signals, albeit with differences in institutional details.

International Financial Markets and Institutions introduces readers to instruments, practices, and institutions of various segments of international financial markets. The book is divided into four parts. Part I, Fundamentals of International Financial Markets, and Part II, The International Capital Markets, consist of eight chapters and introduce the reader to various segments of these markets. Part III, Risk Management in International Markets, consists of four chapters and leads the reader through the principles of risk management in international financial markets. Part IV, in one chapter, focuses on financial institutions in international markets.

When possible, descriptive parts of a segment of international markets have been separated from more analytical parts. For the foreign exchange markets, for example, Chapter 2 describes the operations of the market and Chapter 3 the theory of exchange rates. Similarly, international equity markets are described in Chapter 7 and the theory pertaining to investment in these equities in Chapter 8. This will allow teachers with limited time to choose either the descriptive or the theoretical aspects of the international markets.

This book has two main audiences. First, the book is more suited than the traditional books on international finance for students who want to take only one course in the area of international finance. Most other texts concentrate on corporate financial management with only a scant attention to the international financial markets. This book covers the most important aspect of corporate management, (the management of foreign exchange risk), and also covers the international financial markets in detail. Both these aspects of finance—corporate management and financial markets—are equally important for students. Second, finance professors who have to concentrate most of their course on domestic financial markets can use this book as a supplemental text to cover the details of the international financial markets.

The book will not make an expert out of the reader; curious readers should be left with a lot of questions, accompanied by a desire to seek the answers to those questions. It will certainly not satisfy the curiosity of finance theorists, because questions of whether foreign exchange, international bond, and international equity markets are weak, semi–

strong, or strong form efficient are not included. Similarly, we have not examined the questions of whether or not the micro–structures of various segments of international markets are optimal from the point of view or efficiency. This book is really designed for a student of business organizations who understands the fundamental principles of finance and business and wants to learn about the additional opportunities offered by international markets.

Parts of this book are based on some of my research. The Social Sciences and Humanities Research Council in Ottawa provided funds which made possible the research in Chapters 3, 8, and 9. The Faculty Research and Development Program of Concordia University funded the research that helped produce the material in Chapter 13. Throughout the writing of this book, Annamma provided invaluable support, in addition to a critical first review of the writing. I am grateful to her and the two funding agencies for their support. I would also like to thank Bob Kolb for his patience with my delays, Kateri Davis who typeset the book and managed the production, Andrea Coens for her excellent editorial work, Kristina Rubish for her marketing efforts, Joe Rodriguez who designed the cover, and Sandi Schroeder for compiling the index.

A lot of thought has gone into deciding on the contents and organization of this book. That does not mean, however, that significant improvements are not going to take place in subsequent editions. I invite you to share your opinions, comments, and suggestions for improvements.

Arvind K. Jain

Contents

Chapter 3 The Theory of Exchange Rates   54

Chapter 4 Interest Rates in International Markets   95

Part II The International Capital Markets

Chapter 8 Diversification in International Markets 209

Part III Risk Management in International Markets

Chapter 9 The New Financial Environment and Financial Risk 241

Chapter 10 Financial Derivatives   269

Chapter 11 Managing Foreign Exchange Risk   306

Part I

Fundamentals of International Financial Markets

Part I of the book builds the theoretical foundations on which international financial markets operate. The focus of this section is on operations and theory of foreign exchange markets and on interest rates which link markets in different countries.

The first chapter begins with an explanation of the role of international financial markets in the global economy and then describes how these markets can be divided into various segments. Chapters 2 and 3 explain the working and theory of foreign currency markets, and Chapter 4 explains the basics of international interest rates.

Chapter 1

An Introduction to International Financial Markets

Growing Importance of International Markets

In the early spring of 1992 when the primaries for the U.S. presidential election were in full swing, the campaign had turned very nationalistic and inward looking. Japan bashing was in fashion and even old trusted friends such as Canada were having their lumber exports subjected to tariffs they knew would kill their domestic industries. Many companies had taken to providing incentives to their employees to buy American goods. At the height of this protectionism, there was one silver lining for die–hard internationalists. *The Wall Street Journal,* in a special series on "Going Global with Mutual Funds," recognized what many investment advisors had been saying for some time: "buy foreign."[1] Although the specific recommendation was based on the poor performance of foreign stocks over the previous three years at a time when the U.S. stocks had been rising, American fund managers recognized that capital markets outside the United States could no longer be ignored by U.S. investors looking for attractive returns. Indeed, a stretch of three years of poor performance was a near record, and investment advisors felt that the market could not decline for four consecutive years.

If the advice of these investment counselors was followed by more than a handful of investors in the United States, it would have changed the small role that foreign investments—stocks, bonds, and other instruments—have traditionally played in the portfolios of U.S. investors. Thus, despite the fact that international stock funds accounted for only 10 percent of total stock fund assets in the United States, there is little doubt that this proportion is going to increase over the next few years. What is unclear is exactly how an investor should go about understanding and assessing the potential of foreign capital markets. What should potential investors know about financial markets outside the United States? To raise pertinent questions about these markets from the perspective of an investor, and to provide some answers to these questions, is one of the two objectives of this book. The other aim is to answer some important questions about borrowing opportunities in international markets.

The role that financial markets play in helping individuals invest their savings would not be possible without corporations and individuals who borrow money from these markets. Corporations raise funds by issuing stocks, bonds, notes, and various types of papers and by borrowing from banks. Individuals borrow funds for purchasing homes, cars, and other goods. In particular, international financial markets have become an important source of funds for U.S. and non–U.S. corporations in the last three decades. How can a corporation understand what opportunities exist in markets that extend beyond their national boundaries, and how should it go about exploiting these opportunities? These are some of the important questions that we will attempt to answer.

Study of International Financial Markets

How do we go about studying international financial markets? We will approach the subject in four distinct parts. Part I consists of four chapters. This chapter reviews the role of financial markets within a domestic economy and, therefore, the role of international financial markets in the global economy. The aim of this chapter is to provide the broad framework within which capital markets operate. The next three chapters build the foundations of international financial markets. Our focus is on two sets of variables that have a profound influence on everything else that happens in the international markets: exchange rates and interest rates. Exchange rates are a uniquely international phenomenon, and many readers of this book may be unfamiliar with technical aspects of the foreign exchange market. We explain the operations of this market in Chapter 2 and the theory of exchange rates in Chapter 3. Basics of interest rates are explained in Chapter 4 which also deals with some complexities of international interest rates.

Part II of this book explains how various segments of international markets work. We focus first on short–term and long–term debt instruments and then on equity markets. Our aim is to understand how each of these segments works and some of the economic principles that govern their functions. This section has four chapters, one each for short–term debt, long–term debt, and equity, and one for principles of international investments. Part III of the book is devoted to understanding how modern financial markets create risks for participants and how financial innovations and derivatives facilitate handling risk in international operations. The first two chapters in this section show the reader how financial risk can be understood and measured, and the remaining two chapters focus on management of that risk. We discuss foreign exchange and interest rate risks in separate chapters. Part IV deals with institutions that make these financial transactions possible: the international commercial and investment banks. International supranational institutions such as the World Bank and the International Monetary Fund (IMF) are described in appendixes in chapters where they seem most relevant; the IMF is described in Appendix 2.B after Chapter 2 and the World Bank in the appendix after Chapter 7. The remainder of this chapter introduces readers to the international financial markets.

What Do International Financial Markets Do?

Before we can understand how international financial markets work, we should understand the role these markets play in the global economy. What purpose do international financial markets serve? What do they provide that would not be available to us either at all or at a much higher cost? Do they do something that domestic financial markets cannot do? We begin to answer these questions by first briefly reviewing the contribution that domestic financial markets make to a country's economy and then extending that analysis to financial markets that transcend national boundaries.

The main function of financial markets is to facilitate the production of goods and services in an economy by providing a mechanism that allows money and capital to be transferred between various participants in the most efficient manner possible. Financial markets facilitate this flow of funds between different economic entities by creating and trading in financial assets. The effectiveness of such markets can be measured primarily in terms of how efficiently they facilitate the transfer of funds and financial assets from one party to another.

The importance of financial markets follows from the essential function performed by financial assets in a modern economy. Financial assets serve two purposes: they help transfer funds from "surplus" units in an economy to "deficit" units, and they help redistribute risk from one unit to another. "Surplus" units in the economy are individuals or corporations whose income in a period exceeds their expenditure and, hence, have some savings for the period. The "deficit" units are, of course, the opposite—their expenditures exceed their income in a given period. The funds transfer function is important because individuals or firms (or, generally speaking, "economic entities") that have good ideas for investing funds or expenditures in real assets do not always have sufficient funds to make these investments. They are the units with a deficit of funds. Surplus funds are in the hands of other entities who may have saved some of their income but may not know how to invest these funds in productive real investments. Financial assets in the form of shares, bonds, or loans allow entities with investment ideas to obtain needed funds from the surplus funds by offering the savers some form of reward, either future dividends or interest payments. Without proper financial assets, investments in real assets would be below the levels that maximize the economic growth of the economy because investments of each economic entity would be limited to its own savings.

The second function of financial assets is to redistribute risk between owners of wealth in the economy. Most investments entail some risk, either a risk of failure where all or part of the investment is lost or an opportunity risk where better opportunities become available once the funds have been committed to a particular investment. A real investment, say, a plant to manufacture computer components, has the risk that the investor may not be able to sell the output of the plant or that a better technology may become available once the plant has been built. Without financial assets, investors in real assets will have to take all the risks associated with such an investment. With different kinds of financial assets, risks can be transferred from one party to another. Investors in real assets, for example, may issue shares in their project (thus allowing purchasers of shares to take the full risk of failure), while charging a licensing or management fee for their ideas. Alternatively, they may finance the project by issuing bonds such that bond holders bear the risk of a complete failure of the project. The main function of financial instruments like stocks, bonds, and loan contracts is to redistribute the risk of investments from one party to another. Financial derivatives like futures, options, swaps, and other innovations, on the other hand, redistribute risks of existing assets from one party to another.

How financial assets allow the risk to be transferred between parties—in effect, separating the "creation" of risk from the final "bearing" of the risk—can be illustrated with an example. With financial instruments, those who are responsible for undertaking real economic activities which involve risk can transfer the risk to someone else. Consider the case of a farmer who plants a crop in an economy in which there are no financial instruments. With no financial participation of outsiders, this farmer takes the risk that (a) the crop will grow as expected and (b) the price at the time of reaping (and selling) will be attractive enough to justify the effort. If either the yield is lower than expected, or if the price drops before the farmer has sold the crop, the farmer will suffer a loss. In a more complex economy with financial instruments, the farmer may be able to (a) sell shares in the expected output or (b) sell the crop in the futures market. The farmer may also have a partner who provides the capital and a fixed salary for the farmer and receives the entire crop in exchange for the investment. The risk of crop failure now belongs to the investor, not the farmer. To manage the risk arising from a potential price change, the farmer may sell the entire crop in the futures market at a time when the price seems attractive. If the price drops after this point, the loss will have been transferred to the purchaser of the futures contracts. Therefore, with financial instruments, the person who undertakes the real economic activity (planting the crop) does not have to take the risk that the success of the venture will be marred by events outside the control of the person undertaking the activity.

The main contribution of financial markets in an economy is to provide an institutional framework that makes the exchange of financial assets possible. There are two requirements for a well–functioning market for the exchange of financial assets: financial institutions and the owners of real and productive assets should be willing to offer a large variety of financial assets, and financial institutions should be willing to provide mechanisms and a framework for a secondary market in financial assets. A large variety of assets ensures on the one hand that needs of all kinds of investors (in real assets) can be met, and on the other that wealth owners can adjust their portfolios in response to any kind of change in the economic environment. Thus, well–developed financial markets have mechanisms for issuing a wide variety of assets like stocks, bonds, loans, notes, and commercial paper in the primary markets. They also have a large variety of derivative assets or instruments like futures, options, options on futures, caps, collars, and swaps. These instruments differ from each other as to the credit risk of the issuer of the instrument, maturity of the instrument, and when relevant, the currency in which the instrument is issued. Efficient secondary markets are essential so that the holders of financial assets can sell existing assets to adjust their portfolios in response to changes in the prices of assets. Secondary markets also have to be liquid, that is, they have to have a large number of transactions so that asset holders can exchange or sell assets without having to incur large transactions costs for the intended portfolio adjustments. In addition to liquidity, borrowers and lenders may also be concerned about confidentiality, and borrowers may want to have some confidence that the financial markets will provide them with funds when they need them the most.

In principle, international financial markets carry out the same functions as domestic financial markets, but they do so between economic entities in different countries. Just as some economic units within one country may be short of funds in a certain period, some countries may also face deficits (or surpluses) in their economic transactions with the rest of the world. This is measured and reported as the balance of payments deficits (or surpluses). Appendix I at the end of this chapter introduces the concepts of balance of payments and the relationship between the balance of payments disequilibria and the flows in the international financial markets. International financial markets carry out the critical task of facilitating the flow of funds from the countries with the balance of payments surpluses to those with the deficits. The main task of international financial markets, therefore, is to ensure that sufficient quantities and large numbers of assets with as complete a choice of maturities, risks, and currencies as possible are available for the transactor. In carrying out this function, international financial markets replicate on an international level what domestic financial markets do at a national level: they make it possible for economic entities to transfer funds from one country to another and allow these entities to adjust their financial portfolios by taking advantage of the opportunities available outside the country where the economic entity may be located. Thus, one of the unique contributions of international financial markets is to allow funds to be moved from one country to another. The following box provides an example of how international financial markets have allowed a group of rapidly growing countries to tap into more savings for developing their infrastructures than would have been possible with domestic markets alone.

▼ ▼ ▼

Borrow International–Invest Domestic*

East Asian countries are known for two things: unprecedented growth rates over the last generation and a population that saves a lot. Yet, at the present time, these countries need lots of money. Why does this apparent contradiction exist, and where is the money to come from?

Take Taiwan, for example. The country has moved from being an "agrarian backwater to a manufacturing powerhouse in a generation." The move was made possible in part by a high level of domestic savings estimated to be about 25 percent of personal income. The same is true for Malaysia, Singapore, and South Korea as well.

The development of the infrastructure, that is, roads, railways, airports, communication systems, etc., has not kept pace with the fast growth of personal income. The strains are now being felt, and most of these countries are planning to embark on massive investments to upgrade their economic infrastructures in the next decade. South Korea is planning to spend around $400 billion, Taiwan around $245 billion, Thailand $25 billion, Malaysia $10 billion, and even tiny Singapore plans to spend about $2.4 billion on an underground road. China, whose plans are less well known, may spend probably $92 billion over the next five years.

Where will the money for these investments come from? Although these economies are used to high rates of savings, the amounts needed are beyond the means of the countries themselves. As would be expected, international financial markets will be tapped to provide the bulk of these funds. According to a bank report, East Asian economies, other than Japan, have invested $94.8 billion in international markets over the past five years. Over the next five years, however, they will borrow up to $160 billion from the same markets.

Analysts believe that these funds will be raised in the form of bonds in the international markets. The preference for bonds over bank loans may be a question more of the inability of the banks to supply funds rather than the borrowers' unwillingness to deal with the banks. The banks of the industrialized countries are facing capital restrictions due to recent international regulations concerning bank equity and may not have sufficient funds to lend. Whichever form of borrowing these countries may use, there is little doubt that these economies will be major participants in international financial markets over the next decade.

˙Summarized from "For Thrifty Asia, Rainy Day Has Arrived," *The Wall Street Journal*, July 15, 1993, p. A8.

▲ ▲ ▲

There is another unique function performed by international financial markets. Since the economies of different countries are not yet perfectly integrated with each other or with the global economy, the prices of assets in each country move at least partially independently of the prices of assets in other countries. Such independent movements create opportunities for holders of financial assets to benefit from diversification across national boundaries just as they benefit from diversifying across different assets within an economy. International diversification has an added dimension of risk that domestic investment does not entail—a risk arising from changes in exchange rates—although the principles of diversification that apply to domestic assets also apply to international assets. Since the assets in each country are denominated in the currency of the country, an investor in, say, the United States needs to translate the returns on foreign assets from the foreign currency into the U.S. dollar. If the exchange rate between the U.S. dollar and the foreign currency changes between the time of the initial investment and that of liquidation of the investment, the investor will have to take into account not only what the asset earned in the foreign currency but also the net result of the change in the exchange rate on that return. A study of international investments thus requires one to understand the theory of exchange rates and the reasons for exchange rate changes, as well as the principles of investments.

International financial markets, thus, extend the activities of domestic markets within one economy to the international economy. They provide the framework within which international financial institutions issue a variety of instruments that facilitate economic entities to borrow and invest funds around the world. Our challenge is to understand how various parts of these markets work and connect with each other.

Classification of Financial Markets

Before we proceed with a study of international financial markets, it may be worthwhile to recognize broad differences between various types of capital markets or to classify them into separate categories. International financial markets facilitate capital flows between countries for several reasons. They may do so in response to the balance of payments disequilibria, for borrowing, or for investments opportunities not directly related to the balance of payments. Though international financial markets are subject to the same economic principles that govern domestic markets, there are some differences. The main difference between domestic and international markets arises from the nature of regulations. Most domestic markets—both in the activities that can be carried out in any country and in the financial institutions that facilitate those activities—are tightly controlled by national governments for the purposes of achieving domestic economic or political goals. There is, however, no international government that directly controls or regulates the international financial markets. Some international transactions are subject to regulations because national governments can influence the activities of economic entities under their control. Other transactions in international markets, however, escape regulation completely, giving rise to a set of transactions that are best labelled as "external" market transactions. The extent of regulations that govern the transactions thus provides a convenient dimension for distinguishing and classifying financial markets.

Another convenient dimension for the classification of financial markets is the channel through which capital flows from the entities that save to the entities that make real investments.[2] The main channels through which funds flow are known as direct channels and indirect channels. In the direct flow of funds, the savers or the lenders, that is, those who provide the funds, acquire direct financial claims or assets which are issued by those who use the funds, the borrowers. The most common types of financial assets issued by the borrowers are shares or equity and bonds. With either of these two types of assets, the borrower of funds makes a financial commitment to pay the lender a return in the future, although the exact nature of the commitment is different in the two cases. The important point about these instruments or assets is that the lender of the funds has a direct stake in the performance of the borrower. Direct channels permit lenders of funds to participate in the risks of real investments.

On the other hand, indirect funds flow from the lender to the borrower through a financial intermediary, often a commercial bank. In some situations, the savers of funds prefer to deposit their funds with a bank rather than lend them to an investor in exchange for equity or bonds. The bank, in turn, may lend the same funds to the same borrower in the form of a bank loan. The nature of the risk that the lenders take, however, is quite different. The lenders in this case do not have a direct stake in the performance of the borrower. They have a stake only in the overall well being of the financial intermediary—the commercial bank. The indirect flow of funds thus provides a layer of protection for the lenders of the funds from the risks of real investments. The risk is now shared by the financial intermediary (and hence the shareholders of the financial intermediary).

The two dimensions—regulation and channels for the flow of funds—result in a classification of financial markets that is shown in Exhibit 1.1. Financial markets may face either national regulation, if the market in question is controlled by a national government, or no regulation at all. National regulation applies to two types of transactions. A domestic transaction takes place between a domestic saver and a domestic investor. In a foreign transaction (in which at least one of the transactors is a foreign resident), the transaction takes place in the currency of the country under the rules and regulations of the country. When a transaction takes place in such a way that it completely escapes the regulation of the country whose currency is being used in the transaction—regardless of the nationality of the transactor—the transaction can be said to have taken place in the "external" market. Based on the type of regulation that governs a particular transaction,

Exhibit 1.1
A Classification of Capital Markets

	Regulation		
	Internal		External
	Domestic Segment	Foreign Segment	External Segment
Intermediated Flow of Funds	Domestic Bank Loan	Cross–Border Bank Loan	Eurocurrency Loan
Direct Flow of Funds	Domestic Bond or Equity	Foreign Bonds	Eurobond (Euroequity Markets)

Source: Dufey, G., "International Capital Markets: Structure and Response in an Era of Instability," *Sloan Management Review*, Spring 1981, pp. 35–45.

financial markets can be considered to be domestic markets, foreign markets, or external markets.

Different segments of international financial markets can now be identified according to the type of regulation and the channel for the flow of funds. The domestic–intermediated market is the domestic bank loan market. The domestic–direct market is the market for domestic equities and bonds and various other types of notes and paper that are issued in domestic markets. When a domestic bank lends money abroad, it may be classified as being in the foreign sector of national financial markets. Similarly, when foreigners purchase domestic equities and bonds, the activities fall under the foreign segment of our financial markets.

Our interest in this book will be largely on the external segment of financial markets. The intermediated part of the external segment of financial markets began in the mid–1960s when commercial banks discovered that they could make loans to foreigners by taking various currencies "outside" the countries that had issued the currency. This market became known as the **Eurodollar** market. The title is somewhat of a misnomer, but the name has stuck. There is an external–

intermediated segment for financial markets of all the large industrialized countries. These are the markets in which banks make large volumes of loans to corporations and countries. The most important part of the external–direct flow segment used to be the **Eurobond** market, but now the **Euronote** market is as important as the Eurobond market. Participants issue bonds and notes in this segment of financial markets in various currencies, but the transactions always take place outside the regulatory framework of the country whose currency is being used in the transaction. Finally, there is no true **Euroequity** market, but the term is often used to describe what is essentially an activity in the foreign segment of the financial markets.

Summary

International financial markets provide essentially the same function as do domestic markets. They channel funds from those who save to those who invest. International markets contribute to global economic efficiency in the same manner that domestic ones do for the domestic economy. There is, however, an important difference in one segment of international markets which we call the external segment of capital markets. This segment has a unique feature in that it is an unregulated market. This, and other segments of international financial markets, help investors lower their cost of funds.

International financial markets also contribute by increasing the set of opportunities available to investors. Developments in international markets create more risks for investors on the one hand and provide more opportunities for risk management on the other. Our task in this book is to understand where those opportunities are and to exploit them to our advantage.

Appendix 1.A
Balance of Payments and
International Capital Flows

From a macroeconomic perspective, international financial markets play the critical role of transferring funds from one country to another. Such a funds transfer is required for macroeconomic adjustments that accompany disequilibria in a country's balance of payments. Balance of payments of a country summarize all the economic transactions of the country with the rest of the world. These accounts provide an important indication of how well the country's economy is managing its transactions with the rest of the world and whether or not any problems are likely to emerge in the external economic relations of the country. Two important areas of external economic relations in international financial markets are **international capital flows** and the **exchange rate of the country**. To understand the relationship between balance of payments and these two areas, let us first understand the fundamentals of the balance of payments.

Balance of payments accounts always refer to the economic transactions of a country with the rest of the world during a certain time period, say, a year or a quarter. Although most balance of payments accounts refer to the transactions of one country with the rest of the world, sometimes one country's bilateral balance of payments with one other country may also be prepared. These transactions are separated into three main categories: current account transactions, capital account transactions, and official transactions.

Current account transactions are those which, in an economic sense, are completely settled during the period for which the balance of payments is being prepared. The best known transactions that are included in the current account part of the balance of payments are imports and exports of goods and services; travel and tourism between the country and the rest of the world; unilateral transfers, for example donations, gifts, etc. between the residents of the country and non–residents; and payments of interests and dividends on past investments in and out of the country. All these transactions are completed in one deal and do not necessarily leave any obligation or expectation that future transactions will result from this one transaction, hence the designation of "current" account. In the balance of payments accounting for a country, all these transactions are entered either as an inflow of money or an outflow. The net balance of inflows and outflows over the period for which the balance of payments accounts are prepared gives an indication of whether the country has spent more money abroad during the reporting period than others spent within its own borders. The current account balance for the period indicates how much money the country owes the rest of the world if the current account is in deficit or is owed by the rest of the world if the current account is in surplus. Of course, the counterpart of net expenditure of money abroad is that the country receives goods and services which raise the living standard of the people in the country.

The **capital account** in the balance of payments includes all the transactions in one period which give rise to an obligation or an expectation of a transaction in a subsequent period. These transactions result from investments by residents of one country in another country. An investment may be for the acquisition of real or productive assets (direct investment), or for the acquisition of a financial asset, for example, a bond, treasury bills, or bank loan (portfolio investment). All these investments require transfer of funds in one period for the initial investment and would result in subsequent transfers in the opposite direction as the returns on the investment if the investments are successful.

The third set of accounts in the balance of payments is the **official reserves account** which includes all the foreign economic transactions undertaken by the central bank and the monetary authorities of the country. Details and analysis of this account are usually of interest only to specialists on the balance of payments and will not be discussed in depth here.

The balance of payments is a very useful tool for understanding and analyzing the health of the external sector of a country. The analysis examines the trends in the two main accounts of the balance of payments—the current account and the capital account—and tries to predict consequences of any imbalances that may exist in these two accounts. An imbalance in each of these accounts may be a deficit or a surplus, and the imbalances in the two accounts may or may not be related to each other.

The first step in the analysis of the balance of payments is to explain why an account has an imbalance. Why, for example, does the current account have a deficit (or a surplus)? Why is the country purchasing more goods and services abroad than it is selling? Why is the economy a net consumer of foreign goods and services? Such a deficit may be either temporary or permanent, and it may be driven largely by the consumption of investment goods in the economy or by the consumption of non–investment or consumer goods in the economy. Similar questions have to be raised about the capital account. Suppose a country has a deficit in the capital account. Why is this country investing more funds abroad than foreigners are investing in this country? The answers to this question could be that the country has very few investment opportunities, or that there is some instability in the country which prompts wealthy owners to move their funds abroad, or that the country is so rich that it has surplus funds to invest abroad.

The second step in the analysis is to predict what changes, if necessary, will have to be brought about in the economy to eliminate the imbalances and whether or not the imbalances will continue. How will the financial markets respond to these changes if imbalances are removed? How will the markets respond if the economy is unable to make the necessary changes to solve the payment imbalances? We also need to ask if those in positions of power can bring about the necessary changes.

The answers to both these sets of questions are very complex. To understand the current account imbalances, we have to go beyond the balance of payments numbers and look at the details of goods and services that are being imported and exported. Such information is not easily available from the balance of payments accounts alone. To determine if something should be done about the imbalances, we have to see whether the imbalances are caused by excessive current consumption or by demand for investment, and whether the situation is temporary or permanent. If the imbalances have to be corrected, it would require an appropriate mixture of fiscal, monetary, and exchange rate policies so that the economy in the imbalance can go through an "adjustment process" wherein a balance between the supply and demand of external transactions is restored. A mixture of these policies that will allow for a smooth adjustment is extremely difficult to determine. If the imbalances in the balance of payments are temporary and will disappear without a need for adjustments then mechanisms have to be found for "financing" the imbalances. Financing the deficits requires the country to obtain or borrow funds from the rest of the world to pay for the deficits till the time the deficits disappear.

From the perspective of the study of financial markets, the most important questions pertain to (1) exchange rates and interest rates, i.e., how will these rates change as policies to solve balance of payments problems are implemented, and (2) flow of funds in the international economy, i.e., in what form and between which markets will the balance of payments disequilibria require the flow of international funds?

Appendix 1.B
The Size of International
Financial Markets

How big are international financial markets in relation to domestic markets? Are they really worth paying attention to?

Truly international financial markets are relatively new. Although the foreign sectors of financial markets identified in Exhibit 1.1 have existed for a long time, the external markets began to grow only in the 1960s. Their growth since then has often outpaced that of the domestic markets. Exhibit 1.2 shows how much money was raised in international markets during the past few years in three of the most common forms in which funds are raised. The exhibit shows the growth of international bank lending, gross and net amounts of international bonds, and gross and net amounts of Euronotes. In proportionate terms, the largest growth would seem to be in the Euronote market. These instruments were introduced only in the early 1980s, and the market has grown very rapidly since then. The international bonds market has continued to grow throughout the decade as has international bank lending or the Eurocurrency market. As one would expect, international bank loans and international bonds compete with each other. A decline in growth of international bank loans in 1991, for instance, was accompanied by an expansion of the international bonds market.

International markets are relatively small in comparison with their domestic counterparts. Exhibit 1.3 compares the total volumes of domestic and international bonds outstanding in various currencies. It also provides a comparison of the bond markets in various currencies. Globally, international bonds account for about 11 percent of all the bonds raised in the world. The share of international bonds among all the bonds outstanding in one currency varies from a low of 3.2 percent for bonds raised in Italian lira to 58.7 percent for Swiss francs. The U.S. dollar, yen, deutschemark, sterling, and Swiss franc seem to be the most popular currencies for raising international bonds. The largest bond market in the world is the U.S. domestic market which by itself accounts for about 48 percent of all bonds outstanding at the end of 1992.

Exhibit 1.4 compares similar statistics for the short- and medium-term obligations, that is, commercial paper or Euronotes and medium-

Exhibit 1.2
Funds Raised in International Capital Markets

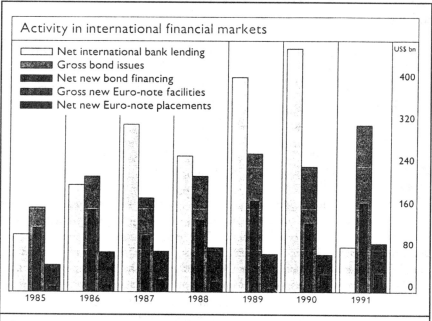

Source: Bank for International Settlements, *Annual Report*, 1992, p. 159.

term notes, for 1986 and 1992. The share of international short–term notes has increased from 7.5 percent in 1986 to 12.8 percent in 1992. The share of international medium–term notes has increased from an almost non–existent market in 1986 to about 25.3 percent in 1992. The U.S. market dominates both these kinds of instruments. All the other currencies account for only about 39 percent of the market for short–term papers. The importance of the international equities markets can be seen from Exhibit 1.5. It compares the growth of total market capitalization of equity markets around the world over the last decade. The exhibit also shows how active these markets are by comparing the growth of the volume equity that is traded on various markets.

Exhibit 1.3
Sizes of Bond Markets, 1992
(billions of U.S. dollars)

Currencies	Amounts Outstanding at End-1992		
	Domestic	International	Intl/Total = %
U.S. dollar	6,672.2	680.5	9.3
Japanese yen	2,888.6	207.5	6.7
Deutschemark	1,234.0	168.5	12.1
Italian lira	734.9	24.2	3.2
French franc	525.0	64.3	10.9
Pound sterling	254.0	121.3	32.3
Canadian dollar	321.7	63.5	16.5
Swiss franc	109.5	155.5	58.7
Other[1]	1,325.6	201.9	13.2
Total	14,069.6	1,687.2	10.7

[1]Including the ECU.

Source: Bank for International Settlements, *Annual Report*, 1993, p. 117.

International markets for financial derivatives have grown rapidly along with the markets for underlying assets. Exhibit 1.6 compares the sizes of the markets for derivatives—those that are available as standardized contracts on exchanges and those that are negotiated as special deals in the over–the–counter market. Both these market segments have grown rapidly since 1986 with the over–the–counter market having grown faster than the exchange–traded market. The largest growth seems to be in the derivatives dealing with interest rate risk as demonstrated by the sizes of interest rate options and futures and interest rate swaps. The last two lines in the exhibit show that financial derivatives have become relatively more important in the 1991 global economy than in that of 1986. The total volume of derivatives as a percentage of the sizes of the economies increased four fold in those six years.

Exhibit 1.4
Domestic and International Markets for
Commercial Paper and Medium–Term Notes
(amounts outstanding at year–end, in billions of $U.S.)[1]

Items	Market Openings	1986	1992
Commercial paper markets			
United States	pre-1960	325.9	545.1
Japan	end-1987	—	98.1
France	end-1985	3.7	31.6
Spain	1982	6.2	29.3
Canada	pre-1960	11.9	24.5
Sweden	1983	3.7	16.6
Australia	mid-1970s	4.1	13.8
United Kingdom	1986	0.8	5.8
Finland	mid-1986	0.4	3.8
Germany	early 1991	—	10.2
Netherlands	1986	0.1	2.6
Norway	end-1984	0.9	2.2
Belgium	1990	—	1.3
Total domestic		357.7	781.9
Euro-commercial paper	mid-1980s	13.9	78.7
Other short-term Euronotes	early 1980s	15.1	37.0
Total		386.7	900.6
Euro/Total (percent)		7.5	12.8
Medium-term note markets			
United States	early 1970s	35.0[2]	175.7
U.K.			4.9
Euro-medium-term notes	mid-1980s	0.4	61.1

[1] Converted at end-year exchange rates, except for Australia.
[2] Estimated.

Source: Bank for International Settlements, *Annual Report,* 1993, p. 112.

Finally, international transactions have become more important in the world economy than they used to be even a decade ago. Exhibit 1.7 shows the relative importance of cross–border bond and equity trades as a proportion of domestic economy for four countries over the last decade. International equity transactions, which were only around 10 percent of GDP in 1980 for these four countries, now amount to between 60 and 600 percent of the total output of these economies.

Exhibit 1.5a
Equity Markets Around the World

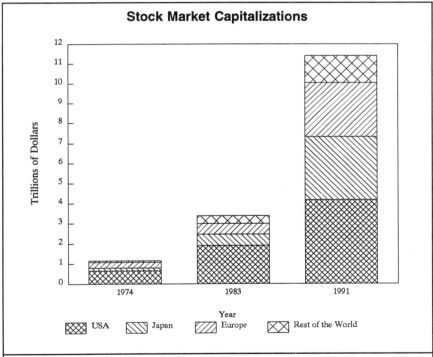

Source: International Finance Corporation, *Emerging Markets Handbook*, various issues, Washington D.C.

Exhibit 1.5b
Equity Markets Around the World

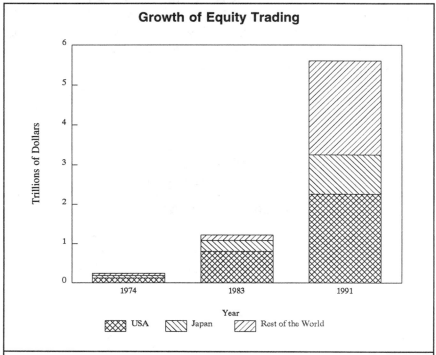

Growth of Equity Trading

Source: International Finance Corporation, *Emerging Markets Handbook*, various issues, Washington D.C.

Exhibit 1.6
The Expansion of Selected
Financial Derivative Markets
(notional principal amounts in billions of $U.S.)

Derivatives Traded on Organized Exchanges Worldwide			
	1988	1992	Open position at end 1992
Interest rate futures	156	335	3048
Interest rate options and options on futures	30	65	1385
Currency futures	22	31	25
Currency options and options on futures	18	23	80
TOTAL	227	454	4538

Derivatives Traded Over–the–Counter			
	1988	1992 H1[1]	Amounts outstanding end 1991
Interest rate swaps	568	1318	3065
Currency swaps[2]	124	156	807
Other swap related derivatives[3]	..	294	577
TOTAL	..	1768	4450

[1] Data for first half.
[2] Adjusted for reporting of both sides, including cross currency interest rate swaps.
[3] Caps, collars, floors, and swaptions.

Source: Bank for International Settlements, *63rd Annual Report,* 1993, pp. 124-25.

Exhibit 1.7
Cross–Border Transactions and GDP

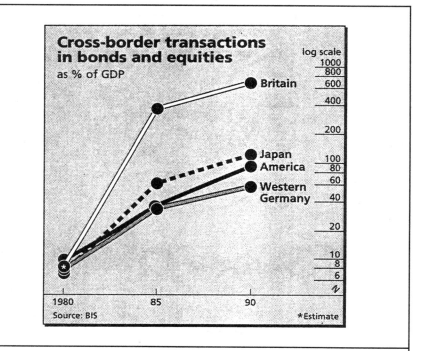

Source: Bank for International Settlements data, as reported in *The Economist*, August 28, 1993, p. 65.

Notes

1. Clements, J., "Going Global with Mutual Funds: 'Buy Foreign' Strategists Urge U.S. Investors," *The Wall Street Journal*, March 3, 1992, p. C1.

2. Dufey, G., "International Capital Markets: Structure and Response in an Era of Instability," *Sloan Management Review*, Spring 1981, pp. 35–45.

Chapter 2
Foreign Exchange Markets: Operations

The middle of September 1992 witnessed one of the most chaotic weeks in international currency markets in recent memory. The chaos was caused by the difficulties that the British and Italian governments faced in maintaining the values of their currencies, the pound and lira respectively, at levels that had been set according to the European Monetary System's Exchange Rate Mechanism. According to those rules, currencies were not allowed to fall more than 2.25 percent below their par values with other currencies of the European Community. High interest rates in Germany had attracted so much capital that the pound, the lira, and some other European currencies were under strong devaluation pressures. The U.S. dollar being free to fluctuate had declined substantially against the German mark over the previous six months. In early September, the European currencies came under renewed pressure from speculators in the market, and governments did what they have always done in times of crisis. They first announced that the crisis was not serious, then, that they planned to defend the values of their currencies, and finally that they were giving up and letting the market take its own course. At the end of that phase of the crisis, the pound, lira, and Spanish peseta had dropped by about 10 percent each. Ironically, the currency that recovered its value was the U.S. dollar; even the German mark fell against it. It is estimated, and of course the authorities will never confirm this, that the Bank of England lost four to six billion dollars in its efforts to save the pound.

Given this information, should international investors be concerned about this chaos? The answer is yes, if investors care about how well their investments do. Investors in domestic stock markets of some of these countries did very well during the week of the crisis. The British market went up by 8.27 percent during one week from September 11 to September 18. An investor in the United States who bet on the British stock market, however, would have lost money because, even as the British stock market went up, the British currency fell by 9.71 percent against the dollar during the same period. A U.S. investor in German stocks would have gained only marginally because even though the stocks went up by 4.03 percent, the mark itself fell by 3.70 percent against the dollar during the same period. The foreign exchange rate changes thus seem to be as important for international investments as the returns earned on the investments in foreign currencies. It is therefore very important for a participant in international financial markets to understand how and why foreign exchange rates change and how, if at all, the changes in foreign exchange rates and the returns on investments in foreign currencies are related to each other. The events of the days from September 10 to 18 illustrate both the importance of taking foreign exchange risk into account in international transactions as well as many of the difficulties we have in understanding foreign exchange markets.

Were the changes during the week of September predictable? Why did the exchange rates change so much during that week? Why were the British and Italian governments so concerned about the values of their currencies? The answers to these questions are difficult and yet very important for international investors. We will provide a framework in this chapter and the next to discover some of the answers. As we will see, the exchange rates for different currencies behave differently. Some exchange rates fluctuate wildly, while others remain stable or move very slowly in one direction or the other. The movements in the values of currencies depend to a large extent upon the economic policies that countries follow, or more precisely upon how the markets perceive those policies. Hence, it becomes necessary to understand the "market."

This chapter explains the workings of the foreign currency markets, and the following chapter explores the reasons for the foreign exchange rates to change. The purpose of these two chapters is to help the reader understand how foreign exchange markets operate and what these markets do for different types of participants, as well as to understand why exchange rates change over time. This knowledge will be useful when we want to assess the impact of these changes on international investments and then take necessary steps to protect the values of our international investments. To understand exchange rate changes and the impact of these changes on international investment and borrowing decisions, we first have to understand what an exchange rate is and the fundamentals of how foreign currencies are traded in international markets. Our aim in this chapter is to become comfortable with dealing in currencies other than our own, to understand what kinds of contracts are available in the foreign exchange market, and to understand how changes in exchange rates are measured.

Exchange Rates and the Foreign Exchange Market

In its most basic form, a foreign exchange rate is simply the price of a foreign currency in terms of our own currency. Just as we denote the prices of hundreds of other items in our economy as so many dollars per unit of the item, we express an exchange rate as the quantity of our currency that equals one unit of the foreign currency. We may find, for example, that the exchange rate for the French franc (ff) is $0.2010/ff. It simply means that one French franc would cost 0.2010 dollars or 20.1 cents. This manner of expressing an exchange rate is called the **direct** quote for a currency. When the price of a foreign currency is given as a direct quote, it is similar to the price of other goods and services in our economy. Thus, the direct quote of $0.2010/ff for the French currency looks very similar in its form to the price of $6.50/person for entrance to a movie theatre.

Our direct quote for the French franc is an **indirect** quote for the dollar in France. The direct quote for the dollar, which is what the French should be using to denote how much a foreign currency is worth, would be the inverse of 0.201, which is, ff4.975/$. A quotation of ff4.975/$ is the direct quote for the dollar in France. Which type of quotation should we use if we want to exchange money with a French company—our direct quote or their direct quote? Although it could depend upon the country in which we happen to be making the exchange, in practice certain conventions have developed that everyone seems to follow. Thus, the French franc is usually quoted as so many ff/$—or in the example here—ff4.975/$. Similarly, by convention, we quote the British pound in $/£ and Japanese yen in ¥/$. Everyone seems to follow these conventions, in the United States as well in Europe and Japan.

Whether we deal in direct quotes or in indirect quotes, banks or foreign currency traders will quote two prices—which are very close to each other—when we ask them for the price of a foreign currency. They are giving us the "bid" and "ask" prices for a currency. A **bid quotation** refers to the price at which the bank will buy the currency, and the **ask quotation** refers to the price at which the bank will sell the currency. The banks may give the two quotations for the French franc as ff4.9745/$ and ff4.9755/$. (In reality, the banks will only say 45-55 over the telephone, that is, the last two digits in the quotation; it is understood among currency traders that the first two or three digits are the same as those currently prevailing in the market.) This implies that if we wanted to sell dollars to purchase francs, we would get 4.9745 francs/$ and if we wanted to purchase dollars, we would pay 4.9755 francs/$.

The difference between the two quotations is equivalent to the transaction cost that we would have to pay. This margin—the difference between the bid and the ask prices—covers the banks' expenditure and profits, as well as compensates them for the risk that after they have purchased a currency from us, its value may fall before they are able to sell it in the foreign exchange market. The risk for the bank arises from the fact that most of the currencies are free to fluctuate at the whim of participants in the market. In the contemporary international monetary system, the exchange rates for most currencies are determined by traders in the foreign exchange market.

The foreign exchange market is not a specific physical location but the interconnected network of computer terminals and electronic signals that the participants generate to make foreign exchange transactions with each other. The main participants in this market are the commercial banks in various countries along with brokers who specialize in dealing in foreign exchange. These commercial banks in turn are connected to corporate and individual clients who are the ultimate users of foreign currencies. Central banks enter this market through their links with commercial banks in their countries. Exhibit 2.1 provides a schematic of

Exhibit 2.1
Participants in the Forex Market

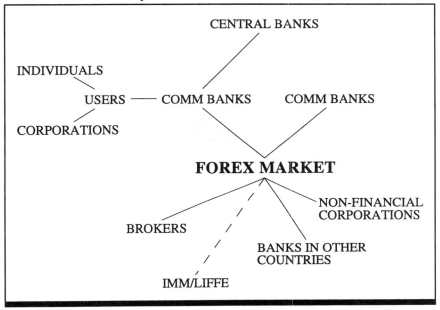

the foreign exchange market. Traders of foreign exchange buy and sell foreign currencies either for their own account to speculate or on behalf of one of their clients who may need to make a payment in a foreign currency.

The volume of trade in the foreign exchange market far exceeds the foreign currencies required for the purposes of settling accounts resulting from international trade or international investments. A large part of the trade in foreign exchange is done by the banks and others for speculative purposes. These speculative transactions make the foreign exchange market the largest market in the world. It is estimated that in the middle of 1992 about 1 trillion dollars worth of foreign currencies were being traded every day in this market. The largest volume of trade takes place in London, with New York in second place. In 1992, the estimated daily trading volume in London was about $303 billion and in New York about $192 billion. Other important foreign exchange markets are in Tokyo,

Hong Kong, Switzerland, Germany, and France. Smaller markets in
Bahrain, Los Angeles, San Francisco, Singapore, Sydney, and other cities

Exhibit 2.2
Foreign Exchange Market
(daily trading volume, $billion, 1989 and 1992)

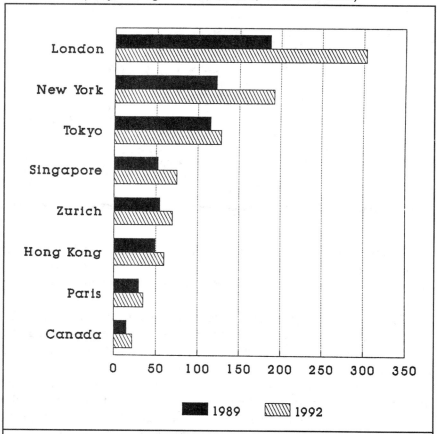

Source: "Summary of Results of U.S. Foreign Exchange Market Survey Conducted in April 1989," Federal Reserve Bank of New York, September 1989, and *The Economist*, December 12, 1992.

around the world create a global foreign exchange market such that the major currencies are always being traded somewhere or another 24 hours a day. Exhibit 2.2 gives an idea of how rapidly these markets have grown over the last decade.

As a measure of comparison for the foreign exchange market, the combined domestic product of the 24 largest Organization for Economic Cooperation and Development (OECD) countries was estimated to be about $17.1 trillion for the whole of 1991,[1] and the global trade in goods and services in 1991 amounted to about $3,442 billion. Thus, the transfer of funds to pay for imports and exports only occupies about four days of the activities of the foreign exchange market in a year, and the entire output of the world would have been traded in 17 days. The rest of the time, the foreign exchange market is busy accommodating international capital transfers between countries and speculative activities of traders, banks, and individuals.

Exhibit 2.3
Trading in Financial Markets in Canada
(total trade in April 1992, $billion)

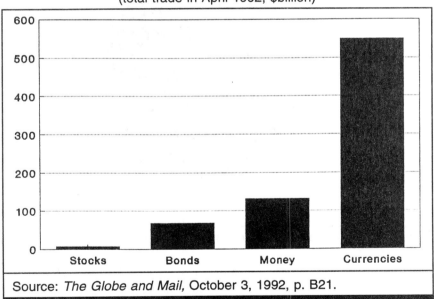

Source: *The Globe and Mail,* October 3, 1992, p. B21.

To put a perspective on the size of the foreign exchange market in relation to other segments of the financial markets, let us compare the sizes of the foreign exchange and the financial markets within one country—Canada. Exhibit 2.3 compares the total trade in April 1992 in the currency, money, bond, and stock markets in that country. The volume of trade in the stock market is merely about 1.2 percent of the trade in the currency market. Even the money market, which is the second largest market in the country, has less than one fourth the volume of trade of the foreign currency market.

Although almost all the currencies of the world are traded in this market, the bulk of the transactions are concentrated in the currencies of

Exhibit 2.4
Foreign Exchange Market
Turnover by Currency (%), 1992

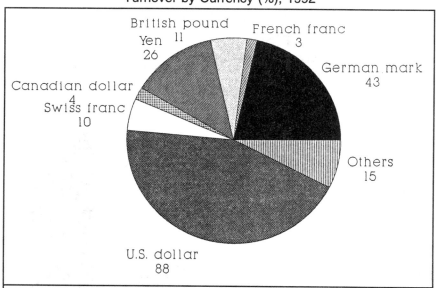

Amounts add up to 200 because there are two currencies in every transaction.

Source: "Summary of Results of the U.S. Foreign Exchange Market Turnover Survey," Federal Reserve Bank of New York, April 1992.

the major industrialized countries. According to recent estimates, the U.S. dollar is involved in about 96 and 99 percent of all transactions on one side of the trade. Exhibit 2.4 shows the breakdown of the currencies on the foreign exchange transactions.

Contracts in the Foreign Exchange Market

The trillion dollar a day trade in the foreign exchange market is done largely in three types of contracts. These contracts are the spot contract, the forward contract, and a simple swap contract. Exhibit 2.5 shows the share of various types of contracts in the foreign exchange market. In addition, specialized exchanges offer futures contracts, options contracts, options on futures, and complex swaps.

The most important contract in the foreign exchange market in terms of volume is the spot contract. In a spot contract, two currencies are exchanged for immediate delivery. Most foreign exchange transactions are now settled on the same business day as the day the contract is made. In a spot transaction, say at $0.201/ff for 10 million francs, one party would deliver 2,010,00 dollars and receive 10,000,000 francs on the day that the transaction is agreed upon. Spot contracts are used for making payments for goods and services and for transferring funds for investments, in addition to meeting all the current needs arising from travels.

The second contract in the foreign exchange market is the forward contract. The forward contract is similar to a spot contract except that the date on which the transaction is settled is different from the date on which the contract is made. The settlement date is agreed upon in advance. Thus, in a forward contract, the two parties will agree to exchange an agreed upon amount of one currency for another at the agreed upon rate at an agreed upon date in the future. If the forward rate for 90 days for the franc were $0.20502/ff, a forward contract for 2 million francs would mean that the party selling dollars would deliver $410,004 (= .20502 × 2 million) on the ninetieth day after the contract is made and would receive 2 million francs on the same day. Later in this book we will examine the reasons why participants would want to enter into forward contracts.

Exhibit 2.5
Foreign Exchange Market
Types of Transactions (%), 1992

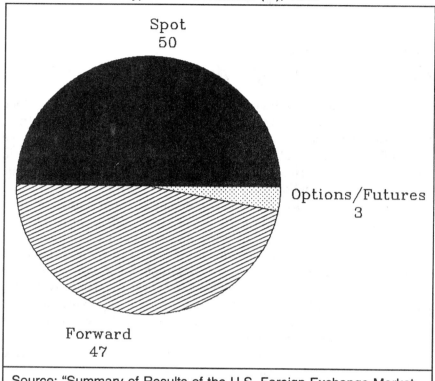

Spot
50

Options/Futures
3

Forward
47

Source: "Summary of Results of the U.S. Foreign Exchange Market Turnover Survey," Federal Reserve Bank of New York, April 1992.

The difference between the spot rate and the forward rate of a currency is known as a **premium** if the currency is worth more on the forward date or as a **discount** if the currency is worth less on the forward date. The premium or the discount is always calculated as an annual percentage rate using the following formula:

$$\text{premuim/discount} = \frac{\text{forward rate} - \text{spot rate}}{\text{spot rate}}$$

$$\times \frac{360}{\text{no. of days}} \times 100\%$$

Using this formula, and the rates given earlier, the premium on the franc can be calculated as being equal to 8 percent.

$$\text{premuim} = \frac{0.20502 - 0.201}{0.201} \times \frac{360}{90} \times 100\% = 8\%$$

The third contract in the foreign exchange market is a simple swap contract (the word *swap* also denotes a complex derivative product that we will deal with later in the book; for the time being swap is used to refer to only the simple transaction described here). In a simple swap contract on the foreign exchange market, a bank buys or sells a combination of a spot and a forward contract, buying one currency for another in the spot market and selling that currency in the forward market. The amounts of the two contracts in one of the currencies are usually the same. The purpose of such a contract is to provide funds in a foreign currency to a participant for a short period of time in such a way that the party does not have to take any risk arising from changing exchange rates. A bank may, for example, sell $10 million for yens in the spot market and buy back the same dollars with a three–month forward contract. The simultaneous sale and purchase at the prevailing spot and forward rates ensures that the buyer of the dollars will know the exact cost of purchasing—actually borrowing dollars and lending yens—in advance. In a more complex swap transaction, the dollars may have been sold for one forward date and purchased back at a later forward date.

Movements in Spot Rates over Time

Exchange rates for currencies change over time, and the changes in the values of currencies are called appreciations or depreciations. When the direct quote increases, that is, when the price of a foreign currency increases in our currency, the foreign currency is said to **appreciate** in value and our own currency is said to **depreciate**. Thus, if the direct quote for the French franc were to change to $0.2211/ff, the French franc would have appreciated—or sometimes be revalued—by 10 percent. The amount of the depreciation—or devaluation—of the dollar, however, has to be calculated from the direct quotes for the dollar in the French franc. Since the value of the dollar would have changed from ff4.975/$ to ff4.5228/$, the dollar would have depreciated or been devalued by 9.09 percent. The change in the value of a currency can be calculated from the following formula:

$$\text{appreciation of franc} = \frac{\text{new rate} - \text{old rate}}{\text{old rate}} \times 100\%$$

$$= \frac{0.2211 - 0.201}{0.201} \times 100\% = 10\%$$

Contracts on Organized Exchanges

In addition to the spot, the forward, and the swap contracts on the foreign exchange market, a host of other contracts generally known as financial derivatives are available either on the organized financial exchanges or in the over-the-counter market. Although we will explain these derivatives in more detail in Chapter 10, we will briefly introduce the concept of future contracts and illustrate how they provide a useful service to the users of foreign exchange markets. These contracts have been created and have become popular because they help firms and investors manage risks that arise from transactions in foreign currencies. In its simplest form, the risk arises when a transactor expects to undertake a transaction in the future which involves converting one currency into another at the exchange rate prevailing at the time of the transaction. Since most foreign exchange rates fluctuate, the transactor cannot be sure of the exchange rate that she will have to pay at the future date. The complex foreign exchange contracts and assorted derivatives are designed to eliminate the risk for the transactor under various situations.

The simplest situation is when someone, for example, an importer, knows the amount and the date of the future transaction. In that case a forward contract would serve the purpose. The importer can then enter into a forward contract to purchase the exact amount of the foreign currency on the required date. Such a forward contract completely eliminates—or, more precisely, hedges—the risk for the importer. Take the example of a wine importer who has ordered ff3 million worth of Bordeaux from the Entre-deux-mers region of France. The contract requires him to pay the francs in 90 days. As of today, given the spot rate of $.201/ff, that amounts to $603,000, but the actual amount of dollars he will have to pay depends upon what the exchange rate will be 90 days later. Since the importer must start selling the wine to his customers even before it arrives, and since he can only do so if he quotes a price in dollars, he needs to know exactly what the wine will cost in dollar terms. He could remove his uncertainty about the dollars he will have to pay and the dollar price he must quote by purchasing a forward contract right now. The contract will allow him to sell dollars and obtain francs. If the forward rate is $0.20502/ff, he will commit to pay $615,060 in 90 days and be sure that he will not have to pay any more (or any less). Thus, the forward contract removes any risk of exchange rate changes for the importer. No matter what the exchange rate is in 90 days, he will only pay at the rate of $.20502/ff.

It is really not correct to say that he is paying more in the forward contract—$ 0.20502 versus $ 0.201—since the spot rate is *today,* and the forward rate is for *90 days hence*; a spot transaction requires dollars today whereas the forward contract will require dollars in 90 days. The two rates cannot be compared without taking the time value of money into account; we will do this under the discussion of interest rate parity in the next chapter.

Suppose, however, that the importer was not completely sure that the foreign currency payment will have to be made and wants a contract that can be easily cancelled. He requires a hedging instrument that is liquid. The correct answer in this case may be a futures contract, or even an option on a futures contract. A futures contract is traded on an organized futures exchange like the Chicago Mercantile Exchange (CME), the Singapore International Monetary Exchange (SIMEX), and many others. It is a standardized contract in that the exchange that trades the contract fixes (1) the amount of one of the currencies, usually the United States dollar, and (2) the future date on which the futures contract will mature. These dates are well known in advance to all the participants. Such a standardized contract makes the futures contract very liquid in that it is easy to find a buyer or a seller for such a contract. Hence, our importer who wanted a contract that could be cancelled with ease may prefer to enter into a futures contract to purchase the foreign currency. If the need to make the payment in the foreign currency were to disappear, the importer would be able to get rid of the futures contracts easily because being a standardized contract, they are much more liquid than forward contracts. We will learn how to use these contracts in the third section of this book.

Now imagine an investor who expects to receive a large interest payment on some foreign currency bonds she had purchased last year. The interest payment will be received in 45 days in the currency of the bond, say deutschemarks. The investor is afraid that her own currency—the dollar—may rise in value against the deutschemark during that time, but she does not want to lose anything if the currency does not rise. In other words, she wants to win both ways. A foreign currency option has been created just for such investors. If she were to purchase what is called a put option contract, she would then have the right to convert her deutschemarks into dollars at a previously agreed upon rate, which she would do if the dollar were to rise. She could also ignore the put option contract if the dollar were to remain steady or even fall against the deutschemark. An option contract, in other words, provides an "option" to the purchaser of the contract: if the exchange rates remain in your favor, ignore the contract; if they move against you, exercise the option contract and obtain the favorable exchange rate. Clearly such an option contract does not come without a cost. The holder of the option pays a premium or a fee to the writer of the contract (the one who agrees to provide the option) in exchange for the privilege of having the choice. We will learn more about option contracts in Chapter 10.

Quotations of Exchange Rates

Exchange rates for foreign currencies are widely quoted in newspapers. Before we leave the subject of foreign exchange markets, let us understand how these quotes can be read. Exhibit 2.6 shows the spot foreign exchange quotes reported in *The Wall Street Journal* on July 21,

Exhibit 2.6
Quotations for Spot Rates for Foreign Currencies

Key Currency Cross Rates
Late New York Trading July 20, 1993

	Dollar	Pound	SFranc	Guilder	Yen	Lira	D-Mark	FFranc	CdnDlr
Canada	1.2783	1.9315	.85419	.66822	.01182	.00081	.75212	.22012	....
France	5.8073	8.775	3.8806	3.0357	.05370	.00366	3.4169	....	4.5430
Germany	1.6996	2.5681	1.1357	.88845	.01572	.00107	....	.29267	1.3296
Italy	1587.6	2398.8	1060.84	829.87	14.679	....	934.07	273.37	1241.9
Japan	108.15	163.41	72.269	56.534	....	.06812	63.633	18.623	84.60
Netherlands ...	1.9130	2.8905	1.2783	....	.01769	.00121	1.1256	.32941	1.4965
Switzerland	1.4965	2.2612	....	.78228	.01384	.00094	.88050	.25769	1.1707
U.K.	.66181	....	.44224	.34596	.00612	.00042	.38939	.11396	.51773
U.S.	....	1.5110	.66823	.52274	.00925	.00063	.58837	.17220	.78229

Source: Telerate

CURRENCY TRADING

EXCHANGE RATES

Tuesday, July 20, 1993

The New York foreign exchange selling rates below apply to trading among banks in amounts of $1 million and more, as quoted at 3 p.m. Eastern time by Bankers Trust Co., Telerate and other sources. Retail transactions provide fewer units of foreign currency per dollar.

Country	U.S. $ equiv. Tues.	Mon.	Currency per U.S. $ Tues.	Mon.
Argentina (Peso)	1.01	1.01	.99	.99
Australia (Dollar)	.6779	.6768	1.4751	1.4775
Austria (Schilling)	.08361	.08323	11.96	12.01
Bahrain (Dinar)	2.6508	2.6522	.3773	.3771
Belgium (Franc)	.02851	.02837	35.07	35.25
Brazil (Cruzeiro)	.0000162	.0000164	61758.02	61011.03
Britain (Pound)	1.5110	1.4985	.6618	.6673
30-Day Forward	1.5072	1.4945	.6635	.6691
90-Day Forward	1.5003	1.4879	.6665	.6721
180-Day Forward	1.4925	1.4800	.6700	.6757
Canada (Dollar)	.7818	.7822	1.2791	1.2785
30-Day Forward	.7811	.7814	1.2803	1.2797
90-Day Forward	.7797	.7800	1.2825	1.2820
180-Day Forward	.7777	.7779	1.2859	1.2855
Czech. Rep. (Koruna)				
Commercial rate	.0342231	.0343053	29.2200	29.1500
Chile (Peso)	.002545	.002548	392.98	392.42
China (Renminbi)	.174856	.174856	5.7190	5.7190
Colombia (Peso)	.001476	.001476	677.50	677.50
Denmark (Krone)	.1525	.1519	6.5590	6.5828
Ecuador (Sucre)				
Floating rate	.000533	.000539	1875.00	1855.01
Finland (Markka)	.17362	.17332	5.7596	5.7697
France (Franc)	.17227	.17181	5.8048	5.8205
30-Day Forward	.17153	.17105	5.8300	5.8461
90-Day Forward	.17031	.16999	5.8715	5.8860
180-Day Forward	.16897	.16869	5.9183	5.9280
Germany (Mark)	.5886	.5860	1.6990	1.7065
30-Day Forward	.5864	.5838	1.7053	1.7130
90-Day Forward	.5828	.5802	1.7159	1.7235
180-Day Forward	.5783	.5757	1.7292	1.7370
Greece (Drachma)	.004302	.004285	232.45	233.35
Hong Kong (Dollar)	.12896	.12891	7.7545	7.7573
Hungary (Forint)	.0106769	.0106769	93.6600	93.6600
India (Rupee)	.03212	.03211	31.13	31.14
Indonesia (Rupiah)	.0004784	.0004780	2090.52	2092.01
Ireland (Punt)	1.4194	1.4137	.7045	.7074
Israel (Shekel)	.3644	.3563	2.7446	2.8070
Italy (Lira)	.0006302	.0006321	1586.87	1582.03

Country	U.S. $ equiv. Wed.	Tues.	Currency per U.S. $ Wed.	Tues.
Japan (Yen)	.009242	.009217	108.20	108.50
30-Day Forward	.009241	.009216	108.21	108.51
90-Day Forward	.009243	.009217	108.19	108.49
180-Day Forward	.009258	.009231	108.02	108.33
Jordan (Dinar)	1.4682	1.4620	.6811	.6840
Kuwait (Dinar)	3.3140	3.3162	.3018	.3016
Lebanon (Pound)	.000578	.000578	1730.00	1730.50
Malaysia (Ringgit)	.3894	.3885	2.5680	2.5740
Malta (Lira)	2.5674	2.5641	.3895	.3900
Mexico (Peso)				
Floating rate	.3203075	.3196420	3.1220	3.1285
Netherland (Guilder) ..	.5230	.5207	1.9122	1.9206
New Zealand (Dollar) .	.5475	.5473	1.8265	1.8272
Norway (Krone)	.1377	.1375	7.2619	7.2753
Pakistan (Rupee)	.0357	.0369	28.05	27.08
Peru (New Sol)	.5053	.4984	1.98	2.01
Philippines (Peso)	.03582	.03697	27.92	27.05
Poland (Zloty)	.00005806	.00005806	17225.00	17225.00
Portugal (Escudo)	.006047	.006051	165.38	165.27
Saudi Arabia (Riyal) ..	.26664	.26664	3.7504	3.7504
Singapore (Dollar)	.6175	.6158	1.6195	1.6240
Slovak Rep. (Koruna) .	.0303306	.0303030	32.9700	33.0000
South Africa (Rand)				
Commercial rate	.2995	.2990	3.3393	3.3443
Financial rate	.2216	.2210	4.5125	4.5250
South Korea (Won)	.0012364	.0012382	808.80	807.60
Spain (Peseta)	.007503	.007498	133.29	133.36
Sweden (Krona)	.1259	.1264	7.9403	7.9139
Switzerland (Franc) ...	.6687	.6664	1.4955	1.5005
30-Day Forward	.6677	.6654	1.4977	1.5028
90-Day Forward	.6661	.6639	1.5012	1.5062
180-Day Forward	.6647	.6624	1.5044	1.5097
Taiwan (Dollar)	.038052	.037615	26.28	26.59
Thailand (Baht)	.03948	.03939	25.33	25.39
Turkey (Lira)	.0000903	.0000902	11072.00	11092.00
United Arab (Dirham) ..	.2723	.2723	3.6725	3.6725
Uruguay (New Peso)				
Financial	.243843	.245398	4.10	4.08
Venezuela (Bolivar)				
Floating rate	.01113	.01109	89.83	90.14
SDR	1.39011	1.38923	.71937	.71982
ECU	1.14510	1.14030	....	....

Special Drawing Rights (SDR) are based on exchange rates for the U.S., German, British, French and Japanese currencies. Source: International Monetary Fund.

European Currency Unit (ECU) is based on a basket of community currencies.

Source: *The Wall Street Journal*, July 21, 1993, pp. c1, c15.

1993. The quotes are for large transactions in the afternoon of the previous trading day, and are obtained from a commercial bank in New York. Direct and indirect quotes are reported for that and the previous trading day, in this case July 20 and July 19. For some countries, the bank also provides forward rates. For other countries, a commercial rate and a financial rate are reported. The difference between these rates is explained in some examples in Exhibit 2.7. In addition, the paper reports the values of an European Currency Unit (in Appendix 2.A) and a Special Drawing Right which is a basket currency unit created by the International Monetary Fund.

▼ ▼ ▼

Exhibit 2.7
Examples of Complex Exchange Rate Arrangements[*]

The simple and straightforward system of exchange rates that exists in the United States and many other industrialized countries is not the general rule around the world. In the simple system in the United States, for example, people are free to buy and sell foreign currencies in exchange for dollars without any restrictions. Anyone can take dollars out of the country or bring them from other countries. The only requirement is that every transaction, or import or export, of over $10,000 must be reported to the Treasury Department (the purpose of this reporting has to do with drug trade, not with government's desire to control the value of the currency). Every participant faces the same exchange rate regardless of the purpose for the transaction. The only difference is that a participant transacting a very large volume of funds will probably pay lower transaction costs. Most other countries have complex exchange rate arrangements where the exchange rate often depends upon the nature of the transaction. The following examples illustrate some of these complexities. In all cases where such an arrangement exists, the central bank (or some other government authority) controls all the transactions. Participants are required to obtain the permission of the central bank to buy foreign currencies (that is, in effect, to buy goods abroad) and are required to turn over any foreign currency they obtain from exports to the central bank.

China
All foreign exchange is controlled by the SAEC (State Administration of Exchange Control). All payments abroad must be approved by SAEC and only SAEC, though the Bank of China, can convert foreign currencies into

the domestic currency, Renminbi. Foreigners travelling in China are issued FECs (Foreign exchange certificates) and they may buy goods and services in China only in FECs. The author, however, encountered a thriving black market in foreign currencies and FECs (which are easily convertible into foreign currencies at the bank) while in China in 1992. Goods were cheaper if paid for in FECs and restaurant service friendlier. The official rate on June 19, 1992, was RMB 547 = US$ 100 and the black market rate was about 15-20 percent better. On January 1, 1994, the government eliminated the FEC, allowing foreigners, as well as Chinese, to transact in Renminbis.

Dominican Republic
Effective January 24, 1991, there are two exchange rates for the Dominican Peso. All foreign exchange transactions carried out in the country are subject to exchange controls imposed by the central bank. In the official market (mercado oficial) the rate is set by the central bank and is pegged to the U.S. dollar. In the private market (mercado privado) the rate is set by the market supply and demand. The official rate is used to convert foreign currency earnings into pesos for all exports of goods and of selected services. All essential imports and debt payments are paid for at the official rate. The private market is used to pay for all imports not considered essential, for foreign travel, and for transferring capital outside the country. This market receives funds from tourist expenditures in the country and from the remittances that foreigners make to citizens. Since March 20, 1992, this rate is also used to convert proceeds from foreign investment in the country and from foreign loans. On May 25, 1992, the official rate was RD$ 12.5/12.75 = US$ 1.00 and the private market rate was RD$ 12.63/12.82 = US$ 1.00. Import or export of national currency is prohibited.

India
The Indian Rupee was made convertible on March 1, 1993. Before that, however, those who received foreign currencies were required to sell 40 percent of the amount to the central bank of the country, The Reserve Bank of India, at the official rate. The other 60 percent could be converted at the market rate. The foreign currencies obtained through the official rate were reserved for certain priority transactions (i.e., the transactions of the government). All others were required to purchase foreign currencies at the market rate. On June 19, 1992, the official rate was IR 25.89 = US$ 1.00 whereas the market rate was IR 29.99 = US$ 1.00. An informal black

market also existed in the country where the rate was close to the market rate. Legally, of course, the black market was illegal.

Kyrgyzstan
Som, the currency of the recently formed republic of Kyrgyzstan of the former Soviet Union, may be one of the youngest currencies in the world. The currency was launched on May 10, 1993, with the help of $62 million credit from the IMF. Initially set equal to 200 rubles, the currency was allowed to float within two weeks of its issue and began trading at about 230 rubles/som, or 4 som/dollar. Other details about the currency were not available.

---

* Details from Union Bank of Switzerland, "Rupiah or Lilangeni: Exchange Rate Arrangements and Currency Regulations," 1992/93 edition, except information on Kyrgyzstan is from *The Wall Street Journal,* May 18, 1993.

▲ ▲ ▲

The quote for Britain begins with the number 1.5110. This means that the pound was quoted on June 20 at $1.5110/pound. The quote for the previous day was $1.4985/pound. The pound appreciated on June 20 because it was worth more in terms of dollars on June 20 than the previous day. The last two columns provide the indirect quotes being given as the units of foreign currency/dollar. These numbers are the inverse of direct quotes.

Note that the newspaper does not report bid or ask prices. The prices quoted are the average of bid and ask prices, and an investor wishing to purchase one of these currencies will have to obtain the bid prices from the bank. The bid-ask spreads will, of course, be different for each currency.

Finally, the exhibit also shows some cross rates. These quotes give the values of two foreign currencies in terms of each other. Thus, the rate for deutschemarks and Canadian dollars is DM 1.3296/C$, which is the same as DM 1.6996/US$ × US$ 0.78229/C$.

Summary

The foreign exchange market is perhaps the largest market in the world. Banks and other institutions that comprise this market offer a variety of contracts that meet various user needs. The challenge for a user is to understand how contracts, spots, futures, forwards, options, and swaps differ from one another and what unique service each contract provides. A spot contract allows money to be transferred from one currency to another immediately. Forwards and futures protect the users from the risks of changes in exchange rates. Options do the same and a little more; they allow users to speculate and hedge. These contracts, however, are not independent of each other. Users must understand how these contracts are related to each other. The biggest challenge for any participant, however, is to understand why and how exchange rates change at all. This is the subject of the following chapter.

Appendix 2.A
The International Monetary System

The current monetary system came into being in 1973 when the Bretton Woods system, which had governed international monetary relations since 1944, came to an end. By an international monetary system we mean explicit or implicit agreements between countries as to how the exchange rates between different currencies are to be determined, and rules and regulations that govern the flow of capital between countries. The system that came into place in 1973 was largely a response to the problems of the previous decade. Under the Bretton Woods system, values of most of the currencies—known as par values—had been fixed in terms of the U.S. dollar. Fluctuations were allowed only within a narrow band of 1.25 percent around the par values. The par value of the German mark in late 1969, for example was 4.0 DM/$. Under the rules of the system, it was the responsibility of the German Central bank, the Bundesbank, to ensure that the exchange rate in the market remained between 3.95 and 4.05 DM/$. The system provided stability for international traders, but proved very restrictive for managing disequilibria in the balance of payments. Governments of the countries that faced balance of payments deficits were either reluctant or unable to change par values of their currencies. This reluctance or inability eliminated the possibility of using foreign exchange rate changes as part of the policy package to adjust domestic economies in order to solve balance of payments problems.

When the balance of payments crises began to appear frequently in the late 1960s and when the United States economy began to have large deficits in its balance of payments, the fixed exchange rate system was abandoned in favor of a floating rate system. It was felt that the flexibility given to the markets to determine what the currencies are worth would allow for faster adjustments in periods of balance of payments troubles. Floating the U.S. dollar also allowed the U.S. economy to have the same tools as the rest of the world to solve its balance of payments disequilibria.

The system has evolved to a point that most currencies are either freely floating or are fixed to another currency, or a basket of currencies, that is floating. Exhibit 2.8 provides a summary of the exchange rate system for most of the currencies in the world. Exhibit 2.7 gives examples of some currencies that have complex exchange rate arrangements. The major exceptions to this are the currencies of the countries of the European Economic Community which have created a European Monetary System (EMS). EMS was created in 1979 in response to what were seen as excessive fluctuations between the values of currencies of the common market countries. An exchange rate mechanism was created at that time that lasted till the fall of 1993 when crisis in the currency markets forced governments to abandon it.

Exhibit 2.8
Exchange Arrangements as of March 31, 1993

Pegged					
Single currency				Currency composite	
U.S. dollar	French franc	Russian ruble[1]	Other	SDR	Other
Angola	Benin	Armenia	Bhutan	Libyan Arab	Algeria
Antigua and	Burkina Faso	Azerbaijan	(Indian	Jamahiriya[7]	Austria
Barbuda	Cameroon	Belarus[4]	rupee)	Myanmar	Bangladesh
Argentina	Central	Georgia	Estonia	Rwanda	Botswana
Bahamas, The[4]	African Republic	Kazakhstan[4]	(deutsche	Seychelles	Burundi
Barbados	Chad		mark)		
		Kyrgyzstan	Kiribati[1]		Cape Verde
Belize	Comoros	Moldova	(Australian		Cyprus[8]
Djibouti	Congo		dollar)		Fiji
Dominica	Côte d'Ivoire		Lesotho[4]		Hungary
Ethiopia	Equatorial		(South		Iceland[10]
Grenada	Guinea		African		
	Gabon		rand)		Jordan
Iraq[4]			Namibia[1, 4]		Kenya[4]
Liberia	Mali		(South		Kuwait
Marshall	Niger		African		Malawi
Islands[1]	Senegal		rand)		Malaysia[9]
Mongolia[4]	Togo				
Nicaragua[4]			Swaziland		Malta
			(South		Mauritania[4]
Oman			African		Mauritius
Panama[1]			rand)		Morocco[11]
St. Kitts and Nevis					Papua
St. Lucia					New Guinea
St. Vincent and					
the Grenadines					Solomon Islands
					Tanzania[4]
Suriname[4]					Thailand
Syrian Arab					Tonga
Republic[4]					Vanuatu
Yemen[4]					
					Western Samoa
					Zimbabwe

[1] Country uses peg currency as legal tender.
[2] In all countries listed in this column, the U.S. dollar was the currency against which exchange rates showed limited flexibility.
[3] This category consists of countries participating in the exchange rate mechanism of the European Monetary System. In each case, the exchange rate is maintained within a margin of 2.25 percent around the bilateral central rates against other participating currencies, with the exception of Portugal and Spain, in which case the exchange rate is maintained within a margin of 6 percent.
[4] Member maintains exchange arrangements involving more than one exchange market. The arrangement shown is that maintained in the major market.
[5] Exchange rates are determined on the basis of a fixed relationship to the SDR, within margins of up to ± 7.25 percent. However, because of the maintenance of a relatively stable relationship with the U.S. dollar, these margins are not always observed.
[6] The exchange rate is maintained within margins of ± 10 percent on either side of a weighted composite of the currencies of the main trading partners.
[7] The exchange rate is maintained within margins of ± 13.5 percent.
[8] The exchange rate, which is pegged to the ECU, is maintained within margins of ± 2.25 percent.
[9] The exchange rate is maintained within margins of ± 5 percent.
[10] The exchange rate is maintained within margins of ± 2.25 percent.
[11] The exchange rate is maintained within margins of ± 3 percent.

Exhibit 2.8 Continued

Flexibility Limited Against a Single Currency or Group of Currencies		More Flexible		
Single currency[2]	Cooperative arrangements[3]	Adjusted according to a set of indicators	Other managed floating	Independently floating
Bahrain[5]	Belgium	Chile[4, 6]	China[4]	Afghanistan, Islamic State of[4] Romania
Qatar[5]	Denmark	Colombia	Ecuador[4]	Albania Russia
Saudi Arabia[5]	France	Madagascar	Egypt	Australia Sierra Leone
United Arab Emirates[5]	Germany		Greece	Bolivia South Africa[4]
	Ireland		Guinea	Brazil[4] Sudan[4]
	Luxembourg		Guinea-Bissau[4]	Bulgaria Sweden
	Netherlands		Indonesia	Canada Switzerland
	Portugal		Israel[9]	Costa Rica Trinidad and Tobago
	Spain		Korea	Dominican Republic Uganda[4]
			Lao People's Democratic Republic	El Salvador Ukraine
				Finland
			Maldives	Gambia, The United Kingdom
			Mexico	Ghana United States
			Pakistan	Guatemala Venezuela
			Poland[4]	Guyana Zaïre
			Sao Tome and Principe	Haiti Zambia[4]
				Honduras
			Singapore	India
			Somalia[4]	Iran, Islamic Republic of
			Sri Lanka	Italy
			Tunisia	
			Turkey	Jamaica
				Japan
			Uruguay	Latvia
			Viet Nam	Lebanon
				Lithuania
				Mozambique[4]
				New Zealand
				Nepal
				Nigeria[4]
				Norway
				Paraguay
				Peru
				Philippines

Source: *Annual Report*, International Monetary Fund, 1993, pp. 132–33.

Currencies that were part of the EMS had fixed par values in terms of each other and could fluctuate within 2.25 percent of the par values. These par values were decided in consultations between the two countries and could be changed as circumstances required. Greater flexibility was allowed for the changes in the par values than was permitted in the Bretton Woods system. This exchange rate mechanism (or ERM) was introduced to reduce the uncertainty created by currency fluctuations for international traders and with the ultimate goal of introducing one currency, ECU or European Currency Unit, in the community. The member countries of the Community signed the Maastricht Treaty in December 1991 that laid out the blueprint for the ultimate monetary unification of the common market and the introduction of one currency. The ERM and the concept of monetary union, however, came under serious stress first in the fall of 1992 when the pound, the lira, and the peseta could not maintain their values and had to be devalued by large amounts. The second threat came about a year later in the fall of 1993 when the foreign currency markets were once again thrown in turmoil. After the second crisis, countries that decided to remain within the ERM agreed that their currencies would be free to fluctuate within a 15 percent band of their par values. At this point it is not clear whether the EEC will continue with the goal of introducing one currency in Western Europe by the end of this decade. Given the increased use of basket currencies in the international financial markets, however, it is important that we understand how a basket currency works.

To understand what a basket currency is, it is best to imagine a basket containing fixed amounts of selected currencies. In the case of the ECU, the basket contains the 12 currencies of the European community. Amounts of the 12 currencies in the ECU basket are shown in column 2 in Exhibit 2.9 against the names of the currencies in column 1. The amounts were chosen based upon the importance of the 12 economies within the community and remain fixed from day to day. On any given day, we can find out the value of the basket in terms of any other currency, say the Canadian dollar, if we know the exchange rate of the 12 currencies in terms of the Canadian dollar. Column 3 in the exhibit shows the exchange rates of each currency as a direct quote in Canadian dollars (that is, $/foreign currency.) Column 4 shows the Canadian dollar equivalents of the currency amounts in column 2 at the exchange rates in column 3, that is, column 2 multiplied by column 3. When the numbers in column 4 are added, they give us the value of an ECU on the date for which the exchange rates were quoted, in this case January 22, 1992.

The advantage of a basket currency is that as exchange rates change, the value of the basket, when measured in any particular currency, will change less than the value of one currency by itself. The lower volatility in the value of the basket results from the fact that as the value of one of the constituent currencies rises, the value of another may fall. Thus, if some of the currencies in an ECU were to rise against the Canadian dollar, it is likely that the others would fall. The value of an ECU, therefore, in terms of Canadian dollars, may fluctuate less than the value of one of these currencies, say the deutschemarks.

Exhibit 2.9
European Currency Unit (ECU)
(value in canadian dollars)

Currency	Amount of Currency (1) in Basket	Exchange Rate: 1/22/92 in C$/unit	Value (2) × (3)
(1)	(2)	(3)	(4)
Deutschemark	0.6242	0.7275	0.4541
French franc	1.332	0.2134	0.2842
Sterling	0.08784	2.0864	0.1833
Lira	151.8	0.000968	0.1469
Guilder	0.2198	0.6463	0.1421
Belgian & Lux. franc	3.431	0.0353	0.1211
Peseta	6.885	0.01153	0.0794
Krone	0.1976	0.1875	0.0371
Irish punt	0.008552	1.9394	0.0166
Escudo	1.04741	0.00845	0.0089
Drachma	1.44	0.006331	0.0091
		1 ECU =	C$ 1.4828

Appendix 2.B
The International Monetary Fund

The International Monetary Fund (IMF) is partly the world's central bank, partly a commercial bank for the governments, and partly a watchdog who steers the wayward finance ministers to the path desired by an absentee shepherd. The IMF was created toward the end of the Second World War at the same conference that ushered in the fixed exchange rate system that came to be known as the Bretton Woods system. The IMF, or the Fund, was created for the purpose of promoting international monetary cooperation and for promoting international trade and growth through maintenance of orderly exchange rate arrangements between the members. Initially the Fund was also supposed to use its financial resources to help member countries manage temporary balance of payments disequilibria. Over the decades, and especially since the fixed exchange rate system was abandoned in 1973 and oil prices increased the same year, the IMF has come to play an important role in evaluation and guidance of the macroeconomic policies of member countries. Although the main focus of the IMF's activity in this area has been toward the developing and emerging countries, the IMF also keeps a close tab on the economic policies of industrialized countries. Over the last decade, its endorsement or criticism of the economic strategies of member countries, industrialized or otherwise, has acquired unprecedented importance in the international financial markets.

Membership in the IMF increased to 178 in 1993 when Micronesia joined the organization in June. The Fund's headquarters are located in Washington, DC but by convention, the managing director of the Fund is a European. Member countries, which form the governing body of the Fund, are allocated votes according to their importance in the global economy. Thus, the United States had 17.8 percent of total votes in 1993, Germany and Japan had 5.55 percent each, and France and the United Kingdom had 4.99 percent each. The remaining votes were divided among the other members. The voting power also determines the proportions in which the members must contribute resources for the Funds.

One of the first tasks given to the IMF was strongly influenced by the time at which the Bretton Woods conference was being held. For about a decade before the Second World War had begun, the world economy had been in a depression during which countries had tried to use devaluation of their currencies as means of escaping the depression. Every country felt that if it could lower the value of its currency, its exports will be stimulated and domestic economy would grow. When every country tried to use that strategy and engaged in competitive devaluations, volume of world trade, and hence the global economic output, declined. Participants at the Bretton Woods conference wanted to prevent a repetition of that vicious cycle. Thus, the IMF was mandated to facilitate the expansion of world trade by, among other things, promoting exchange stability, maintaining orderly exchange arrangements, and avoiding competitive devaluations. Indeed for the first two decades of the Fund's existence, member countries found it difficult to devalue their currencies even if they were facing serious balance of payments disequilibria. The Fund also encourages members to have full convertability for current account transactions, allowing international trade to take place without hindrance. In 1993, 77 members of the IMF had made their currencies fully convertible.

The second important task given to the IMF in its earlier days was to ensure that the international monetary system had sufficient liquidity. A monetary system, whether national or international, requires a sufficient quantity of a reserve asset. This reserve asset, which can be gold, currencies, or something else, provides the users of the monetary system with a mechanism for saving funds which they can use in times when their expenses exceed their incomes. After the Second World War, the U.S. dollar had become the main international reserve, with gold and some other international currencies playing secondary roles. In the mid-1960s, it was felt that, on the one hand, the dollar should not have such a prominent position and, on the other hand, the supply of dollars in the hands of the international community was increasing fast enough. The IMF responded to the situation by creating its own reserve asset, known as Special Drawing Rights (SDRs) which were allocated to member countries in proportions to their quotas in the organization. These SDRs could be used by central banks of the countries to settle accounts with each other. In 1973, the value of an SDR was defined in terms of a basket of currencies which, after some changes, has consisted of the following currencies since 1991:

SDR Valuation

Since January 1, 1991

Currency	Amount of Currency in the Basket	Weight on January 1, 1991
U.S. dollar	0.572	40
Deutschemark	0.453	21
Japanese yen	31.8	17
French franc	0.800	11
Pound sterling	0.0812	11

At the present time, the IMF's main task would seem to be to provide policy advice and financial assistance to members that face unusual difficulties. As part of policy advice, the Fund may also provide technical assistance to countries for building institutions that are ultimately responsible for macroeconomic management of a country's economy. The Fund may carry out a surveillance of the global economy as well as of the economies of specific member countries before offering policy advice.

The IMF played a critical role in the first half of the 1980s when a number of developing countries were unable to meet their obligations arising from their international debts (we will discuss some aspects of this third world debt crisis in Chapter 13). The IMF recommended adjustment programs for the borrowing countries which were used by private commercial banks as preconditions for rescheduling the loans of the indebted countries. Although these adjustment programs allowed the loans to be rescheduled, and thus averted bankruptcy of the commercial banks on the one hand and defaults of the countries on the other, they were severely criticized in the developing countries as having imposed too large a burden on the poor sections of the populations. The IMF has played a similar role for the transformation of the formerly centrally planned economies of Europe over the last few years.

The Fund has created a number of different programs for financing needs of its members over the last two decades. The most recent of these programs is the establishment of a temporary systemic transformation facility (STF). This facility has been designed to help the formerly centrally planned economies to transform their economies to market

Exhibit 2.10
Total Fund Credit Outstanding to Members,
Financial Years Ended April 30, 1981–83
(in billions of SDRs; end of period)

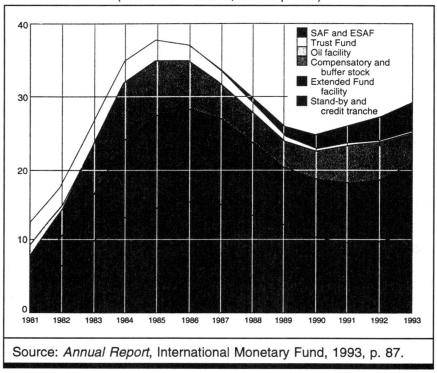

Source: *Annual Report*, International Monetary Fund, 1993, p. 87.

economies. STF funding is meant to help countries stabilize their situation so that they can borrow under Structural Adjustment Facility (SAF) or under Enhanced Structural Adjustment Facility (ESAF). The fund has a number of other sources which allow it to fund different types of member needs. Exhibit 2.10 provides an overview of how large these programs, and the resources of the IMF, are.

Note

1. "Survey: World Economy," *The Economist*, September 19, 1992, p. survey–9.

Chapter 3
The Theory of Exchange Rates

We began the previous chapter with a brief description of how foreign currency markets were thrown in a turmoil in the fall of 1992. Foreign exchange rates for some of the European currencies changed suddenly, and by large amounts, in spite of concerted efforts from the central banks of these countries. Although a number of reasons can be advanced for why these changes came about during those days, it is far from clear that most market participants had noticed any fundamental reasons for the exchange rates to change even a few days before the events of that week. In fact, the central banks of some of the countries whose currencies dropped in value were so confident of the values of their currencies that they invested large sums of money (not their own) and lost billions of it when currencies did drop in values. Why do exchange rates change at all, and why do they seem to change so unpredictably? In this chapter, we want to address these questions and raise the importance of forecasting future values of exchange rates for international investors. In order to forecast exchange rates, we have to understand the economic relationships between exchange rates and other macro economic variables, and since we have to contend with markets which react to events as they did in the fall of 1992, we also have to understand the importance of "market sentiment" or the behavior of speculators in the market.

The turmoil in the currency markets in the fall of 1992 may have caught the markets by surprise partly because we had come to expect some semblance of stability in the exchange rates between the currencies of the European Common Market. Since 1979 when the European Monetary System was established, the exchange rates of the larger common market economies had fluctuated less and less with respect to each other. For exchange rates other than those of the common market, however, high volatility had become the norm rather than an exception since the floating exchange rates era began in 1973. The increased volatility of exchange rates over that period can be demonstrated if we examine the actual behavior of some of the currencies over the last three decades. Exhibit 3.1 compares two measures of volatility for six of the major currencies during the fixed and floating exchange rate periods. All the exchange rates are measured as the value of one SDR in terms of each of the six currencies. The first measure, the range divided by the mean, shows the difference between the maximum and the minimum value of each of the six currencies divided by its mean during two five–year periods of the fixed exchange rate system and four five–year periods during the floating rate period, in addition to the two years, 1971 and 1972, when the international monetary system was in a turmoil. The second measure, the coefficient of variation, is a ratio of the standard deviation of the month–end values divided by the mean of those values over the same time period, expressed as a percentage.

The exhibit provides an indication of the fluctuations in the values of the currencies and an increase in the volatility in the markets since the floating regime began in 1973. Consider the fluctuations in the French franc. During the entire decade from 1961 to 1970, its value fluctuated between 4.9 ff/$ and 5.78 ff/$. The range of fluctuations in the second half of the decade was about 13 percent of the average value of the currency. Over a five–year period in the late 1970s, however, the franc changed by about 40 percent of its average value. A similar pattern is observed for all the other currencies also. There is a dramatic increase in the range of fluctuations after 1972 for every currency. The coefficient of variation provides a good measure of how much currency values have fluctuated in terms of the value itself. A dramatic increase in the values of this measure shows that the volatility in the markets has increased since 1973. The values of these two measures for the 1980s show further that the increased volatility was not limited to a period soon after the introduction of the floating rate system.

Exhibit 3.1
Volatility of Selected Exchange Rates[*]

Range/Mean Over the Period (in percent)						
Period	USA	UK	France	Germany	Canada	Japan
1961-65	0.0000	1.1326	0.3203	5.1572	9.5881	1.2071
1966-70	0.0000	15.9787	13.2709	10.0576	7.0988	1.4132
1971-72	8.1907	14.7538	4.3982	9.3396	8.4506	9.0545
1973-77	14.7148	45.9957	21.7977	29.3777	20.2718	23.1469
1978-82	23.3658	26.6308	39.7635	20.4811	18.7342	32.0980
1983-87	41.0277	27.3306	27.2452	35.0923	37.4903	37.1718
1988-92	17.6911	24.0772	17.7050	17.2481	23.1928	22.6968
Coefficient of Variation (in percent)						
1961-65	0.0000	0.2795	0.0711	0.89689	2.5857	0.4114
1966-70	0.0000	7.3099	5.3824	3.82327	1.7462	0.5641
1971-72	4.1689	4.6727	0.9976	2.64020	3.2917	3.8522
1973-77	2.7061	13.3334	5.0287	7.01755	4.2029	5.9044
1978-82	6.6647	6.7021	12.0769	5.89984	5.0996	7.5713
1983-87	10.2413	6.1644	7.1493	9.77603	11.8362	12.7379
1988-92	4.1526	4.9779	4.7186	4.58593	5.3217	5.3764

[*]All exchange rates are measured as the value of one SDR in the currency of the country. This measure of the exchange rate, rather than the value of another currency, say the U.S. dollar in terms of the national currency, allows for a more stable base against which changes in the values of a particular currency can be measured. If volatility were measured against the U.S. dollar, say for the French franc, both the measures would show higher volatility in the post 1973 era than the table above because the U.S. dollar itself was not changing in value till 1973.

Source: The analysis is based upon exchange rates in *International Financial Statistics,* International Monetary Fund, Various issues.

Our aim in this chapter is to understand why exchange rates change. In a freely fluctuating exchange rate system, the exchange rate for any currency is determined by an equilibrium between its supply and its demand. This is true only as long as the government of the country, through its central bank, does not interfere with the functioning of the market. It is, however, very difficult to measure the precise supply and demand. The difficulties arise due to the nature of the majority of transactions which were identified in Chapter 2 as being based largely upon speculative motives and not on a need to make a payment in a foreign currency for imports of goods or services. The foreign exchange rates thus become dependent upon the expectations of speculators. Since expectations can change very quickly and in response to the slightest bits of relevant information, foreign exchange rates can become very volatile for those freely floating currencies which are used by the market participants as speculative vehicles. The speculators, however, do not base their decisions on arbitrary whims. They are guided by relationships between exchange rates and other macroeconomic variables. Our challenge, therefore, is first to understand which macroeconomic variables influence the value of an exchange rate, second to understand how speculators would assess those variables and their relationships, and finally to understand if and when central banks would intervene in foreign exchange markets to influence the values of their currencies.

We will study the theory of exchange rates in three stages. The first section discusses the macroeconomic determinants of exchange rates. We will discuss three economic concepts or variables that are known to influence exchange rates: interests rates, inflation rates, and balance of payments. The subsequent section examines the influence of speculation on exchange rates, and the third section discusses the role of central banks.

Economics of Exchange Rates

The price of any commodity in a free market depends upon supply and demand. The same is true of foreign exchange rates. For the freely fluctuating currencies, the exchange rates are determined such that supply and demand for currencies are equalized. That may sound simple in theory, but in reality, it is impossible to measure supply and demand. We can, however, analyze origins of supply and demand for currencies. If we could understand how the factors that determine supply and demand change, we could begin to understand why foreign exchange rates change.

We will study the sources of supply and demand for currencies in three ways. First we look at what are called "parity relationships" in the foreign exchange market. Parity relationships in this market arise from possibilities of arbitrage between the foreign exchange market on the one hand and the money markets or real goods markets on the other hand. Arbitrage dictates equilibrium relationships between exchange rates and either the interest rates or prices of goods and services in the economy. These relationships arise from the possibilities that, if parity did not exist, profitable and sometimes risk–free arbitrage would be possible. Since the existence of such arbitrage opportunities is inconsistent with efficient markets, exchange rates and other variables will maintain relationships with each other such that arbitrage opportunities do not exist.

Second, we look at the balance of payments transactions as sources of supply and demand for foreign currencies. Since all balance of payments transactions involve payments or receipts in foreign currencies, absence of equilibrium in balance of payments accounts is a good indication of whether the supply and demand for foreign currencies are creating pressures for changes in exchange rates.

Finally, we look at some macroeconomic theories that establish relationships between exchange rates and other macroeconomic variables by modelling the value of an exchange rate either in terms of supply and demand or as one of the prices in a macroeconomic system. These three approaches to the study of determination of exchange rates are not independent of each other; they are driven by the same fundamental changes in the economy, but they posit different channels through which the variables cause changes in exchange rates.

Parity Relationships

Interest Rate Parity Theorem

The interest rate parity theorem postulates that the difference between interest rates in two countries must have a known and predictable relationship with the exchange rates. More precisely, it states that the interest rate differential between two countries that do not have restrictions on capital flows should equal the difference between the spot and the forward exchange rates. The theorem is based on the idea of arbitrage according to which markets do not allow unexploited profit opportunities to exist for any length of time.

The interest rate parity theorem can be best understood with an example. Consider an investor in the United States who has, say, one million dollars to invest for a period of three months. The investor is indifferent as to where she invests but is not willing to take any risk with the money. In the absence of any other investments, she is willing to buy U.S. government Treasury bills which are currently yielding 5.0 percent per annum. Now suppose that a broker informs her that the interest rate on German government Treasury bills is 9 percent and assures her that the bills are at least as safe as the U.S. government bills. Should she not be investing in Treasury bills in Germany where she can earn 4 percent more? To help her decide, look at the situation as depicted in Exhibit 3.2.

The exhibit depicts two investment alternatives available to the investor. The investor has money in the United States at time T_0 and wants to end up at time $T_{3\text{-months}}$ in the United States with dollars. She has two routes to go from the time T_0 to time $T_{3\text{-months}}$ (or any other time

Exhibit 3.2
Interest Arbitrage

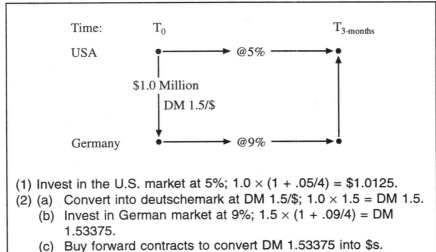

(1) Invest in the U.S. market at 5%; $1.0 \times (1 + .05/4) = \$1.0125$.
(2) (a) Convert into deutschemark at DM 1.5/\$; $1.0 \times 1.5 = $ DM 1.5.
    (b) Invest in German market at 9%; $1.5 \times (1 + .09/4) = $ DM 1.53375.
    (c) Buy forward contracts to convert DM 1.53375 into \$s.

period). First, she can invest the million dollars in the United States and obtain interest at the rate of 5 percent per annum, which would result in her having $1,012,500 at the end of 3 months. Alternatively, she could convert the money into German marks, buy German T–bills, and then plan to convert the money back into dollars at the end of three months. The exact number of dollars she would receive at the end of three months would depend upon the exchange rate that should prevail at the time of maturity of the T–bills—which is three months later. Since she is risk averse, that is, she wants to take as little risk as possible, she would sell the marks in the forward market and fix the amount she will receive in dollars.

Following through on the steps in the transactions, we can determine the amount that will be received in dollars. Exhibit 3.2 shows that the spot exchange rate is 1.5 marks/$. Thus, at time T_0 one million dollars would yield 1.5 million marks if we assume that there are no fees or charges associated with the transaction. 1.5 million marks invested for three months at 9 percent would yield 1.53375 marks. Now suppose that the forward rate is the same as the spot rate, that is, the market does not expect the spot rate to change in three months. The investor can buy a forward contract to convert 1.53375 million marks into dollars at 1.5 marks/$ and expect to receive $1,022,500 at the end of three months. Note the differences between the two alternatives. The first alternative promises an amount of $1.0125 million without any risk other than the credit risk of the U.S. government. The second alternative promises an amount of $1.0225 million (provided the forward rate is 1.5 marks/$) without any risk other than the credit risk of the German government. Since we have been told that the German government is as safe as the one in the United States, the two alternatives seem to have the same risk, but the second alternative offers a higher return. Since our investor is a rational investor, she will obviously choose the second alternative and transfer her funds to the German money market for three months.

Are other investors likely to follow her example? Undoubtedly yes! The money markets in Germany offer better returns than those in the United States. Every investor in the United States will now have the incentive to take his funds to Germany. In fact, given the rapidity of information flow in the financial markets, it will only take a short time before the U.S. money markets lose all funds to the German money markets—unless something changes.

The supply and demand forces in the financial markets will begin to work. Three changes are possible. As the funds flow out of U.S. markets, U.S. interest rates may begin to rise. Simultaneously, German interest rates may begin to fall. Thus, one solution to the disequilibrium situation is that the interest rates in the two markets will be equalized.

What is of greater interest to us is what may begin to happen in the foreign currency markets—the third change that may take place. Suppose that the money markets in the two countries are too large to take note of money going out or coming in. The attention will shift to the foreign exchange markets. At time T_0 there is a great demand for the marks and there is a great demand for dollars at time $T_{3-months}$. These demands will create imbalances in the supply and demand and will cause both the spot and the future rates to change. Due to the excess demand for marks in the spot market, the mark will rise in value and the exchange rate will become less than 1.5 marks/$. In the forward market there is a demand for dollars which will make dollars more expensive and the exchange rate will rise above 1.5 marks/$. The changes in the spot and the forward rates will now alter the returns that an investor would be able to obtain if he were to take his dollars for investment in Germany. A rising value of marks in the spot market will mean that he will have fewer marks to invest at time T_0 and a rising value of dollars in the forward market will mean that the marks obtained from the investment in the financial market in Germany will convert to fewer dollars at time $T_{3-months}$. What will the exchange rates be when the markets settle down, that is, when equilibrium is re–established in the markets? The condition for equilibrium in this case is that the arbitrage incentive that had motivated investors to move funds from one market to another should disappear. In other words, calm will be restored only when the exchange rates (or exchange rates together with interest rates) change such that the investor ends up with the same number of dollars whether she keeps the money in the United States or she takes it to Germany.

Since we are interested in exchange rates, we will assume that the interest rates remain fixed and only the exchange rates change to bring about the equilibrium. To simplify the analysis even more, let us further assume that the spot rate also remains fixed and it is only the forward rate that will change. Let us now return to the first investor who had $1.0 million to invest for three months. What must be the new forward rate such that she is indifferent between the two alternatives she has? The general answer to this question is that the forward rate must be such that the investor's gains due to higher interest rates in Germany are completely negated by any loss in the foreign exchange market. Since the interest rate differential between the two markets is 4 percent per annum in favor of Germany, the forward rate must reflect an equal loss against the spot rate. As we saw in the previous chapter, this means that the forward rate for marks must be at a discount of 4 percent per annum from the spot rate. We can confirm this by looking at the numbers once again. To be indifferent between the two alternatives, the forward rate must be such that the marks obtained from the investment yield the same number of dollars as the investment in the United States. This implies that the forward rate must be:

$$\text{forward rate} = 1.53375 \div 1.0125 = 1.51482 \text{ marks/\$}$$

At the forward rate of 1.52482 marks/\$, the investor, who would have received 1.53375 million marks by investing the 1.5 million for three months, would obtain \$1.0125 million, the same amount as would be obtained if the amount were invested in the United States. At this forward rate, there is no incentive for people with money to arbitrage. If the forward rate were below 1.51482 marks/\$, say 1.51 marks/\$, investors would earn more by investing their money in Germany. If, however, the rate were to be higher than 1.51482 marks/\$, say 1.525 marks/\$, the incentive would be for German investors to take their money to the United States. They would now earn more money if they invested it in the United States instead of in Germany, even though the interest rates were higher in Germany. You may wish to verify this by calculating the amount of marks that a German investor would have at the end of three months if she has 3.0 million marks at time T_0. The following box provides the answer.

▼ ▼ ▼

Incentive for the German Investor to Invest in the United States

A German investor who starts with 3.0 million marks at time T_0 would have 3.0675 million marks at the end of three months if the funds were invested in German money markets.

$$3.0 \times (1 + 9/100 \times 3/12) = 3.0675$$

If, however, he converts them into dollars, he would receive $ 2.0 million to invest. This would yield $2.025 million at the end of three months. This would then be converted into 3.088125 million marks:

$$2.025 \times 1.525 = 3.088125.$$

Clearly, the incentive is now for the German investors to take their money to the United States.

▲ ▲ ▲

What will happen in equilibrium? The forward rate will have to be such that the investors in neither country have incentive to take their funds to the other country. At this point, a parity relationship would have been established between the interest rates and the exchange rates. At the point of equilibrium, the advantage of higher interest rates in one country is offset by the disadvantage of expected depreciation in the exchange rate of that country in the future. The general form of this relationship is derived in the following box.

▼ ▼ ▼

Formal Derivation of the Parity Relationship

Let S_0 represent the spot exchange rate and F_0 the forward rate with both rates being quoted as direct quotations (not the indirect quotation used in the earlier numerical example), and let i_d and i_f be the domestic (the United States in the earlier example) and foreign interest rates. Let the investor begin with one unit of domestic currency in the period T_0. The two alternatives can now be represented algebraically as follows:

(i) Invest in the domestic market:

$$\text{Amount at the end of 1 year} = 1 \times (1 + i_d) = 1 + i_d$$

The Theory of Exchange Rates   63

(ii) Invest in the foreign country:

$$\text{Amount to invest in foreign currency} = 1 / S_0$$

$$\text{Amount in foreign currency at the end of one year} = (1 / S_0) \times (1 + i_f)$$

$$\text{Amount in domestic currency at the end of one year}$$
$$= (1 / S_0) \times (1 + i_f) \times F_0 = (F_0 / S_0) \times (1 + i_f)$$

In equilibrium, the two amounts must be equal:

$$1 + i_d = (F_0 / S_0) \times (1 + i_f)$$

Simplification results in the following equation:

$$(F_0 - S_0)/S_0 = (i_d - i_f)/(1 + i_f) \qquad (3.1)$$

The left–hand side of this equation represents the discount or the premium on the forward rate. If the interest rates are small and we measure this equation for short periods of time, the quantity $(1 + i_f)$ is nearly equal to 1 and the right–hand side of the equation becomes the difference in the interest rates in the two markets. With the simplifying assumption, the equation can now be written as:

Forward discount or premium = Difference in interest rates

This relationship represents the general form of the covered interest rate parity theorem.

▲ ▲ ▲

Up to this point, we have talked about an investor who does not wish to take any risk. To avoid risk, the investor protected, or covered, her investment in the forward market. For this type of investor, the relationship between the interest rates and the exchange rates is known as the **covered interest rate parity theorem**. Before we discuss the importance of this theorem from the point of view of predicting exchange rate changes, let us recognize that the investors could also undertake a risky investment in the foreign country, following the uncovered interest rate parity. The full meaning of that term is explained in the accompanying box.

▼ ▼ ▼

Uncovered Interest Rate Parity

The U.S. investor has the choice of investing her money in Germany without purchasing the forward contract to convert the proceeds back into U.S. dollars. She will have to wait for three months to find out the rate at which marks will be converted into dollars. The investor could gain or lose depending upon the movement in the exchange rate between the time the investment is made and the time it matures. If the forward rate is an unbiased predictor (more on this later in the chapter) of the future spot rate, the investor's expected value from the investment in the foreign country would be the same as in the case of covered interest rate parity, but unlike that situation, there is a risk that the return will be different. Since there are investors who are willing to take risk (for example, risk neutral investors) if the interest rate differential between the two countries were to be different from the expected change in the exchange rate, there would be opportunities for arbitrage—albeit with risk. In equilibrium, the interest rate difference between the two countries will be equal to the expected appreciation or depreciation of the domestic currency.

▲ ▲ ▲

Empirical Evidence. Do the interest rate and exchange rates in the financial markets really move according to this theory? The answer to that question is yes—whenever the assumptions required for the theorem are met. The assumptions were not very stringent: the risks of the two instruments—the treasury bills of the two governments—must be the same, there should be no restrictions on investors and arbitrageurs to move funds in and out of the two countries, and, for ease of exposition, there must not be any transactions costs. These conditions are not difficult to satisfy in contemporary financial markets, and we find that the interest rate parity theorem is one of the few relationships derived from theory that actually works in practice. A number of studies have been carried out to test this theorem. The main conclusion that emerges from these studies is that the interest rates and exchange rates are constantly adjusted by the market such that, once transactions costs are taken into account, there are no opportunities for arbitrage. In other words, the interest rate parity theorem is a valid theorem.

Interest Rate Parity Theorem and Determination of Exchange Rates

What does the interest rate parity theorem tell us about future exchange rates? To answer that question, we must recall that this relationship is based upon the potential for arbitrage, not on the market's expectations or ideas (to be more precise, that of the participants in the market place) about what the exchange rates or interest rates should be. We can therefore expect that the two sets of variables, exchange rates and interest rates, will always maintain a certain relationship with each other, but this relationship by itself does not tell us what will be the value of exchange rates in the future. This parity relationship, moreover, only tells how much the exchange rate is expected to change in the future, but says nothing about the level from which it will change. To understand this point, consider an example.

The Canadian market is closely integrated with U.S. financial markets. At any time, the interest rate parity theorem holds, that is, the opportunity for arbitrage rarely exists. In early 1993, the three–month T–bill rates in the United States and in Canada were 3 percent and 5 percent respectively. On a particular day, the spot rate for the U.S. dollar in Canadian dollars was C$1.2500/U.S. dollar when the forward rate was 1.2565. This forward rate implied an annual premium on the U.S. dollar of 2 percent, the exact difference between the corresponding Treasury bill rates. But about a month later, the spot rate was C$1.2709/U.S. dollar whereas the premium on the forward rate and the two interest rates were exactly the same. (As a matter of fact, the spot rate had fluctuated between C$1.1829/U.S. dollar and C$1.2875/U.S. dollar over the previous 12 months.) Thus, the U.S. dollar appreciated in value by about 1.7 percent in one month, far more than the interest rate parity had dictated, but the parity still held at the new levels of the exchange rates. Did something go wrong? The answer is no. The example simply illustrates the applicability of the interest rate parity relationship: at any point in time, the forward rate indicates how much the exchange rate is expected to change from the *current* level of the spot rate, but does not necessarily promise any particular level of the spot rate.

This relationship merely states that, given a certain interest rate differential between two countries, the spot and forward exchange rates must also maintain the same difference. The interest rate parity does not make any statements about the *level* at which the exchange rates must remain. Thus, in the case of Canadian dollars, the forward rate remained at 2 percent discount with respect to the spot rate, regardless of the level of the spot rate. If the market has strong expectations of what the exchange rate will be in the future, it will then adjust the spot and forward rates such that the interest rate parity is maintained.

We can now summarize our discussion about the interest rate parity. It tells us merely that if there are no restrictions in financial markets, the forward exchange rate will have a fixed relationship with the spot exchange rate. We cannot say what the actual exchange rates will be based only upon our knowledge of the interest rate parity theorem. We will look at the influence of interest rates on the exchange rates once more in a section below.

Purchasing Power Parity Theory

One of the most enduring theories of exchange rates is known as the purchasing power parity theory. First proposed in the early 1900s, this theory is based on two ideas: in the absence of trade restrictions, the prices of real goods should be the same in two countries, and since an exchange rate is merely the price of one currency in terms of another, it should equalize the prices of real goods in the two countries. Another way to say the same thing is that the exchange rates must adjust such that it is not possible to conduct profitable arbitrage in goods in different countries. To understand this concept, and its implications for changes in exchange rates, let us start with the simple idea of the law of one price.

Law of one price.   The law of one price states that in open economies, prices of individual commodities (when compared in the same currency), should be the same in two different countries. If the prices were not the same, it should be possible to purchase the commodity in the market where it is cheaper and sell it for a profit in the market where it is more expensive. This assumes the absence of any transaction costs arising from shipping or from trade barriers. We will relax this unrealistic assumption very shortly. If the prices were not equal, someone would undertake this risk–free arbitrage till prices rose in the market where they were low and fell where they were high. In equilibrium, we will observe the following relationship:

$$p_t = p_t^* \times S_t \qquad\qquad (3.2)$$

where p_t is the domestic price of a commodity, p_t^* is the foreign price of the same commodity quoted in the foreign currency, and S_t is the exchange rate, quoted as a direct quote (domestic currency/foreign currency). In the absence of transactions costs, arbitrage will ensure that the relationship between the two prices is one of strict equality. The equation can then be used to determine the value of the equilibrium exchange rate once we know the prices in the two countries. If the price in one market were to change, equilibrium would require that either the exchange rate or the price in the other market change also. The equilibrium exchange rate in this situation is given by:

$$S_t = p_t^* \,/\, p_t \qquad\qquad (3.3)$$

In a real world situation where the transaction costs are not negligible, we can expect the following relationship to hold:

$$p_t = p_t^* \times S_t \pm T \qquad\qquad (3.4)$$

where T represents the transaction cost of purchasing the commodity in one market and selling it in the other, expressed in units of the domestic currency. Existence of T creates "arbitrage bands" around strictly equal prices such that prices in the two markets can deviate from each other between these arbitrage bands whose width is T. Thus, the domestic price will not be exactly equal to the foreign price times the exchange rate, but could be higher or lower than that by an amount not exceeding T. The equilibrium exchange rate in this situation could be written as:

$$S_t = (p_t^* \,/\, p_t) \pm T' \qquad\qquad (3.5)$$

where T' is derived from T (it is not necessary to derive its exact value at this point). The equation states that the actual exchange rate could deviate from the exact equilibrium value in Equation 3.3 by an amount of up to T'.

Extensive research has been done to test if the law of one price is valid in the real markets. The general conclusion from this research is that, when allowance is made for the transportation costs, and when standardized goods or commodities are compared, this relationship indeed reflects the reality of the global marketplace. This conclusion forms the basis for aggregating the prices of individual commodities into a price index for an economy as a whole and to develop a more important relationship for our purpose: the purchasing power parity.

Absolute Purchasing Power Parity. The previous relationship, the law of one price, was stated in terms of prices of individual commodities. Can we make similar statements for price aggregates for economies as a whole?

In open economies, that is, in economies which are open to trade and investments from other economies, the value of an exchange rate can be stated in terms of prices in the two economies. To see how, consider first the idea of a "consumption basket." Define a consumption basket as a combination of goods and services which a typical individual consumes. We could define this basket over a day, a month, or any other period. This basket would contain proportionate amounts of all the goods and services that an individual would consume over the period for which the basket is being defined. The basket would, thus, contain some food, clothing, housing, medical services, and entertainment. The value of this basket in any country can be measured by pricing each component of the basket at the current prices and adding up the values of each of the components.

We now have the value of a consumption basket in one country. Similarly, we can calculate the value of a similar consumption basket in the second country. What should be the relationship between the two prices, that is, the prices of the same basket, in the two countries? Given our assumption of the open economies, and given that we have found the law of one price to be a valid relationship, we would expect that the two baskets should be priced equally when compared at the prevailing exchange rate—since each component of the basket sells for the same price in the two countries. Turning this statement around, we can now define the equilibrium exchange rate. The exchange rate between two countries can be defined as the ratio of prices of a consumption basket denominated in the respective currencies of the two countries. The price of a typical consumption basket in a country can be called the price level of that country. Thus, in more general terms, the purchasing power parity theorem states that an exchange rate is the ratio of price levels in two countries (for the moment, note that we are talking about price levels, not price indexes; the distinction will soon become clear):

$$S_t = P_t / P_t^*$$ (3.6)

where P and P^* now represent price levels in the countries, not prices of individual commodities.

The **purchasing power parity** (PPP) represents a very useful relationship for determining exchange rates. In its strictest form, known as the absolute version of purchasing power parity, exchange rates are defined as in Equation 3.6. This version of the PPP provides a precise definition of the value of an exchange rate based upon the actual levels of prices in two countries. The relationship is based upon the assumption that successful arbitrage will eliminate any discrepancies between prices between the two countries. Given the importance of arbitrage in maintaining the relationship, it is important to examine the validity of the assumptions that form the basis for the existence of arbitrage.

A number of conditions must be met before arbitrage in the real goods markets can successfully equate prices in the two countries and allow the absolute PPP to hold. The most important of these conditions are as follows:

1. **Homogeneous commodities.** Arbitrage can only take place if the commodities are standardized. If the consumers in the two countries prefer somewhat different products, arbitrage would not be easy. This requirement would seem to render the purchasing power parity concept inapplicable, since almost all products consumed in modern economies are adapted according to the specific needs of each country. In practice, however, research has shown that such differences can be priced as a fixed gap or a fixed band between the prices of the two countries. Also, arbitrage can ensure that the prices move together even when the product specifications are not exactly

the same. In summary, the requirement for standardized commodities makes it difficult, but not impossible, to enforce purchasing power parity.

2. **Non–tradable commodities.** Derivation of the purchasing power parity was based on the possibility that if the prices of the same product or service differ from one country to another, trade will eliminate the difference. The same, however, cannot be true for non–tradable products and services, like houses, restaurants, or retailing. If the consumption basket for a country included a large proportion of these non–tradables, we could not hypothesize the relationship in Equation 3.6. The existence of non–tradables would thus seem to invalidate the concept of purchasing power parity. It is likely, however, that the inputs for non–tradable commodities, that is, the products that are used to produce the non–tradable commodities (lumber, fixtures, paint, etc. for houses, food for restaurants, and all the products sold by the retail outlet) are themselves traded. The prices of non–tradables in these circumstances cannot differ except by the difference in the costs of assembling the non–tradable services from the traded inputs. The presence of non–tradable commodities, therefore, does not completely invalidate the concept of purchasing power parity but introduces some deviation from the exact equality of Equation 3.6.

3. **Transaction costs.** As in the case of the law of one price, transaction costs can remove the incentive from arbitrage. Transaction costs include the cost of shipping, costs of any trade barriers, and the cost of buying and selling the product. As before, we find that the transaction costs create an arbitrage band around prices so that the prices between two countries are not exactly equalized but can differ from each other by the width of an arbitrage band. If the price in one market were to rise, however, the price in the other market would also rise, keeping the width of the arbitrage band constant. Again, the existence of transaction costs does not invalidate the concept of purchasing power parity but merely makes the equality less precise.

4. **Similar consumption baskets.** We derived the equation for purchasing power parity, Equation 3.6, assuming that the consumption baskets for the two countries were exactly the same. Consumption baskets of two countries, however, can differ for two reasons: they may contain different goods, including some non–tradables, or they may contain different proportions of the same goods. For both these reasons, we would not expect the price levels in the two countries to be equal, even if the prices of each specific commodity were equalized by arbitrage. These differences in the typical consumption baskets of countries represent the most serious challenge to the purchasing power parity relationship. If, however, the consumption baskets remain stable over time, the changes in the prices of individual commodities should have equal effects on the overall price levels of the two countries. In this case, even if the price levels in the two countries are not equalized, *changes* in the price level in one country should be equal to the changes in the price level in the second country. The following example illustrates the importance of the constitution of the consumption baskets.

5. **Relative price changes.** The final challenge to the purchasing power parity concept arises from the possibility that when consumption baskets in different countries are not the same, PPP may seem to be violated if the price of one commodity changes relative to the price of another commodity. The effects of relative price changes on the PPP are best illustrated with an example.

Purchasing Power Parity: An Illustration

Consider two countries, Westland which uses dollars and Eastland which uses marks. There are only three products in the economy: rice, cotton and lumber. The amounts of each product consumed in each economy and their prices are given in the Table 3.1. In addition to the information in the table, we know that the exchange rate is $1.00 = 4.00 marks. At this exchange rate the law of one price holds. The price for each commodity in marks in Eastland is exactly what we would expect: its price in dollars in Westland times the exchange rate. Does the purchasing power parity also hold?

Table 3.1

	Westland		Eastland	
	Amount	**Price**	**Amount**	**Price**
Rice	10	5.00	20	20.00
Cotton	5	15.00	15	60.00
Lumber	8	30.00	10	120.00

To examine if the absolute purchasing power parity holds, we first calculate the price level in each economy. The price level can be defined as follows:

$$P_t = \sum w_i \times p_i$$

where w_i is the weight of each commodity in the economy. In our example, these weights can be calculated by taking the ratio of the total value of each commodity (its quantity times its price) to the total value of all commodities. The value of the first commodity, rice, in Westland is 50 (10 × 5), that of cotton is 75, and that of lumber is 240. The weight of rice, therefore, is 50/365 (365 = 50 + 75 + 240). The weights for cotton and lumber are 75/365 and 240/365. The price level in Westland is:

$$P_{\text{Westland}} = \frac{(50 \times 5)}{365} + \frac{(75 \times 15)}{365} + \frac{(240 \times 30)}{365}$$

$$= 23.5 \text{ dollars}$$

Similarly, you should verify that the price level in Eastland is 82.4 marks. The PPP exchange rate, according to Equation 3.6, should be 3.506 marks/\$ (= 82.4 / 23.5), not the actual rate of 4.0 marks/\$.

Does the difference between the actual and the PPP exchange rate mean that the theory is not correct? In this case, the difference arises because at least one of the conditions for the theory to be valid has not been met. In our example, the weights of the three commodities are not equal in the two countries. Although the prices of the three commodities are the same in the two countries, Westland consumes more lumber and Eastland more cotton. Lumber has a weight of 0.658 in Westland (240/365) but only 0.48 (1200/2500) in Eastland. Similar differences exist for rice and cotton. The different weights of the three commodities in the two countries violate one of the conditions for the PPP, condition 4, similar consumption baskets. Therefore, the inequality between the actual and the PPP exchange rates does not invalidate the theory.

What would happen if a forest fire were to result in the price of lumber doubling when the other prices remain the same? The price of lumber would increase in absolute terms as well relative to the other commodities. The new prices, and the new price levels in each economy, are shown in Table 3.2. At the new prices, the exchange rate should be 3.46 marks/$. Why does the PPP exchange rate change when the actual exchange rate remains the same? This has happened because the condition for relative price changes, condition 5, has not been satisfied. After a price increase, lumber which was twice as expensive as cotton before now becomes four times as expensive. When relative prices change, the PPP relationship cannot provide us with the correct value for the exchange rate.

These objections to PPP seem to indicate that this theory would have little application in the real world where prices change all the time and

Table 3.2

	Westland		Eastland	
	Amount	**Price**	**Amount**	**Price**
Rice	10	5.00	20	20.00
Cotton	5	15.00	15	60.00
Lumber	8	60.00	10	240.00
New Price Level		49.90		172.43
New PPP exchange rate = 172.43/49.9 = 3.46 marks/$				

the commodity baskets in the different countries are obviously not the same. Fortunately for the theory, the extent of changes in relative prices is not very large. Although prices change, given that we have thousands of products in our consumption basket, the effects of changes in any one price are often negligible from the point of view of the price level of the economy as a whole. Except in rare circumstances, the increases in the price of oil in the 1970s for example, relative price changes do not affect the PPP relationship in any significant manner. The different constitutions of commodity baskets also present less of a problem for the theory than would appear at first sight. Although each country has a unique consumption basket, the weights of thousands of products that make up the consumption basket change only very slowly. Thus, even though the consumption baskets between different countries may be different, the baskets themselves do not change very much over time. The differences, in other words, tend to remain stable over time.

The stability of these differences allows us to redefine PPP so that the essence of the idea of purchasing power parity can be retained without the rigid form of the relationship outlined in Equation 3.6. The renewed form of PPP is known as the **relative purchasing power parity**. This version of PPP states that *changes* in exchange rates over time should compensate for the difference in the changes in the price levels of the two countries. Relative PPP can be represented by the following equation:

$$\frac{P_{t+1}}{P_t} = \frac{P_{t+1}^*}{P_t^*} \times \frac{S_{t+1}}{S_t} \qquad (3.7)$$

where all the terms have the same meaning except that P can now be the price *index* in a country, not necessarily the price level. According to this equation, the exchange rate will change such that the relationship between the prices in two countries will be maintained. The relationship does not have to be one of equality. To understand relative purchasing power parity, let us look at an example.

Mexico experienced high rates of inflation during most of the 1980s. Let us see if the exchange rate for Mexican currency, the peso, followed the predictions of relative PPP during that time. In January 1986, the wholesale price indexes for the United States and Mexico were 100.0 and 137.6 respectively (remember that the price index numbers are arbitrary—these two numbers do not imply that Mexican prices were 1.376 times those in the United States). The exchange rate at that time was 414 pesos/$ (note this is an indirect quote from the U.S. perspective). By July of 1987, the Mexican price index had risen to 454.1, whereas the U.S. index was at 100.3. The exchange rate had changed to 1420 pesos/$. To see if the relative PPP would have predicted the same exchange rate in July 1987, we can calculate the exchange rate by substituting the values in Equation 3.7. To calculate the exchange rate, however, we rearrange the equation to bring only S_{t+1} on the left–hand side:

$$S_{t+1} = \frac{P_{t+1}}{P_t} * \frac{P_t^*}{P_{t+1}^*} \times S_t \qquad (3.8)$$

The time t in this equation refers to January 1986 and the time $t + 1$ to July 1987. Since our exchange rate is in terms of pesos/$, we have to remember that P now refers to Mexico and P^* to the United States. Substituting the values, we get:

$$S_{t+1} = \frac{454.1}{137.6} \times \frac{100.0}{100.3} \times 414.0$$

or 1362 pesos/$. This is not exactly equal to the actual rate of 1420 pesos/$, but it is close considering that the Mexican government was trying to control the exchange rate at that time.

Empirical Validity and Implications for Determination of Exchange Rates

Since it was first proposed in the early 1900s, PPP has been a subject of much research—both academic and applied. Tests have been carried out for many currencies and for many time periods. The fact that a large number of studies have been required indicates that each study contradicts previous studies in some manner. It seems possible, however, to draw three generalizations from these studies. First, it is rare that PPP holds over very short periods of time. Second, it seems to hold for currencies during periods of high inflation. Third, over long periods of time, exchange rates tend to move in the direction indicated by purchasing power parity. This implies that although PPP cannot be used to forecast currencies to any degree of accuracy, it provides the bounds within which an exchange rate should move in the future. The farther an exchange rate moves from its PPP value, the more will be the pressure for the exchange rate to return to the PPP value. PPP values of exchange rates provide the long–run equilibrium values of currencies but say nothing about their short–run movements.

Balance of Payments and Exchange Rates

In Appendix 1.A, we examined the basic concepts of a country's balance of payments. We emphasized the importance of a surplus or deficit in the current account. The current account of a balance of payments summarizes a country's net balance of purchases and sales of goods and services (both being defined very broadly) from the rest of the world. Since for most countries the volume of transactions in the current account far exceeds the volume of transactions in capital and other accounts, the current account balance becomes a good barometer of the health of the external sector of a country. Moreover, since almost all transactions of either a purchase or a sale of goods or services involve a payment between residents of two countries, all current account transactions become intimately tied with foreign exchange markets. Before a payment can be made in a foreign currency, the domestic currency must be converted into the foreign currency through the foreign exchange market. Since all current account transactions must go through the foreign exchange market, supply and demand of foreign currencies, and hence the exchange rate, become closely dependent upon the current account. For countries which have a large volume of transactions in the capital account, the exchange rate depends upon both the current and the capital account.

Balance of payments influence the exchange rates in three ways. The first and most obvious influence is through supply and demand of foreign currencies to make payments. A deficit in the balance of payments results in an excess supply of the domestic currency and hence in its depreciation. Second, imbalances in balance of payments accounts require the government to take steps to correct the imbalances, including changes in exchange rates. Other policies such as monetary and fiscal constraints may also influence exchange rates. Third, participants in foreign exchange markets look to a country's balance of payments accounts, among other things, to assess the future prospects of a country. These assessments form a part of the information that speculators use to assess future values of a currency, and to make decisions to buy or sell currencies at that time. These decisions will, of course, influence the current exchange rates.

The most obvious impact of balance of payments accounts on the exchange rates is through supply and demand of domestic currency on foreign exchange markets. When domestic residents purchase goods and services abroad, they must pay for those goods in the currency of the exporter (it does not make a difference to our analysis if the foreign exporter accepts the domestic currency and converts it into the foreign currency). Similarly, when domestic residents sell goods and services abroad, they receive foreign currencies which they convert into domestic currency. Every other current account transaction, such as tourism, transfer payments, payments of dividends or interest, as well as every capital account transaction, such as portfolio or direct investment, results in either some supply or some demand of foreign currency for domestic currency in the foreign exchange market. Since each transactor is only concerned with his or her transaction, there is no guarantee that the supply will exactly equal the demand. If there is disequilibrium and if the exchange rates are freely fluctuating, the rates will change such that supply and demand are equalized. If there was too much demand for the foreign currency at the existing exchange rate, the foreign currency will rise in value. This increase will now require domestic importers to pay more domestic currency for imports, thus raising the prices of imports. Some importers will now find it more attractive to purchase competing products in the domestic market, thus reducing the level of imports. Simultaneously, domestic goods will now cost less in terms of foreign currency, stimulating their demand in the foreign countries. Both these effects of an appreciation of the foreign currency, that is, decrease in imports and increase in exports, will move the supply and demand of the foreign currency toward equilibrium. In fact, the exchange rate will continue to change until the supply and demand are equalized.

A freely floating exchange rate, therefore, adjusts such that the balance of payments is in equilibrium. If we were interested in forecasting the value of an exchange rate, we would have to estimate the levels of imports and exports (and other items in the balance of payments) at various exchange rates and determine the exchange rate at which the two are equalized. Such an analysis requires a system in which the government does not interfere very much with the foreign exchange market and speculators generally leave the currency alone. We will discuss the influence of these speculators very shortly.

If the government plays an active role in the external sector of the economy, it will want to follow some policies that bring about an equilibrium in the balance of payments. Although a complete discussion of how different policies achieve such an equilibrium is not necessary for our analysis of exchange rates, we should note that the gamut of policies employed by governments include changes in monetary and fiscal policies, as well as interference in the foreign exchange markets. What is of concern to us is how these policies will influence the determination of exchange rates.

Monetary policy may influence exchange rates directly by affecting the money supply and, hence, the inflation in the economy. Expected inflation will then influence exchange rates through purchasing power parity and interest rate parity relationships. The link between monetary policy and these two relationships is shown in Exhibit 3.3. Monetary as well as fiscal policy influences exchange rates indirectly by affecting national income and, hence, the demand and supply of goods, domestic as well as foreign. A restrictive fiscal policy, for example, reduces income in the hands of domestic residents. With reduced income, they demand fewer imported, as well as fewer domestic goods. Reduction in imports influences exchange rates as discussed earlier. Availability of more domestic goods provides incentives to export more goods (through price effects in Keynesian analysis and through reduced absorption of goods in Monetarist analysis), once again influencing the exchange rates. The challenge for market participants who attempt to forecast exchange rates is to predict first what the government policies will be and then how those policies will influence exchange rates. Clearly, both these tasks are complex and fraught with uncertainty. Is it any wonder then that opposite views can be heard about any currency at any time in the marketplace?

Exhibit 3.3
Exchange Rates, Interest Rates, and Inflation

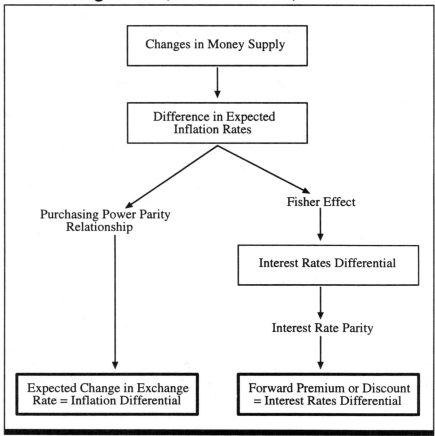

The difficulty in predicting the government's response to the balance of payments imbalances leads us to the third link between the balance of payments and the exchange rates: market participants', especially speculators', prognosis of the future state of a country's balance of payments. Since speculators are concerned mainly with what will happen to a currency rather than what the value of a currency is at the present time, they want to understand how a country's external sector will perform in the future, not only at the present time. They are, thus, more interested in what imbalances in a country's balance of payments say about its future than about its present.

This analysis is certainly not easier than the analysis of government policies regarding these imbalances. Consider the example of the United States. For most of the last decade, the U.S. economy has had current account deficits of between 1 to 3.5 percent of the GNP. Such persistent and large deficits indicate that, over the last decade, U.S. residents have been buying considerably more goods and services from the rest of the world than they have sold.

What does that mean for the U.S. economy and for the U.S. dollar? Has the U.S. economy lost its ability to produce goods at prices that others find attractive? If that is the correct interpretation, and certainly the current account deficits could justify that conclusion, then the U.S. economy and the U.S. dollar should have nowhere to go but down. But is that the whole picture? Let us also look at the capital account balance. For almost the entire time that the current account was in deficit, the capital account was in surplus. In other words, foreigners were investing more money in the United States than U.S. residents were investing abroad. Why would foreigners do that? The probable answer is that they felt optimistic about the future of the U.S. economy and wanted to invest in that country. The investments they made may have stimulated U.S. imports. First, the investments required them to purchase machinery and equipment, some of which had to be imported. Second, since they purchased existing assets and real estate, it put a lot of money in the hands of U.S. residents, some of which was spent on imports. The increased imports from these two sources may have caused the current account deficits!

This appears to paint quite a different picture for the prospects of the U.S. economy. If foreigners find the U.S. economy an attractive place to invest, what is wrong if Americans spend some of their money on imports? The future does not look bad. The U.S. economy and the U.S. dollar should be going up.

This example highlights the difficulty in linking balance of payments accounts with exchange rate changes. Although the two are intimately connected, it is difficult to establish the causal link between the two. It is even more difficult to predict the future course of events. Predictions depend not just upon numbers—whether the accounts are in deficits or in surpluses—but also on why they are in deficits or in surpluses. If the second interpretation of the U.S. economy is correct, then we have reasons to be bullish; if the first explanation is closer to the truth, then we would have to be bearish.

In conclusion, although balance of payments analysis provides useful insights into what may happen to exchange rates, we have to look far beyond the numbers themselves to understand what is really happening. Balance of payments analysis, in other words, must be used with caution.

Macroeconomics and Exchange Rates

Macroeconomic analysis is based on a general economic equilibrium in which the value of each economic variable, including the exchange rate, adjusts so that its demand and supply are equalized. Each economic variable is dependent upon a set of other variables and, in more complex analysis, feedback effects of variables on each other are recognized. Since most macroeconomic analyses are carried out in terms of real (versus the monetary) values of economic variables, we must return to one of the concepts we discussed under purchasing power parity to define a "real" exchange rate. A real exchange rate is defined as the nominal exchange rate (that is, the exchange rate quoted by the market as the domestic currency price of foreign currency) multiplied by the ratio of domestic to foreign price levels. Price levels were defined in the discussion of the absolute version of purchasing power parity and refer to the prices of typical consumption baskets in an economy. The objective of macroeconomic analysis is to identify economic variables which influence the values of exchange rates and to determine the exact relationship between these variables and the exchange rates. Armed with this knowledge, we should be able to predict how exchange rates will change as economies go through changes.

Most macroeconomic models begin analysis of exchange rates from the same variable that we have seen before: inflation rate. Starting from the premise that the most important role of exchange rates is to determine relative prices of goods and assets between two economies, these models recognize that relative price movements between economies, that is, different rates of inflation in two countries, should also affect exchange rates to maintain equilibrium. The main contribution of these models comes in explaining inflation rates themselves in terms of other variables in the economy. In general, price changes are found to be a function of monetary policy (that is, changes in money supply) and rate of growth of the economy (which is really a function of increase in productivity). If the money supply increases faster than the output in one economy, that economy will have higher inflation than others, and its real exchange rate will fall.

The other sets of variables that explain exchange rates in macroeconomic models revolve around the balance of payments. Exchange rates will be set such that these accounts will be in equilibrium in the long run, and all the factors that affect supply and demand of goods and assets that enter the balance of payments will also influence the exchange rates. These factors include income levels, changes in income levels, and changes in relative prices, among other variables.

Macroeconomic models of exchange rates, thus, do not differ significantly from the other models of exchange rates that we discussed earlier. In fact, empirical tests of models do not have much more success in explaining exchange rates than do the purchasing power parity or balance of payments models. The general consensus is that, in spite of all the work that has been done on the theory of exchange rates, we know very little about why exchange rates change.

Speculation and Exchange Rates

While discussing the size of the foreign exchange market in the previous chapter, we noted that the total volume of international trade in a year can be paid for by about four days of transactions in this market. For the rest of the time, transactions in the market represent either capital flows between countries or speculative transactions. Speculative transactions are pure risk–taking transactions in which the speculator's total expected gain is derived from a change in the value of an asset. In efficient markets, the price that a speculator will pay to purchase an asset will depend upon the speculator's expectation of the future price of the asset. In fact, the speculator will first form an expectation of what the price of an asset will be at some future date, and then derive the maximum price that can be paid for it at the time of purchase. The difference depends upon the risk associated with the asset and alternatives available for investment.

Speculation in foreign currencies follows the same general principles as above. One speculator may purchase a currency that he expects will rise in value, and another may sell a currency that she expects will fall. In either case, the speculator forms an expectation of what the currency will be worth in the future and then estimates the maximum price that can be paid given the risk and the alternatives. Since the alternatives in the form of stocks, bonds, etc., are freely available in the financial markets, and speculators can form reasonable expectations of the risk, the critical task in foreign currency speculation becomes one of forming expectations regarding the values of currencies.

How do speculators make judgments about the values of currencies given the difficulties we had in describing how exchange rates are determined? The answer to this question requires understanding the role and the importance of information. Speculators trade and deal on information—information about global events that may have even the most remote connection with economies and hence with the foreign currency markets. To understand how information affects the market, consider a currency market in which news arrives at a time when the market had been calm before the arrival of the news.

We begin with a situation where the market has accepted the exchange rate as being in equilibrium. The calm in the market indicates that all the participants, that is, speculators, hedgers, traders, etc., have taken a position in the market that is consistent with their belief about how the exchange rates are supposed to change in the future. Now suppose that some news that has relevance for exchange rates arrives in the market. How would a specific speculator respond to this news? What actions would she take?

The speculator has to assess the impact of the news in two ways. First, what does the news indicate about the expected change in the exchange rate of a currency in which our speculator deals? Second, what will be the market's reaction to the news? The answer to these two questions will determine the action that the speculator takes in the market.

Will the exchange rate go up or down? How much? To answer this question, the speculator will probably rely upon an implicit model in her head, rather than on complex theoretical models on paper or in computers. For instance, how will the value of the dollar change when the president of the United States announces that he will not commit U.S. troops to war–torn Bosnia? Our speculator may see that as increasing the value of the dollar because she believes that a strong statement like that indicates that the president wants to focus his attention on domestic economic issues and will have more time to implement his policies for economic growth. With all the attention on the domestic economic situation, his policies will be implemented effectively and the U.S. economy will grow rapidly. A high growth rate will be partly due to high productivity which will lower the costs of export goods. Increased competitiveness of export goods in turn will raise export volumes more than the increase in imports resulting from higher income levels. The balance of payments will thus move toward a surplus situation which will put pressure on the dollar to increase. Since it is more than likely that, with all the attention on the domestic economy, the monetary policy will not be inflationary, the purchasing power parity relationship will supplement the pressure for the revaluation of the dollar. For these reasons, our speculator is confident that the news points to an appreciation of the dollar.

Should the speculator then go out and buy dollars? Before taking that action, she has to answer the second question we had raised above: how will the market react to the news? Will everyone in the market analyze the news in the same way? An alternate analysis could be that the president's announcement indicates that he is unable to take control of the situation in a global crisis and it is likely that he will also lose control of the domestic economy. If that were to happen, the recovery of the U.S. economy would halt and the dollar would decline.

Suppose our speculator has made her analysis along the lines of the first scenario. How should she act in response to the new information? Since she expects the dollar to appreciate, she should buy the currency because when the value of the dollar goes up, she will have profited from her speculative activity. But whether the dollar goes up or not depends also upon what the market (that is, the other participants in the market) thinks about the situation. If the other participants had made the same analysis, they would also expect the dollar to go up and no one would be willing to sell the dollars to our speculator. The only way she can speculate is by trying to find someone who has not yet heard the news or someone whose analysis is along that of the second scenario. With the market as a whole believing the first scenario, every speculator expects that the dollar will go up as a result of the news and will now revise his or her estimate of the future value of the dollar, and, hence, the current value of the currency.

Exhibit 3.4
Information and Exchange Rates

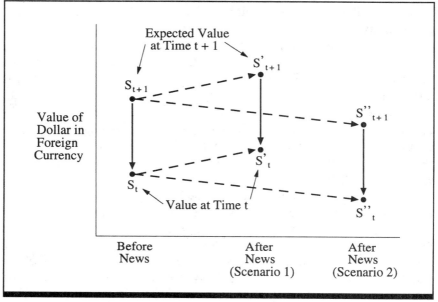

The situation is depicted in Exhibit 3.4. Before the news came to the market, the equilibrium spot value of the dollar was set such that if the currency were to be purchased at the spot exchange rate of S_t and held for one time period, this speculative position would yield an expected rate of return which was comparable to other investments available in the economy, allowing for the differences in the risk associated with the position. The spot exchange rate is derived from the expected future value of the currency—S_{t+1}. (Readers with previous knowledge of finance theory will recognize that we are talking about an asset pricing model like the capital asset pricing model. The relationship between S_{t+1} and S_t is governed by the risk free rate, the rate of return on a market portfolio, and the "beta" for the currency as an asset.) After the news, the expected future value of the currency—S'_{t+1}—changes and, given the new expected future value of the currency, the current spot rate—S'_t—is derived from that.

Since every market participant has revised the estimate of the future value of the currency, no one is willing to sell the currency at a price less than S'_t, and because that is the maximum price our speculator is willing to pay, there will be no trade. What has happened is that once the news came, and once there was consensus in the market about the impact of the news, the price of the dollar increased without a single trade taking place. This is how an efficient market should work.

What if the market believed in the second scenario while our speculator held the first view? Also suppose that, from a purely theoretical perspective, she was right and the market was wrong. There is now an opportunity for our speculator. Since every one else believes that the dollar will fall, they would be willing to sell it at any price above S'''_t. Our speculator, on the other hand, believes the correct spot rate should be S'_t. She can now purchase currency at S'''_t and hold it until it reaches S'_{t+1}. Theoretically, this would be possible, but the reality of the market place does not allow that to take place. In the real financial markets, the value of the currency will fall to S'''_t just because the market believes it should. Our speculator will be isolated and will have to maintain a risky position in the market for a long time. Although in the long run she will be proven correct, she may face financial ruin in the mean time.

Speculators, thus, act on information in two ways. On the one hand they make their assessment of the impact of new information coming in to the market, and on the other hand they make an assessment of how the market will react to the same news. They must react to the news instantaneously. In making their analysis, they take into account all the theoretical considerations that we have discussed earlier, but more often than not their models are very informal and based on their experience, rather than on sophisticated theory. Given the importance of speculators in the foreign exchange markets, however, their actions dominate the changes in the exchange rates in the marketplace. Their self interest ensures that the exchange rates at any instant reflect all available information.

Central Banks and Exchange Rates

The main role of a central bank in the foreign currency markets is to influence the value of its currency to bring the exchange rate closer to what the central bank thinks it should be. This is achieved mainly by the central bank purchasing its currency if it has fallen too far in value or by selling it if it has risen too much. The central banks that wish to interfere with the market values of their currencies maintain reserves of foreign currencies which they can use to purchase their own currency. The International Monetary Fund estimates that at the end of 1992, the global foreign currency reserves stood at about $916 billion.

Central banks enter foreign exchange markets through one of their commercial banks. They usually ask designated commercial banks to buy or sell foreign currencies on their behalf. The success of the operation depends upon how serious the market thinks the central bank is and, if it is perceived to be serious, does the market think that the bank has sufficient resources to fight the market if the market were to resist the efforts of the central bank.

At other times, the central banks may try to "talk" the market into changing its perception of what the value of an exchange rate should be. In early 1993, for example, the Japanese currency increased from about 120 yen/$ to 110 yen/$ over a period of about two weeks. The increase was in response to statements by U.S. officials, including the Secretary of the Treasury, that the yen was undervalued and that the U.S. government would have liked to have seen the Japanese do something about the value of their currency. The statements were taken seriously by the market because it was generally perceived that the government was under strong public pressure to force Japan to reduce its trade surplus with the United States. The new administration had taken to waving the possibilities of imposition of various types of trade barriers which would hurt Japanese exports to the United States. The market believed that the Japanese government would take steps to raise the value of the yen to alleviate some of the balance of payments problems. Anticipating intervention in the foreign currency markets, the markets raised the rates even before the Japanese government had to do something.

In general, however, central banks are not very successful at influencing the markets. Their resources are too small compared to the size of the foreign exchange market. By the nature of the transaction, the central banks are "leaning against the wind." The efficacy of central banks' actions is illustrated by the events of April 27, 1993. Central banks in the United States and Canada intervened in the foreign exchange markets to influence the values of their currencies, albeit with very different results. Let us first review the events that led to the substantial interventions on that day.

The U.S. dollar had been declining against the major currencies but especially against the Japanese yen since about the beginning of February. The dollar was worth about 110 yen on April 26, after having been as high as 133 yen/$ during the past 12 months. The rise in the value of the yen was not totally unplanned; just a few weeks earlier, officials in President Clinton's administration had made it clear that the yen was undervalued and that they were going to help revalue the yen. The market had taken the cue and acted on it. By the end of April, however, the dollar had begun to decline against other currencies as well, and the administration in Washington seemed not to want to tolerate such a decline. On the Canadian side, the events were triggered by the announcement of a new budget by the federal government on April 26. The finance minister, Mr. Mazankowski, had built expectations over the previous few weeks that this was going to be a tough budget attacking the problem of federal debt which was seen at that time as creating an excessive burden for the national economy. The actual budget on April 26, however, was seen as a "re–election" budget that would help the conservative government win a re–election, expected at that time to take place in the fall, rather than as a tough budget that would put their house in order. Markets responded to the budget by dropping the Canadian dollar by 0.86 U.S. cent on April 27, the largest drop in a single day in about the last five years.

On April 27, the Federal Reserve Bank of New York and the Bank of Canada intervened in the foreign exchange markets. Both aimed to prevent declines in the values of their respective dollars. The Federal Reserve's actions "brought the dollar's skid to a sudden halt . . ." and reversed the downward trend of the dollar against the yen that had continued since the beginning of the year. The Fed purchased dollars at 109.50 yens/dollar in the market. The market saw the Fed's actions as a shift in the Clinton administration's policy from one of benign neglect to one of active management.

More important, however, the market believed that the Fed was serious, viewed the intervention as "well–timed and deftly executed" and interpreted it as persistent. The Fed purchased dollars in small lots of about $10 million each at a time when investors in the foreign exchange market had sold dollars against yens. The Fed's activities were viewed as "highly significant" by the market because they were coordinated with other efforts to influence the market. Treasury Secretary Bentsen told a Senate subcommittee hearing on the same day that "there's been some misinterpretation about the U.S. exchange–rate policy." One economist felt that the intervention would succeed because "it has increased uncertainty in the market as to what the U.S. wants." At the end of the day, the U.S. dollar had risen to 111.67 yen compared to 110.55 yen the previous day and to 1.5830 marks against 1.5688 marks the previous day.[1]

The Bank of Canada also intervened in the foreign exchange markets on April 27 to protect the value of the Canadian dollar. Market participants had been disappointed by the budget and the market mood was bearish when the market opened on April 27. One of the obvious targets for the market bears was the Canadian dollar. By the early evening, the Canadian dollar had dropped to 78.21 cents in terms of the U.S. dollar, a drop of 1.30 cents for the day. The Bank of Canada had made a number of interventions and had raised its Bank of Canada rate by 33 basis points during the day to boost the confidence in the Canadian dollar. By the end of the day, however, the Canadian dollar closed at 78.65, a loss of 0.86 cents for the day. The intervention by the Bank of Canada had not stopped the decline of the currency. Obviously, the market did not think that the Bank of Canada had sufficient desire or the resources to back up the value of its currency.

Exactly a month later, however, a somewhat similar intervention by the Federal Reserve failed to sway the market. On May 27, the dollar was in the middle of another decline against the yen and the Fed tried to prevent the decline by purchasing the dollar at around 108.40 yen/$. The intervention failed and the dollar had fallen to below 108 yen/$ by the afternoon. The market traders felt that the tide against the dollar was too strong for any central bank to stop it.

In summary, all we can say is that it is very difficult to assess the impact of the intervention by central banks. Their intervention seems to work in smaller currencies where only a few speculators are active in the market. It also seems to work when the market is divided, that is, when the speculators are not all of the same opinion. It also works when speculators see that a number of central banks are united in their efforts to change the value of a particular currency. In all cases, speculators seem to make money off the central banks.

Forecasting Exchange Rates

With all this uncertainty about the correct model for the value of an exchange rate and with the unquantifiable activities of speculators, what is an investor to do about predicting where the exchange rates may be going? How is an investor to decide if he or she should invest the money abroad? What if the exchange rates fall?

The answer to this question requires us to understand the last box in Exhibit 3.3—the one dealing with forward premium or discount. The equilibrium relationships shown in that exhibit indicate that the forward premium or discount should exactly equal the change in the exchange rates. In other words, the economic relationships imply that if the exchange rate is expected to devalue by, say, 4 percent in three months, the forward rate should indicate a discount of 4 percent. Does that really happen?

A large number of researchers have attempted to answer that question. If the economic models of exchange rates are valid, the actual change in an exchange rate over, say, three months should be equal to the forward rate premium or discount three months ago. We can thus measure the change in the actual exchange rate over three months and compare it to the premium or discount three months ago. The relationship can be tested with the following equation:

$$S_{t+1} = a + b \times F_{t,1} + e_t \qquad (3.9)$$

where S_{t+1} is the spot rate at time $t + 1$, $F_{t,1}$ is the forward rate quoted at time t for one period ahead (that is, for $t + 1$) and e_t is the error term. a and b are regression coefficients such that we would expect a to equal 0 and b to equal 1.0 if the forward rate were an accurate predictor of the future spot rate. This formulation assumes that there is no risk premium in the foreign exchange market. Results of this test provide only partial support for the contention that forward rates reflect expectations of the future rate. More advanced tests which incorporate possibilities of a risk premium and a test that the spot rate itself may be the best predictor of the future exchange rate also yield very mixed results.

From the point of view of an investor, it would seem that the most effective strategy is to accept the contention that forward rates provide the best estimates of future spot rates. The systematic error due to the presence of a risk premium is very small, and it varies by time and by currency, making it difficult to use that information in any systematic fashion. At least it is known that there is no other measure or model that performs better than the forward rates.

Expected versus Unexpected Exchange Rate Changes

While we may not be able to improve upon the forward rate as a forecast for future exchange rates, we have to recognize that this forecast accounts for only one of the two sources of change in exchange rates. These two changes may be separated into expected and unexpected exchange rate changes.

When we accept the forward rate as our forecast of the future exchange rate, we are merely saying that given the information at the present time, the forward rate is our best estimate of the future spot exchange rate. The difference between the current spot rate and the current forward rate is how much we expect the exchange rate to change. This expectation is based upon our analysis of all the information that is available at this point in time.

We are, however, aware that as information arrives in the foreign exchange market, the market participants will respond to that information and will revise their estimates of the future exchange rates. Since information arrives in markets at random intervals, and if we knew what information were going to arrive we would incorporate that information in our estimates of current exchange rates, we must accept that exchange rates will change in the future due to surprises contained in the new information. Therefore, we must expect that some exchange rate changes will take place in the future that are unpredictable at the present time. Moreover, we should expect that these changes will take place at random time intervals. These changes are really unexpected exchange rate changes.

The actual change in any exchange rate may, therefore, be separated into two parts. One part consists of the change that we had expected. The second part is the surprise; we did not expect it to take place, and we could not predicted the timing or the magnitude of this component of change.

Although, by definition, it is not possible to predict when the unexpected exchange rate changes will take place, it is possible to make some statements about the magnitude and distribution of these unexpected changes. These unexpected changes were estimated by the distribution of the error term, e_t, in Equation 3.9. Most of the tests of that equation reveal that it is reasonable to assume that the error terms, e_t, and hence the unexpected changes, have a mean of zero and that a normal distribution is a fair approximation for the distribution of these changes.

The results of these tests have very important implications for forecasting exchange rates. If the unexpected changes are distributed with a mean of zero, then the best we can do is to try to forecast the expected exchange rate changes. If our forecast of expected changes is accurate, then on the average, our forecast will provide an unbiased estimate of the future spot rate. In view of the unexpected changes, however, it also means that our forecast will almost never be right; it only means that sometimes we would have overestimated the future exchange rate, sometimes underestimated it. Our error, on the average, will be zero.

Summary

In spite of being one of the largest markets in the world, we have a great deal of difficulty in understanding what determines exchange rates. The difficulty arises from the conflict between economic theory and reality. Economic relationships derived from theory predict that inflation rates, interest rates, and international trade should influence exchange rates. The effect of higher inflation, measured through purchasing power parity, should result in devaluations. Although this relationship may hold over long periods of time, the relationship is of little comfort to investors who must make decisions with short planning horizons.

Interest rates have a similar influence on the exchange rates. Arbitrage ensures that effective interest rates, particularly those adjusted for exchange rate changes, are equalized over countries. The main influence on exchange rates in the short run seems to come from the activities of speculators. Since most speculators risk their own funds, however, they tend to be very fickle and markets become a guessing game—every speculator is trying to outguess the others. In the long run, however, economic theory seems to prevail, providing bounds within which speculators can operate. The long–term forces of economic theory may offer the best protection for less informed investors. The investor can operate with the assumption that, in the long run, exchange rates will move to their equilibrium values—thus disciplining speculators in the short run. This discipline is what allows investors to base their investment decisions on the forward rate.

Note

1. This summary of Federal Reserve's action and the market's reaction is from, "FED Halts Dollar's Slide on Exchange Markets," *The Wall Street Journal*, April 28, 1993, pp. C1, C15.

Chapter 4
Interest Rates in International Markets

The study of interest rates in international markets is based upon the same fundamental principles as the study of domestic interest rates. Interest rates represent the price of money in international markets just as they do in the domestic ones. There is, however, one complication. Since borrowers and lenders have a choice of going from one market to another, interest rates in international markets or in various countries cannot be independent of each other. The interdependence derives from the flow of funds and from exchange rates. We have already seen in the previous chapter that interest rate parity ensures a certain relationship between interest rates and exchange rates. In this chapter, we want to extend that discussion to create a more complete picture of how interest rates are determined in international markets.

We begin with a review of the theories of interest rates: what are interest rates and what is the relationship between interest rates for various maturities. We then discuss some terms pertaining to interest rates that will explain how we can manage risks in financial markets, the subject of the third part of this book. Finally, we examine some relationships among interest rates in international markets.

Basics of Interest Rates

Nominal Interest Rate

To understand why interest rates change and why these changes create risks for some participants in financial markets, let us first understand the role of interest rates in the economy.

Consider an individual who has some surplus funds after having paid for all the essentials of life. His choice now is either to go on a vacation or to lend the funds to his neighbor for a year. The neighbor has a plan to develop a lawn mover with an electronic sensor which cuts the grass but removes any weeds that do not resemble grass blades. The guarantees she is providing are good enough for the investor. Should he lend the money, thus postponing his vacation a year, or should he go now? What incentives would he require to postpone his vacation?

Assuming that the investor is not interested in charity, the minimum he would want from the inventor is that he should be able to take the same vacation next year as he would have taken this year. Given that prices in the economy keep rising, the inventor will therefore have to provide a compensation that is at least equal to the rate of inflation. Thus, in one year, our investor would receive enough money to be able to go on the same vacation he would have taken the previous year.

A compensation at this rate, however, requires the investor to postpone his pleasure for one year. Why should the investor postpone his vacation? To motivate the investor to do this, the inventor will have to offer something more—an incentive that the vacation next year will include a little more than would have been possible this year. The inventor, or the borrower, is thus compensating the investor, or the lender, for two things: first, enough compensation to maintain the purchasing power of the funds, and second, some compensation for postponing the satisfaction to a future period. The compensation would also have had to include a compensation for risk if we had not made the assumption that the inventor's guarantee is good enough.

Why should the inventor agree to pay such an interest rate? Why could she not use her own money if the investment is so good? There are two parts to the answer to the second question. First, remember what we had said in the first chapter: people (or economic entities) who save money in the economy are not necessarily the people who have ideas for investments. Financial markets help transfer funds from the savers to the investors, but that can be done only at a cost. Second, there is a slightly more complex answer related to risks: using borrowed money allows the risk of the project to be shared between different entities. Given that the investor has to use other people's money, what interest rate should she be willing to pay?

The answer lies in the scale and the profitability of the project. Most ideas for business opportunities are such that, the bigger the scale of the project, the lower will be the rate of return on the investment. Economic projects, in other words, have decreasing returns to scale. Our investor, who starts with a certain amount of her own capital, can decide on the size of the project by borrowing the remainder of the required investment. If she invests only the funds she has, she will earn a high rate of return. If she were to expand the scale of the project by borrowing, say $1,000, she knows that additional profits will be over and above what she has to pay to borrow the funds. Hence, she will borrow at least the first $1,000. As she expands the scale of the project using borrowed funds, her share of additional profits decreases as the marginal profits from expansion decrease but the cost of funds increases. She could borrow a lot more, but given the decreasing returns to scale, she will borrow just enough money until the size of the project is such that investing one more dollar in the project will earn exactly what has to be paid for the money. The interest rate that the inventor is willing to pay determines the size of the project, but the existence of such projects in the economy collectively determines the interest rates in the economy.

The compensation paid here, or the interest rates in the financial markets, thus consists of two elements, assuming there is no risk:

Nominal interest rate = Real interest rate + Expected inflation   (4.1)

Equation 4.1 was first proposed by Irving Fisher in 1930 and is now known as the Fisher effect. The "real interest rate" part of the nominal interest rate is the equivalent of the risk adjusted rate of return in constant prices. This is the part of the interest rates that the borrower has to pay the lender to persuade the latter to postpone the use of funds for the duration of the loan. It includes a compensation for the risk that the lender has to take, that is, the risk that the borrower will default on the loan agreement and the lender will lose part of the funds. In our example here of the investor and the inventor, we had assumed that there was no risk. The "expected inflation" part of the nominal interest rate provides a compensation for the inflation. Since the interest rates have to be decided for every period in the beginning of the period before the actual inflation for the period becomes known, the nominal interest rate includes compensation for the *expected* rate of inflation.

This description of interest rates, although useful for understanding what interest rates are about, is not an exact relationship. A more precise description is given by the following equation:

$$(1 + i) = (1 + r) \times (1 + \pi) \tag{4.2}$$

where i is the nominal interest rate in fractions that the borrower has to pay, r is the real rate of return or the real interest rate, and π is the expected rate of inflation. To calculate the nominal rate i that must be paid, all three, i, r, and π, have to be expressed as fractions. Thus, if we expected a real return of 4 percent and the expected inflation to be 3 percent, we would calculate the interest rate as follows.

$$(1 + i) = (1 + .04) \times (1 + .03) = 1.0712$$

The nominal interest rate would therefore be 7.12 percent.

Term Structure of Interest Rates

In the example given, we assumed that the inventor wanted the funds for one year. In the real world, there is a wide range of borrowers with needs for funds for maturities ranging from one day to 30 years or even longer. To allow borrowers and lenders to make a decision as to the period for which they wish to make a transaction, we need to provide interest rates for all possible maturities. The term structure of interest rates refers to the relationship between the interest rates for different maturities for instruments of equal risk and provides information on the interest rates for different maturities—short term as well as long term. Some typical term structures are shown in Exhibit 4.1. The most common term structures are those in which the interest rates are either rising or falling

Exhibit 4.1
Term Structures of Interest Rates

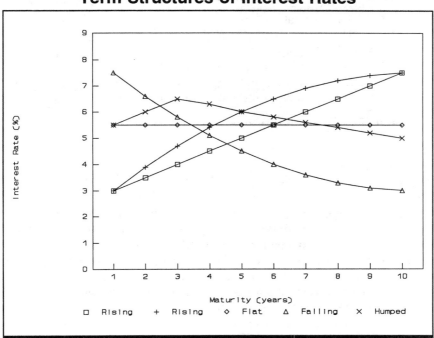

with maturity, but any other structure is possible. Why should the interest rates for different maturities be different?

Theories of term structure attempt to explain the relationship between interest rates for different maturities. There are three possible explanations for why the interest rates for different maturities may differ from each other, and what the possible relationships between the interest rates for different maturities are.

Expectations Theory

This theory is based on the principle of arbitrage. According to the expectations theory, interest rates are set such that an investor's expected return over any length of time is the same whether the funds are invested in long–term instruments or whether they are invested in short–term instruments and the proceeds are continuously rolled over at each maturity. Since the interest rates at the time of roll overs are not yet known, the equality relationship is based on the expected future interest rates. If the investment over a certain time horizon using one maturity were to offer higher returns than investment over the same time horizon using another maturity, funds would be transferred to instruments of the maturity offering higher returns. Such a flow of funds would force the interest rates to change in a way that the returns over a certain time horizon using any maturity would be equalized.

▼ ▼ ▼

The expectations theory makes two important assumptions. It assumes that investors are risk neutral and that instruments of all maturities have the same risk.

The risk neutrality assumption for investors allows the theory to treat the implied forward interest rates as unbiased predictors of future interest rates. Without this assumption, we would have to recognize that since there is some risk that the predictions about future interest rates may not turn out to be true, risk averse investors would demand a risk premium for investing in short–term instruments. This is because with short–term instruments, they will be taking the risk that the interest rate may turn out to be lower than expected. Risk neutral investors, on the other hand would not demand such a premium. There is as much a chance of the future interest rates being higher than the expected rates as of their being lower than the expected rates. Being risk neutral, investors derive as much satisfaction from higher than expected rates as they suffer from lower than expected rates.

Assumptions that instruments of different maturities have the same risk does away with a need to calculate the present values of cash flows of different maturities at different discount rates.

The representation of expectations theory presented here is somewhat simplified. A more precise interpretation of this theory merely implies that all instruments of equal risk, regardless of maturity, will have the same yield over a given period. Thus, an investor should expect to earn the same return whether he holds a three–month Treasury bill to maturity or a six–month bill for three months. The same should be valid for an investment for one year or five years or any other maturity.[1]

▲ ▲ ▲

Let us look at this principle with the help of an example. To keep the example simple, let us assume that the market offers instruments with maturities only in multiples of three months, that is, maturities of three, six, nine, twelve, fifteen, etc., months. Suppose an investor has surplus funds for six months which he wants to invest for maximum returns. Suppose also that the three–month bills are offering 7 percent (annual) return and those for six months are offering a return of 8 percent. Should he then invest in six–month bills because they have a higher interest rate? The answer according to expectations theory is that it would not matter. This is because although the three–month bill is now offering only 7 percent, the market expects that three months later, when the first investment of three months matures and the funds from the first investment have to be reinvested for another three months, the rates would have moved in such a way that the total return after six months would be exactly the same as would have been received if the funds had been invested for six months right from the start. In fact, it is possible for us to calculate what that interest rate would be. Let us denote the three–month interest rate that is expected to be offered three months from now as $F_{3,3}$, where the first number after the forward interest rate F denotes the time period for which the interest rate is quoted, and the number after the comma denotes the maturity, in number of months, for which the interest rate will be offered. Thus $F_{6,3}$ indicates that six months from now, the three–month interest rate will be F. Let $I_{0,m}$ denote the interest rate in the market at the present time, time 0, where m denotes the maturity for which the interest rate is being offered. Using this notation, we have the following relationship according to expectations theory:

$$(1 + I_{0,6}) = (1 + I_{0,3}) \times (1 + F_{3,3}) \qquad (4.3)$$

Since the six–month interest rate in our example was 8 percent and the three–month rate was 7 percent, we expect that the three–month interest rate three months from now will be:

$$(1 + F_{3,3}/4) = \frac{(1 + .08/2)}{(1 + .07/4)}$$

which yields a value of 8.845 percent for $F_{3,3}$. To verify this, note that $1,000 invested today for three months at 7 percent would provide $1,017.5 at the end of three months, which when reinvested at 8.845 percent would provide $1,040, exactly the amount that would be obtained if the funds were invested for six months today at 8 percent.

In its general form, the expectations theory can be extended to any maturity as shown in the equation below. For the ease of exposition, all interest rates are annual rates. This theory will later help us understand how risks arising from changes in interest rates can be managed.

$$(1 + I_{0,n}) = (1 + I_{0,1}) \times (1 + F_{1,1}) \times$$
$$(1 + F_{2,1}) \dots (1 + F_{n-1,1}) \tag{4.4}$$

Liquidity Preference Theory

Whereas the expectations theory was based on the assumption that investors are risk neutral, other theories that explain the term structure of interest rates make the more realistic assumption that investors are risk averse. The liquidity preference theory states that investors consider long–term investments risky and hence demand a premium for holding longer term instruments. The longer the maturity, the higher the risk premium. The risk premium is what the borrowers need to pay the investors to compensate for the risk.

This theory implies that long–term interest rates will always be higher than those implied by expectations theory. For any long–term maturity, investors will require some premium over the rates indicated by expectations theory because they consider long–term investments to have higher risk. The general equation for the expectations theory can be modified as follows:

$$(1 + I_{0,n}) = (1 + I_{0,1}) \times (1 + F_{1,1} + L_2) \times$$
$$(1 + F_{2,1} + L_3) \dots (1 + F_{n-1,1} + L_n) \tag{4.5}$$

$L_2, \dots, L_n$ represent the liquidity premiums that investors demand. These risk premiums will be such that:

$$L_2 < L_3 \ldots < L_n \qquad\qquad (4.6)$$

Preferred Habitat or Segmentation Theory

It may be possible that some investors as well as borrowers really prefer to deal only with a limited range of maturities. Investors may be planning to use their funds and borrowers may wish to commit themselves only for certain specific periods for their debts. If that is indeed the case, these investors and borrowers will not compare interest rates for different maturities in order to choose the maturity that offers them the most attractive rates, but will compare instruments only within a very narrow range of maturities. Most individuals, for example, would prefer to borrow long–term funds to finance their houses. During the last few years, short–term interest rates have been below long–term rates and yet most mortgages have been fixed rate mortgages with commitments for five years or thereabouts. Homeowners seem to prefer long–term commitments rather than take interest rate risks with floating rate mortgages. This indicates their preferred habitat of long–term security.

If investors or borrowers have their preferred habitats of maturities, then the long–term and short–term funds markets would not operate as one integrated market. The two sectors of the market will then be segmented and interest rates in the two segments of the market may not necessarily bear any relationship to each other. If there were to be excess demand for short–term funds, interest rates for the short term may rise above those for long–term funds without implying that short–term rates are expected to fall in the future below long–term rates.

Regardless of the term structure theory, it is clear that interest rates for different maturities are linked to each other through arbitrage. Even if some investors or borrowers prefer certain maturities over others, there are others who will take advantage of differences in yields that are not justified by economic considerations. If, for example, the return for long–term bonds were to rise above the return on a series of short–term instruments of equal risk, an arbitrager or a speculator would be able to borrow short term, lend long term, and earn arbitrage profits. The potential for such arbitrage will keep interest rates for different maturities in equilibrium. This is especially true since the introduction of derivative products like swaps and options that are flexible enough to take advantage of any discrepancy in the marketplace. We will return to these instruments and the knowledge of the term structure in subsequent chapters.

Some Terminology of Interest Rates

Simple Interest Rate

Simple interest rate is the nominal rate that is the contract payment on a loan or a bond, expressed as a percentage or in decimals. If a loan of $100 will have to be settled by a payment of $108 in one year, the simple interest rate is given by:

$$1 + i = \frac{(108)}{100} = 1.08$$

$$\therefore \text{ simple interest rate, } i = .08 = 8\%$$

Compound Interest Rate

Compound interest rate is measured over more than one time period and refers to the rate at which the amount grows, assuming that whatever interest is received in any period also earns the same interest rate as the original amount. If we invest $1,000 in a fixed term deposit for a period of three years with a bank which promises to pay $1,225 at the end of that period, the compound rate of interest will be given by:

$$1,225 = 1,000 \times (1 + i) \times (1 + i) \times (1 + i)$$

$$\therefore i = (1,225/1,000)^{1/3} - 1 = .07 = 7\%$$

Note that at a simple rate of interest of 7 percent, the bank would have paid $70 at the end of first and the second years and $1,070 at the end of the third year.

Coupon Rate

Coupon rate refers to the promised rate of interest on a bond. When the bond is first issued, the issuer notes the rate at which the interest will be paid through the life of the bond. The rate is applied to the face value of the bond. Thus, a 10–year bond with a face value of $1,000 and an 8.5 percent coupon will pay interest of $85 every year for the ten years. This does not mean, however, that the holder of the bond will earn 8.5 percent return on the bond every year. The price of the bond may change from year to year, and the return on the bond will change along with the price. The actual return on the bond is referred to as the **yield**.

Yield to Maturity

Yield to maturity refers to the rate at which future cash flows associated with the bond must be discounted to equal the current price of the bond (or any other instrument). The cash flows of a bond are the periodic interest payments at the coupon rate, and the redemption of the face value at maturity. Yield to maturity and the current price of the bond are interdependent; we must know one to find the other. Consider a World Bank deutschemark bond with a coupon of 5–7/8 percent, maturing in exactly four years and currently selling at 99.64 (for every 100 deutschemarks of the face value), that is, slightly below its par value. If the face value of the bond is DM1000, the bond will pay 5.875 percent of DM 1000, or DM 58.75 at the end of every year for three years and DM 1058.75 at the end of the fourth year. The yield to maturity, y, can be calculated by discounting the first year's flow of DM 58.75 by $(1 + y)$, the second year's flow by $(1 + y)^2$, the third year's flow by $(1 + y)^3$, and the final year's flow of DM 1058.75 by $(1 + y)^4$.

$$996.4 = \sum_{n=1}^{3} \frac{(58.75)}{(1 + y)^n} + \frac{1058.75}{(1 + y)^4}$$

Solving the equation for a yield of 5.98 percent, we obtain:

$$996.4 = 55.43 + 52.31 + 49.36 + 839.26$$

The bond, therefore, has a yield to maturity of 5.98 percent. The yield is slightly different from the coupon because the bond is not selling at its face value.

In the marketplace, the calculations will proceed in the opposite direction. For any bond, the yield to maturity will have to be the same as the yield on other instruments of equal risk. Given the required yield and face value, a trader will then calculate the price of the bond given its coupon rate and the frequency of payments. The following table gives the price of a World Bank bond for different required yields.

Required Yield	Price of the Bond in Deutschemarks
5.0%	1031.0
5.5%	1013.1
5.75%	1004.4
5.8%	1002.6
5.875%	1000.0
6.0%	995.7
6.25%	987.1
6.5%	978.6
7.0%	961.9

Notice that if the required yield is higher than the coupon of the bond, the bond sells at a discount, and if the coupon is the higher one, the bond sells at a premium.

Yield of a Zero–Coupon Bond

The yield of a zero–coupon bond is calculated in the same fashion as the yield to maturity except that the only cash flow to be discounted is at the maturity of the bond. Thus, the yield of a zero–coupon bond equates the current price of the bond to the discounted face value of the bond. The yield of a zero–coupon bond is also equivalent to the compound interest rate defined earlier and is calculated in exactly the same fashion. For a zero–coupon bond, the yield and the compound interest rate become equal.

International Interest Rates

The theory of international interest rates is a simple extension of the theory of interest rates in one country. The theory and principles for the explanation of interest rates discussed earlier do not depend upon the institutional details of a specific country. They are applicable to all countries where market forces determine prices and interest rates. We can therefore expect that the interest rates in each country will be governed by these relationships. But what about the interest rates for the same maturity in two countries? What would be the relationship between the three–month Treasury bill rate in the United States and that in Germany?

The interest rate parity theorem helps answer these questions for situations in which forward rates are available. In this section, we will provide an explanation for situations in which forward rates are not quoted and, hence, risk free arbitrage is not possible.

Exhibit 4.2
Yields on Government Bonds, June 1993

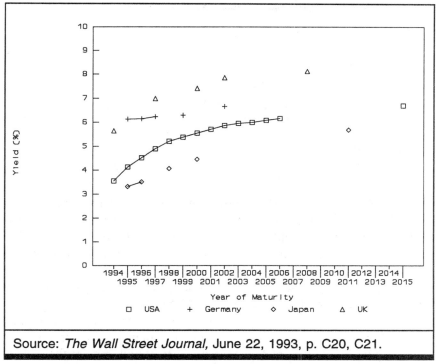

Source: *The Wall Street Journal*, June 22, 1993, p. C20, C21.

Exhibit 4.2 shows the plots of the term structures for the yields of government bonds in four countries during June 1993. All the curves are rising, indicating that interest rates increase as maturities lengthen. Yet there are some differences among the interest rates in these countries. Rates for different maturities do not differ very much from each other in Germany, but both in the United Kingdom and the United States, long–term rates are much higher than short–term rates. What explains these different term structures?

Let us begin with the simple description of an interest rate given by Equation 4.1 in the beginning of this chapter. An interest rate was defined as consisting of two components: a real rate of return and expected inflation. We can define the interest rate for any maturity in two countries using the Fisher effect. Disregarding the exact maturity for the moment, we can describe the interest rate for each country, the United States and Germany, as:

$$i_{U.S.} = r_{U.S.} + \pi_{U.S.}$$

and

$$i_{Ger} = r_{Ger} + \pi_{Ger}$$

The difference between the interest rates in two countries can be written as:

$$i_{U.S.} - i_{Ger} = (r_{U.S.} - r_{Ger}) + (\pi_{U.S.} - \pi_{Ger}) \qquad (4.7)$$

Thus, the difference between nominal interest rates in two countries is the sum of the difference between the real rates of interest in the two countries and the difference between their expected rates of inflation.

Let us examine the first term on the right–hand side of Equation 4.7, that is, the difference between the real rates of interest in the two countries. Remember that a real rate of interest represents the extent to which the real value of an asset increases when a real rate of interest, or return, is obtained. What would the investors in one country do if they observed that funds can be invested in another country at higher real rates of return? In the absence of capital controls, they will transfer their funds to the second country and invest them in that country. As a result of the outflow of funds from the first country and the inflow of funds in the second country, the real rates of interest will change in both places. The rate in the first country would rise because the supply of funds has decreased and that in the second country would fall because the supply of funds has increased. Equilibrium will be re–established only when the real rates of interest in the two countries have been equalized through this flow of funds. In the absence of capital controls that restrict the flow of funds, equilibrium will imply equal rates of interest. The following box provides evidence that, as financial markets begin to be liberalized, and funds begin to flow without restrictions, real interest rates between countries begin to converge also.

▼ ▼ ▼

Liberalization of Financial Markets and Convergence of U.S. and Japanese Interest Rates[*]

In the early 1980s, the Japanese government commenced the process that led to almost complete elimination of restrictions on capital movements in and out of Japan and to an integration of Japanese financial markets with the international financial markets. One of the consequences of this integration has been that the differential between the real interest rates in Japan and those elsewhere has tended to move toward zero, indicating that *ex ante* real interest rate differentials may be disappearing.

In a study of real interest rates in Japan and the United States, Hutchison compared the *ex post* real interest rate differentials over the 1980s. *Ex post* real rates are calculated as nominal interest rates minus the actual inflation. Since the actual inflation may not equal the anticipated inflation, the *ex post* real interest rate may not equal the *ex ante* real rate. If the prediction error associated with the inflation rate, however, is random, the differential between the real interest rates will slowly disappear. It was found that changes in the real rate in one country tend to be completely incorporated in the real rate of the other country within four to eight quarters. The effect, moreover, is symmetrical: changes in U.S. interest rates affect those in Japan and changes in Japanese interest rates affect those in the United States.

The author concludes that the "results indicate a very high degree of real interest rate linkage between the U.S. and Japan since the early 1980s. . . . Gaps in real interest rates between the two countries also appear to close quickly, and Japan seems to play an important role in the determination of rates in the U.S." (page 3.)

The research supports the contention that, *ex ante,* the real interest rate differential in Equation 4.7 in the text can be assumed to be zero.

* Summarized from Michael M. Hutchison, "Interdependence: U.S. and Japanese Real Interest Rates," Federal Reserve Bank of San Francisco, *Weekly Letter,* Number 93–23, June 18, 1993.

▲ ▲ ▲

The second term in Equation 4.7 is the difference in the expected inflation rates between the two countries, and it leads us to the relationship between interest rates and exchange rates. Given that the expected value of the first term in that equation is zero, the difference between the interest rates becomes equal to the difference between the expected rates of inflation. Since, as we saw in the previous chapter, the inflation differential also equals the expected change in the exchange rates, we have the relationship that was shown in Exhibit 3.3 between the three sets of variables–interest rates, exchange rates, and rates of expected inflation.

The purchasing power parity relationship dictates that the expected change in exchange rates will equal the inflation differential between the two countries. As we saw earlier, the inflation differential also determines the difference between interest rates. From the interest rate parity theorem we also know that the difference in the interest rates between two countries will exactly equal the forward rate premium or discount. What happens, however, if there is no forward rate in the market, that is, if the banks are not willing to quote a forward rate?

In the absence of a forward rate quotation for exchange rates, interest rate differences will become equal to the expected changes in the exchange rates. Instead of a riskless arbitrage situation that ensured the interest rate parity relationship, we will now have risky arbitrage in which market participants will be taking a risky position with the expectation of a profit. To illustrate this relationship between interest rates and exchange rates, let us return to the Exhibit 4.2.

Consider the interest rates shown in that exhibit for Germany and the United States for short maturities, say bonds maturing in 1995. This implies a maturity of two years, since the exhibit shows the rates prevailing in June 1993. German bonds have a yield of 6.13 percent, and those for the United States have 4.13 percent. Why would an investor be willing to hold U.S. dollar bonds when it is possible to earn 2 percent more by holding German bonds of the same maturity and with the same risk? The answer lies in the expected exchange rate changes. Market participants expect that, over the next two years, the deutschemark will depreciate with respect to the dollar at an annual rate of 2 percent. If the deutschemark were to depreciate by that amount, investors in dollars and those in deutschemarks would end up with the same returns at the end of the two years. Consider next the maturity of 2002. The yield on those German bonds is 6.66 percent compared to the U.S. yield of 5.88 percent. The difference, 0.78 percent per annum, represents the market's expectation of the average annual depreciation of the deutschemark over the next nine years. Comparing the two estimates of the changes in the

Exhibit 4.3
Bond Yields and Exchange Rates

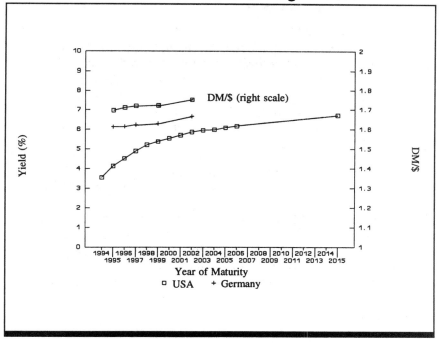

values of the deutschemark, we notice that the rate of depreciation is expected to slow down considerably. Over the next nine years, the expected cumulative depreciation is 7.24 percent $\{ = (1 + 0.0078)^9\}$. However, the expected cumulative depreciation over the next two years is 4.04 percent $\{ = (1 + 0.02)^2\}$. This implies that between 1995 and 2002, the market expects the deutschemark to depreciate only by about 3 percent $\{ = (1 + .0724)/(1 + 0.0404) -1\}$. Exhibit 4.3 shows the term structures of bond yields for the two countries and the expected path of the deutschemark, given that the spot rate on the day was DM 1.63/$.

The expectations of exchange rates that are built into the international interest rates can give rise to opportunities, or pitfalls, in international markets. An example of such a situation is provided by a recent innovation in the financial markets called PERLS. Details of one such innovation, and some dangers of ignoring some fundamental principles of economics in international financial markets, are described in the following box.

▼ ▼ ▼
Innovative Ways to Bet on Interest Rate Parity . . . and Lose[*]

Financial innovations sometimes help prove that the theory is not altogether ignored in efficient capital markets. Innovative instruments that came to be known as Principal Exchange–Rate Linked Securities, or PERLS, illustrate the dangers of ignoring predictions of interest rate parity. We may remember from Chapter 3 that, according to this theory, interest rates in two countries can differ only by the amount of expected exchange rate changes.

PERLS were first offered by Morgan Stanley & Co. in March 1987, and the investment banking firm had offered a total of $3.7 billion of these instruments until August 1992. Other banks, including J.P. Morgan, Bankers Trust, and First Boston had sold an additional $4 billion.

The attraction of PERLS was that they offered higher interest rates than those available in the U.S. markets for instruments of equal risk. In exchange for the higher risk, however, the investor was required to take an exchange risk. The principal of the notes was payable not in dollars, the currency in which the principal and the interest amounts were denominated on the notes, but in a mixture of some other currencies. The complexity of PERLS is best illustrated with an example.

Sallie Mae (Student Loan Marketing Association) raised $135 million on June 28, 1990, by issuing PERLS with a maturity of five years. These notes paid an interest of 11.75 percent which represented a premium of 3.34 percent over the treasury notes of equal maturity. (Given that Sallie Mae notes are the obligations of a U.S. government agency, they are almost as good as treasury notes. The interest rates on these notes, therefore, should be very close to the interest rate on treasury notes. By way of confirming this, we may note that, at the time of this writing, the yields on two–year maturity notes of Sallie Mae as well as those of the treasury were exactly 3.68 percent.)

In exchange for the higher interest rates, the investors had to take some risk on the exchange rates for British pounds and German marks. This is because at maturity, investors will be repaid the principal not as $135 million, but as 155 million pounds minus 225.6 million deutschemarks. These amounts are the equivalent of $270 million in pounds minus the equivalent of $135 million in deutschemarks at exchange rates prevailing at the time the notes were issued. The amounts of 155 million pounds and 225.6 million deutschemarks were derived by dividing the original principal of $135 million in two parts: $270 million minus $135 million. The first part, $270 million, was equivalent to 155 million pounds at the end of June 1990 at the then prevailing exchange rate of $1.7416/pound, and the second part of $135 million was equivalent to DM 225.6 million at an exchange rate of DM 1.6715/$. Thus, on June 28, 1995, when the notes mature, the investors will receive not $135 million but an amount that is the dollar equivalent of 155 million pounds minus 225.6 million deutschemarks at exchange rates prevailing on *that day.*

The investors gambled that the pound and the deutschemark exchange rates will not change in a way that will offset their gains from higher interest rates. In 1990, given that both these currencies were a part of the Exchange Rate Mechanism (or ERM that we discussed in Chapter 2), that seemed like a reasonable assumption. ERM would require the currencies to fluctuate only within a narrow range of each other. Central banks would intervene if one of the currencies were to come under market pressure for a large change. Obviously, the bankers who advised Sallie Mae to offer higher interest rates had taken into account the probabilities of a devaluation of the pound and revaluation of the deutschemark. The bankers may have been proven right by the currency crises in the fall of 1992 and it seemed that the investors had lost. At the end of December 1992, the pound was worth only $1.5022/pound and the deutschemark had been revalued to DM 1.5935/$. The worst nightmare of the investor had come true. If the notes had to be repaid at the end of 1992, the investors would have received only $91.2 million ($232.8 million for 155 million pounds minus $141.6 million for 225.6 million deutschemarks).

It is, of course, still possible that between December 1992 and June 1995, exchange rates will move back to levels that will benefit the investors. On the other hand, things could get even worse! The market, taking into account potential changes in exchange rates, valued these PERLS only at $88.5 million in early March 1993.

PERLS illustrate the principles of interest rate parity. In the example of Sallie Mae, the issuer offered higher interest rates in exchange for potential for gains from changes in exchange rates. They, of course, could not be sure that they would not lose money on these notes, but the proper estimation of the probabilities and amounts of expected changes in exchange rates allowed their bankers to determine the interest rate that made these instruments attractive to investors without costing the issuer an excessive amount. The issuer in this case, moreover, had been able to hedge the exchange risk involved in the transaction. The hedging, through forwards, swaps, and options, would yield enough revenue for Sallie Mae to offset the cost of higher interest rates.

Note, however, that the story is not yet finished. The notes will mature in 1995. It is quite possible that within the next two years, the exchange rates will move in a direction that the original investment in these notes would not appear to be such a foolish move.

Source: "Currency Instability Tarnishes PERLS," *The Wall Street Journal*, March 9, 1993, page C1.

▲ ▲ ▲

Summary

Interest rates consist of two components: inflation and real rate of compensation. The two components are essential to motivate lenders to part with their funds. Since investors evaluate opportunities only in terms of real rates of return, arbitrage will ensure equality of real rates of returns across countries. Nominal rates, however, can differ from country to country because of different rates of inflation. The differences in interest rates for various maturities across countries, that is, the term structures of interest rates, will also differ by expected rates of inflation for those maturities. Since the inflation differentials also affect exchange rates, interest rates across countries have an intimate relationship with exchange rates. This relationship will become very important for managing financial risks arising from changes in interest and exchange rates.

Note

1. Campbell, T. S. and W. A. Kracaw, *Financial Risk Management: Fixed Income and Foreign Exchange*, New York: HarperCollins, 1993, pp. 86–90.

Part II

The International Capital Markets

The second part of the book describes various segments of the international financial markets. Institutional details as well as economic principles for the operations of international money, bond, and equity markets are explained. Main instruments and techniques within each market segment are described, and economic fundamentals that govern the use of each instrument are explained where necessary. Chapter 5 explains the growth of the Eurocurrency deposits and then explains the functioning of international money markets. Chapter 6 describes the international bond markets. The last two chapters of this part deal with international equity markets. Chapter 7 describes how international equity investments can be made and Chapter 8 discusses the economic principles of international investments.

Chapter 5
International Money Markets

The development of what is now known as the Eurodollar market would have to be recognized as one of the most significant innovations in capital markets over the last three decades. As investors began to look beyond financial markets in their own countries in the 1960s, a new concept of offshore or Eurodollars was developed. Banks seized upon the opportunity presented by these unregulated dollars and soon mandates for syndicated loans became much sought–after prizes. Once the glamour of loans had worn off, banks found other applications for these dollars—first, the Eurobonds and then more exotic instruments like Revolving Underwritten Facilities and Eurocommercial papers.

Our objective in this chapter is to understand how these Euromarkets work. We will begin by examining the creation of a Eurodollar and then study how these accounts are used for channelling savings in international financial markets. After understanding how these accounts are created, we will look at the Eurocurrency loans and then at other money market instruments such as Euronotes.

Eurocurrency or Eurodollar Markets

A more appropriate term for this market would have been "external–currency" market, reflecting the fact that what characterizes this market is the external nature of the accounts, a location anywhere in the world, and availability in many international currencies. The term "Eurodollar," however, was used in 1959 by one of the first economists who wrote about this market, and the name stuck. Following common practice, we will use the term Eurodollar as a generic term to refer to all segments of the Eurocurrency market. The term "euro" is used here to designate all the markets that deal in credit transactions in a currency other than that of the political jurisdiction in which the transaction takes place. Thus, a bank loan for U.S. $10 million will be a Eurodollar loan if the transaction takes place anywhere outside of the United States. Such a transaction could take place in London, Zurich, Singapore, the Cayman Islands, Panama, or Ouagadougou. In a more precise interpretation, the term "Eurodollar" refers only to that portion of the Eurocurrency markets which deals with U.S. dollars. The other major segments of this market are EuroDMs, Euro–French franc, Euro–Swiss francs, Euroyen, etc., and accounts in about 15 currencies are currently available in this market. Besides the major financial centers in the industrialized countries, Bahrain, Singapore, and Hong Kong, international banking centers in exotic places like the Cayman Islands, the Bahamas, Netherlands Antilles, and Turks and Caicos Islands accept Eurocurrency deposits. It must be noted, however, that the banking centers in these locations exist in name only; the real activity is carried out in places like New York or London. The accompanying box describes a typical international banking center.

The term "Euromarkets" refers to the network of financial institutions and intermediaries and participants, whether individuals, corporations, or governments, that buy and sell credits in Eurocurrencies. These external credit markets may be divided into two broad categories based upon the nature and the maturity of the claims: the Eurocurrency or money markets and Eurobond markets. The Eurocurrency markets consist largely of commercial banks that accept deposits and make loans, as well as commercial and investment banks that issue securities of short and medium maturities in many currencies in international markets. Typical instruments in this market are known as "syndicated Eurodollar loans," "Euronotes," or "Eurocommercial paper." The Eurobond market consists of the network of banks and distributors that facilitate corporations and public entities to issue long–term bonds. Euromarkets of each currency are closely tied to domestic money markets of that currency and foreign exchange markets.

▼ ▼ ▼

Have International Banking Centers.
Will Solve Your Unemployment Problems!

An "offshore" or international financial center is merely a location where the government allows financial transactions in foreign currencies between non–residents to be carried out without being subject to the regulations of domestic monetary authorities or being subject to domestic taxation. The only exception to the requirement that the currency be a foreign currency is in the United States: the U.S. government has allowed banks to set up International Banking Facilities or IBFs. With an IBF within the United States, certain transactions may be designated as "offshore" transactions and hence may not be subject to the U.S. regulations or taxation.

The main motivation for allowing an international banking center is employment and marginal revenues from taxation. Although the governments in these centers exempt the transactions from income taxes, they still charge a small fee for banks to register themselves and sometimes even a small fee based upon the transactions. For some governments, for example some islands in the Caribbean or the Pacific, these revenues can be a substantial proportion of their gross revenues. The other motivation for these governments' allowing the international banking centers is creation of employment. The governments believe, quite reasonably, that banks at any location will require some incentives to carry out transactions between non–residents from that location. These transactions would normally be carried out at a location where one of the transactors is resident. These transactions between non–residents, moreover, have no influence on the monetary policy that the government may wish to follow. Allowing these transactions to take place from a domestic (to the government) location would not have any effect on the domestic economic policies, but the fact that an activity that was carried out outside the country is now carried out within the country will generate some employment. Hence, the motivation for opening the international financial centers.

To the users, these centers offer the advantage of confidentiality and a chance to avoid the regulations of their own governments. Many financial centers offer a higher degree of confidentiality to their transactors than their respective countries. Although it is becoming more and more difficult for financial authorities in one country not to cooperate with financial and taxation authorities in other countries in large criminal or fraud cases, investors can still expect to shield some of their transactions from their own governments for minor transactions. In some cases, the investors may also be able to escape or delay paying taxes on some of some of their income by going through these financial centers. The governments in these centers, however, have to balance the confidentiality advantage over the risk that too much secrecy will tarnish the image of the center as a place for high quality legal operations. Too much secrecy may also result in the government of a leading industrialized country, the United States for example, to bar their institutions from carrying out operations in that center. No center would be able to survive such a ban. Recognizing the importance of having the tacit approval of the major governments, the Cayman Islands, which has been a leading international banking center for a long time, has signed agreements with the U.S. and U.K. governments to prevent laundering of illegal money.

Banks operating in these centers find that they have far fewer reporting requirements at these centers compared to the requirements imposed by their own governments. Absence of these requirements can mean substantial savings for the banks. Banks may also be able to save some labor costs. On the one hand, they have to pay higher compensations to expatriates who are employed in these centers, but on the other hand, there are substantial savings to be had from the employment of local employees. This is especially true for locations in low wage countries where jobs with foreign banks are considered very prestigious, and these banks may have access to a much higher quality of worker than would be possible at

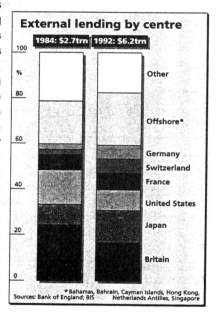

home. All these factors have resulted in an increase in the market share of these centers for international lending activities—as shown in the accompanying box. The government that desires to have an international banking center within its territory must be able to offer a stable political environment and advanced and modern transportation and communication networks. In addition, it does not hurt if the location is known for its golf courses and other recreation facilities for the expatriates that work for the banks.

At the present time, the following international banking centers are widely used by banks around the world:* London, the United States in the form of international banking facilities, Zurich, Paris, Frankfort, Tokyo, Malta, Hong Kong, Singapore, the Bahamas, Bahrain, Bermuda, the Cayman Islands, Cyprus, Guernsey, Isle of Man, Jersey, Madeira, Netherlands Antilles, Puerto Rico, Turks and Caicos Islands, and the British Virgin Islands.

* Main offshore financial centers are described in: Euromoney, *The 1992 Guide to Offshore Financial Centers*, Research Guide, 1992. The graph is from *The Economist*, May 22, 1993, p. 116.

▲ ▲ ▲

This chapter deals with the Eurocurrency markets consisting of syndicated loans, Euronotes, and Eurocommercial papers; Eurobonds are the subject of the following chapter. This chapter explains how international money markets work in three steps. After a brief history of the growth of the Eurodollar market, the first part of the chapter deals with how money moves from domestic markets to the external market, in effect creating the Eurodollar accounts. Creation of these accounts is motivated by costs of doing business in domestic markets; hence it is necessary to understand how and why interest rates in these markets differ from those in the domestic markets. The second part of the chapter explains the lending process in international money markets with a focus on the process of syndication. The third part of the chapter deals with short– and medium–term securities that have come to dominate the attention of participants in these markets. Although money markets within each country—countries foreign to a particular investor—could also be considered as a part of international money markets, we ignore these foreign money markets because in terms of economic principles, foreign money markets would operate in the same way as domestic money markets. This does not imply that all domestic money markets offer the same mixture of short– and medium–term instruments or that they follow the same borrowing and lending practices, just that the differences between domestic and external money markets are more complex than those between various domestic money markets.

Growth of Eurodollar Markets

Although there is some evidence that foreign currency deposits were held by banks before World War II, it is only since the late 1950s that Eurocurrency markets have grown rapidly and consistently. The total size of the market as measured by the amount of credit outstanding to non–banks (or the net size of the market) grew from a mere U.S. $9.0 billion in 1965 to about U.S. $3,610 billion at the end of 1991.[1] It is, however, a very difficult market to measure, and these numbers must be interpreted with caution. The cause for the existence and growth of the market has been attributed to U.S. balance of payments deficits, the erstwhile U.S. capital control program, mysterious multipliers, and even the financial machinations of the Russians. And while there is a kernel of truth to all these allegations, the most important reason is perhaps that Eurocurrency markets are simply the response of competitive banking to regulatory distortions in domestic markets.

To understand why the Eurocurrency markets did not start growing until the late 1950s, we must recognize three necessary conditions for the functioning of external markets identified by Dufey and Giddy:[2]

1. Foreign–based entities must possess the freedom to maintain and transfer demand deposit balances in, say, New York; that is, there should be no restrictions on nonresident inpayments, outpay-ments, and transfers. This had existed for the United States at least since World War II.

2. Eurobanks must be able to offer external deposits and loans at competitive rates in a convenient location. While the absence of reserve requirements and the like made Eurobanks potentially competitive with their U.S. counterparts, the widespread currency restrictions during the decade following World War II eliminated most suitable locations outside the United States.

3. There must be a demand for external currency deposits and loans. In other words, non–Eurobank entities must be willing and able to place dollar funds with banks outside the United States and to employ dollar funds borrowed from such banks. Prior to the restoration of convertibility of major European currencies in

1957, this ability was lacking for most non–U.S. depositors and lenders.

These conditions were not satisfied until the late 1950s. Growth in international trade had increased the demand for international vehicle currencies. Given the importance of the U.S. dollar within the contemporary international financial system—the Bretton Woods system—and given that the United States had been the main source of funds for investments in Europe through its Marshall plan, and due to the need to finance its balance of payments deficits, the U.S. dollar had become the main vehicle currency for global trade. The dollar was used not only for trade with the United States, but also by third countries for their trade with each other. In addition, U.S. multinationals needed dollars to fund their foreign direct investments. Thus, the dollar was in great demand and, given the strength of the U.S. economy, fully convertible.

Although the U.S. dollar had been a convertible currency, the restoration of convertibility for major European currencies after 1958, and the formation of the European Economic Community that year, allowed the market to develop a confidence that exchange restrictions would not undermine investments in major industrial countries. The convertibility of currencies reduced the perceived political risk of the different European currencies. Further, the dismantling of exchange control regimes allowed holders to move their currency balances freely from one country to another. This movement of currencies created a competition among the banks for deposits and forced them to look for ways to cut their costs and offer more attractive returns to investors. One of the areas where banks could see cost savings was in avoiding costs of domestic regulations on banking activities. Banks took advantage of the absence of reserve requirements on their foreign exchange balances and began to shift their domestic currency balances to markets outside the country. Absence of regulatory and other costs allowed the banks to offer deposit rates on external market deposits above the domestic rates and lower the loan rates on external market loans below those in the respective domestic markets. These differences in rates created demand for Eurocurrency funds which allowed the market to grow at a rapid rate.

The stage for the rapid growth of the Eurodollar market was finally set in the early 1960s when the U.S. government first imposed the Interest Equalization Tax in 1963 and then introduced a Voluntary Credit

Restraint Program in 1965.[3] The aim of both of these programs was to keep U.S. funds in the United States. The response of borrowers, of course, was to find ways to circumvent the controls. One way in which the borrowers could obtain dollars and not be subject to the controls of the United States government was to make the transactions outside the United States. This was all that was needed at that time for the Eurodollar market to take off. By 1972, the market had grown to about 10 times its size of 1964.[4]

The second impetus for the growth of the Eurodollar market came with the oil price shocks of 1973–74 and 1979–80. The oil exporting countries found large volumes of surplus funds in their hands without the expertise to either invest in their own economies or the know–how to invest them in the economies of the industrialized world. They found it attractive to deposit the funds in the form of Eurodollar market certificates of deposits with the large commercial banks around the world. These deposits offered good enough returns for their purposes. Banks, of course, were anxious to obtain these deposits because the oil importing countries were anxious to finance their balance of payments deficits caused by the oil price increases. The Eurodollar market provided a convenient medium for recycling the funds from the oil exporting/surplus countries to the oil importing/deficit countries. The market grew another tenfold during the decade to a net size of about $1,285 billion by the end of 1982.[5]

The folly of recycling came home to roost in 1982 when a large number of developing countries that had been borrowing heavily in the market realized that they were unable to service their Eurodollar market debts. Ironically, the fall of dominos began with an oil exporting country—Mexico, which had borrowed heavily to build its oil industry—in the fall of 1982. The banks which had lent the funds were now viewed by investors as very risky because of impaired balance sheets, significant parts of which were loans from countries nearing default. The increased perception of risk associated with the deposits of banks in the external markets slowed the growth of the Eurodollar market in the 1980s. The growth was slowed further because of the development of innovative instruments such as Euronotes and Eurocommercial paper which competed directly with bank loans. It was only in the latter part of the 1980s that investors regained their confidence in the international markets and the banks. At the present time, the Euroloan, Euronote, Euro–

commercial paper, and Eurobond markets compete with each other for the investor's attention.

Creation of a Eurodollar Account

Contrary to the popular and romantic impressions, Eurodollars are created not when drug dealers take suitcases full of U.S. dollars out of the country but as a result of legal transactions of private investors looking for the best returns on their investments. Eurodollars are created when someone holding a dollar account in the U.S. banking system transfers that account to a bank outside the United States. The bank outside the United States begins to transact in a currency that is not the currency of the country where the bank is located. Since at the present time most governments control only the accounts in their own currencies, the above account falls outside the regulation of the country where the bank is located. Since the dollar account is physically outside the United States, there is very little that the U.S. government can do about it—at least directly. Hence, the dollar account becomes a non–regulated account. This absence of regulation creates distinctions between an external account and a domestic account. It has a profound influence on the cost of doing business with these accounts.

Exhibit 5.1 helps us understand the steps involved in a typical set of transactions that result in the creation of a Eurodollar account. We start with a U.S. corporation—AUS Corp.—making a payment to a foreign company—Afor Co.—for some parts it has purchased a few months back. The payment is made by a check drawn on a U.S. bank. Afor Co. may have a U.S. bank account and may deposit the check in that account at least temporarily. Very soon, however, the company will have to decide what to do with that money. It may convert the money into its own currency in which case the dollars go back into the U.S. banking system after the appropriate amount of foreign currency has been delivered to the Afor Co., and the transaction ends at that point. Let us suppose that the company wants to keep the U.S. dollars because it anticipates needs for dollars in a short time. It may, however, find it inconvenient to deal with a bank located in the United States for reasons of distance and may prefer that a local bank—Eurobank, Inc.—agree to open and manage a current account in U.S. dollars. If the local bank agrees to open such an account, the Afor Co. will write a check on its U.S. bank and give it to the

Exhibit 5.1
Creation of a Eurodollar Account

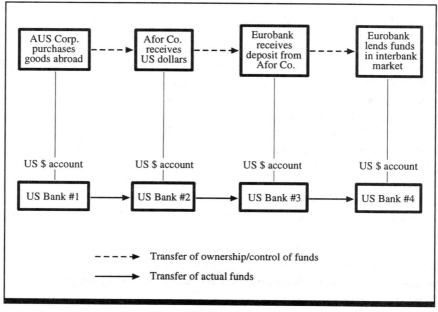

Eurobank. The Eurobank, in turn, will deposit the check in its own U.S. dollar account within the United States.

These transactions have created what we call an external market account which has several characteristics that distinguish it from a dollar account within the United States. First, the Afor Co. has opened a U.S. dollar account outside the United States. Second, although the account is with the Eurobank, the Eurobank does not really have the actual U.S. dollars—not even a fraction of the value of the account as a U.S. bank would. All it has is dollars in its account with a U.S. bank in the United States. Every time the Afor Co. wants to make payments in U.S. dollars, it will issue instructions to the Eurobank and the bank will then make a payment out of its U.S. account with a bank in the United States. Third, the amount of U.S. dollars in the account has moved outside the direct control of the U.S. government. As it happens, the monetary authorities of the country in which the bank holding the account is located, say the

Netherlands, also does not really put any requirements on the Eurobank about reserve requirements on the dollar account. To understand the last point, imagine what would have happened if Afor Co. had left its account with its U.S. bank instead of transferring the account to the Eurobank; the U.S. bank would have held a current account for Afor Co. and would have had to hold a portion of the account as reserves because of U.S. government regulations. The Eurobank is not subject to those regulations and its own government does not regulate the U.S. dollar account—or, for that matter, an account in any other foreign currency. An account has been created which is unregulated by any government.

It is worthwhile to note that the reliance placed on the nationalities of some of the transactors in the above example was purely for purposes of illustration and is not a requirement for a Eurodollar account. The account could have been transferred to a Eurobank by a resident of the United States. The Eurobank does not have to be a non–U.S. bank; many of the banks are branches of U.S. banks in foreign countries. In fact, it is not even necessary that the Eurobank be outside the United States. In view of the large growth of the Eurodollar market, the United States government recognized that banks that carried out Eurodollar market activities created some employment in the location where the activity was carried out. To bring some of the benefits of these activities back to the United States, the government allowed the banks in the United States to open International Banking Facilities in 1981. Under these facilities, a bank can open a Eurodollar account from its offices within the United States if the transaction meets some of the conditions that would have allowed it to become a Eurodollar account in the normal course. Thus, if an investor were in a position to open a Eurodollar account with a bank outside the United States, she could now open a similar account with a bank inside the United States. The investor would get the same interest as if she went to a Eurobank, and the activity would be carried out within the United States.

What has been said about the creation of an external account in U.S. dollars is true for other currencies also. An external account can be created in British pounds, French francs, Hong Kong dollars, or any other currency. One requirement for creating such accounts is that the currency should be convertible, that is, the government of the country should not place any restrictions on who can own the currency and who cannot own it. Along with convertibility, there must be sufficient demand for accounts in that currency so that the banks have the incentive to develop the necessary infrastructure that is required to open and maintain accounts in a particular foreign currency.

Transactions in Eurodollars do not end with a Eurobank acquiring a foreign currency deposit. Since the bank has to pay interest on the account, it must invest the funds in income–bearing investments. Most of the funds in the Eurodollar market are deposited with banks in the form of banks' certificates of deposits or CDs. These deposits may have a very short maturity—as short as overnight—or long maturities of up to one year. Most of the deposits are made in the form of negotiable CDs so that the depositor can at least sell the deposit in the secondary market, even if the funds cannot be withdrawn from the bank itself. Since the bank commits itself to pay interest on these deposits, banks have to look for borrowers of funds who are willing to pay slightly more than the interest the bank has to pay on the CDs. Sometimes the bank does not have a ready borrower when the funds are received. In that case, the bank will lend the funds to another bank in the interbank market. The interbank market is the network through which banks borrow and lend money to each other when they have a shortage or surplus of funds. The interest rate at which the top tier banks lend money to each other in the interbank market in London has become a reference rate for this market and is known as London InterBank Offer Rate, or LIBOR. LIBOR represents the interest rate at which a bank will be willing to lend funds to a bank considered very safe or a top tier bank. If there is some risk that the bank will have some difficulty repaying the funds on maturity, the rate will be above LIBOR.

Interest Rates in the Eurodollar Market

We had mentioned earlier that the growth of the Eurodollar market was largely due to the attractive interest rates offered by this market. We will analyze two aspects of the interest rates in the Eurodollar market. First we want to understand the link between interest rates for the Eurocurrency segment of a particular currency and interest rates in the domestic segment of the same currency. Second, we want to understand the link between the interest rates in the Eurocurrency segments of two different currencies.

Euromarket versus domestic interest rates. To understand the link between these two segments of any currency, let us examine the interest rate for the deposit side separately from the interest rate on the lending side. In other words, let us first treat the Eurocurrency deposits as completely independent of the Eurocurrency loans.

For the analysis of interest rates we assume that depositors are perfectly rational and will always prefer a higher return to a lower one with the same risk, and lower risk to a higher one with the same return. We also assume that investors have a known trade–off between risk and return. Naturally, the trade–off is such that investors will accept higher risk only if they are compensated for it in the form of a higher return. Given these assumptions, what would depositors of funds require to put their money in the Eurocurrency market rather than in the domestic market?

An investor will first assess the risks of the two markets. The risk of the deposit in the domestic market is that the bank in which he deposits his funds will become bankrupt and the depositor will lose part or all of his money. The risk of bank failure is mitigated first by the existence of deposit insurance in many countries and second by the possibility that the government of the country will come to the rescue of a bank under its jurisdiction and the depositor will not lose any money at all.[6] There is precedence for such intervention by governments. The Federal Reserve Board in the United States intervened in the financial markets in 1985 when Continental Illinois Bank of Chicago faced illiquidity in the international markets. The Fed guaranteed the deposits of the bank and the bank was able to avoid bankruptcy. The second risk of domestic deposit is that the government will change its monetary policy and the particular deposit will become subject to some controls that do not exist now.

The Eurocurrency deposit, on the other hand, faces slightly higher risks.[7] First, there is no insurance for offshore or Eurocurrency market deposits. Second, it is not clear that governments will protect the offshore branches of their banks as well as they would protect the domestic ones. Governments like to be vague about their intentions because it leaves a lot to their discretion. There are precedents both for governments having come to the rescue of their depositors and for governments having let the depositors suffer a loss. In the Continental Bank case, the U.S. government protected both the domestic as well as the offshore deposits of the bank. In the case of the BCCI scandal, however, governments did not protect even the domestic depositors. Third, depositors in the Eurocurrency market face risk of intervention from two governments, one of which is the country whose currency is being used in the transaction and the other of which is the country where the Eurocurrency deposit is being made. Even if these risks are small, we must remember that they are not equal to zero. Lastly, depositors in the Eurocurrency market face a convertibility risk. There is always a risk that the government whose currency is being used for the particular transaction may impose exchange controls at some point in the future. This will make it difficult to use the Eurocurrency funds in that currency freely. Although the investor will eventually receive his funds, the inconvenience is a risk from the point of view of the investor. In addition, some investors, albeit a small minority, may consider the offshore location of banks as an inconvenience.

For all these reasons, an investor will view a Eurocurrency market deposit as carrying a slightly higher risk than the deposit in the domestic market. For this reason, he will require a slightly higher return on a deposit of a certain size in the Eurocurrency market than on a deposit of equal size in the domestic market. It should be noted that some depositors may find an offshore market more attractive than the domestic or "onshore" market since the transactions are somewhat hidden from the government whose currency is being used. The proportion of such depositors, however, is very small, and they do not influence the economics of the Eurocurrency market to any significant extent.

The depositor's demand for a higher risk, however, cannot be satisfied unless the deposit–holding bank finds it worthwhile to pay a higher return on the Eurocurrency deposit than on an equal–sized deposit in the corresponding domestic market. There are a number of factors that make it possible for banks to satisfy depositors' demands.

First, there are no reserve requirements in the Eurocurrency market. Governments that require banks in their jurisdiction to hold a small percentage of demand and time deposits in the form of a reserve with the central banks make no such demands on foreign currency deposits. The reserve requirements in the domestic market allow banks to lend less than 100 percent of the deposit they have received to a lender. The interest to be paid on the proportion of the deposit that is set aside as a reserve has to be earned by increasing the interest charged on the loan. This represents a cost to the bank. In the Eurocurrency market, however, there is no reserve requirement and, consequently, banks are free to lend almost 100 percent of the Eurocurrency deposits they receive. For the bank, this represents a cost saving.

Second, since banks do not accept small deposits in the Eurocurrency market, they do not need the institutional infrastructure that is required for domestic operations. This results in significant cost savings for banks. Third, banks accepting deposits in the Eurocurrency market save from the absence of portfolio restrictions on the use of funds. Most governments place some restrictions on banks that they must lend a certain proportion of their domestic funds to designated borrowers. Since legal restrictions are required because banks do not find these borrowers attractive in the first place, the absence of these requirements for offshore funds represents a cost savings for banks.

As a result of all these savings, banks are indeed able to satisfy the demand of depositors for a higher interest rate in the Eurocurrency market than in the corresponding domestic market. Consequently, the Eurocurrency deposit rates are higher than domestic market rates.

Let us turn to the lending side of the Eurocurrency markets. From the point of view of borrowers, it should not matter where the funds come from—the Eurocurrency market or the domestic market. There is, however, a slight risk that some government restriction will be imposed between the time a borrower has been promised a Eurocurrency loan (and the borrower has made plans according to the expected receipt of these funds) and the time the funds are actually received by the borrower. Such restrictions do not create any financial obligation for the borrower but do require him to negotiate a loan from some other source. This risk is very small and a borrower will accept almost the same interest rate in the Eurocurrency market as he would in the domestic market. Lending banks, however, have some cost savings in the Eurocurrency market arising from the large volume of transactions in this market. Due to the large size, banks benefit from economies of scale and the competition in the market ensures that these savings are passed on to the borrowers. Consequently, the lending rates in the Eurocurrency market are lower than corresponding rates in the domestic market.

The net result of interest rate differentials on the two sides of a Eurocurrency market transaction is shown in Exhibit 5.2. The deposit rate in the Eurocurrency market is higher than that in the domestic market and

Exhibit 5.2

Eurocurrency and Domestic Interest Rates

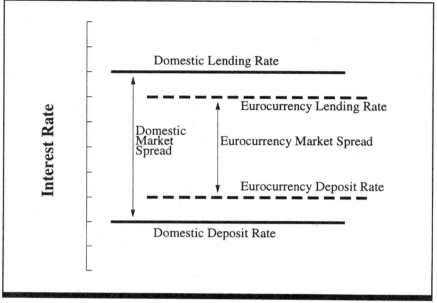

the lending rate is lower. Consequently, the spread between the deposit and the lending rate is lower in the Eurocurrency market than that in the domestic market. This represents the efficiency of the market.

Interest rates in two Eurocurrency markets. The relationship between domestic and Eurocurrency interest rates described here does not depend upon the characteristics of a particular currency. It is valid for all currencies. In other words, we expect that Eurocurrency deposit rates for all currencies will be higher than the corresponding domestic rates and the Eurocurrency lending rates will be lower than the domestic lending rates. We will now extend this analysis to see how the interest rates for two Eurocurrencies would be linked to each other.

Actually we have already discussed this relationship in the previous chapter. You may recall that we examined the relationship between bonds denominated in different currencies—the U.S. dollar and deutschemarks.

We found that the difference between the interest rates in these two currencies was equal to the expected change in the exchange rates. The reason for this equality was the presence of potential arbitrage: if the interest rate in one currency is such that an investor can earn more in that currency compared to another, after taking into account the expected changes in exchange rates, that investor will move funds between countries until the returns on the two currencies are equalized.

The same argument will also hold for deposits in the Eurocurrency market. The deposit rates for two currencies will have to be such that the difference between the two deposit rates exactly equals the expected change in the exchange rate between the two countries. In other words, the interest rate parity theorem should fully explain the difference between the interest rates in two Eurocurrencies.

Lending Procedures in the Eurodollar Market

Commercial banks were able to further cut the costs of operations in Eurocurrency markets by developing the technique of **syndication**. Syndication allows a number of banks to pool their resources to offer very large loans, and this has two effects. First, it allows further cost reductions, and second, it enables banks to extend credits to individual borrowers that exceed legal lending limits of individual banks. When the borrowers are individual countries, syndication procedures provide some security to individual banks in that the default risk is spread between a number of banks. If a borrowing country did attempt default, it would face resistance from commercial banks as well as central banks of all the countries from which banks had participated in the original syndicate. Moreover, since the credit risk in these syndicated loans is borne by banks that provide the funds, smaller commercial banks have the additional security of being able to rely upon the credit analysis performed by the large banks that lead the syndicate. Small banks lack the resources or the know–how to assess risks of individual countries. Participation of large banks in a syndicate provides a signal that large banks consider the borrower to be safe. Borrowers also find it to their advantage to deal with a syndicate because a single negotiation results in a large loan.

In a typical syndication procedure, **lead banks** negotiate the amount and terms of a loan with a borrower. Once the terms are agreed upon, the lead banks invite commercial banks around the world to participate in lending to the borrower. Each participating bank accepts the terms agreed upon between the lead banks and the borrower and agrees to provide funds for the predetermined period at interest rates stipulated in the original agreement. The lead banks receive front end fees for their service and may receive a management fee for arranging repayments of interest and principal by the borrower. The interest rate paid by the borrower consists of two parts: a **base rate** and a **spread**. The base rate is usually LIBOR, (London Interbank Offer Rate), the rate at which prime banks can raise Eurocurrency funds in the London market. The spread reflects the risk premium for the borrower. The loans are arranged for maturities of three to 12 years. The interest to be paid over the life of the loan, however, is arranged on a floating basis. Every three or six months (depending upon the agreement) the base rate is changed according to the prevailing LIBOR. The spread, on the other hand, remains constant over the life of the loan.

Country Risk Assessment

Almost from its beginning, the Eurocurrency market has attracted sovereign borrowers because of its ability to offer a large volume of funds. The syndication procedure allows lending banks to share the risk of these borrowers and allows large amounts of funds to be lent to them. With increasing indebtedness, especially for governments of developing countries, banks become increasingly concerned about the risk of these borrowers and a near industry has developed around the idea of "country risk" assessment.

It was only natural that increasing exposures of developing countries in international credit markets should increase the concern of the lenders about the ability of these countries to repay the loans. Although many countries have had high levels of external debt in the past, almost all of that debt was owed to governments or to international agencies. That kind of debt was usually extended for reasons other than profit motives, and if the debtor country had repayment problems, renegotiation of repayment terms was easily accomplished. In contrast, the borrowing from Euromoney markets represents loans from private banks. These banks, being profit–seeking economic entities, are more concerned with repayments.

The main concern of the lenders is to understand, and evaluate, the country risk or sovereign risk involved in any loan. The country risk, or creditworthiness of a country, is an attempt to measure that country's capacity to meet punctually the financing commitments stemming from a credit agreement. In assessing country risk, lenders are trying to estimate the probability of a country defaulting on interest or amortization payments. The concept of country risk involves assessing commercial risk of the borrower as well as transfer risk that the country will have enough foreign exchange earnings to meet its debt obligation. Commercial risk has to be assessed for the borrowing entity, whether private or public, and then the debt service capacity for the country in which the borrower is located has to be estimated. Even if a private borrower is able to generate local currency funds to meet repayments, the country in which the borrower is located may not have sufficient foreign exchange earnings to repay the banks. In that case, a **transfer risk** exists even though there is no credit risk.

If a country fails to meet its repayment obligation, a **rescheduling** of the debt is generally carried out. In a rescheduling agreement, the terms of repayment are renegotiated to accommodate the needs of the borrowing country. The alternative to rescheduling is an outright default by the country. During the last three decades, however, there have been no examples of outright default in which a country has refused to repay the loan. The rescheduling may represent a loss to lenders because the lender has to readjust its portfolio and, invariably, the renegotiated terms may involve at least some concessionary element. Rescheduling fees, on the other hand, usually more than compensate the banks for any costs they incur. The rescheduling country usually also has to accede to severe limitations on its future economic policies and to strict belt tightening.

In addition to the problem of riskiness of return on any particular loan to a country, the banks are also concerned about the concentration of developing–country loans on their portfolio. Banks attempt to manage the composition of their assets and liabilities according to modern portfolio theory. According to this theory, an efficient portfolio combines all available assets such that unsystematic risk or diversifiable risk is minimized. This requires optimum amounts of each asset to be held, with optimum amounts being determined by the return, risk, and covariance characteristics of any particular asset. For banks, this theory requires that assets, or loans, of the bank be distributed so that loans to various types of borrowing entities have an optimal mix. It follows that loans to countries should be a certain optimal proportion of the total loans of the bank. The optimal proportions will depend upon how attractive (that is, the return on the loan) and risky (considering both the probability of non–payment or partial payment and covariance of a country's repayment problems with world economic problems) the loans to that country are. In practice, it is very difficult for banks to determine these optimal proportions primarily because data are so difficult to obtain. In practice, banks try to set up "exposure limits" by which they determine the maximum amount that they can lend to any particular country.

In setting up these exposure limits, banks are concerned with the riskiness of their entire portfolio and the contribution that each country's loan makes to that risk. They may look at each country individually or look at geographical regions or groups of countries based on their economic or political status. Thus, banks may separate their international loans by industrialized, OPEC, semi–industrialized, non–oil–developing, and emerging economies.

In addition to commercial banks, the bank regulatory authorities in which banks are located are also concerned with the loans of commercial banks to developing countries. If a few borrowing countries with large loans fail to repay their loans, the viability and liquidity of their commercial banks may come under serious doubt given the importance of these loans in the portfolios of the banks. The regulatory authorities are concerned about the prospect for two reasons.

First, the entire financial sector of the economy may be threatened if a few commercial banks fail. The shock of the failure of the Franklin National Bank in the United States is a grim reminder of that possibility, although the failure was not caused by loan defaults. Second, to avoid bank failures, the central bank or monetary authorities may be faced with the prospect of taking over the loans of defaulting countries, especially developing ones. The repayments, or rescheduling, then become the direct concern of central banks. In those circumstances, it becomes very important for central banks to understand the process of country risk assessment.

Although the two concepts, the bankers' concept of creditworthiness of a country and the macroeconomists' concept of external debt capacity of an economy, focus on the idea of the ability of a country to repay its foreign loans, there may be differences in the two concepts from a practical viewpoint. Bankers are concerned with cash flow problems which may occur even though there are no fundamental problems. A fundamental problem occurs when the investment for which the borrowed funds are used is not able to generate, on an expectations basis, enough funds to repay the interest and the principal. In other words, a fundamental problem occurs when investment is made in economically unsound projects.

An economically sound project must have a rate of return that exceeds the cost of borrowing. But cash flow problems can occur even for an economically sound investment in certain periods. It is possible that interest and amortization payments required by the loan agreement exceed the cash generated from the investment during those periods. This is likely to happen when a long–term investment is funded with medium–term loans. This mismatch may be necessitated by conditions in financial markets, or may represent the hesitation of bankers to take long–term risks. Whether the reason is bad management, that is, mismatch of maturities, or market determined, the country will have a cash flow problem. The country, however, may be able to meet its payment obligations from its regular export earnings or from cash flows from investments made in the past. Indeed, if the country has no other means of meeting its obligations, bankers may not provide the loans. The cash flow problem for the country can become serious if a number of investments with such cash flow problems are bunched together. Inadvertently, or through bad management, a number of loans may be bunched together such that they become due at the same time.

The second reason for cash flow problems for an economically sound project has to do with "externalities" or who derives the benefits of the project. This issue can be best illustrated with an example. The rate of return on a socially productive overhead investment, the education system for example, may far exceed the cost of funds. The returns, however, will be highly diffused, and the government may not be able to charge a "price" for education. The higher growth effects of education will accrue to different individuals in the economy. Thus, although the economy as a whole benefits, the investor of the funds in education is not able to recoup the investment and meet the payments for the loans. Once again, the government will have to rely on general tax revenue and exports to repay the loan. The problem of diffusion of gains in this case is exacerbated by the first problem in that the length of period over which the benefits are received far exceeds the period over which the repayments have to be made.

Third, a cash flow problem may occur as a foreign exchange constraint. The investment may generate sufficient domestic funds, but may not stimulate, directly or indirectly, sufficient exports (or other foreign exchange generating cash flows) to help meet the repayment requirements of the loans.

In all cases where cash flow problems occur in spite of economically "sound" investments, the effect of aggregation of loans must be considered. Excessive cash flow requirements of one loan may be met by surplus cash flows from other loans. Problems will arise only when the loans are bunched together such that the combined cash outflows exceed cash inflows.

A borrowing country has to understand both concepts, that of credit–worthiness and of debt capacity. The goal of the country should be to maximize its growth by obtaining the optimal level of external debt. The optimal amount is based upon the opportunities available to the country and the cost at which the debt can be obtained. The optimal amount of debt, however, can be raised through external sources only if the lenders, mostly bankers, are convinced that the country is creditworthy. Thus, an understanding of how banks determine the creditworthiness of a country is of critical importance to the borrowing country.

The main concern of lenders in international money markets is recuperation of the principal and interest payments. Since commercial banks have to handle a large number of loans for a large number of countries, their main concern has been to ensure that the borrowing countries have sufficient earnings or resources in foreign currencies to meet debt obligations, regardless of actual use to which the funds are put. To this end, they relied very largely on their analysis of one or more statistical ratios or indicators. Such analysis is much simpler and faster than a qualitative and thorough analysis of economic, political, and social conditions of the country, which may give indications of the country's ability to repay its loans.

By far the most common individual indicator has been the debt service ratio. **Debt service ratio** (or DSR) is defined as the ratio of interest and amortization payments in any period to the exports of goods and services during the same period. The ratio attempts to measure, without looking at the imports, the proportion of a country's exports that would be required to pay for the debt. The smaller the ratio, the less the risk of default.

The weakness of this ratio stems from the fact that it ignores, on the one hand, the importance of other forms of financial resources (mostly foreign investments), and on the other hand, the flexibility the country has to reduce its imports. Thus, a country with a small DSR may have already cut its imports to a minimum and may have no leeway to pare them any more. Moreover, the country may attract little or no foreign capital, private or public. Such a country will have a far greater difficulty in meeting its debt obligations than a country with a high DSR but with high levels of capital inflows and a great degree of flexibility in cutting imports if necessary. The country with a high DSR, moreover, may be planning to use the funds from a particular debt for a highly productive investment which would raise sufficient foreign exchange to pay for itself. This country, obviously, would be more creditworthy from the point of view of lenders than one with a low DSR, but with little ability to reduce imports or attract foreign capital and without opportunities for productive investments. The debt service ratio at any point in time, thus may give a false impression by itself.

Changes in DSR over time also have to be interpreted with caution. If this ratio increases for any country, the reasons for the increase may be more important than the fact of an increase in DSR. If increased debt payments reflect borrowing which has been used for productive investments, there is no cause for alarm. If, however, the debt has been used for consumption purposes, increasing the DSR may be a signal for an impending crisis.

The problems in the use of debt service ratio resulted in the use of a number of other indicators relating different elements of debt obligation, or payments, to various measures of revenues from which the payments have to be made. Ratio of interest payments to total exports measures only the cost element of the debt to revenues. This measure is in no way superior to DSR, and far inferior in that it ignores the burden of amortization payments. The criticisms of DSR apply to this ratio also. Two variations of this ratio are the total debt to total exports ratio and current account deficit to total exports ratio.

A conceptually different ratio is the total debt outstanding to total output ratio. On one hand the amount of external debt may have only an indirect relationship with the gross domestic output. On the other hand, this ratio relates the size of the debt to the size of the economy. This ratio has been used by borrowers to estimate an optimal level of debt.

The ratio of interest payments to the levels of international reserves of any country tries to measure the ability of a country to meet its interest obligations from non–current income. Higher levels of reserves indicate that the country may be able to meet debt obligations for some time even though it may not have sufficient earnings from the investment during that time. A lower interest payment to the international reserves ratio (or total debt payments to the international reserves ratio) will indicate that a country wishing to make investments in projects with a long payback period may be considered creditworthy by lenders. This ratio is only an indication of a country's ability to meet temporary shortfalls. In the long run, current earnings must be sufficient to repay the loans.

Another ratio which is more an indication of mismanagement of a country's debt than of creditworthiness is the ratio of debt amortization payments in any year to the total debt outstanding at the beginning of the year. If the maturities of a number of loans are bunched together, a country may face large amortization payments during a given year. But a large amortization payment to total debt ratio merely indicates that the maturities have not been properly scheduled and that too many debts have been allowed to mature in any given year. This ratio is only useful if it is high for a number of years and the country has little resources to meet its payment obligations. A high ratio for one year may not be a sign of trouble if the country expects to have sufficient export earnings in the following years. The blame for bunching of maturities goes to both borrowing economic planners and lending financial institutions for not foreseeing the problem. It may also reflect a situation when borrowers have no choice but to accept terms of loans which would bunch their maturities; the market conditions at the time of borrowing may have dictated that.

Most of the ratios or indicators outlined above are very difficult to measure and even more difficult to interpret. There is a lot of room for judgmental analysis in which a lending banker tries to assess the quality of borrowers' decisions based on factors other than financial ratios. It is for this reason that bankers like to think of country risk assessment both as an art and a science.

Euronote and Eurocommercial Paper

In 1981, Citicorp offered a new kind of facility to raise funds for the government of New Zealand that caught the eyes of the market. This segment is known by its generic name of "Note Issuance Facilities" or NIFs, or by specific brand names used by some financial institutions, "Revolving Underwriting Facilities" or RUFs, note purchase facilities, or Euronote facilities. These facilities have now grown into a very significant segment of the international financial markets. In substance, they are all variations of the same basic theme. These facilities differ from non–underwritten short–term sources of funds generally known as Eurocommercial papers. The main differences among various instruments are shown in Exhibit 5.3.

A note issuance facility has three characteristics. The borrower obtains medium–term funds (typically five to seven years), financial institutions guarantee that the borrower will not be stranded without funds at some point in the future, and investors who supply the funds commit only for a short period of time. Let us elaborate on each of these three

Exhibit 5.3
Differences Among Euronotes,
Euro–CPs and Domestic–CPs

	Euronotes	Euro–CPs	Domestic–CPs
Issuer	Sovereign/ banks/MNCs	MNCs	Banks/MNCs
Underwriting Commitment	Banks' commitment	None	None
Cost	High	Lowest (of the three)	Low
Maturity of Paper	Standard — 1, 3, 6 months	Odd dates, 7–365 days	Odd dates 14–45 days
Secondary Market	Small	Small	Very High

aspects of a typical NIF. NIFs are attractive for borrowers who are looking for funds for the medium term.

The borrower is interested in a source of funds which he can tap into any time without having to negotiate another deal with the financial institutions. Instead of taking a loan from a bank, however, the borrower may feel that it is cheaper to raise funds directly from investors—that is, the people who have the savings. At the same time, the borrower feels that, at certain points within this medium term, he may not need the funds for a quarter or for six months or so. The borrower, therefore, does not want to issue long–term or medium–term bonds because, once the bonds are issued, interest has to be paid on them whether or not the funds are really needed. The borrower can also not depend upon the short–term commercial paper market because, although it is a very good source of funds, commercial papers have a short maturity. Also, every time new papers have to be issued, there is some degree of renegotiation with the financial institutions that help raise the funds. A note issuance facility satisfies various requirements of the borrower. It provides a medium–term source of funds, without the obligation of having to pay for these funds whether they are used or not, and it raises funds directly from the savers—thus keeping the cost down.

The main advantage of an NIF over other short–term sources of funds is that banks underwrite, that is, guarantee, the funds. They guarantee to the borrower that when he tries to raise the funds from the savers in the form of short–term notes and the savers refuse to buy all or part of these notes, the banks will then provide the funds. The borrower is thus assured of funds. If the notes are offered at a good price, the savers, that is, the investors, will buy the notes and provide the borrower with the funds. If the investors refuse to buy the notes, banks will lend the funds. This guarantee is very valuable when the borrower does not want to have to depend upon the vagaries of financial markets for his investment plans. Eurocommercial papers differ from Euronotes in this important characteristic: banks do not underwrite Eurocommercial papers.

The funds are raised in the form of short–term notes with maturities of, say, 30 days or three months or even longer. The borrower issues the short–term notes which are distributed to the investors by the financial institutions. At the maturity of these notes, the borrower reissues the notes. At this point investors may purchase the new notes, or may take their funds back. This process is repeated at every maturity of the notes.

The advantage of this maturity from the point of view of investors is that they are committing their funds to a particular borrower only for a short period of time. If at the maturity of one set of notes the investors feel that the credit conditions of the borrower have deteriorated significantly, they are under no obligation to lend their funds to this borrower. They simply withdraw from the NIF. In global markets where the situations of borrowers can change very rapidly, investors may prefer to commit their funds only for short maturities. Short maturities also give investors a flexibility whereby they can switch from one type of investment to another very quickly without incurring large costs that may result, for example, with bonds. The differences among three short–term instruments available to the investors are summarized in Exhibit 5.4.

Euronotes are usually distributed through placing agents. In some cases, one sole agent, the lead manager of the deal, has the right to place all the notes. The underwriting banks then either buy the notes that may not be sold by the placing agent or provide loans according to the underwriting agreement. With a technique called tender–panels, the notes are distributed by a panel of banks who have bid for the right to distribute the notes to the investors.

Exhibit 5.4
Differences Among Euronotes,
Bank–CDs, and Euro–CPs

	Investor's Point of View		
	Euronotes	**Bank CDs**	**Euro–CP**
Credit Risk	Issuer	Issuer	Guarantor
Diversification of Funds	High	Low	Low
Liquidity	Low	High	High
Yield	High	Low	Low
Knowledge Required	Low	High	High

The Euronote market has grown rapidly since its inception in 1981. Exhibit 1.4 in Chapter 1 provided some data on this market, along with some data on the domestic commercial paper markets in various industrialized countries. Exhibit 5.5 gives some idea of how various segments of this market have developed in 1992.

Exhibit 5.5
Euronote Market, 1992

	Activity During the Year		Stock at End of December 1992
	1991	1992	
Net issues:	32.5	37.5	176.9
Euro–CPs	9.0	0.2	78.7
Other short–term notes	7.4	11.8	37.0
Medium–term notes	16.0	25.4	61.1
Currency of issue:			
U.S. dollar	17.1	25.8	126.9
Australian dollar	1.2	1.0	10.5
ECU	3.6	–2.4	9.2
Japanese yen	0.6	3.4	6.8
Deutschemarks	1.5	4.6	6.2
Others	8.5	5.1	17.3

Source: Bank for International Settlements, International Banking and Financial Market Developments, Basle, May 1993, p. 10.

Summary

Creation of Eurocurrency accounts and the growth of international money markets have been among the most remarkable developments in financial markets during the last few decades. Eurocurrencies are created when banks are able to trade in the currency of a country outside the regulatory environment of that country. Contrary to popular myths, Eurocurrencies do not represent illegal flows of money. They represent intermediation of funds in the freest possible circumstances.

The development of Eurocurrencies accounts has given rise to a number of instruments and techniques to facilitate the flow of funds between economic entities. Among the first of these techniques was the syndicated or Euroloans. The process of syndication of loans was an innovation of the Euromarket. Syndicated loans at revolving interest rates grew at a rapid pace during the 1970s. Simultaneously with growth of Euroloans, the banking industry developed techniques for country risk analysis, and when a large group of borrowers came close to defaults, banks had to learn quickly about rescheduling loans and negotiations with countries. On the money market side of the transactions, international financial institutions developed note issuance facilities in the early 1980s. This market has now become a very significant part of international capital markets.

The market used Eurocurrencies for long–term debt instruments also. These instruments, or Eurobonds, are the subject of the following chapter.

Notes

1. Bank for International Settlements, *Annual Report,* 1992, p. 162.

2. Dufey, G. and I. Giddy, *The International Money Market*, 2nd Edition, Englewood Cliffs, NJ: Prentice Hall, 1994, p. 10–11.

3. Interest Equalization Tax was imposed in 1963 to equalize the cost of funds raised by foreigners on the U.S. capital markets to those paid by U.S. borrowers. The Voluntary Credit Restraint Program in 1965 imposed voluntary controls on the volume of funds U.S. banks could lend to U.S. multinationals for their foreign investments.

4. The estimates of this market are notoriously difficult to obtain. The main problem arises due to the difficulty of defining precisely which of the liabilities of commercial banks can be treated as external market accounts. At the present time, only the Bank for International Settlements in Basle provides some estimates of the size of this market. In the past, Morgan Guaranty Trust Company of New York used to provide detailed estimates of the size of this market.

5. Estimate of Morgan Guaranty Trust, *World Financial Markets*, New York, various issues.

6. The following table summarizes the availability of deposit insurance in some countries in early 1990:

Country	Est.	Condition of Membership	Deposits Covered	Level of Protection
USA	1933	Voluntary	All	$100,000
Belgium	1985	Voluntary	Bfr only	BFr 0.5 million
Britain	1982	Comp.	£ only	75% up to £20,000
France	1980	Comp.	FFr only	FFr 0.4 million
Holland	1979	Comp.	All	Guilder 35,000
Ireland	1989	Comp.	IR punt	80% of first IR£5,000, 70% of next IR£5,000, 50% of next IR£5,000
Italy	1987	Voluntary	All	100% on claims to 200m, 90% between 20m lira and 1.0 billion lira, 80% between 1.0 billion and 3.0 billion lira
Japan	1971	Comp.	Yen only	10 m yen
Spain	1977	Voluntary	All	Ptas 1.5m

Source: Summarized from *The Economist*, March 10, 1990, p. 86.

7. For a detailed treatment of these risks, see Dufey, G. and I. H. Giddy, "Eurocurrency Deposit Risk," *Journal of Banking and Finance*, 8, 1984, pp. 567–89, North Holland.

Chapter 6
International Bond Markets

International bonds come in two forms: Eurobonds and foreign bonds. **Eurobonds** refers to the bonds issued in the external sectors of financial markets—sectors that were identified in Exhibit 1.1 as falling outside the regulatory environment of national authorities. Thus, "Euro" bonds are issued outside the country in whose currency they are denominated. **Foreign bonds** are bonds issued in national capital markets by foreign residents. Foreign bonds, of course, fall under the regulatory jurisdiction of national authorities. On a global basis, international bonds account for less than 11 percent of all bonds outstanding, but they may be more important than domestic bonds for some countries. Exhibit 6.1 compares the volumes of domestic and international bonds issued in 1992 as well as the total amounts of these bonds outstanding at the end of 1992 for selected countries. International bonds are important segments only for the United Kingdom and Switzerland; for most of the other countries, these bonds account for less than 15 percent of the total bond activity.

International, and especially Eurobonds, differ from domestic bonds mainly in terms of how these bonds are issued and why investors are attracted to these bonds. Although this chapter will concentrate largely on Eurobonds, some characteristics of foreign sectors of the bond markets in some countries are identified in Exhibit 6.2. Before we discuss some economic foundations of these bonds, we should look at who issues these bonds and in what forms.

Exhibit 6.1
Issuing Activity in the Bond Markets, 1992
(net issues adjusted for exchange rate movements,
in billions of U.S. dollars)

Currencies	Bonds Issued in 1992		Amounts Outstanding at End–1992		
	Domestic Markets[1]	Intl. Markets	Domestic	Intl.	Intl/ Total = %
U.S. dollar	558.6	35.0	6,672.2	680.5	9.3
Japanese yen	141.6	4.8	2,888.6	207.5	6.7
German mark	188.8	20.5	1,234.0	168.5	12.1
Italian lira	71.6	6.2	734.9	24.2	3.2
French franc	36.1	21.7	525.0	64.3	10.9
Pound sterling	44.0	11.2	254.0	121.3	32.3
Canadian dollar	24.3	7.5	321.7	63.5	16.5
Swiss franc	11.8	–6.4	109.5	155.5	58.7
Other[2]	104.6	17.0	1,325.6	201.9	13.2
Total	1,181.4	117.5	14,069.6	1,687.2	10.7

[1] OECD countries only, excluding Iceland and Turkey.
[2] Including the ECU.

Source: Bank for International Settlements, *63rd Annual Report,* Basle, Switzerland, 1993, page 117.

Composition of the International Bond Market

At the end of March 1993, the total volume of international bonds outstanding was estimated to be $1,742 billion. Let us examine the composition of this outstanding amount to understand who issues these bonds, what types of bonds are issued, and what currencies are used for these bonds. Exhibit 6.3 divides the amount of $1,742 billion in four ways: by the country of issuer of these bonds, by the type of issuer, by the type of bond, and by the currency of issue—which, except in the case of international currencies, shows who purchases these bonds.

Exhibit 6.2
Comparison of Euro– and Foreign–Bond Sectors of Selected Countries

	Eurobond Sector	Domestic/Foreign Bond Sector
Deutschemarks	Euro–DM bonds issued in bearer form. Coupon paid annually. Maturities—2 to 10 years. Fixed rate issues about 60% of total. Floating rate notes linked to LIBOR.	Most bonds are bearer bonds. Bonds issued by banks—54% of market by the end of 1991. Straight fixed rate issues—80% of the market. Primary market: A practice of three–tranches to bond syndicates, by tender, and to Bundesbank. Investor structure fluctuates between domestic and foreign holders.
U.S. Dollar	Private issuers account for 70% of volume. Fixed rate issues about 60% of total. No registration or queuing requirements. Bearer instruments. No withholding taxes on interest or principal. No restriction on the price for initial offering. Issuer is free to choose the exchange where the issue is to be listed.	Called the Yankee bond market. Registration and queuing required. Registered bonds. Bond income is taxed. Most bonds are fixed rate bonds. Interest is paid semiannually unlike the Eurobond sector which pays interest annually. Most bonds are not amortized.
Yen	Market opened in 1977; almost restriction–free since 1989. Euroyen bonds popular with supranationals who account for 21% of these bonds. Permission of MOF needed for all issues. Market dominated by few lead managers; 5 had 90% market share in 1991 (50% for Eurodollar bonds); foreign firms allowed to lead manage only since 1984.	Called the Samurai bond market. Permission of MOF needed for all issues; administered through Bond Floatation Committee. Bond market is dominated by four big securities firms: Nomura, Daiwa, Nikko, Yamaichi.
U.K. Pound	Similar to other Eurobonds sectors in most respects. Permission of Bank of England needed for all issues. Japanese firms face some restrictions in lead managing sterling issues. Corporations can raise long–term fixed rate issues.	Called the Bulldog bond market. Government securities—gilts— are the dominant securities. Fixed coupon—fixed maturity bonds—85% of all bonds.

Source: "The 1991 Borrower's Guide to Financing in Foreign Markets" *Euromoney*, 1991.

Exhibit 6.3
Breakdown of International Bonds Outstanding—March 1993

(All amounts in the table in billions of U.S. dollars)

Volume of International Bonds Outstanding: $1,741.8

Breakdown by Country of Issuer		Breakdown by Type of Issuer		Breakdown by Type of Bond		Breakdown by Currency of Issue	
Country	Amount	Issuer	Amount	Type of Bond	Amount	Currency	Amount
Japan	346.9	Banks	337.8	Floating Rate	228.4	U.S. dollar	689.1
U.K.	159.3					Japanese yen	229.5
U.S.A.	153.6	Governments and State Agencies	336.6			German mark	180.5
Canada	138.5			Straight Fixed Rate	1279.4	Swiss franc	148.5
France	132.5	International Institutions	237.2			U.K. pound	125.3
Eastern Europe	10.8						
OPEC and LDCs	53.9	Private Corporations	830.2	Equity–Related	234.0	ECU	101.8
International Institutions	237.2						
Other Developed Countries	509.1					Others	267.1

Source: Bank for International Settlements, *International Banking and Financial Market Developments*, May 1993, various pages.

Exhibit 6.4
Net New International Bond Issues—by Type
(1988–92, all amounts in billions of U.S. dollars)

Type of Bond	1988	1989	1990	1991	1992	Stock at End–1992
Straight Fixed Rate Issues	99.0	89.7	80.5	142.7	113.6	1211.4
Floating Rate Notes	5.9	11.0	28.3	3.2	23.7	221.6
Equity–Related Issues	34.1	74.8	23.1	25.2	–19.8	254.2
TOTAL	139.0	175.5	131.9	171.1	117.5	1687.2

Source: Bank for International Settlements, *63rd Annual Report*, Basle, Switzerland, 1993, p. 115.

The Japanese are the largest issuers of international bonds, more than twice as much as issued from any other single country. Developing countries, including the countries of Eastern Europe, seem to have only a limited access to this market. Together, developing countries account for only 3.7 percent of the total market. The small share of these countries may indicate that bond holders, who have to bear the credit risks of bonds, like to deal only with relatively safe and well–established borrowers in this market. Government agencies and private banks from developed countries each have about a 20 percent market share, with the bulk of the bonds having been issued by private industrial corporations. Bond holders seem to prefer mostly straight fixed–rate bonds, which account for almost three–fourths of all bonds outstanding. This trend appeared to be changing in the late 1980s, but the most recent data indicate that the market has gone back to its preference for straight issues.

Exhibit 6.4 shows the breakdown of bonds issued in recent years. The proportion of equity–related issues has decreased so much so that, during 1992, the volume of equity–related issues that were redeemed exceeded the volume of new issues by about $ 20 billion. Equity–related issues, however, were very attractive in some markets. The accompanying box describes how in the middle of 1993, Japanese investors were willing to pay large premiums to acquire convertible bonds. The equity feature of the bonds becomes attractive when it is able to offer something unique to the investors, something they can obtain elsewhere only at a high cost. Finally, the U.S. dollar seems to be the most popular currency for denominating the bonds, although the issuers in the United States account for less than 9 percent of all bonds. ECU, or the European Currency Unit that we had studied in Chapter 2, accounts for a very small proportion, less than 6 percent, of all bonds.

▼ ▼ ▼

Innovative Bonds to Help Manage Stock Market Volatility

Bonds and stocks may seem to be different and independent instruments, but their intimate connection was demonstrated in 1993 when Japanese corporations recognized that investors were attracted by certain features of convertible bonds. Convertible bonds give bond holders an option to convert the bonds into stocks at pre–set prices. If the stock prices rise above these pre–set prices, bond holders would gain by converting the bonds into stocks. If the stock prices remain below this level, the bond holders receive only the interest on the bonds. Due to this option to convert, the interest rate on convertible bonds is lower than that on straight bonds.

In the middle of 1993, these bonds became very attractive for investors due to the volatility of the Japanese stock market. The Japanese stock market had declined for most of 1991 from its historically high levels. The market began its recovery in 1992 and the Tokyo Nikkei index had reached a level of about 16900 in the beginning of 1993. The market reached a level of just below 22000 by the beginning of June and then dropped by about 2500 in the last two weeks of June after the Japanese parliament, the Diet, passed a no confidence motion in the government, requiring new elections the following month. The future prospects for the stock looked very uncertain and the traders expected volatility in the markets before the elections in July.

In this environment, Japanese investors were attracted to convertible bonds. Bonds worth about 300 billion yen ($2.8 billion) were expected to be issued in June of 1993, compared to about 30 billion yen in January of the same year. Given the uncertainty about the stock markets, investors want to play the stock market when it goes up, but be protected if it falls. In exchange for such a possible play, the convertible bonds pay an interest of only 1.5% when the Japanese postal savings accounts, which are more flexible, pay 3.6%. Bank loans, at the same time, would cost a company about 6%. These bonds are priced such that the holders are expected to gain if share prices increase in the neighborhood of 10 to 20%.

Summarized from "Wary Japanese Bet on Convertible Bonds," *The Wall Street Journal*, June 28, 1993, p. C1.

▲ ▲ ▲

Evolution of the International Bond Market

Foreign bond markets, the segment of financial markets in which foreigners can come and issue bonds under the regulations of the country, have existed as long as bond markets have been around. London and Switzerland in the nineteenth century and New York in this one have attracted foreigners who needed far more funds for long–term investments than their domestic markets were able to supply. Modern Eurobonds, however, are more recent instruments. They owe their birth to the balance of payments problems of the U.S. economy in the early 1960s.

In the first few years of the 1960s, the U.S. economy had moved from a surplus to a deficit in its external payments. One of the contributing factors was the outflow of long–term funds from the country in the form of bonds. Europeans, it seemed, were financing some of their investments by raising funds in the U.S. capital markets. One of the reasons for the attraction of New York was the low rates of interest in the U.S. markets compared to those in the European ones. U.S. government officials began to hint at that time that free access for foreigners to the U.S. capital markets may not have been in the American interest. In July 1963, President Kennedy imposed an interest equivalization tax on foreign issuers, that is, on the foreign bond issues, to stem the flow of U.S. capital. The tax was payable by U.S. investors who purchased foreign securities and was charged as a percentage of the purchase price of the instrument. The effect of the tax was to raise the interest rate on foreign bonds by about 100 basis points, thus almost equaling the rates prevailing in the European markets. The tax was extended a number of times before being abolished in 1974, but the rate of equalization had been brought to zero in 1970. The purpose of the tax was to make foreign securities unattractive to U.S. investors and close the foreign bond sector of the capital markets.

The financial institutions and the Europeans, however, had other plans. In early July, an Italian company that had no U.S. or any other international operations raised $15 million in the form of U.S. dollar denominated bonds. This issue was to launch the Eurobond market. The Italian company was Autostrade, an operator of toll highways in Italy. A special feature of this issue was that, although the issue was denominated in U.S. dollars, the funds were not raised on the U.S. capital markets. The company was advised and helped, that is, the issue was lead managed, by banks in London and co–managed by banks in Belgium, West Germany, and the Netherlands. U.S. banks were not involved in this issue and the bonds were funded out of Eurodollar accounts that had proliferated all over Europe by this time. The manner in which the bonds were issued was quite unique: bonds were denominated in one currency, the funds to be used by a borrower located in a second currency, and the banks who managed the deal and the investors who provided the funds were located

Exhibit 6.5
Volume of Eurobonds Issued in Selected Years
(billions of U.S. dollars)

Year	Total Volume	Dollar Bonds	Deutschemark Bonds	Basket Currencies
1963	0.1475	0.0905		0.043
1965	0.8095	0.6075	0.105	0.0644
1970	2.7619	1.703	0.569	0.104
1975	7.2816	3.3655	1.7231	0.5858
1980	18.72	12.932	0.898	0.094
1985	134.5	94.67	9.82	6.72
1990	131.0	39.4		
1992	117.5	35.0	20.5	17.0

Sources: 1963, 1965, 1970, 1975 data from F.G. Fisher, *The Eurodollar Bond Market*, Euromoney Publications, 1979; 1980, 1985, 1990: OECD, *Financial Market Trends*, various issues: 1992; BIS, *Annual Report*, 1993.

in places where none of these two currencies was the native currency. These features were to become the characteristic of the Eurobond market except that investors, issuers, or banks were not barred from participating in bond deals in their own currencies; it was just not the norm. Thus, U.S. banks would help manage Eurodollar bond issues, and U.S. investors would invest in these bonds, but their participation would be just like any other bank or investor, not a necessary condition for the issue of these bonds as it would have been in the domestic markets. What distinguished Eurobonds from domestic bonds in the same currency is the location of issue: domestic bonds are issued within the country whose currency is being used to raise the needed funds whereas Eurobonds are issued outside that country.

The Eurobond market grew in spurts since the initial issue in 1963. Eurodeutschemark bonds were the first European currency bonds to be issued followed by bonds in French francs and Dutch guilders. Exhibit 6.5 shows the total volume of Eurobonds issued in selected years in various currencies since 1963. The U.S. dollar segment of this market has been the largest segment, but its importance has decreased over the years.

Issuing Eurobonds

Eurobonds are issued through a syndicate that is led by a **lead manager** who takes the primary responsibility for the entire issue. This lead manager helps the issuer decide the price of the bonds and the role that other banks would play in the distribution process. The lead manager also stands ready to support the price of the bond during the issuing period so that an orderly market is maintained. The lead manager may be supported by a "co–lead manager." **Underwriters** of the bonds agree to distribute the bonds to the investors and in case the bonds are not sold, they commit themselves to purchase a certain proportion of the bonds. **Members of the selling group** agree to sell the bonds but do not commit themselves to purchase any bonds if they are left unsold at the end of the distribution period.

The total fees for a Eurobond issue may be between 2 and 2.5 percent of the amount raised, depending upon the maturity of the issue. The largest share of the fee, up to 1.5 percent, goes to the bank that sells or distributes the bonds to the investors. The remainder of the fee is shared by the managers and the underwriters. One bank may, of course, play more than one role in one issue. Thus, the lead manager may also be an underwriter and a seller.

Secondary markets for Eurobonds are provided by most banks that act as lead managers. These transactions are settled seven days after the

Exhibit 6.6
Lead Managers for Eurobond Issues
(January to mid December, 1992)

Rank in 1992	Bank	Amount*	Number of deals
1	Nomura Securities	24.9	84
2	Deutsche Bank	23.0	70
3	Merrill Lynch Capital Markets	19.5	55
4	Goldman Sachs	18.6	55
5	CSFB/Credit Suisse	17.9	68
6	JP Morgan	17.1	41
7	Banque Paribas	12.3	45
8	Union Bank of Switzerland	12.1	50
9	Daiwa Securities	11.4	66
10	Industrial Bank of Japan	10.4	23
11	Yamaichi Securities	9.1	55
12	Nikko Securities	7.9	51
13	Morgan Stanley	7.8	29
14	Salomon Brothers	7.8	29
15	Dresdner Bank	7.7	23

* Lead managers and co–managers receive full credit for the amount of the issue.

Source: *Euromoney*, January 1993, p. 93.

trade in the secondary market. Eurobonds settlements are done either through Euroclear in Brussels or Cedel in Luxembourg. In 1991, there were about 4,000 Eurodollar bond issues being traded in the secondary markets.

Banks compete fiercely with each other to obtain mandates from borrowers to manage new issues of Eurobonds. Winning these mandates is a sign for the bank that customers view it as providing a good service. Rankings of lead banks are prepared according to the total volume of funds they manage and are published frequently. Exhibit 6.6 shows the rankings for 1992. One of the criteria that borrowers use for judging the quality of a potential lead manager is his or her ability to provide secondary trading in the bonds once the bonds have been issued. A survey conducted by Euromoney magazine ranked Deutsche Bank as the best trader in the area of Eurobonds. The bank seemed to have won its position based on a well–focused strategy, a large global network, and a number of specialist trading rooms that can specialize in one or two issues and create a market for those issues.[1]

Private Placement in Eurobond Markets

One of the features of the Eurobond market is the practice of private placement of an issue. In a private placement, a select group of investors purchases all the bonds that a company issues at a particular point in time. The issuing company finds a private placement more desirable if the total volume of funds to be raised is not very large. Since public placements require that the company file necessary information with the stock exchange, the fixed costs of meeting the regulatory requirements for public issues are quite high. With a private placement, the company does not have to go through these costs. Although the total size of private placements may be small, each bond can often be of much larger denomination than would be possible with a public issue. Private placements are preferred by large institutional investors who have specific needs for certain types of debt instruments in their portfolios. These investors prefer private placements because they can often dictate very specific conditions for the bonds, such as maturity and currency of denomination. In most cases, private placements begin by assessing the needs of the interested investor by the investment bankers. These bankers then search for a company that can meet the requirements of the investors. Bankers receive higher fees, between 1 and 2 percent of the amount, for private placements. Privately placed bonds, however, are not as liquid as publicly issued bonds because they do not meet all the requirements of the exchanges on which the trade could take place.

Bought Deals

The norm for the Eurodollar bond market is a **bought deal**, especially for straight issues. In a bought deal, the lead manager of the deal agrees to all the conditions of the issue with the borrower—most important of which is the issue price. In this case the underwriter is the lead manager, taking the risk that market conditions will not change between the time the agreement has been made and the bonds are sold to the public. If the market conditions change in such a way that the bonds become less attractive, the underwriter could suffer big losses. In the initial years, bought deals were accompanied by large fees for underwriters. Since August 1989, however, the issuing procedures in the Eurodollar bond market have become similar to those in the U.S. domestic market. Under this fixed price re–offer system, a select group of underwriters decide the price, and the bonds are sold at a fixed price during the initial offering period of around 24 hours. The underwriters are compensated by a fee.

Floating Rate Notes

One important innovation in the Eurobond market in the early 1970s was the introduction of floating rate notes or bonds. The interest rates had become more volatile at that time, and investors were hesitant to lock in their capital for long periods of time. Eurobonds, which were usually issued for long maturities, were becoming difficult to sell. The market responded to the needs of the investors by issuing long–term bonds but made the interest rate on these bonds flexible. The first floating rate note, as these bonds have come to be called, was issued in 1970 for Ente Nazionale per L'Energia Electrica (ENEL). Two U.S. banks, Bankers Trust and S.G. Warburg, lead managed the issue and helped ENEL raise $125 million for ten years. The interest rate on these notes was to be reset every six months at six–month LIBOR plus 3/4 percent. The cost of the funds, thus, was set as the cost of a Euroloan would be set, but the borrower had commitment for ten years. Investors found the note (or the FRNs), desirable because, unlike bank loans, these notes were tradable in the secondary market. As shown in Exhibit 6.4, these notes are a small but important segment of the Eurobond market.

Global Bonds

A recent development in the international bond markets is the introduction of global bonds. These bonds are offered for sale simultaneously in several markets around the world. The first such issue was a World Bank issue in September 1989. The World Bank raised US$ 1.5 billion through a five–year issue that was offered in the U.S. as well as in the Euromarkets. To accommodate the U.S. market requirement of registered bonds, and the preference of Euromarket investors for bearer bonds, these bonds were issued in a targeted registered form. While global bonds follow the domestic market practice of registration of bonds, they follow the Euromarket practices regarding the fee structure. Secondary market trading in these bonds can be cleared either through the Euroclearing systems (CEDEL and Euroclear), or through the domestic bond clearing systems. The second global bond issue by the World Bank in February 1990 was sold in Japan, in addition to the markets where the first issue was sold.

Since global bonds are listed in a number of markets, they are more liquid than purely domestic bonds or Eurobonds that are listed in one country. This liquidity makes them very attractive to institutional investors who are willing to give up some yield in exchange for this liquidity.

By the end of 1992, the total volume of global bonds outstanding was estimated to be $37 billion. The World Bank alone had issued about $15 billion of that amount. Global bonds were initially issued only in the U.S. dollar but now issues in Canadian and Australian dollars are also available.

Summary

The Eurobond market started in response to regulatory restrictions in the mid–1960s, but once the market opened, the removal of restrictions did not stop the market from continuing to grow. Eurobonds are differentiated from domestic bonds because they are offered in a jurisdiction which is not of the currency of the bonds.

Like most other financial markets, this market has also had its share of innovations. These bonds are now offered in the currencies of most industrialized countries and are offered in the form of floating rate notes or bonds and as straight bonds. Moreover, they offer a variety of innovations and options, such as bonds with warrants. The most recent of the innovations of this market is the issue of the global bond.

Note

1. "Why Deutsche Is Top at Eurobond Trading," *Euromoney*, May 1993, pp. 30-36.

Chapter 7

International Equity Markets

International equity markets may be the youngest segments of international financial markets. The term "international equity" would hardly have been recognized a little more than a decade ago. From its humble beginning in the early 1980s, international equities, like international and Euromoney and bond markets, have become an important segment of financial markets.

In contemporary terminology, international equity refers to two related activities and instruments. The term **international equity**, sometimes referred to as Euroequities, is used for a simultaneous offering of a new issue of equity by a company in a number of countries. The company may decide that a new issue of its equity will be attractive to investors in a number of countries and may offer the shares directly to those investors rather then require them to acquire the shares by having to make a purchase in a foreign country, usually the country where the company is domiciled. We may also use this term to describe foreign shares that are registered and traded on a country's stock exchanges. Shares of 153 foreign companies, for example, are traded on the New York Stock Exchange besides the shares of U.S. companies. These foreign companies have decided that for the convenience of their American stock holders, they will meet the stringent requirements of the NYSE and list their stocks on the exchange. Listing on a U.S. exchange

Exhibit 7.1
International Equity Offerings by Geographical Origin
($ figures are in millions)

| | 1987 | | 1988 | | 1989 | | 1990 | | 1991 | | 1992 | | |
	# of Issues	$	# of Issues	$	# of Issues	$	# of Issues	$	# of Issues	$	# of Issues	$	% of Total
North America	49	3,800	44	1,600	59	1,900	83	3,000	166	6,300		8,300	34.0
Western Europe	93	11,400	60	4,900	145	10,600	74	6,000	61	8,000		7,100	29.1
Australasia	12	900	23	500	15	500	2	400	5	1,100			
SE Asia/Far East	5	700	12	900	10	1,000	34	2,500	22	900			
Latin America /Caribbean	8	200	9	1,100	19	2,500	16	800	43	4,300	31	3,600	14.8
Other	4		3		6		9	300	19	900			
Total		17,000		9,000		16,500		13000		21,500		24,400	

Source: *Euromoney*, various issues.

will make it easier for U.S. stockholders to buy or sell the stock. Although foreign listings are a relatively new phenomenon in the United States, some European stock exchanges have thrived on listings of foreign companies. Exchanges in the Netherlands and Switzerland, for example, had more foreign companies listed than domestic ones even ten years ago when there were only about 50 foreign firms listed on the New York stock exchange as against almost 1,500 domestic ones.

The distinction between the two uses of the term international equity parallels the distinction between primary and secondary markets. The term **primary market** refers to the initial offering of a security, whether a stock, a bond, a loan, or a derivative instrument. **Secondary market** refers to the market and institutional framework within which existing securities can be traded between investors. The primary market for international equities seems to have begun in 1983 when six Euroequity issues worth about $300 million were offered on the international markets. The growth of this market since then is shown in Exhibit 7.1.

To put a perspective on the volume of the international equity market, the data in that exhibit should be compared to the data in Exhibit 1.5a. Compared to the total sizes of the stock markets around the world, international equity markets are quite small. The international equity market had been growing very rapidly until the global stock market crash of October 1987. It has recovered slowly since the crash and now surpasses the levels attained previous to the crash. U.S. firms have been the most active issuers of international equity in the past and are expected to maintain their leading position in this segment of the international financial markets. The secondary market activities are most developed in London. Although stocks of foreign firms are traded on a number of exchanges, financial institutions in London have developed a reputation for providing liquidity for a large number of foreign stocks. Exhibit 7.2 provides an indication of the extent of trade in foreign shares in that market. By comparison, trading by foreigners accounts for a much smaller, albeit growing, proportion of the trade on the U.S. exchanges.

The term **international equity** may have been used only for the two activities described above, but there are other activities that relate to international investments in equity. From the point of view of an investor, international equity investment refers to the acquisition of equities in a foreign country. In our study of international equity investments, we will include two activities that help investors acquire equities in foreign firms.

Exhibit 7.2
Composition of Foreign Equity Turnover
(London, 1990)

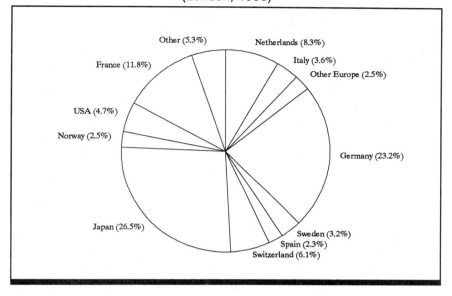

First, investors can ask financial institutions in their own country to purchase foreign stocks for them by making a trade on the stock exchange of the country which the investor wishes to enter. Second, investors can contact a financial institution in a foreign country and ask it to acquire shares in its domestic market. Before the introduction of international equities, individual investors had little choice but to follow one of these two routes if they wanted direct ownership of stocks of foreign companies. They, however, had an indirect method for acquiring stake in some firms established in foreign countries; they could acquire stocks of multinational companies which owned foreign subsidiaries.

The study of international equity investments also raises some questions about the appropriate mix of domestic and foreign assets in an efficient portfolio. We will defer these questions to the following chapter. In this chapter we want to become acquainted with the institutional details of international equity investments: where are the international markets for the investors and how can investors enter foreign equity markets.

International Equity Investments

There are a number of reasons why international equity markets have grown rapidly over the last decade. Corporations have realized that accessing the pool of international investors lowers their cost of equity as well as provides good public relations benefits. As stock exchanges began to list foreign stocks, they realized that turnover of these stocks was very important for them. Foreign investors are also becoming larger investors in domestic securities listed on national stock exchanges. The growing interest of investors in foreign securities is a reflection of the growing investor awareness of the benefits of international diversification. Finally, as was shown in Exhibit 1.5, U.S. stock markets are becoming relatively less important in the world. The growing size of foreign stock markets has attracted the attention of the largest pool of investors in the world–those in the United States. The pull for international equities has been supported by regulatory and technological factors. Advances in tele-communication and computer technologies have made it possible for traders to obtain current information and to trade in far off markets without delays that inhibit trading. Regulators in most countries have also realized that the system under which national markets were isolated from each other and national regulatory authorities had full control over the activities of their investors is increasingly obsolete. Regulators have responded to the pressures of a globalized securities market by making necessary adjustments. In the U.S. market, regulation 144A, which allows trading in American Depository Receipts, is an indication of such adjustments.[1]

International equities satisfy an important need in financial markets: they provide investors in a country with vehicles for benefitting from economic opportunities in other countries. Investors of one country are interested in investment opportunities in foreign countries for two reasons. First, some foreign markets may offer higher rates of return than domestic markets. Second, even if the rates of return are not markedly different from those in the domestic markets, the fluctuations in the prices in the foreign markets may not be correlated with those in the domestic markets. From the perspective of an investor who wants to increase the value of her or his portfolio and minimize the risk, such uncorrelated markets may be very attractive. We will deal with the theoretical issues regarding international diversification in the following chapter.

The international investor's desire for making equity investments in economic activities of foreign countries is not new. Before international equities became available, investors had a number of other mechanisms which allowed them to earn the rewards that go with equity investments, along with the risk that these rewards entail. These mechanisms were, of course, not as efficient as the direct purchase of international equity. A brief understanding of each of these mechanisms will allow us to recognize the advantages of such international equities.

The flow of international equity capital could be separated into two broad categories: foreign direct investment and portfolio investment. Foreign direct investment involves acquisition of productive assets in a foreign country with a view to actively manage the assets to produce goods and services in the foreign country. Portfolio equity investment involves purchasing the stock of a company without intending to interfere with the running of the company.

Foreign Direct Investment

When a U.S. machine tool company acquires or establishes a subsidiary, say, in Spain, to manufacture and sell one of its models, the company is said to have made a foreign direct investment. The U.S. company acquires a significant proportion of the shares of the subsidiary in Spain and aims to manage the subsidiary as it sees fit. The investment is referred to as foreign direct investment because it involves control of the stocks of the company in the foreign country and it involves management of the foreign operations. This arrangement does not preclude the involvement of a joint venture partner who shares either in equity or in management, or in both. The U.S. company takes the risk associated with equity investment: if the investment is successful, the company is expected to earn good returns; if the investment fails, the company could lose even all of its original investment. From the perspective of the investor, the advantage of foreign direct investment is that the investor receives full rewards associated with the investment and is able to control the operations. The disadvantage for the investor is that managing operations in a foreign country requires a very high degree of commitment to the investment. It places great demands upon the expertise, skills, and time of the investor. These requirements increase the risks associated with foreign direct investment.

Given the requirements and risks of this type of investment, it is not surprising that foreign direct investment flows are very sensitive to political and economic events and the volume of funds coming under this category tends to fluctuate considerably. Exhibit 7.3 compares the flows of foreign direct investment over the last two decades with the growth of world economies and exports. Although foreign direct investment flows have grown much more than the global economic output and world trade, they also exhibit much larger fluctuations than the other two variables. It is noteworthy that almost all of these foreign direct investment flows originate in industrialized countries and about 80 percent of these flows are directed toward other industrialized countries. Data on foreign direct

Exhibit 7.3
Some Patterns of World Foreign Direct Investment

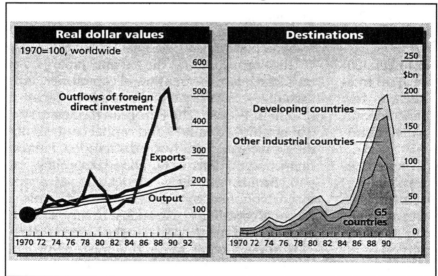

Source: "A Survey of Multinationals," *The Economist*, March 27, 1993, p. 8.

Exhibit 7.4
U.S. FDI Abroad by Country, 1990
Historical Cost Basis
(millions of dollars)

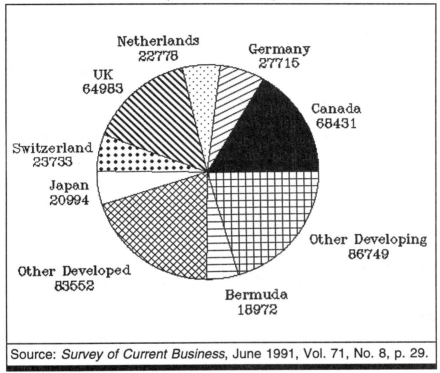

Netherlands 22778

Germany 27715

UK 64983

Canada 68431

Switzerland 23733

Japan 20994

Other Developing 86749

Other Developed 83552

Bermuda 18972

Source: *Survey of Current Business*, June 1991, Vol. 71, No. 8, p. 29.

investment by U.S. firms conforms to the same patterns. Exhibit 7.4 shows the destination of direct investment of U.S. companies. Most of it is directed to a few countries, and developing countries receive about 20 percent of the total investment.

In the days before investors were allowed to expand their portfolios to include stock in foreign countries, multinationals offered the only vehicle through which an investor could benefit from the economic activities in foreign countries. The connection, however, was somewhat indirect. Consider the example of a U.S. multinational company which has 50 percent of its sales outside the United States. The 50 percent foreign sales may be divided between a number of foreign countries. What determines the price of the stock of this company? Let us assume for simplicity's sake that the company is in an industry whose sales rise and fall in direct proportion to the state of the economy. In other words, if the economy is growing by 3 percent in real terms, the sales of the company will also increase by 3 percent in real terms. In times of recession, the sales of the company will fall by the same percentage as the decline in the level of the economy. Assuming that the stock price reflects the sales of the company, half of the price of the stock of this company should fluctuate with the rise and fall of the U.S. economy and the other half with a weighted average of the rise and fall in the economies in which this company operates. The weights of the economies will be the proportions in which the company's sales are divided in the foreign countries. Thus, the stock price of the company fluctuates half in response to the swings of the U.S. economy and half in response to the swings of the global economy excluding the United States. An investor who buys the stock of this company is able to participate in the swings of the global economy. If the investor felt that the rest of the world would grow faster than the United States, he would increase the proportion of shares of this firm, and others with large non–U.S. components in their sales, in his portfolio. He would sell the stock of this firm and purchase stocks of purely domestic companies if he believed that the U.S. economy would grow faster than the rest of the world. The more an investor wanted to participate in the international economy, the more he would build his portfolio with the shares of multinational companies.

Availability of other vehicles may have reduced the importance of multinational companies for investors wishing to invest in foreign economies, but the shares of these companies remain important to some investors for international diversification. In mid–1993, when the U.S. economy had very modestly rebounded from a prolonged recession, European countries were still struggling for signs of an upturn in their economies. At that time, a leading investment banking firm in the United States was recommending a strategy of purchasing the shares of America's Euro–industrials. These shares were considered to be attractive for investors who were hesitant to invest directly in foreign countries and preferred to keep their money invested with U.S. firms. The firms being recommended for investment tended to have a very large proportion of their total sales in Europe. The specific strategy outlined below by one advisor highlights the importance of shares of multinationals as vehicles for taking advantage of a lack of synchronization in various economies:

"When stock–picking, investors should pay close attention to a company's overseas exposure, [the advisor] suggests. For instance, an investor who likes auto stocks may have started last year by buying Chrysler, whose sales are concentrated in the U.S. But then, the investor would have been wise to move onto Ford, which has greater exposure to the United Kingdom. The U.K. was one of the first European countries to ease interest rates, and as a result its auto sales are already picking up momentum. Finally, when the European economies are starting to show faint signs of a recovery, the investor would be smart to snap up some shares of General Motors. Unlike Ford, GM offers investors the opportunity to savour a smorgasbord of European countries."[2]

Portfolio Investment

Portfolio investment refers to the acquisition of bonds or equity in a foreign country, without an intention of playing any role in the management of assets. The aim of portfolio investment is for investors to benefit from the appreciation of financial assets and receive the interest or the dividend payments. Precise data on the extent of international portfolio investment in equities is very hard to obtain. Exhibit 7.5 compares the volumes of direct and portfolio investments by the major industrialized countries over the last two decades. The exhibit shows that portfolio investments have been at least as important as direct investment in terms of the volume of funds, and have become more important than direct investments in recent years.

A study by Baring Securities quoted in Euromoney indicates that at the end of 1991, 8.1 percent of equities around the world were held by international investors. The study expected that the number would have risen to 9 percent by the end of 1992 and to 20 percent in the next five years. Moreover, equities seem to be becoming an ever–increasing part of portfolios of private investors around the world. According to the same study, "Private global portfolio flows accounted for 15 percent of cross

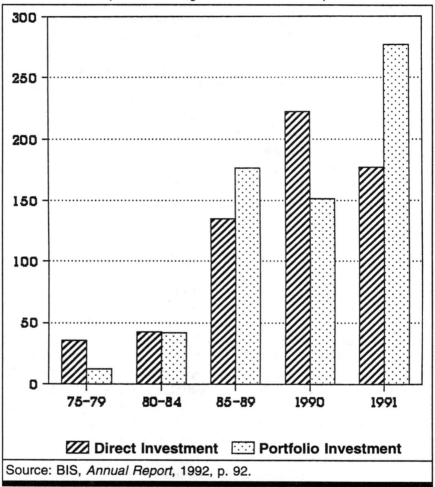

Exhibit 7.5
Global Pattern of Capital Movements
(annual average in billions of dollars)

Direct Investment   Portfolio Investment

Source: BIS, *Annual Report*, 1992, p. 92.

border investment in 1975–79: today, that figure is nearly 75 percent. Equities which constituted 5 percent of total portfolio flows in 1979 make up 36 percent."[3] One less significant indicator of the increasing

Exhibit 7.6
Major Stock Market Indexes

Exchange	12/30-31/91		12/30-31/92		ROR-1991-92	
	Stock Ind.	Ex. Rt.	Stock Ind.	Ex. Rt.	LC	in $
Tokyo Nikkei Ave.	22983.77	0.007962	16924.95	0.008026	-26.36	-25.77
Tokyo Topix Index	1714.68	0.007962	1307.66	0.008026	-23.74	-23.12
London FT 30-Shares	1891.30	1.8695	2185.2	1.5145	15.54	-6.40
London 100-Shares	2493.1	1.8695	2846.5	1.5145	14.18	-7.51
London Gold Mines	140.1	1.8695	63.9	1.5145	-54.39	-63.05
Frankfurt DAX	1577.98	0.659	1545.05	0.6188	-2.09	-8.06
Zurich Credit Suisse	450.1	0.7405	2107	0.6835	45.30	34.12
Paris CAC 40	1765.66	0.19305	1857.78	0.18104	5.22	-1.33
Milan Stock Index	981	0.0008715	884	0.0006765	-9.89	-30.05
Amsterdam ANP-CBS General	191.4	0.5845	198	0.5508	3.45	-2.52
Stockholm Affarsvarlden	917.6	0.1802	912.6	0.1416	-0.54	-21.85
Brussels Bel-20 Index	1092.72	0.03196	1127.02	0.03015	3.14	-2.70
Australia All Ordinaries	1651.4	0.76	1549.9	0.6878	-6.15	-15.06
Hong Kong Hang Seng	4297.33	0.12858	5512.39	0.12916	28.27	28.85
Singapore Straits Times	1490.7	0.6171	1524.4	0.6098	2.26	1.05
Johannesburg J'burg Gold	1131	0.3153	799	0.2062	-29.35	-53.80
Madrid General Index	246.24	0.010354	214.25	0.008708	-12.99	-26.82
Mexico I.P.C.	1431.46		1759.44	0.0003209	22.91	
Toronto 300 Composite	3512.36	0.8654	3350.44	0.7865	-4.61	-13.31
Euro, Aust, Far East MSCI-p	868.9		748.2		-13.89	

Source: *The Wall Street Journal*, various issues; the data are for the last day of trading in the calendar years which is December 30 for some countries and December 31 for others.

importance of international equities may be that the leading financial newspaper in the United States has finally entered the foray by announcing the creation of its own world stock market index. The contents of this index are described in the accompanying box. The newspaper *The Wall Street Journal* had, however, reported prices on other stock markets for a long time. A list of international stock indexes whose prices are reported daily in the newspaper, and the movements in the indexes during 1992, are shown in Exhibit 7.6. The exhibit also provides the returns earned on these indexes, in local currencies as well as in dollars, for the year 1992.

▼ ▼ ▼

The Wall Street Journal Enters the World of World Stock Markets

In early January 1993, *The Wall Street Journal* finally recognized the importance of global equity markets and launched its own "World Stock Index." The index was to include 2,200 companies around the world in 120 industry groups. According to the announcement, the index was to initially include companies from 10 countries: U.S. (which would be represented by the Dow Jones industrials), Canada, Britain, Germany, France, Italy, Japan, Hong Kong, Singapore, and Australia. Other countries would be added as they permit foreign investors to hold their stocks.

The stock prices would be calculated in four currencies: dollar, pound, mark, and yen. Stock prices included in the index would be translated into each of these currencies so that investors could track the changes in the price of the global index in any of these currencies.

▲ ▲ ▲

American investors are somewhat latecomers to the game of international equity and bond investments, although the first few years of the 1990s have seen a dramatic change in the activities of these investors. Exhibit 7.7 supplements that information by showing the trend in the expansion of U.S. investments abroad. U.S. investors increased their net purchases of foreign stocks and bonds in 1992 by 10 percent over the 1991 levels. Of the total $51.5 billion invested abroad, $32.3 billion went to stocks and the remainder to bonds.[4] The bulk of the stocks purchased were in Europe. The largest recipient countries were the United Kingdom, Japan, Hong Kong, Mexico, Switzerland, and Brazil.

Exhibit 7.7
The Lust to Go Abroad
(U.S. net purchases of foreign securities, in billions of dollars)

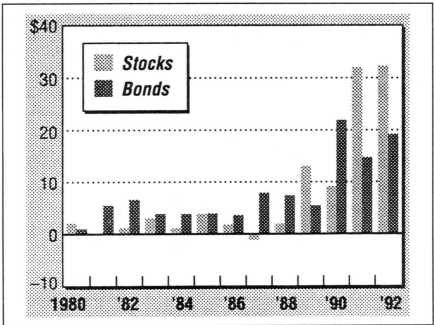

Source: Securities Industry Association, "Foreign Stock and Bond Markets Lured Record Levels of U.S. Investments in '92," *The Wall Street Journal*, May 4, 1993, p. C1.

Investors' motivations for entering these markets were somewhat different for each country. The U.K. has traditionally been a large receiver of U.S. portfolio investments. Hong Kong was prominent in 1992 because it is an entry to China which is seen as a "burgeoning economy." Mexico is attractive because of the forthcoming North American Free Trade Agreement which would remove trade and investment barriers between the United States, Canada, and Mexico. Investment advisors sometimes also feel that they can spot highly undervalued stocks in the foreign countries.

Investors can make portfolio investments in one of two ways: they can enter foreign stock markets or they can invest money in their home markets in vehicles that represent ownership of foreign assets. We will first discuss the stock markets and then two vehicles that permit investors to invest in foreign equities without having to deal with an institution in a foreign country. The two vehicles that we discuss are mutual funds and American Depository Receipts. Since developing and emerging markets have become a new and important category of investments, we will discuss these markets separately.

Exhibit 7.8
Shares of Stock Markets

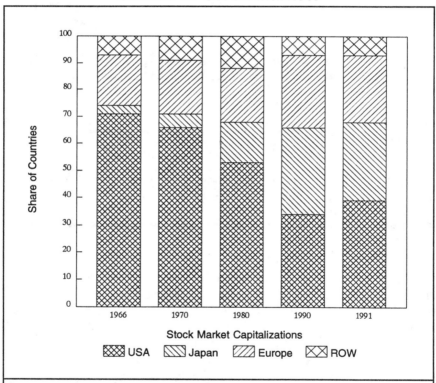

Source: International Finance Corporation, *Emerging Stock Markets Factbook*, Washington, DC, 1992.

Stock Markets Around the World

The stock markets in the United States are known to be the largest stock markets in the world. As shown in Exhibit 7.8, their reputation is well deserved, although their relative importance in world markets has been decreasing as other stock markets have grown faster than those in the United States. The size of a stock market can be measured by the capitalization of the stock market, which is the total value of all the shares (number of shares of each company times the price of each share) listed on the stock exchange. The capitalization of the U.S. stock markets accounts for almost 40 percent of the total capitalization of all stock markets in the "developed" world, and about 37 percent of the capitalization of all the markets around the world. Exhibit 7.9 shows the sizes of the U.S. and 22 other stock markets known as developed markets and Exhibit 7.10 shows the sizes of 32 markets that have come to be known as emerging stock markets. New stock markets have been opening around the world at a fast pace since the political changes in Eastern Europe in 1989–90. A more recent listing included 67 stock markets, having excluded very small exchanges in Ecuador, Uruguay, Iceland, Malta, Iran, and Papua New Guinea.[5] Exhibit 7.11 provides the names and locations of the major stock exchanges in the emerging markets along with the information on the extent to which these exchanges are accessible to foreign investors. The exhibit also shows the tax burden that U.S. investors will have to bear in these markets.

Exhibits 7.9 and 7.10 show the market capitalization of the stock exchanges in 1982 and 1991 (as well as in 1972 in some of the developed markets), the number of companies listed on the exchanges of each country in 1991, and the turnover of the stocks in 1991. The two exhibits provide data for the dollar value of trading on the exchanges of each country as well as the turnover as a percentage of the total capitalization of the stock market. The percentage figure provides an indication of how frequently the stock holders in a country reallocate their portfolios as well as how liquid these markets tend to be. Higher turnover indicates that markets are liquid and foreign investors have good chances of purchasing or selling shares at fair prices.

The two exhibits distinguish the data based on the classification of the stock exchange into developed markets and emerging markets. The distinction is commonly used in financial markets since the International

Exhibit 7.9
Developed Equity Markets

	No. of Listed Companies	Market Capitalization (billions of U.S. dollars)			1991/1982	Value Traded	
	1991	1972	1982	1991		Billion $ 1991	% of Market Capitalization
Australia	957	26.0	41.5	144.9	3.5	46.8	32.3
Austria	105		1.5	25.6	17.1	14.1	55.1
Belgium	176	9.2	8.5	71.3	8.4	6.2	8.7
Canada	1,086	57.0	103.5	266.9	2.6	78.2	29.3
Denmark	294		5.5	53.6	9.7	10.6	19.8
Finland	63		2.8	14.2	5.1	1.6	11.3
France	839	31.0	28.0	374.1	13.4	118.2	31.6
Germany	667	43.0	68.9	393.5	5.7	818.6	208.0
Hong Kong	333	9.4	18.8	122.0	6.5	43.0	35.2
Israel	286		15.9	12.1	0.8	8.4	69.4
Italy	348	14.0	19.9	154.1	7.7	43.3	28.1
Japan	2,107	152.0	430.8	3,130.0	7.3	996.0	31.8
Luxembourg	70		4.7	11.4	2.4	0.2	1.8
Netherlands	284	14.0	25.7	169.3	6.6	77.0	45.5
New Zealand	139		(6.2)*	14.3	2.3	3.1	21.7
Norway	112		2.4	22.0	9.2	11.7	53.2

Exhibit 7.9 Continued

South Africa	758		77.8	124.0	1.6	8.1	6.5
Singapore	157	8.1	31.2	47.6	1.5	18.1	38.0
Spain	433		11.1	147.9	13.3	40.6	27.5
Sweden	127	7.5	18.6	97.5	5.2	20.6	21.1
Switzerland	182	17.0	36.8	179.5	4.9	68.8	38.3
United Kingdom	1,915	140.0	196.2	1,003.2	5.1	317.9	31.7
United States	6,742	864.0	1,520.2	4,180.2	2.7	2,255.0	53.9
Developed Markets	18,150	18,150	2,670.2	10,760.0	4.0	5,005.8	46.5

*Data for 1984.

Source: International Finance Corporation, *Emerging Stock Markets Factbook*, Washington, DC, 1992; Market Capitalization for 1972: Morgan Stanley Capital International data.

Exhibit 7.10
Emerging Equity Markets

	No. of Listed Companies	Market Capitalization (millions of U.S. dollars)		Value Traded		
	1991	1982	1991	1991/1982	Billions $ 1991	% of Market Capitalization
Argentina	174	974	18,509	19	4,824	26.1
Bangladesh	138	34	269	8	3	1.1
Brazil	570	10,249	42,759	4	13,373	31.3
Chile	221	4,395	27,984	6	1,900	6.8
Colombia	83	1,322	4,036	3	203	5.0
Costa Rica	82	(118)[3]	311		9	2.9
Cote d'Ivoire	23	321	567	2	7	1.2
Egypt	(573)[1]	654	(1,835)[1]	0	(126)[1]	
Greece	126	1,923	13,118	7	2,443	18.6
India	6,500	7,058	47,730	7	24,295	50.9
Indonesia	141	144	6,823	47	2,981	43.7
Jamaica	44	177	1,034	6	95	9.2
Jordan	101	2,845	2,512	1	432	17.2
Kenya	53	(474)[4]	638		11	1.7
Korea	686	4,408	96,373	22	85,464	88.7
Kuwait	(52)[2]	(10,108)[5]	(9,932)[2]		(1,709)[2]	
Malaysia	321	13,903	58,627	4	10,657	18.2

Exhibit 7.10 Continued

Mexico	209	1,719	98,178	57	31,723	32.3
Morocco	67	292	1,528	5	49	3.2
Nigeria	142	1,458	1,882	1	9	0.5
Pakistan	542	877	7,326	8	645	8.8
Peru	273	685	1,135	2	135	11.9
Philippines	161	1,981	10,197	5	1,506	14.8
Portugal	180	92	9,613	104	2,818	29.3
Sri Lanka	178	(365)[6]	1,998		120	6.0
Taiwan, China	221	5,086	124,864	25	365,232	292.5
Thailand	276	1,260	35,815	28	30,089	84.0
Trinidad and Tobago	29	1,357	671	0	80	11.9
Turkey	134	952	15,703	16	8,571	54.6
Uruguay	26	24	44	2	2	4.5
Venezuela	66	2,415	11,214	5	3,240	28.9
Zimbabwe	60	355	1,394	4	77	5.5
All Emerging Markets	11,827	66,960	642,852		590,993	91.9

Source: *Emerging Stock Markets Factbook*, IFC, 1992.

[1] Data for 1990.
[2] Data for 1989.
[3] Data for 1983.
[4] Data for 1988.
[5] Data for 1986.
[6] Data for 1985.

Exhibit 7.11
Equity Investment in Emerging Countries

Country	Stock Exchanges in the Country	Access to Foreign Investors	Repatriation		Tax Rates for U.S. Investors		
			Income	Capital	Interest	Dividends	Capital Gains
Argentina	Mercado de Valores de Buenos Aires	Free	Free	Free	20	20	0
	Bolsa de Comercio de Rosario						
Bangladesh	Dhaka Stock Exchange	RFE	SR	SR	—	—	—
Barbados	Securities Exchange of Barbados	—	—	—	15	15	0
Bolivia	Bolsa Boliviana de Valores	—	—	—	—	—	—
	Bolsa de Valores de Santa Cruz de la Sierra, S.A.						
Botswana	Stockbrokers Botswana Ltd.	—	—	—	15	15	0
Brazil	Bolsa de Valores Minas–Espirito Santo e Brasilia	Free	Free	Free	15	15	15
	Bolsa de Valores de Rio de Janeiro						
	Bolsa de Valores de Sao Paulo						
Bulgaria	First Bulgarian Stock Exchange	—	—	—	—	—	—
Chile	Bolsa de Comercio de Santiago	RFE	Free	SR	35	35	35
China	Shanghai Securities Exchange	SCS	SR	SR	10	10	0
	Shenzhen Stock Exchange						

Exhibit 7.11 Continued

Country	Exchange						
Colombia	Bolsa de Bogota S.A.	Free	Free	Free	7	20	0
	Bolsa de Occidente						
	Bolsa de Medellin S.A.						
Commonwealth of Independent States	Moscow Intl. Stock Exchange	—	—	—	32	32	0
	St. Petersburg Stock Exchange						
Costa Rica	Costa Rica Stock Exchange	RFE	SR	SR	—	—	—
Cote d'Ivoire	Abidjan Stock Exchange	—	—	—	—	—	—
Cyprus	No official stock exchange, but over the counter market	—	—	—	25	30	0
Czechoslovakia	Bratislava Stock Exchange	—	—	—	—	—	—
	Stock Exchange of Prague						
Ecuador	Bolsa de Valores	—	—	—	—	—	—
Egypt	Alexandria Stock Exchange	—	—	—	—	—	—
	Cairo Stock Exchange						
El Salvador	El Salvador Stock Exchange	—	—	—	—	—	—
Ghana	Ghana Stock Exchange	—	—	—	30	15	0
Greece	Athens Stock Exchange	RFE	SR	SR	10	42/45	0
Honduras	Bolsa Hondurena de Valores S.A.	—	—	—	—	—	—
Hungary	Budapest Stock Exchange	—	—	—	40	40	40

Exhibit 7.11 Continued

		AIO	SR	SR	10	10	10
India	Bangalore Stock Exchange Ltd.						
	The Bombay Stock Exchange						
	The Calcutta Stock Exchange						
	Madras Stock Exchange Ltd.						
	The Delhi Stock Exchange Assoc. Ltd.						
Indonesia	The Jakarta Stock Exchange	RFE	SR	SR	20	20	20
	Surabaya Stock Exchange						
Iran	Tehran Stock Exchange	—	—	—	—	—	—
Jamaica	Jamaica Stock Exchange	RFE	SR	SR	33	33	0
Jordan	Amman Financial Market	Free	Free	Free	0	0	0
Kenya	The Nairobi Stock Exchange	RFE	SR	SR	12.5	15	0
Korea	Korea Stock Exchange	SCS	Free	Free	25	25	25
Kuwait	Kuwait Stock Exchange	—	—	—	—	—	—
Malaysia	The Kuala Lumpur Stock Exchange	Free	Free	Free	20	0	0
Malta	The Malta Stock Exchange	—	—	—	—	—	—
Mauritius	Stock Exchange Commission	—	—	—	0	0	0
Mexico	Bolsa Mexicana de Valores S.A. de C.V.	RFE	Free	Free	0	0	0
Morocco	Casablanca Stock Exchange	Closed	—	—	20/30	15	40
Nigeria	Nigerian Stock Exchange		SR	SR	15	15	20

Exhibit 7.11 Continued

Country	Exchange						
Oman	Muscat Securities Market	Free	—	—	—	—	—
Pakistan	Karachi Stock Exchange Lahore Stock Exchange	—	Free	Free	10	10	0
Panama	Bolsa de Valores de Panama	—	—	—	—	—	—
Paraguay	Bolsa de Valores y Productos de Asuncion	—	—	—	—	—	—
Peru	Lima Stock Exchange	Free	Free	Free	10	10	37
Philippines	Makati Stock Exchange, Inc. Manila Stock Exchange	SCS	Free	Free	15	15	.25
Poland	Gielda Papierow Wartosciowych	—	—	—	0	5/15	0
Portugal	Bolsa de Valores de Lisboa Bolsa de Valores de Porto	Free	Free	Free	20	20	0
Sri Lanka	Colombo Stock Exchange	RFE	SR	SR	0	15	0
Taiwan, China	Taiwan Stock Exchange	AIO	Free	Free	20	20	0
Thailand	Securities Exchange of Thailand	RFE	Free	Free	15	10	0
Trinidad & Tobago	Trinidad & Tobago Stock Exchange	RFE	RF	RF	30	10	0
Tunisia	Tunis Stock Exchange	—	—	—	—	—	—
Turkey	Istanbul Stock Exchange	Free	Free	Free	0	0	0
Uruguay	Bolsa de Valores de Montevideo	—	—	—	—	—	—
Venezuela	Bolsa de Valores de Caracas	RFE	SR	SR	20	20	20

International Equity Markets   187

Exhibit 7.11 Continued

Yugoslavia	Belgrade Stock Exchange Ljubljana Stock Exchange, Inc. Zagreb Stock Exchange	—	—	—	—	—
Zimbabwe	Zimbabwe Stock Exchange	SCS	Rest.	Rest.	10	20	30

RFE: Relatively free entry.
SR: Some restrictions.
SCS: Special classes of shares.
AIO: Authorized investors only.
Rest.: Restricted.
—: Information not available.

Source: International Finance Corporation, *Emerging Markets Yearbook*, 1992, various pages.

Finance Corporation, an arm of the World Bank in Washington D.C., used that classification for data collection as well as for policy making. This distinction is, however, somewhat arbitrary, since it is based neither on size nor capitalization, nor on liquidity nor on any other observable variable. Some of the "emerging" market stock exchanges, for instance, are much older than those in developed countries: India's exchange was established in the 1870s. Further, the markets of Taiwan and Korea, which are classified among emerging markets, are much bigger than those of Finland, Norway, Israel and some others which are included in the list of developed stock markets. The emerging markets of Taiwan, Thailand, Korea, Turkey, and India turn over much larger percentages of their capitalization than do most developed markets, especially markets like Luxembourg, South Africa, Finland, and Belgium. Observers agree that some of the emerging markets are ahead of some of the developed markets in terms of regulations of activities; some of the emerging markets permit unlimited access to foreign investors whereas some of the developed markets do not.[6] In general, though, developed market exchanges have more derivative products available than do the emerging markets, with the possible exception of Malaysia.

The distinction between the developed and emerging markets should be seen as a reflection of investment opportunities on these markets. During at least the last two years, the highest, and the lowest, returns have been obtained on the emerging stock markets. Exhibit 7.12 shows the annual changes in price indexes, measured in terms of U.S. dollars, for stock exchanges around the world for 1991 and 1992, with the countries being ranked in terms of their returns in 1992. The highest ranking developed market stock exchange is thirteenth on the list with the United States being in the sixteenth position.

The two exhibits, 7.9 and 7.10, show quite clearly that stock markets have grown very rapidly over the last two decades. The capitalization of the U.S. markets has grown almost five times from 1972 to 1991. The most phenomenal growth has been on the Japanese market. Between the same two years, that is, between 1972 and 1991, the Japanese exchange grew about 20 times. In 1972, as in 1991, it was the second largest stock market in the world based upon the total capitalization on the exchange. But whereas in 1972, the Japanese market was only about 18 percent of the U.S. market, in 1991 it was almost 75 percent of the size of the same market. By 1991, the developed markets as a group had grown to be

Exhibit 7.12
World Stock Market Performance
(percent change in U.S. dollars)

	1992	1991		1992	1991
Jamaica	202.0		UK	−7.2	16.0
Peru	124.9		Hungary	−11.4	
China	109.6		Germany	−11.8	8.8
Israel	75.2		Austria	−12.0	−11.9
Colombia	36.1	191.5	Australia	−13.2	35.6
Thailand	35.9	36.1	MSCI EAFE	−13.9	12.5
Hong Kong	27.4	49.5	Canada	−14.2	12.0
Malaysia	24.6	12.3	Finland	−14.4	−17.4
India	22.1	18.1	Sweden	−16.4	15.4
Jordan	21.1	15.6	Pakistan	−20.5	172.3
Mexico	20.0	107.3	Poland	−21.5	
Philippines	17.2	59.3	Japan	−22.1	9.1
Switzerland	15.6	16.8	Portugal	−22.6	2.3
Chile	12.3	99.2	Luxembourg	−22.7	
Singapore	4.4	25.0	Norway	−23.4	−15.1
US	4.2	31.3	Ireland	−23.4	
IFC Latin America	4.0	134.0	Italy	−24.0	−0.7
Korea	3.5	−14.4	Spain	−24.9	17.0
Indonesia	1.0	−40.4	Argentina	−27.5	396.6
France	1.0	18.5	Taiwan, China	−27.7	−0.6
IFC Asia	−0.1	−0.7	Denmark	−29.2	17.0
Netherlands	−1.0	19.1	Greece	−33.3	−18.7
IFC Composite	−1.4	19.2	Sri Lanka	−36.0	
Brazil	−1.5	173.0	Nigeria	−38.8	37.8
New Zealand	−5.2	20.7	Venezuela	−42.7	48.4
Belgium	−5.3	15.3	Turkey	−54.8	−26.9
MSCI World	−7.1		Zimbabwe	−61.6	−52.2

Sources: 1991 data: International Finance Corporation, *Emerging Stock Markets Factbook*, Washington, DC; 1992 data: *Euromoney, World Equity Markets*, Research Report, March 1993.

about 6.5 times their size in 1982. The emerging markets grew about 28 times during the same time period, albeit from a very small base. The fastest growth over this time period was in some of the emerging markets such as Indonesia, Mexico, and Portugal, which grew to be more than 50 times their sizes over this decade. It is noteworthy that the markets have grown without a dramatic increase in the number of companies listed on the exchanges. In one case at least, the growth in trading of stocks has taken even the government by surprise. The accompanying box provides an account of how the Chinese have taken to the stock markets so much that they are finding innovative ways to circumvent government controls.

▼ ▼ ▼
Stock Markets Do Not Have to Be Legal!

Having won the honor of being the first communist country to have a stock market, China may now be on its way to adding another feather in its cap: having the first illegal stock market. The illegal market, however, is not located in one specific place unlike the official exchanges of Shenzhen and Shanghai. The illegal market seems to be operating in far off places including the "grasslands west of Mongolia." The government seems unable to control these activities.

Ironically, the government itself may have given the impetus for the start of the illegal market when it encouraged thousands of state–owned enterprises to issue stocks. The aim of the government was to separate the ownership of these enterprises from management. Large proportions of the newly issued shares were held by the government, with the employees or other companies holding a small number of these shares. Trading in these shares was, however, discouraged because they were not allowed to be listed on the two organized exchanges.

Two over–the–counter trading systems, however, have developed in Beijing: the Securities Trading Automatic Quotation System, which is designed for bonds but also lists eight shares, and the National Electronic Trading System, which lists four shares. Legally only companies can trade in the shares listed on these two systems, but like other things in the country, well–connected investors seem to be able to sidestep the regulations. In addition to these two exchanges, there are reports that shares can also be bought alongside the vegetables in ubiquitous street markets in China.

The main concern of the authorities is that this informal market undermines the securities regulations in the country, not to mention that it draws funds away from the organized exchanges. The prices on the organized exchanges have fallen while those on the informal market have gone up by about 50 percent in the last two months.

Not to be outdone by their rivals on the mainland, the Taiwanese have an illegal market in something more exotic than stock: financial futures. About 500 illegal futures brokers were supposed to be active in the 1980s, but the number may have dropped to between 100–150 at the present time. The government has finally announced that it will allow legal traders to set up operations within Taiwan and will allow Taiwanese investors to deal in futures contracts on 11 exchanges around the world. The legalization, however, is not expected to cause the illegal traders to disappear although there is widespread fraud among them. These illegal traders are known to gamble against their clients and may even disappear with the customers' money. The only disadvantage of legal traders will be their high fees—expected to be about five times those of the illegals—and the unfortunate risk that the taxman will be aware of the profits being made on these trades.

Information on China summarized from "Alongside China's Official Exchanges, Booming Illegal Stock Market Operates," *The Wall Street Journal*, June 22, 1993, p. A11. Information on Taiwan is from "Future Imperfect," *The Economist*, August 7, 1993, p. 66.

▲ ▲ ▲

Mutual Funds

The most common, and the fastest growing, form of portfolio investment is through mutual funds. Both closed–ended and open–ended mutual funds that specialize in investments abroad are available for U.S. investors. Closed–ended funds offer only a fixed number of their shares and invest the proceeds according to their mandate. Open–ended funds do not place a limit on the volume of funds and invest all the funds that they receive according to their investment philosophy.

Mutual funds offer investors opportunities for international investments in four ways.

Global Funds. Global funds invest in stocks all over the world. These funds are generally designed for investors in the country where the fund is located and hence tend to have a significant proportion of the assets within the country.

International Funds. International funds tend to specialize in stocks outside the country where the fund is located. These funds are attractive for investors who may want to handle their investments within the country themselves, but who may lack the expertise to follow international markets. They may, thus, prefer a mutual fund that takes care of the international diversification on their behalf.

Regional Funds. Regional funds specialize in one particular region of the world or in one type of market, say, the emerging markets. A regional fund may specialize in the Far East, including stocks from the countries in Southeast Asia, Latin America, or Europe, etc. One of the most popular regions in the last few years has been the fastest growing region of the global economy—Southeast Asia.

Country Funds. Country funds specialize on one country. Along with the increase in the role of the emerging markets, country funds have been a growth industry. Whereas many banks and investment companies offer Japanese or Canadian or other established country funds, more exotic country funds like the Malaysia fund or the India Growth fund are also available. In fact, one such country fund, the Turkish Investment Fund, had the highest return of any mutual fund, almost 60 percent, for the most recent 12 month–period ending in May 1993. To balance the picture, however, five country funds were listed among the 10 worst performers during the same period.

As an illustration of what a typical firm may offer, the following is a list of international funds offered by one company—Templeton International—to investors in Canada. The company offers a similar array of funds in the United States and in some other countries (note that Canadian investors do not consider U.S. stocks to be really "international" since the U.S. and Canadian economies are highly integrated).

Growth Fund invests in stocks in Canada and the United States.

Emerging Markets Fund invests in about a dozen emerging markets.

Global Smaller Companies Fund specializes in companies around the world that have a small capitalization.

Global Income Fund focuses on high current income, in contrast to the growth fund which emphasizes long–term performance.

International Stock Fund focuses on long–term growth from investments **outside** the United States and Canada.

American Depository Receipts

American Depository Receipts, or ADRs, are the market's response to a demand that cannot be satisfied directly due to regulations. At a time when U.S. investors desire to hold more and more foreign stocks, foreign firms whose stocks are in demand find it difficult and costly to list their stocks on exchanges which would be easily accessible to U.S. investors. The difficulties arise due to very stringent requirements imposed by the exchanges in the United States for data and information which sometimes are not collected in foreign countries and sometimes are treated as confidential by foreign firms. Since the investors show a willingness to hold foreign assets in spite of what would appear to be incomplete information from a U.S. perspective, banks have created American Depository Receipts. The Securities and Exchange Commission, which regulates all stock trading in the United States, has allowed ADRs to be used to smaller, first–time foreign issuers in the U.S. securities markets. In the beginning of 1993, there were about 800 issues of ADRs which together raised about $10 billion in 1992.

These receipts represent the ownership of underlying stocks which are held in custody by the bank that issues the ADRs. Since ADR's are not actual stocks, they are more easily traded within the United States. The holder of an ADR, however, is entitled to all the privileges of a stock holder including the receipt of the dividends. The banks that issue the ADRs usually collect the dividends and transfer the equivalent in dollars to the owners. Each ADR often represents ownership of a number of shares since the trading volumes and amounts tend to be somewhat higher in the United States than in Europe. ADRs are traded on the over–the–counter market as well as on the organized exchanges, especially the NYSE. In early 1993, ADRs from 34 countries were available in the United States. The United Kingdom, Australia, Japan, and South Africa were the largest issuers of the instruments. By the early 1990s, ADRs had become popular enough that companies began to issue Global Depository Receipts, or GDRs. GDRs are similar instruments to ADRs, but can be simultaneously issued on stock exchanges all over the world.

Exhibit 7.13
Real Aggregate Net Resource Flows
to Developing Countries

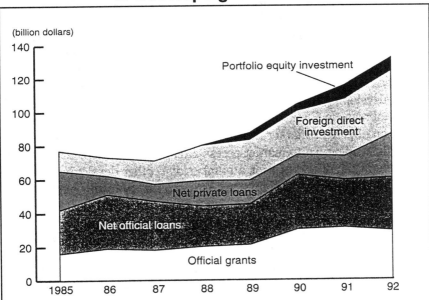

Note: All flows are deflated by the import unit value index (IMF: WEO) at constant 1992 dollars, 1992 deflator is a World Bank staff estimate; data for portfolio equity investment are World Bank estimates, available since 1989 only.

Source: World Bank Debt Tables 1991–1992, *Finance and Development*, March 1993, p. 9.

One of the advantages of ADRs is that the investor need not be concerned about dealing in foreign currencies; ADRs are quoted and traded in U.S. dollars. Thus, the quoted prices in the United States take into account the changes in the value of the share in its own market as well as the changes in exchange rates.

Portfolio Investment in Developing Countries

One area of interest to investors is the potential of developing countries as suitable places to invest money. These countries had traditionally relied either upon government to government flows in the form of aid or loans, or upon bank loans. As shown in Exhibit 7.13, private portfolio flows to these countries have become very important over the last decade. Moreover, equity investments would seem to be the fastest growing form of capital flows to the developing countries since 1989. Between 1989 and 1991, the flow of equity funds seems to have grown almost 20–fold, from $0.4 billion to $7.6 billion. These flows come as ADRs, as country or regional funds, or as direct purchases of equity. The breakdown of these flows is shown in Exhibit 7.14. The popularity of ADRs is quite clear from the exhibit.

The growth in the popularity of developing countries is explained by a number of factors. Perhaps the main reason for this growth is the sweeping economic reforms that have been carried out in some of the countries. These reforms have included privatization of previously publicly held organizations and a greater reliance upon market forces to determine prices and patterns of productions. These changes have signalled to investors that their investments will not be subject to arbitrary government actions, but rather to the economic risks of doing business. Investors feel more comfortable about their ability to assess the latter and generally prefer to avoid the former. In addition, developing countries have removed many barriers to investments by foreign investors. We have already listed the existing barriers in Exhibit 7.11, and the following chapter gives a concrete example of how even some communist countries are making some signs of wanting to attract private capital. In addition, portfolio flows to developing countries have been aided by the return of "flight capital" that had left some of these countries

Exhibit 7.14
Gross Portfolio Investment Flows
to Developing Countries
(billions of dollars)

	1989	1990	1991	1992 (est)	Total 1989–92
Portfolio equity investment, of which:	3.5	3.8	7.6	8.2	23.0
Country funds	2.2	2.9	1.2	0.6	6.9
Depository receipts	0	0.1	4.9	5.6	10.7
Direct equity investment	1.3	0.8	1.5	1.9	5.4
Debt instruments*	4.1	9.3	12.7	19.1	41.5
Total	7.6	9.3	20.3	27.3	64.5

*Debt instruments consist of bonds, commercial paper, and certificates of deposit, but "new money bonds" that were issued in Brady–type debt service reduction operations are excluded.

Source: *Finance and Development*, March 1993, p. 12; data from World Debt Tables, 1992–93.

after the debt crisis hit international bank loans in 1982. The box on page 200 provides an example of how one country is attracting foreign capital. Exhibit 7.15 shows a list of country and regional funds offered for emerging markets in 1991. As the exhibit shows, none of these funds was in existence before 1981 and most of them have started within the last two to three years. Most of these funds are also quite small.

Exhibit 7.15
Information on Selected Closed-End Country Funds for Emerging Markets
(Values in U.S. $; End September 1991)

Fund Name	Market Listed	Date of First Offering	Gross Initial Size(M)	Offering Price Per Share	Market Price Per Share	Net Asset Value Per Share	Premium/ Discount to NAV(%)	Total Market Value(M)
Regional Funds								
EMGF, Inc. (I,II,III)	Luxembourg	May 86	383.21	20.75	.	33.46	.	754.66
Templeton E.M. Fund	AMEX	Feb 87	115.00	10.00	19.25	18.17	5.9	221.38
EMIF, Inc. (I,II,III)	Luxembourg	Feb 88	230.74	11.59	.	17.08	.	340.18
New World Inv. Fund (I,II)	-	May 89	71.47	10.13	.	19.98	.	144.82
Commonwealth Equity Fund	-	Sep 90	56.56	10.00	.	10.85	.	61.37
Asian Devel. Equity Fund	Luxembourg	Jan 88	100.00	10.00	.	13.57	.	135.70
JF Asia Select Fund	Hong Kong	Dec 89	103.00	1.03	0.72	1.06	-32.1	72.00
Brazil								
Equity Fund of Brazil		Sep 87	77.90	106,293.06	.	131,435.88	.	96.28
Brazil Fund	NYSE	Mar 88	150.00	12.50	15.13	13.51	12.0	181.50
Brazilian Inv. Fund (I,II)		Jun 91	43.14	53.08	.	56.67	.	46.07
Chile								
Chile Fund, Inc.	NYSE	Oct 89	80.50	15.00	31.75	38.35	-17.2	170.39
Five Arrows Chile Fund	London	Feb 90	75.00	10.00	14.25	22.11	-35.5	106.68
GT Chile Growth Fund	London	Feb 90	106.00	10.60	15.50	26.58	-41.7	155.00
India								
India Fund	London	Jul 86	192.28	2.04	3.06	4.41	-30.2	290.20
India Growth Fund	NYSE	Aug 88	60.10	12.00	15.13	16.08	-5.9	75.78
Indonesia								
JF Indonesia Fund (I,II)	Hong Kong	Mar 89	67.52	1.35	.	0.98	.	49.00
Jakarta Fund	London	Aug 89	42.00	21.00	.	8.57	-19.8	13.75
Nomura Jakarta Fund	Hong Kong	Sep 89	30.00	10.00	.	6.31	.	18.93
Indonesia Fund Inc.	NYSE	Mar 90	60.00	15.00	8.75	7.98	9.6	35.00
Korea								
Korea Fund (I,II,III)	NYSE	Aug 84	150.00	10.88	14.50	10.50	38.1	312.56
Korea Growth Trust	Hong Kong	Mar 85	31.50	10.50	40.00	33.16	20.6	120.00
Korea Int'l Trust (I,II)	-	Nov 81	27.25	10.48	54.50	44.83	21.6	141.70
Korea Trust (I,II)	-	Nov 81	26.03	14.87	65.50	54.39	20.4	114.63
Korea Europe Fund (I,II,III)	London	Mar 87	116.13	4.04	6.05	4.28	41.4	173.70
Seoul Int'l Trust	-	Apr 85	31.35	10.45	43.00	35.28	21.9	129.00
Seoul Int'l Trust	-	Apr 85	31.35	10.45	39.00	32.54	19.9	117.00
Malaysia								
Malaysia Fund	NYSE	May 87	96.60	12.00	11.88	12.57	-5.5	95.59
Malaysia Growth Fund		Apr 89	45.25	10.00	.	10.55	.	47.74
Malacca Fund (I,II)	London	Jan 89	89.68	13.80	6.88	10.94	-37.2	44.69
Mexico								
Mexico Fund	NYSE	Jun 81	147.31	7.47	22.38	24.28	-7.8	447.30
Equity & Income Fund	NYSE	Aug 90	72.00	12.00	13.13	15.03	-12.7	78.75

Exhibit 7.15 Continued

Fund Name	Market Listed	Date of First Offering	Gross Initial Size(M)	Offering Price Per Share	Market Price Per Share	Net Asset Value Per Share	Premium/ Discount to NAV(%)	Total Market Value(M)
Philippines								
Manila Fund	London	Oct 89	52.00	10.40	4.63	8.01	-42.3	23.13
First Philippine Fund	NYSE	Nov 89	100.10	12.00	8.00	10.04	-20.3	66.74
Portugal								
Portugal Fund	London	Aug 87	42.32	10.58	4.00	5.02	-20.3	16.00
Oporto Growth Fund	London	May 88	37.10	10.60	5.50	7.16	-23.2	19.25
Portugal Fund, Inc.	NYSE	Nov 89	69.00	15.00	10.63	10.94	-2.9	48.87
Portuguese Inv. Fund	London	May 90	31.00	100.00	70.50	71.76	-1.8	21.85
Taiwan, China								
Formosa Fund	London	Mar 86	25.70	10.28	75.50	75.75	-0.3	188.75
Taipei Fund	London	May 86	25.70	10.28	57.00	57.30	-0.5	142.50
Taiwan Fund (I,II,III)	NYSE	Dec 86	94.31	23.46	22.38	20.13	11.2	89.97
R.O.C. Taiwan Fund	NYSE	Oct 83	42.13	10.28	10.13	10.25	-1.2	303.90
Thailand								
Bangkok Fund (I,II,III)	London	Aug 85	44.17	17.72	65.00	72.68	-10.6	162.50
Siam Fund	;	Feb 88	95.04	11.88	17.50	20.56	-14.9	140.00
Thai Fund, Inc.	NYSE	Feb 88	114.96	12.00	16.88	14.44	16.9	161.66
Thailand Fund	London	Dec 86	31.14	10.38	-	31.40	-	94.20
Thai Euro Fund	London	May 88	80.25	10.70	11.75	17.58	-33.2	88.13
Thai Prime Fund	Singapore	Sep 88	155.00	10.00	13.00	14.99	-13.3	201.50
Thai Int'l Fund	London	Nov 88	80.03	10.67	11.75	17.52	-32.9	88.13
Turkey								
Turkish Investment Fund	NYSE	Dec 89	84.00	12.00	7.38	5.64	30.8	51.63
Total			4,112.82					6,700.26

Notes:
• 'Gross initial size (US$ millions)' means the total capital (US$ millions) raised by the fund through one or more offerings.
• 'Offering price per share' means the weighted averageprice per share, including fees, of shares sold by the fund in one or more offerings, adjusted for stock dividends and splits.
• 'Market price per share' means the last transaction price (in US$) for the share, or - if the share is not actively traded.
• 'Premium/discount to NAV(%)' shows the premium or discount of the present market price per share to the present net asset value(NAV) per share, where a trading price is available.
• 'Total market value(US$ millions)' means the market value of the fund (US$ millions), calculated using the number of shares issued and outstanding, multiplied by the last price per sha
  Where no trading price is available, the NAV per share is used.

Source: International Finance Corporation, Emerging Market Data Base, 3rd Quarter, 1991.

International Equity Markets 199

▼ ▼ ▼

101 Ways to Own Stocks in an Emerging Market

In early 1992, Mexico had become the favorite of stock brokers. The Bolsa Mexicana de Valores had gone up by 103 percent the previous year in terms of dollars. In the first six weeks of 1992, the Bolsa had gone up by 13 percent compared to 2.6 percent for Dow Jones. Predicting total returns of between 35 and 45 percent for the year, analysts were recommending stocks that were selling at low price–earnings ratios. The prospects for Mexico looked especially good in view of the likely approval of the North American Free Trade Agreement between the United States, Canada, and Mexico. The potential of the Mexican Bolsa had attracted $2.39 billion from U.S. investors in the first nine months of 1991 compared to $90 million in 1990 and $8 million in 1989. There had been no U.S. investment in Mexican stocks for a number of years prior to that. U.S. investors had four choices for acquiring equity in Mexico.

- **Directly**. U.S. investors could buy one of the three types of shares issued by Mexican companies: shares that can be owned by Mexicans or foreigners. Other types of shares are ones that can be owned only by Mexican nationals, and shares that carry limited or no voting rights.

- **ADRs**. In early 1992, ADRs on 22 Mexican companies were available, 14 of which traded either on the New York Stock Exchange, the American Stock Exchange, or NASDAQ. These ADRs, like all others, are priced in dollars. In 1991, 14 Mexican companies raised $2.68 billion in the form of these receipts.

- **Mutual funds**. As was the case in other countries, a number of mutual funds specialized in Mexico: Mexico Fund, Inc., Emerging Mexico Fund, and Mexico Equity and Income Fund.

- **Other**. U.S. securities firms and banks were designing special indexes that would reflect a selected number of Mexican shares. Investors would be able to buy warrants on these indexes, thus speculating on the movements of the Mexican stock market.

Summarized from "Mexico's Red Hot Stocks Can Still Excite, but Buying Blind Might Burn Investors," and "U.S. Brokers Seek Wider Access to the Shielded Mexican Market," both from *The Wall Street Journal*, February 12, 1992, page C1.

▲ ▲ ▲

Issuing International Equity

Investors hold international equities because they obtain benefits of diversification. What advantages do firms obtain from issuing international equities?

The most important advantage of international equities from the point of view of the companies is that access to international markets expands the pool of investors available to the company and hence reduces the cost of raising equity. In some cases, it also reduces the time required to raise the funds. In addition, when equities are issued in more than one market, they are also listed in more than one market. Active trading of a company's securities in more than one market seems to provide liquidity for the stock, although at the present time, the most important location for the trade in an equity seems to be its home market. Companies find that international issues and international listing adds to the prestige of the company and is well worth the additional costs involved. A recent survey found that European firms consider raising capital as the primary reason for issuing international equities, followed by considerations of international image, creation of a wider shareholder base, ability to fund company investments, creation of an international reference price, extension of the trading zone, and legal restrictions on domestic stock exchanges. The main deterrent to international listing was the cost of being present in many markets. This was followed by tax and regulatory differences and lack of standardization between markets. Firms were also afraid the equities issued abroad could be sold back to domestic investors and a supply of a firm's equity in a foreign market could create conditions for a takeover.[7]

Firms are aided by securities firms and investment banks in their issues of international equities. As noted earlier, the largest issuers of international equities are U.S. multinationals. In keeping with the nationality of the issuers, the largest lead managers, that is, the firms that manage the issue of these securities on behalf of the issuing company, were also American firms. In the first four months of 1993, Goldman Sachs had managed the largest volume, followed by Merrill Lynch, CSFB/Credit Suisse, JP Morgan, and Morgan Stanley.[8]

Institutional Investors and the
Future of International Investments

Two trends would indicate that international equity and bond investments will grow at a very rapid pace in the near future. First, the institutional investors in the United States as well as in the rest of the world control more and more of the financial assets within their economies. Institutional investors are the organizations that have large pools of funds which they control on behalf of others. Included among institutional investors are pension funds, insurance companies, mutual funds, and investment banks. Their market power gives them access to information that will lead to more international diversification than has been made in the past. Second, decreased intervention by governments in their economies has led to greater attention to private activities, and hence to greater importance of securities of firms owned by the public. This increased importance of securities has led to increased flow of information about these securities which in turn encourages investments in these securities. The decreased role of governments also shows a liberalization of the regulatory environment that used to restrict the behavior of investors. Both these factors will provide an impetus for an existing trend which has seen greater international investments by investors in all countries.

The first point made here can be illustrated with the help of data from the United States. Direct stock holdings of individuals in the U.S. have been going down steadily over the last quarter century. In 1965 individuals controlled 84 percent of all the stocks in the United States. Mutual funds controlled about another 3 percent on behalf of these individuals. In 1991, individuals had direct control over 53.1 percent of stocks and about another 10 percent in mutual funds. Stocks worth nearly $400 billion were held by mutual funds, out of a total market capitalization of $4.37 trillion.[9] The remainder of the funds were controlled by institutional investors. Further, these institutional investors have some resources that individual investors cannot possess. The large investors have access to timely and sophisticated information about developments in international markets and the ability to understand and manage risks that are inherent in international investments. Large investors, for example, can have access to information about developments in stock and foreign exchange markets which will allow them to assess when and if currency risks become excessively high to jeopardize the potential gains from foreign investments. With better information on how to manage currency and, in some cases, political risks inherent in these investments, these investors are much more willing to accept the risks of these investments at prices (that is, higher expected returns) that would be acceptable to the issuers of international equities. These large investors can also diversify most of the unsystematic risks associated with each foreign market by investing in a large number of markets in a large number of currencies. Such diversification of portfolios helps manage both the unsystematic risk of foreign stock markets as well as currency risks.

Even without the growth in the relative importance of institutional investors, the last decade has seen greater internationalization of

Exhibit 7.16
Foreign Assets of Pension Funds

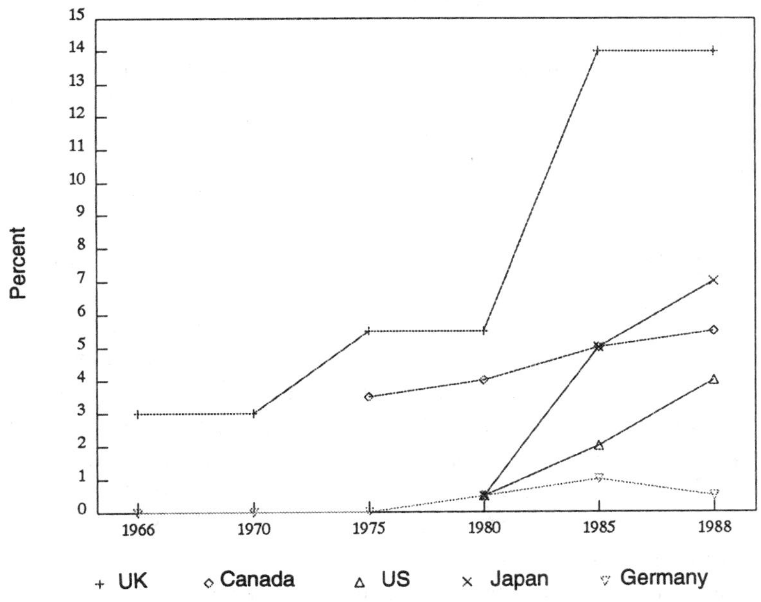

Source: Bank of England, *Quarterly Review*, 1991.

portfolios. This is true even for large institutional investors who are sometimes bound by regulations. Exhibit 7.16 provides a rough idea of the extent of internationalization of the portfolios of pension funds in selected countries. The information is sketchy, but the trends are clear. Other studies indicate that Swiss funds increased their foreign investments between 1991 and 1992 from 24.7 percent of their assets to 27.3 percent, with Irish funds showing a more dramatic increase from 25.7 percent to 42.9 percent.[10] One study for the United States estimates that U.S. pension funds will increase their holdings of foreign equities from $53.1 billion, or 5.6 percent of their portfolios, in 1991 to $119.7 billion, or 9.5 percent of their portfolios, in 1993.[11] The information in Exhibit 7.16 is supported by more detailed information in Exhibit 7.17, which shows the breakdown of the portfolios of pension funds for four countries. This information is supported by other data. One study estimates that "across continental Europe, . . . the total assets of pension funds will double over the period 1990–1995, from $675 billion to almost $1000 billion. . . . the increase in competitiveness . . . will mean that investors look increasingly to overseas markets to maximize returns."[12]

All through this chapter, we have talked about the second of these trends, that is, increasing involvement of investors in international equities. If the two trends continue even mildly, the study of international equities will become a much more important and relevant subject over the next decade.

Summary

International equities are a relatively new form of international portfolio investments. Investors and firms have long sought fortunes in foreign markets. Avoiding all other indirect forms, firms have now begun to offer their shares directly to investors in foreign countries. Even before international equities became available, investments in foreign equity were being made through mutual funds and by direct purchases of equity abroad. With increasing interest in ownership of foreign equities, financial institutions have developed many forms of funds and other vehicles that facilitate the international diversification process. This chapter has provided the institutional framework within which international investments take place; the following chapter looks at the economic benefits of such investments.

Exhibit 7.17
Portfolio Allocation
(pension fund assets, end 1991)

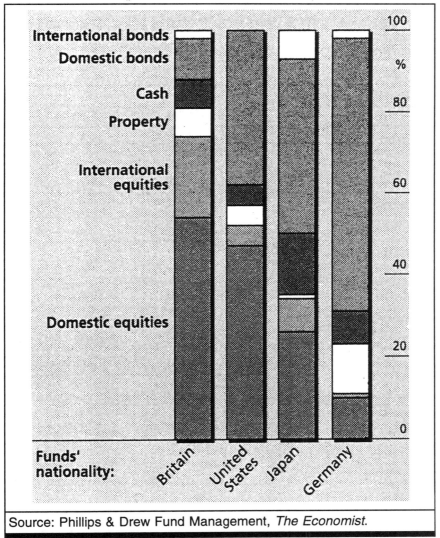

Source: Phillips & Drew Fund Management, *The Economist*.

Appendix 7
The World Bank Group and Other Development Banks

Formally known as the International Bank for Reconstruction and Development, the World Bank Group consists of three somewhat separate organizations: the World Bank, the International Development Agency (IDA), and International Finance Corporation (IFC), all located in Washington D.C. The main objective of this group is to channel financial resources available in the developed world to the developing areas of the world. The Bank came into existence at the end of World War II to help the reconstruction in war-torn Europe. Within the first two decades of its existence, however, the bank became the main conduit for the flow of multinational developmental aid to the developing countries.

The World Bank does not aim to compete with the private sector, and it normally finances long–term developmental or infrastructure projects which have a long gestation period. It raises funds through the contribution of member industrialized countries and lends funds to the borrowing countries at commercial or market interest rates. Projects which would not result in cast flows that can be used to make interest payments may qualify for IDA assistance, which is known as the soft-loan arm of the group. IDA finances projects that support development in a country but which, due to externalities, cannot be undertaken by the private sector, projects are often in the fields of education, health, and infrastructure.

IFC, on the other hand, undertakes projects in cooperation with private sector firms. It tries to play the role of a catalyst that brings together private sector organizations in the industrialized and the developing countries. Over a few years, IFC has emphasized the role that stock markets can play in the developing process and has played a leading role in the development of the emerging stock exchanges.

The World Bank relies on two sources of funds. Subscriptions of its members constitutes the primary source of funds for the organization. In 1992, these subscriptions totalled $152 billion. The Bank also raises funds in international capital markets largely in the form of bonds. In its funding activities, World Bank has been somewhat of a pioneer. It is an active user of swaps and the first ever issuer of global bonds.

A number of other institutions, known as development banks, also channel development assistance to developing countries. These banks (for example, Inter-American Development Bank, Asian Development Bank, and African Development Bank) attempt to meet the development needs of specific geographic regions. Of these banks, European Development Banks for Reconstruction and Development was established in 1990 to help modernize the economies of countries in Central and Eastern Europe. By the fall of 1993, however, this bank had only managed to draw public uproar over its president, Jacques Attali's modernization of bank's headquarters in London which had used up more funds than the entire amount that had been spent on the modernization of the countries that it was supposed to help.

Notes

1. Regulation, as we had discussed in the first chapter of this book, is critical for financial transactions. For details on the regulation of international equity markets, see Joseph A. Grundfest, "International-ization of the World's Securities Markets: Economic Causes and Regulatory Consequences," in Marvin H. Koster and Allan H. Meltzer, (eds.), *International Competitiveness in Financial Services*, Kluwer Academic Publishers, 1990, pp. 349-378.

2. "Searching for Overseas Stock Plays? Consider U.S. Multinational, Some Say," *The Wall Street Journal*, June 1, 1993, p. C1–C2.

3. Euromoney, *Markets 1993*, Supplement in March 1993, page 6.

4. "Foreign Stocks and Bond Markets Lured Record Levels of U.S. Investment in 1992," *The Wall Street Journal*, May 4, 1993, p. C1.

5. Euromoney, *World Equity Markets*, May 1993.

6. For some more details, see Euromoney, *World Equity Markets*, May 1993.

7. Arthur Anderson & Co., *European Capital Markets: A Strategic Forecast*, Special Report No. 1161, 1989.

8. Euromoney, *Key Figures*, May 1993, p. 158.

9. "Small Investor Continues to Give Up Control of Stocks," *The Wall Street Journal*, May 11, 1992, p. C1.

10. Euromoney, *World Equity Markets,* May 1993, p. 4.

11. "More Pension Cash Goes Overseas," *Fortune,* November 18, 1991, p. 14.

12. Ibid.

Chapter 8

Diversification in International Markets

The three previous chapters have explained the workings of three important segments of international financial markets: short–term debt or money markets, long–term debt or bond markets, and equity markets. When we discussed these markets, our focus was on both lenders and borrowers. In this chapter we want to limit our perspective to that of investors, that is, the lenders of funds, and discuss some issues concerning the role that these markets should play in the overall investment strategies of the investors.

Simply stated, we want to discuss the importance of including international money, bond, and equity market instruments in the portfolios of investors. The advantage of investing in international instruments derives from the basic principles of diversification: an investor can improve the performance of a portfolio by including assets whose returns are uncorrelated with each other. In this chapter, we want to highlight the importance of searching for assets with uncorrelated returns not only within one economy but in different economies. We will show that economic activities in different countries in the global economy are themselves uncorrelated with each other. Hence, including assets from different economies will reduce the systematic risk of a portfolio below what would be possible with domestic investments alone.

We begin with a quick review of the theory of portfolio investments, reminding the readers of the importance of diversification and the concepts of systematic risk and optimal portfolios. This is followed by a discussion of the importance of international diversification. We then discuss the evidence for the lack of perfect correlation between various economies of the world. The chapter ends with a discussion of the importance of exchange risk associated with international portfolio investments and the gains that an investor can derive from international diversification.

Fundamentals of the Theory of Investments

The most fundamental concept in investments is the idea of risk–return trade–off. Since every rational investor would like as high a return as possible and as low a risk as possible, competition between investors creates a hierarchy of assets such that assets with higher returns also have higher risks. This trade–off, that higher returns are expected to be accompanied by higher risks, affects how investors make their investment decisions, which in turn determines the prices at which assets sell in the marketplace. Let us first be clear about how risk and return are measured and the idea of trade–off between the two.

We measure the return on an asset as the percentage increase in the price of the asset, taking into account any payments (interest or dividends) that may have been made during the period. When an asset is purchased, we expect it to have a certain return over a certain period of time. We will call this the *ex ante* or expected return on the asset. After we have held the asset for the stipulated time period, we may find that the asset has not appreciated by the amount we expected. The *ex post* or actual return may not equal the *ex ante* return. The risk that the return will change from period to period is measured by the standard deviation of the return. The trade–off between risk and return can now be shown graphically as in Exhibit 8.1.

The exhibit shows the risk–return profiles of a number of assets. Consider first only the three points A, B, and C. Asset A has the highest return and the highest risk. Asset C has the lowest risk and the lowest return. Asset B, however, has the same return as Asset C, but the same

Exhibit 8.1
Trade–off Between Risk and Return

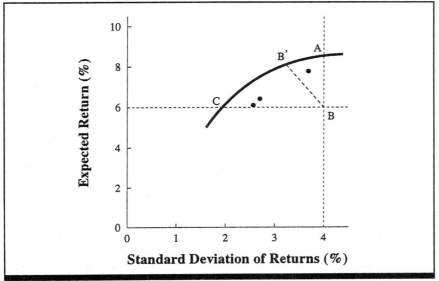

Standard Deviation of Returns (%)

risk as Asset A. The choice between B and either one of the other two assets is quite clear. An investor has no incentive to hold B since Asset A can give a higher return for the same level of risk and Asset C can give the same return for a lower level of risk. The investor's choice is only between A and C. We will return later to how the investor makes the choice between these two. No rational investor will buy Asset B. The seller of this asset, therefore, will either have to sell the asset at a discount such that the expected return on the asset rises to the level of A or provide some guarantees so that the risk falls to the level of C. It is also possible that the seller may do a bit of both such that the risk falls a bit and the return rises a bit. The risk–return profile of B will have to shift to B' at which point it falls on what is called the efficient frontier. At B' the choice for the investor becomes difficult and includes three assets—A, B' and C.

Which of these assets an investor chooses depends upon the nature of the investor. Most investors are known as "risk averse," that is, they prefer not to take risk. Due to their aversion to risk, these investors will pay some price for not having to take risk. One way to look at this price is that, given a choice between receiving $100 with certainty or receiving "x" dollars with a probability of 50 percent (such as in a fair coin toss where "x" dollars are paid if the coins turns up heads and zero dollars if the coin turns up tails), risk averse investors will accept the uncertain payment only if "x" were more than $200. In contrast to risk averse investors, there are gamblers who like to take risks. Gamblers will accept less than $200 in the coin toss since they like the thrill of gambling. The third kind of investors are called risk neutral investors. These investors neither like nor shun risk. Such an investor would set the value of "x" at exactly $200. Since most of the investors are known to be risk averse (at least for large sums of money relevant for financial decisions, even though they may be classified as gamblers for small sums such as those involved in lottery tickets or horse races), financial theory in large part is developed with the assumption that investors will pay to get rid of risk. The theory of investments centers on determining the price that most investors will pay to get rid of risk.

We begin our discussion of the theory of investments with the simple notion that the objective of every investor is to maximize the value of her or his portfolio. This objective must be attained with the help of various assets available in the financial markets. We must, therefore, understand on the one hand how investors choose assets, given the prices of all the assets, and on the other hand, how the decisions of investors affect the prices of assets.

Let us make a simplifying assumption at the beginning of the analysis. We will relax this assumption very soon. Let us assume that each asset can be chosen independently of all other assets, that is, we assume that each asset's contribution to the portfolio is completely independent of all the other assets in the portfolio. (We could have also made the assumption that each investor is allowed to purchase only one asset; either of these assumptions would lead us to the same conclusion.) Given this assumption, the only thing that the investor can do is choose the asset that offers the best trade–off between risk and return. If we allow for the fact that each investor will have a different price of risk, that is, investors will have different degrees of risk aversion, there will be one asset that offers the best combination of risk and return from the point of view of each investor.

Exhibit 8.2
Choice Between Risky Assets

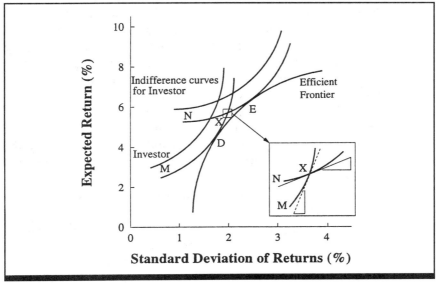

Each investor's trade–off between risk and return can be shown as an indifference curve as in Exhibit 8.2. An investor's indifference curve shows the trade–off between risk and return that the *investor* is willing to accept, the rate at which the investor is willing to substitute risk for return. The exhibit shows indifference curves for two investors—M and N. Which of these two is willing to take more risk? The answer, if not obvious from the shape of the curves, can be derived by looking at a point of intersection X. Tangents to the indifference curves at point X show that for 1 percent increase in risk, investor M wants the return to increase by more than does Investor N. Hence, M is more risk averse than N. Each investor's choice, given the shape of the indifference curves, is clear. Investor M receives the best combination of risk and return from Asset D and Investor N from Asset E. Thus, given our assumption that returns on assets are independent of each other, each investor will purchase only one asset for the portfolio—M will purchase only Asset D and N will purchase only Asset E.

Diversification in International Markets   213

The assumption of independence of the returns on assets, however, is not a realistic assumption. Recognizing that the returns on assets are related to each other gives rise to benefits of portfolio diversification. The idea of diversification of portfolios derives from the observation that different assets respond in different ways to changes in economic conditions. Consider two stocks for a moment: one in a company manufacturing new autos and the other in a garage that specializes in rebuilding old autos. How would these two shares respond to an economic recession? To an economic boom? The stock in the auto manufacturer's firm will rise and fall with the economy; as the economy booms, demand for new autos will increase and the company's stock will rise. The stock of the garage, however, should respond in exactly the opposite fashion; demand for its services will increase in a recession and fall in an economic boom. Which stock should an investor buy if we are not sure of whether the next period will be a boom or a recession? The answer for an investor who wants to play it safe would be to include a bit of both in her or his portfolio. In this way, at least one of the stocks will rise regardless of which way the economy turns. The investor would, in effect, be diversifying her or his portfolio and would end up with a portfolio with a better risk–return profile than if she or he would have purchased only one stock. The diversification benefit was obtained because the returns on the two stocks are negatively correlated with each other—as the return on one stock goes down, the return on the other goes up.

The benefit of diversification can be shown more rigorously with some notations. If there was only one asset in the portfolio, say, Asset C from Exhibit 8.1, the expected return and risk of the portfolio would be the same as those of Asset C. If the risk is measured as the variance (or the standard deviation), and if E represents the expectations, then:

$$E(R_p) = E(R_c)$$

and

$$\text{Var}(R_p) = \text{Var}(R_c)$$

With two assets, say A and C, with the portfolio divided between A and C in weights w_a and w_c such that $w_a + w_c = 1$, the return and the risk of the portfolio will be given by:

$$E(R_p) = w_a \times E(R_a) + w_c \times E(R_c)$$

and

$$Var(R_p) = (w_a)^2 \times Var(R_a) + (w_c)^2 \times Var(R_c)$$
$$+ 2 \times w_a \times w_c \times COV(R_a, R_c)$$

(8.1)

$COV(A, C)$ is the covariance of the returns of A and C and is obtained from the standard deviations (σ) of the returns of A and C:

$$COV(R_a, R_c) = \sigma(A) \times \sigma(C) \times r_{a,c} \qquad (8.2)$$

where $r_{a,c}$ is the correlation between the returns of the two assets. If the correlation is negative, the last term in Equation 8.1 becomes negative and hence the variance of the portfolio becomes less than the weighted average of the variance of the two assets. To understand the benefits of diversification, suppose that the two assets, F and G, have exactly the same expected return and the same risk (as measured by their respective variance), but that their returns are negatively correlated. A portfolio created by combining these two assets (and the weights w_f and w_g do not really matter) will have exactly the same return as either of the two assets, but the variance of the portfolio will now be less than that of either asset because the last term, the term for the variance of the portfolio, in Equation 8.1 will be negative. By combining assets with negative correlations, the investor is able to reduce the risk of the portfolio without sacrificing any return.

It is actually not necessary that the correlation between two assets be negative. If the correlation is less than one, the variance of the portfolio will be reduced by mixing the two assets. In the example of the two assets with the same returns and the same risk, the variance of the portfolio will be less than the variance of either asset as long as the two assets are less than perfectly correlated.

We can extend the idea of diversification to more than two assets. It should be obvious that as we combine more assets, we will be able to reduce the risk of the portfolio even more. Adding more assets, however, will reduce the risk of the portfolio by lesser and lesser amounts since it will become more and more difficult to find assets which offer some benefits that are not already offered by existing assets in the portfolio. When all assets in an economy are combined in a portfolio, there will still be some risk left in the portfolio. The extent of diversification that can be achieved with the help of a large number of assets in one economy, say the United States, is shown in Exhibit 8.3 by the curve "U.S. Assets." The vertical axis of the exhibit shows the risk of a portfolio of more than one asset as a percentage of the risk of the one

Exhibit 8.3
Systematic Risk:
Domestic and International Portfolios

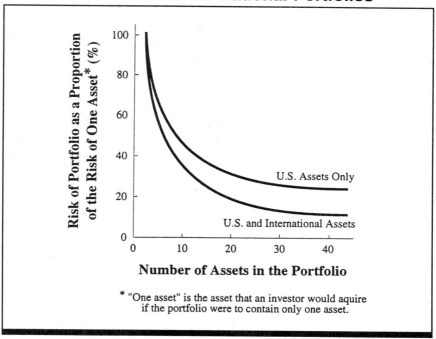

Number of Assets in the Portfolio

* "One asset" is the asset that an investor would aquire
if the portfolio were to contain only one asset.

asset that an investor would purchase if she or he could purchase only one asset. Research shows that the benefit of diversification within the United States becomes very small once between 15 to 20 well–chosen stocks have been included in a portfolio.[1] Whatever risk remains in the portfolio after all of the possible assets have been included is called the **systematic risk** of the portfolio. In Exhibit 8.3, this risk is shown as the risk when the curve becomes horizontal. With a portfolio of only U.S. stocks, the systematic risk of the portfolio would be about one fourth of the risk of the most attractive single asset. Diversification into different assets removes the **unsystematic risk** from the portfolio.

With a large number of assets available, the challenge for an investor is to choose assets in such proportions that the best combination of risk and return is obtained. Given that each investor may have a different indifference curve, each portfolio may end up looking different. However, since investors' choices of assets affect asset demand and supply, market prices of assets settle down in equilibrium in such a way that the market–place as a whole ends up having one optimal portfolio. Individual investors end up choosing the right mix of risk and return by combining different proportions of a risk free asset and the market portfolio. For the purpose of understanding the benefits of international diversification, we do not need to demonstrate the construction of this market portfolio.

Benefits of International Diversification

If a U.S. investor can obtain most of the benefits of diversification by investing in about 20 stocks, what possible benefits could be had from investing abroad? Although a legitimate question, it is answered by referring to the idea of systematic risk. For a U.S. investor, systematic risk can be understood by imagining an investor who has enough wealth to purchase every single asset in the country. Although this investor's risk is diversified as much as is possible within the United States, there is still the possibility that the U.S. economy will face swings and the value of the investor's wealth will fluctuate. The only risk that is left in this investor's portfolio is systematic risk. To reduce the risk even further, the investor must look for assets that are not correlated with the U.S. economy. Therefore, the investor will have to look at other countries for these investments. Non–U.S. economies will be able to offer U.S. investors benefits of diversification that are not available within the

United States because at any point in time, most of these economies are in a different phase of the economic cycle than the United States. Diversification into foreign economies will reduce the systematic risk for U.S. investors to levels less than would be possible with U.S. investments alone. The curve marked as "U.S. and International Assets" in Exhibit 8.3 gives an idea of what the new levels of systematic risk may be. With a portfolio of U.S. and international stocks, an investor is able to reduce the systematic risk of the portfolio to about one eighth of the risk of the single most attractive asset. Non–U.S. investors would also benefit from investments in the United States and other countries in addition to investments in their own economies.

Whether or not benefits of diversification into international markets are real depends upon the correlations of the returns of these markets with those of the United States. We must examine the actual returns to answer the questions regarding the potential for diversification benefits.

Exhibit 8.4 provides estimates of simple correlations between the monthly returns of the stock markets for 12 countries for the period of 1960–92. All the returns for this exhibit are calculated in terms of the currency of the country, without making any corrections for changes in the exchange rates of the countries. The monthly returns are calculated as the percentage change in the stock market indexes reported by the International Monetary Fund without making adjustment for dividends that may have been declared. The numbers in this exhibit, therefore, must be interpreted with caution. Each number in the exhibit shows the correlation between the monthly returns of the stock market of the country on the left of the number with the monthly returns of the stock market of the country above the number. Clearly, the number in the cell with the same country on the left and at the head of the column is 1.0. The correlation coefficients reported in the exhibit demonstrate quite clearly that none of these 12 economies is perfectly correlated with any other economy. The highest correlation is about 0.64—between Germany and the Netherlands. The highest correlation for the U.S. economy is with Canada—a correlation of about 0.63.

From the perspective of an investor in a specific country, the relevant rates of return will be those calculated in the investor's currency. To calculate these returns from the perspective of a U.S. investor, we convert the value of the stock market index from its local currency value into dollars at the beginning and end of the month. The percentage change

Exhibit 8.4
Correlations of Returns in Local Currencies
1960–1992

	US	France	Germany	Japan	Canada	Netherlands
US	1.00000					
France	0.33561	1.00000				
Germany	0.38440	0.32844	1.00000			
Japan	0.32394	0.17713	0.22613	1.00000		
Canada	0.62582	0.35638	0.23615	0.24780	1.00000	
Netherlands	0.60434	0.37556	0.64377	0.35399	0.34790	1.00000
Denmark	0.16960	0.12656	0.18739	0.17805	0.19896	0.19969
Finland	0.12946	0.21526	0.20691	0.20688	0.12418	0.25516
Austria	0.14439	0.18554	0.32174	0.10123	0.10836	0.25615
Spain	0.27417	0.18447	0.23736	0.20286	0.20183	0.28618
Switzerland	0.52245	0.39733	0.52363	0.29168	0.37658	0.61848
UK	0.52386	0.21927	0.31288	0.29452	0.33414	0.46877

	Denmark	Finland	Austria	Spain	Switzerland	UK
Denmark	1.00000					
Finland	0.10553	1.00000				
Austria	0.08062	0.16882	1.00000			
Spain	0.21793	0.24172	0.11731	1.00000		
Switzerland	0.17363	0.18167	0.25031	0.24211	1.00000	
UK	0.16319	0.16416	0.11779	0.23654	0.37004	1.00000

in the dollar value of the index then provides an estimate of the monthly rate of return in dollars. Correlations between rates of return calculated in this manner are summarized in Exhibit 8.5. The correlations lead to almost the same conclusions as those from Exhibit 8.4. Most correlations are less than about 1/3 and many are as small as .10 or 10 percent. Most of the high correlations are between economies that are generally known to be well integrated with each other: the United States and Canada, Germany, the Netherlands, and Switzerland, etc. The United States stock markets seem to be well connected to those in Canada, the Netherlands, and the United Kingdom, and not very well connected to those in Finland and Austria. Likewise, some of the European economies seem to be integrated with each other—a reflection of the close trade and investment ties between the economies as well as of close coordination of economic polices between these countries. The two Scandinavian countries included in this study—Finland and Denmark—seem to be more independent of other countries. This is not surprising for Finland but it is for Denmark. Denmark is one of the first countries to have joined the European Common Market. Interestingly, there are very few cases of negative correlations.

We would also like to know if the pattern of correlations between countries has been undergoing some changes over the past two or three decades. Exhibit 8.6 summarizes the correlations of the returns on the U.S. stock market with those of other countries over each of the past three decades: 1960 to 1969, 1970 to 1979, and 1980 to 1992. The division based on the 1960s and 1970s is somewhat arbitrary but illustrates some trends quite well. In many cases we observe an increase in the value of the correlation over time. For many of these countries, the correlation is the lowest in the 1960s and the highest in the 1980s. This is partly an indication of the increased globalization of the financial markets around the world—financial markets in different countries are becoming more and more integrated over time. As markets become more integrated, same global events affect prices in all stock markets and investors and speculators have more information and opportunities for removing price discrepancies. Their actions ensure that the stock markets in different countries move in tandem.

The pattern of correlations indicate that investors in any of these countries would gain from diversification into other countries. To see if an investor would really benefit from international diversification, let us

Exhibit 8.5
Correlations of Returns in Dollars
1960–1992

	US	France	Germany	Japan	Canada	Netherlands
US	1.00000					
France	0.30001	1.00000				
Germany	0.32780	0.42041	1.00000			
Japan	0.28613	0.27608	0.31486	1.00000		
Canada	0.61546	0.34768	0.23954	0.22959	1.00000	
Netherlands	0.52215	0.43281	0.73031	0.41899	0.34460	1.00000
Denmark	0.16231	0.24934	0.33754	0.29616	0.23627	0.35354
Finland	0.10523	0.24802	0.27215	0.26518	0.15871	0.28933
Austria	0.12270	0.30643	0.47689	0.19275	0.12313	0.41843
Spain	0.24018	0.24867	0.27843	0.26834	0.20467	0.33018
Switzerland	0.43564	0.46158	0.61875	0.38053	0.35314	0.69930
UK	0.48420	0.27906	0.36535	0.34372	0.35911	0.48338

	Denmark	Finland	Austria	Spain	Switzerland	UK
Denmark	1.00000					
Finland	0.18956	1.00000				
Austria	0.25489	0.25052	1.00000			
Spain	0.28244	0.26401	0.17726	1.00000		
Switzerland	0.33518	0.23391	0.38444	0.25725	1.00000	
UK	0.25758	0.17719	0.19461	0.28360	0.39803	1.00000

Exhibit 8.6
Correlations Between the U.S. and Other Markets by Each Decade

Returns in Local Currencies

	France	Germany	Japan	Canada	Netherlands	UK
1960–69	0.30084	0.30710	0.12772	0.68436	0.67784	0.34906
1970–79	0.21118	0.39147	0.44590	0.56275	0.52485	0.56158
1980–92	0.46730	0.46315	0.40945	0.65911	0.61879	0.59666

	Denmark	Finland	Austria	Spain	Switzerland
1960–69	−0.06309	0.09398	0.01118	0.00144	0.52660
1970–79	0.18737	0.19787	0.16152	0.24080	0.48594
1980–92	0.24840	0.10430	0.21561	0.35432	0.56074

Returns in Dollars

	France	Germany	Japan	Canada	Netherlands	UK
1960–69	0.30168	0.30857	0.12252	0.68797	0.67987	0.37724
1970–79	0.22461	0.36292	0.42414	0.55527	0.49078	0.54410
1980–92	0.37551	0.32566	0.29226	0.64102	0.46827	0.48847

	Denmark	Finland	Austria	Spain	Switzerland
1960–69	−0.04433	0.08715	0.01156	0.04352	0.52363
1970–79	0.22898	0.22968	0.17942	0.19613	0.43153
1980–92	0.18934	0.03978	0.15415	0.31467	0.39231

make some decisions on behalf of a hypothetical investor. Let us imagine that Paul had foreseen the benefits of international diversification in the early 1980s and was interested in investing abroad. In the early months of 1980, he had data on how the various stock markets had performed over the previous two decades. In addition to our Exhibits 8.4 and 8.5, he had the left half of Exhibit 8.7, which shows the performance of each stock market during the 1970s (the right half—which only became available in 1993—will be used later in this example). Making the best possible assumption that the markets will perform in the future more or less as they had done in the 1970s, and not knowing much of sophisticated finance theory which would have helped build an optimal portfolio, he decided to choose only a few countries in which to invest. First he chose Japan because of its excellent performance in the 1970s. Then he chose Finland and Austria as two out of three markets with very low correlations with the U.S. market, and then France because he valued the French government's rhetoric about its need to be independent of the

Exhibit 8.7
Performance of Stock Markets
Monthly Returns in U.S. Dollars

| Country | Performance in 1970s | | Performance in 1980s | |
	Mean Return	Standard Deviation	Mean Return	Standard Deviation
US	0.225691	3.833348	0.998250	3.763597
France	0.839204	8.324360	0.986661	7.096404
Germany	0.520295	4.552429	0.731960	5.467630
Japan	1.268226	4.864170	1.285379	5.963574
Canada	0.539333	5.123973	0.498007	5.558130
Netherlands	0.461869	5.030282	1.036542	4.841923
Denmark	0.873354	5.372403	1.161964	5.936114
Finland	0.789579	4.130834	1.019089	5.733731
Austria	0.852160	3.629077	0.911649	6.999583
Spain	−0.332660	5.837958	0.993456	7.352613
Switzerland	0.738113	5.094587	0.818588	5.309926
UK	0.625154	7.708095	1.008056	5.190702

rest of the world in its economic policies. He decided that he would keep half his portfolio in the United States and divide the rest equally between the four countries. He also decided to leave that portfolio untouched for at least ten years.

How would this global portfolio perform compared to the single country portfolios? Exhibit 8.8 plots the performances of the 12 markets and of Paul's portfolio. The global portfolio ends up with a mean return of 0.96 percent/month with a standard deviation of 3.32 percent, compared to the U.S. portfolio with a mean return of 1.00 percent/month and a standard deviation of 3.76 percent. With the global portfolio, Paul ended up with a return which was about 4 percent less than what he would have received by investing only in the United States, but the risk of his portfolio decreased by almost 12 percent (as measured by the

Exhibit 8.8
Means and Standard Deviations
of the 12 Markets, 1980–1992
(monthly returns in dollars)

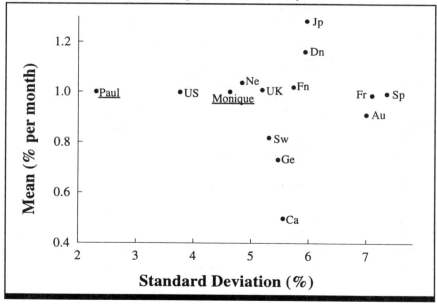

standard deviation). The advantage of the lower risk for him is that had he needed the funds before the end of 1992, there was a greater chance that he would have received a return closer to his average return with a global portfolio than with a purely domestic one.

What if the investor had been French? Assume that Monique had also decided to invest globally and had followed a strategy similar to Paul's: invest half the funds within her domestic economy—France—and divide the remainder equally between the four other countries. Her global portfolio will provide a mean monthly return of 0.98 percent with a standard deviation of 4.76 percent, a far superior performance than that of the French stock market over the same period. The French market had a risk of 7.10 percent for almost the same level of return.

This example, although somewhat arbitrary, illustrates two important points about international diversification. First, it seems clear that investors in all countries gain from international diversification of their portfolios. We were able to illustrate this with diversification into only four countries and with arbitrary weights assigned to the investment in each country. Second, the example illustrates the problem of data: we have to make decisions based on past data without being sure that the past data are a fair reflection of what will happen in the future. As Exhibit 8.6 demonstrates, the correlations among various markets in the 1980s were very different from those in the 1970s. Even the average returns and standard deviations of the markets in the two periods, as shown in the right half of Exhibit 8.7, were very different. The correlation between the average return of a market in the 1970s and that in the 1980s was an insignificant 0.28 for the sample of 12 markets.

This example may have given the impression that an investor has to be lucky to find the best international portfolio. That is not the case. Investment theory provides the exact methodology for determining an optimal portfolio. The calculations, however, become very complex when the number of assets increases because the correlation between every pair of assets has to be taken into account. We will return to the issue of the optimal portfolio in a later section.

Are the Diversification Benefits Transitory?

One of the observations we made in the previous section was that increased globalization of financial markets seems to be increasing the correlations between various markets. We could discern a weak support for this trend in higher correlations between markets during the 1980s that was not there during the 1960s. Can we then draw a conclusion that if globalization of markets continues, the benefits of international diversification will disappear? Will international diversification become irrelevant, especially because we had also remarked that an investor can reduce most of the unsystematic risk by investing in no more than about 15 to 20 stocks? In integrated global markets, prices of all assets will be determined as if they were in an international market, and an investor would not have to buy more than a few domestic stocks to acquire a fairly safe portfolio.

Although this would seem like a plausible scenario, there are other factors that will make international diversification relevant. Recent research has identified three reasons, the first one of which is a mere technicality, that indicate that there will always be a need for international diversification, at least in the foreseeable future.[2] First, the stock market indexes in different countries will not have a perfect correlation because they are constructed in different ways. Some indexes are based on a wide selection of stocks from the country, and others are chosen from only some of the firms. Thus, if we compare the stock market indexes for countries reported by the Financial Times of London, which are known as FT Actuaries/Goldman Sachs National Equity Market indexes, we find that the index for the United States is made of 553 firms, whereas that for Mexico contains only 13 firms. Although some difference between the number of firms included in the index can be expected based upon the size of the economies, the proportions used in the FT/Goldman Sachs indexes do not reflect those differences. In addition to the number of firms, these country indexes represent different concentrations of industries. Some indexes, for example those for the United States and the United Kingdom, include a large number of industries whereas others, for example those for Mexico, New Zealand, and South Africa, include only a few industries from these countries.

The second, and perhaps the main reason, why the stock market returns will not be perfectly correlated for a long time to come has to do with the industrial structures of the countries. Industrial structures, that is, the importance of different industries within a country, are known to differ from country to country. The differences are explained by resource endowments of countries, that is, natural resources that exist in a country, as well as by differences in the levels of development and the structures of demand within the countries. The stock markets of countries reflect the composition of the industries within those countries or the industrial structures of the countries. In so far as the importance of a particular industry varies across countries, the fluctuations of activity in that industry will affect the stock market indexes of these countries by different amounts. Until such time when industrial structures of countries become identical, the stock markets of different countries will continue to have some degree of independence from those of other countries.

Third, the exchange rate changes influence the returns of a country's stock market when measured in another currency, say, the dollar. If the exchange rates continue to change at least partially in a random fashion, the stock market returns measured in a foreign currency will also show some degree of independence from that of other countries. We will discuss the impact of exchange rate changes on portfolio investments in more detail in the following section.

In summary, the economic structures of countries are different enough that rates of return on stock market indexes will continue to offer some degree of diversification benefits for investors. Over time, as industries and financial markets across the world begin to integrate, the benefits of diversification will be incorporated in the prices of the stocks themselves, and investors will not have to think about international diversification as much as they may need to now. There will, however, still be some benefits to such diversification.

Unique Risk of International Investments

All investments involve some degree of risk, either a credit risk that the funds will not be repaid in full, or an opportunity risk that once the funds have been committed to one investment, better opportunities will become available. International investments are no exception. In addition, however, these investments involve an additional risk that is absent, at least directly, in domestic investments: the foreign exchange risk.

Exchange risk arises because the investor and the investment are in different countries. By definition, we are talking about investments in a foreign country (except when we refer to "euro" markets—Eurocurrency or Eurobonds). In the contemporary global economy, each country uses its own currency and, hence, when an investor in one country has to purchase an asset in another country, it is necessary to convert one currency into another. Exchange rates at which funds are converted tend to fluctuate and change. Since investments mature in a different time period than the one in which they are made, chances are that the exchange rate at the time the investment capital has to be repatriated will be different from the one that was in existence when the funds were invested. Hence, the exchange risk.

For international portfolio investments, exchange risk means that the investor has to take into consideration not only the return of the asset in its currency of denomination, but also the change in the exchange rate. Consider an investment of I_o in a foreign asset which is made by converting dollars at an exchange rate of e_o. The investment yields a cash flow of I_t a year later when the exchange rate is e_t. The return on the investment can be calculated as:

$$R_{lc} = \frac{(I_t - I_o)}{I_o}$$ (8.3)

and

$$R_\$ = \frac{I_t \times e_t - I_o \times e_o}{I_o \times e_o}$$ (8.4)

where R_{lc} represents the return in local currency (the currency in which the investment is made) and $R_\$$ is the return in dollars. Over short periods of time, when the exchange rate changes are not very large, the above equation can be reduced to:

$$R_\$ = (1 + R_{lc}) \times (1 + R_e) - 1$$ (8.5)

where R_e represents the change in the exchange rate. Equation 8.5 merely states the obvious: the rate of return in dollars on an investment in a foreign currency is the net of rates of return in the foreign currency and the return on the exchange rate. The importance of this equation, however, is in measuring the risk of this investment. When the returns are measured over small periods of time, the previous equation can be reduced to:

$$R_\$ = R_{lc} + R_e \qquad (8.6)$$

The risk of this investment, as measured by the variance of $R_\$$, will be given by:

$$\text{Var}(R_\$) = \text{Var}(R_{lc}) + \text{Var}(R_e) + 2.SD(R_{lc}).SD(R_e).\text{Corr}(R_{lc}, R_e)$$
$$(8.7)$$

The value of this equation is in highlighting that it is not only the change in the exchange rate that matters, but also the correlation between the exchange rate changes and the price of the asset. The equation points out the importance of recognizing the links between exchange rate changes and the changes in the stock and the bond markets. It is possible that the same factors that cause exchange rates to change also cause the prices of assets to change. The exchange risk associated with an international investment cannot be assessed independently of the risk associated with the foreign currency value of the assets. When we evaluate the desirability of purchasing a stock in, say, Japan, we need to assess (1) how the Japanese stock market will perform, (2) how the yen will perform, and (3) whether the unexpected changes in yen offset or compound the unexpected changes in Japanese stock markets.

To assess the exchange risk associated with international investments appropriately, we have to assess the extent of the correlation between the foreign exchange and asset markets. The theoretical answer to this query, unfortunately, is not any easier than our question in Chapter 3 regarding the determinants of exchange rates. You may recall that we offered a number of explanations for what causes exchange rates to change, without being able to identify the variables that would allow us to forecast exchange rates with any confidence. Our main conclusion from the discussion of economic theory was that the values of currencies which have become international currencies are determined very largely by the actions of speculators. These actions are not predictable, and we had to conclude that most of the fluctuations in the exchange rates are random fluctuations. Values of currencies that are not used by speculators tend to follow predictions of traditional economic models a little better. These conclusions are also helpful in assessing the exchange risk of international investments. We can expect that the correlations between exchange rate changes and the changes in stock prices will be unpredictable for the currencies of the major industrialized countries. For the smaller countries, both the exchange rates and the stock prices may change in predictable fashion, and we can expect somewhat higher correlations between the two.

For most of the countries, however, it is very difficult to estimate and manage the exchange risk. Investors can manage the exchange risk by purchasing futures or forward contracts on foreign currencies to hedge their investment exposure in the foreign currencies. Empirical evidence seems not to support this approach. We will return to this issue for a more detailed analysis of the hedging techniques in Chapter 11.

Optimal Allocation of Assets in International Markets

Once an investor recognizes that international diversification is beneficial, how can he or she decide what the optimal portfolio should look like? The answer to this is very similar to the answer for our same question concerning domestic investments. We will briefly review the theory regarding building the optimal domestic portfolio and then extend it to international investments.

With the choice of a number of domestic assets, the selection of the optimal portfolio depends upon the indifference curves of the investor on the one hand and the characteristics of the assets on the other. Exhibit 8.9 illustrates the interaction between these two for the case of two assets, A and C. The set of choices for the investor depends upon the correlations between the two assets. If the two assets are perfectly correlated, that is, the correlation is 1.0, an investor has the choice of allocating the portfolio

Exhibit 8.9
Correlation Between Assets
and Portfolio Choices

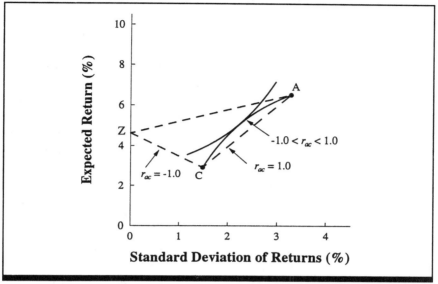

anywhere on the line joining A and C. The risk and return of the portfolio will be given by the line AC depending upon what proportions were invested in each of the two assets. If the correlation were −1.0, that is, the assets moved in exactly opposite directions, the investor's choices will be given by the lines AZ and ZC. Notice that in this case, the investor is able to build a risk free portfolio at point Z by investing half the amount of funds in each of the two assets. For a more realistic case when the correlation between the two assets is somewhere between −1.0 and +1.0, the choices are given by the curve AC. The point of tangency between this curve and the investor's indifference curve gives the point where the investor has the best possible combination of risk and return, given the choice of two assets for investment.

The design of the optimal portfolio, thus, depends upon the risks, returns, and correlations between the assets available and the preferences of the investor regarding the price he or she is willing to pay for risk.

The same holds true when there are more than two assets. The investor will first derive the opportunity set available given the choice of assets and then choose the point on the opportunity set that provides the highest level of satisfaction. In practice, it is possible to construct a market portfolio that reflects market consensus regarding the price of risk, and each investor can then choose any level of risk and return by combining the market portfolio and a risk free asset. Since the market equilibrium is not of concern to us, we will not deal with that extension of the theory of investments.

The extension of this analysis to international investments is quite straightforward. Instead of only domestic assets, the investor will have to take into account all the assets available in the global market place. The optimal portfolio will be built in exactly the same fashion as the optimal domestic portfolio. The only difference is that, with an international portfolio, the investor will also have to think of the exchange risk. All the returns will have to be calculated in the investor's currency. Changes in exchange rates can make very important differences in what the optimal portfolios will look like.

In an important study carried out to demonstrate the importance of exchange rate changes for international portfolios, Choel Eun and Bruce Resnick built optimal portfolios for residents of different countries. They allowed investors to own country funds rather than individual stock in the countries. Their analysis shows that because of exchange rate changes, investors in different countries will hold very different portfolios. U.S. investors, for example, will hold a portfolio consisting of Japan, the Netherlands, and Sweden country funds. Swedish investors, on the other hand, will hold their country's assets in addition to those in the Netherlands, Hong Kong, and Singapore.[3] The optimal portfolios for each country's investors, in other words, depend upon the interaction of the characteristics of the assets, exchange rate changes, and the indifference curves of the investors themselves. Their study, however, confirms unequivocally that investors will gain from international diversification.

Exhibit 8.10, reproduced from their study, shows the mean return and standard deviations for domestic as well as the optimal international portfolios for residents of 15 countries. In addition to these statistics, the authors also calculated a Sharp performance measure (SHP). This SHP is

Exhibit 8.10
Gains from International Diversification by Country

Investor's Habitat	Domestic Portfolio			Optimal International Portfolio			
	Mean (%)	S.D. (%)	SHP	Mean (%)	S.D. (%)	SHP	SHP*
Australia	0.76	7.12	0.048	1.24	4.54	0.1809	0.1327
Belgium	0.82	4.40	0.092	1.08	3.83	0.1718	0.0802
Canada	0.93	5.94	0.086	1.21	4.40	0.1806	0.0942
France	0.64	6.62	0.034	1.08	3.93	0.1695	0.1358
Germany	0.61	3.87	0.024	0.85	4.50	0.0965	0.0716
Hong Kong	1.11	13.48	0.051	1.17	4.47	0.1682	0.1175
Italy	0.92	7.84	0.064	1.68	4.34	0.2899	0.2257
Japan	0.55	4.10	0.032	0.87	4.64	0.0971	0.0647
Netherlands	0.76	4.83	0.071	0.88	4.29	0.1078	0.0368
Singapore	0.80	9.70	0.040	0.86	4.70	0.0945	0.0550
Spain	0.04	5.26	−0.072	1.61	4.91	0.2438	0.3156
Sweden	1.52	5.42	0.204	1.34	3.78	0.2443	0.0408
Switzerland	0.32	4.56	−0.021	0.77	5.07	0.0688	0.0901
UK	1.26	8.40	0.100	1.32	4.27	0.2118	0.1114
US	0.57	4.84	0.032	1.09	4.87	0.1391	0.1075

*For monthly returns: January 1973–December 1982.
Source: Choel S. Eun and Bruce G. Resnick, "Currency Factor in International Portfolio Diversification," *Columbia Journal of World Business*, Summer 1985, pp. 45–53, Table 4.

an indication of the rate of substitution between risk and return and is estimated from the following equation:

$$SHP_i = \frac{(R_i - R_f)}{\sigma_i} \qquad (8.8)$$

SHP for an asset or a portfolio depends upon its rate of return, R_i, the risk free rate in the economy, R_f, and the standard deviation of the return, σ_i. For the calculations in Exhibit 8.10, it was assumed that the risk free rate was 5 percent per annum. Thus the SHP for the domestic portfolio of Australia will be:

$$SHP_{Australia} = \frac{0.76 - (5/12)}{7.12} = 0.048 \qquad (8.9)$$

A high SHP for an asset indicates that the asset provides a high return for each unit of risk associated with the asset. Exhibit 8.10 provides the values of SHP for domestic as well as international portfolios, and the change in SHP for the investors of any country that results from holding an international portfolio over a purely domestic one. In all cases, the change in SHP, shown in the last column of the exhibit, is positive. The SHP for Australian investors increases from 0.0482 to 0.1809 if they hold an optimal international portfolio rather than a purely domestic one. The SHP value for the U.S. increases more than four times. The best improvement may be for Spanish investors, whose SHP changes from a negative value (indicating that Spanish investors earned less from taking risk over the 1973–82 period than they would have gained from holding a risk free asset) to a large positive number.

The analysis for the research mentioned here was carried out by using the market index for each country rather than individual stocks. Indexes are used frequently in the United States because they seem to perform better than actively managed funds in the long run. There is a general perception that foreign market indexes do not perform as well. A skeptical investor may ask if the theory that demonstrates the benefits of international diversification would work in practice if the indexes were not reliable. The following box summarizes an investigation regarding the usefulness of foreign stock market indexes.

▼ ▼ ▼

Do Foreign Stock Market Index Funds Perform Well?

Investors who believe that markets are efficient are content to invest in funds that track market indexes instead of trying to outguess the markets by choosing stocks that may outperform the market. A market index represents a weighted average of all the shares in the market. A market index portfolio will have all the stocks in the market in the same proportion as the market itself. A market index portfolio is thus a miniature replica of the market itself. Evidence favors these conservative investors; many investors who actively manage their portfolios fail to do as well as the market as a whole. Foreign stock market indexes, however, are supposed to be more volatile and hence not very reliable.

Evidence suggests that the international index funds have done better than actively managed international funds over the long run. Index funds generally tend to outperform the managed funds when the markets are rising. Over the last few years, however, actively managed funds seem to have done better. Actively managed funds have an advantage when the manager of the fund can correctly anticipate the price peaks and take actions to avoid a loss in the value of the portfolio from a fall in the prices.

Investors need to consider indexing not only within one foreign market, but also among various foreign markets. Indexing among markets would require combining individual country indexes in some proportion that represents the importance of the country. Stock market capitalizations offer a convenient measure for the weights for mixing various country indexes. One problem with this measure, however, has been that Japan, which has a large stock market, ends up with a much larger share of the internationally indexed portfolio than many investors would desire. These investors can, of course, lower the weight for Japan, substituting stocks from Europe.

Summarized from "Foreign Index Funds Are Long Term Bets," *The Wall Street Journal*, June 24, 1993, p. C1.

▲ ▲ ▲

Why Have Investors Not Diversified in the Past?

If international investments are so attractive, why have investors shunned them for such a long time? The main reasons for the lack of extensive international diversification include capital controls, lack of information, and lack of suitable vehicles for investments.

At the present time, we talk of a globally integrated financial market in which investors and speculators are free to move their funds around the globe. This freedom, however, is a recent phenomenon. Although some countries like the United States have had very open capital markets for a long time, other industrialized countries have operated with restrictive regimes until the early 1980s. Countries used to control the inflow as well as the outflow of capital from their financial markets. It was not until the early 1980s that the Japanese government allowed Japanese investors some freedom to invest their funds in international markets. Britain imposed similar controls on its residents until 1984, although foreigners were free to carry out financial transactions in London in foreign currencies without any interference from the British government. The accompanying box provides an example of an industrialized country that had strict restrictions on capital movements until the end of 1991. Exhibit 7.11 in the previous chapter lists restrictions imposed by governments on foreign investors in emerging markets.

▼ ▼ ▼

Capital Controls: Not a Relic of the Distant Past

It was not until November 4, 1991, that Austria lifted the last of its restrictions on capital movements, a process that it had begun in 1986. Austrians will now be free to open bank accounts abroad, borrow money in foreign markets, and buy stocks and bonds abroad without having to deposit them in an Austrian bank. Foreigners will now be free to access the foreign sector of the country's financial markets without having to check with the central bank first. On the same day, Cuba announced that it is finally going to be opened for foreign investments and that investment profits will be allowed out of the country. Thus, as one country is completing the process of opening its capital markets completely, another is just beginning the process.

Summarized from *The Wall Street Journal*, November 5, 1991, p. A14.

▲ ▲ ▲

International portfolio investment levels have also been influenced by restrictions governments impose on pension funds. In the past when information on foreign stocks was not available as readily as in the United States, the U.S. government, like most other governments, had placed restrictions on the percentage of the portfolios of pension funds that could be invested in non–U.S. assets. The lack of information, as well as lack of channels through which investors could acquire foreign securities, prevented individual investors from entering foreign markets in any significant way.

The last decade has seen changes on these fronts. As we have discussed in the previous chapter, international equities are now common-place, and a number of funds are now available that allow investors to target their investments to areas that they feel will provide them with desirable rates of return. Capital controls seem to be becoming relics of the past. All the indications are that international investments will come into full bloom in the next quarter century.

Summary

The objective of an investment strategy is to maximize the value of a portfolio. The performance of an investment strategy is measured by the return that is expected to be earned, allowing for the risk associated with that return. Including a number of different assets improves the performance of a portfolio. Such a diversification can reduce risk, increase return, or both.

With the opening of international markets, diversification benefits are possible over and above what can be achieved in domestic markets. International diversification can also reduce the systematic risk of a portfolio. Such a reduction is possible because economies of different countries are not fully integrated with each other, and movement in prices of assets show significant degrees of independence. Research shows that, in spite of the globalization of economic activities in the 1980s, diversification into global markets can bring benefits to investors. Such diversification, however, introduces new types of risks, at least two of which, exchange rate risk, and interest rate risk, will be the subject of the next part of the book.

Notes

1. See E. F. Fama, *Foundations of Finance*, New York: Basic Books, 1976.

2. The remainder of the discussion on this issue is summarized from R. Roll, "Industrial Structure and the Comparative Behavior of International Stock Market Indices," *The Journal of Finance*, March 1992, pp. 3-41. Interested readers should see that article for details.

3. Choel E. Eun and Bruce Resnick, "Currency Factor in International Portfolio Diversification," *Columbia Journal of World Business*, Summer 1985, pp. 45-53.

Part III

Risk Management in International Markets

The third part of this book is devoted to risk management in international markets. Our focus is on two types of risk: foreign exchange risk and interest rate risk.

We first discuss sources of risks in international financial markets along with instruments that have been developed to manage various types of risks. Chapter 9 explains the sources of risk for different types of investors. Basics of instruments like futures, forwards, options, swaps, and other derivatives are explained in Chapter 10. The last two chapters of this section discuss how various types of risks can be managed. Chapter 11 discusses the management of foreign exchange risks, and interest rate risk is the focus of Chapter 12.

Chapter 9

The New Financial Environment and Financial Risk

The Changing Environment of Financial Markets

Financial markets around the world went through some dramatic and irreversible changes during the 1980s. With some simplification, it could be said that the world of finance went from being a series of back room deals in an old boys' network to wheeling and dealing in a Sunday morning village market. Not that a village market does not have deals under the table; it is just that the consequences of those deals are felt in the marketplace very quickly. Shocks are transmitted to the markets immediately and participants can turn to the marketplace and shop around for information and for ways to protect themselves from the consequences of these shocks in the marketplace. A village market, moreover, makes all the wares visible to all shoppers.

The changes contributed to increased volatility in the financial markets. Financial variables like prices of commodities, interest rates, and exchange rates began to fluctuate more than had happened before. These fluctuations increased financial risks for market participants, whether corporations or individuals. Financial institutions, however, responded to the increased financial risk by developing new instruments that helped participants manage risks in the financial markets. The third part of this book is devoted to understanding the financial risk: why has it increased, how can it be measured, and how can it be managed.

The first section in this chapter examines how the financial environment has changed over the previous decade and how these changes have contributed to increased risk. The subsequent section examines some evidence for the increased volatility in the foreign exchange rates and in interest rates. We then turn to the measurement of risk. The first section in this part examines ways to measure interest rate risk and the second section examines the measurement of foreign exchange risk. For each of these variables, we examine three types of situations: an investor who owns one single financial asset or a single financial liability, an investor who owns a portfolio of financial assets and liabilities, and an investor who owns real assets. The last section in this chapter examines a question that could be raised by our discussion in the previous chapter: if investors can diversify away the unsystematic risk, then why bother about managing this risk? The following three chapters are devoted to management of these risks.

New Financial Environment

A number of factors are responsible for the changes in the external environment of financial markets. With some simplification, we may link these developments in the following sequence as shown in Exhibit 9.1. These factors of change may be included under three broad categories: government regulations, globalization, and technology. Changes in the external environment have led to an increase in both competition and volatility, that is, the variability of financial variables like prices, interest rates, and exchange rates. The increase in volatility (perhaps exacerbated by an increase in competition) heightened the risk faced by the users of financial assets. These users began looking for ways to manage their risks. Fortunately for them, the increased competition in the marketplace prompted financial institutions to vie for customers by providing better services. One of these services came in the form of financial innovations that allowed financial risks to be better managed. Further, this process of innovation was aided by advances in computer and communication technologies that allowed for complex information manipulation required

Exhibit 9.1
Financial Environment and Risk

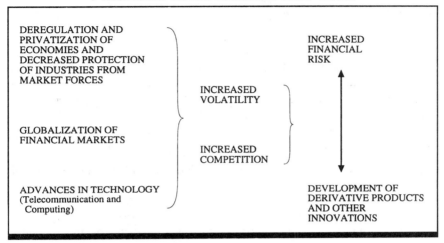

for these innovations. Thus, changes in the competitive environment and advances in technology not only caused the problem (increased financial risk) but also provided the solutions (the financial innovations themselves).

Let us first elaborate on the changes in the environment, the first of which is the change in the regulatory environment of financial institutions. Government regulations in two areas are important here. At the macroeconomic level, governments were confronted with the failures of government bureaucracies to manage their economies in general, and productive enterprises in particular. This led a number of governments to loosen their hold on the economies and let market forces dictate the process of resource allocation. A necessary component of this liberalization, which is the second important change in the environment, was the opening of national economies to global competitive forces. Industries became globalized. To serve the financial needs of these globalized industries, financial institutions like banks also had to become global. National financial institutions could no longer expect that their domestic markets would be safe from outside competition. In addition to the liberalization at a macroeconomic level, the financial sectors in a number of countries also saw liberalization of their own. More and more governments took away the monopoly powers that financial institutions derived from legislated restrictions to entry in different sectors of financial markets. The competition, in other words, sneaked up from a number of directions.

The third change in the environment can be attributed to technology. Technological changes have had a dramatic impact on the management of what is perhaps the most critical non–human resource for this industry: information. Advances in telecommunications have provided access to information in amounts and at speeds that could not have been possible even a decade ago. Advances in computers have made it possible to process that information at ever–increasing speeds and have, moreover, placed that computing power in the hands of people in direct touch with customers or markets.

Two of the most important consequences of these changes in the environment have been the increase in competition in the financial services industry and the increase in the volatility in the financial markets. Again, increased competition has taken two forms. First, financial institutions are able to offer services in areas that they were barred from entering even a decade ago. In most industrialized countries, barriers and walls that separated various types of financial activities—commercial banking, investment banking, insurance, and trust services—are being removed. Old neighbors have become competitors. Second, barriers to entry of foreign financial institutions are being eroded, slowly but surely. Thus, foreign financial institutions have now become predators in domestic markets.

The second consequence of the changes in the environment of financial markets has been an increase in the volatility in the markets. Volatility refers to the fluctuations in the prices of financial and real assets—prices of various commodities and products, interest rates, and exchange rates. Since our interest in this book is only in financial assets, we will examine only the volatility in exchange rates and interest rates.

Exchange and Interest Rate Volatility

We briefly examined the volatility of exchange rates in Chapter 2 and recognized that exchange rates became more unstable in the 1980s than they were earlier. We will look further at how the volatility of exchange

Exhibit 9.2
Volatility of Spot Exchange Rates
(currency units/dollar)

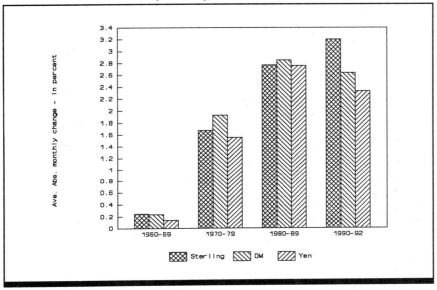

rates has increased over the last few years and also examine the volatility of interest rates.

Exhibit 9.2 illustrates the dramatic increase in the volatility of exchange rates over the last three decades. It shows the average absolute monthly percentage changes in the price of the dollar in terms of three currencies—the pound sterling, the deutschemark, and the yen. The volatility has increased in every decade, although it may have stabilized over the last few years. The information in the graph is supplemented by the data in Exhibits 9.3 and 9.4. Exhibit 9.3 shows the maximum change in the value of a U.S. dollar in terms of seven currencies within a year, and a measure called the coefficient of variation. This measure is a ratio of the standard deviation to the mean of a variable. In Exhibit 9.3, the coefficient of variation was calculated for every year. The exhibit compares the range, that is, the difference between the highest and the lowest values during the year, and the coefficient of variation for fixed

Exhibit 9.3

Movements in Exchange Rates Within a Year

	Highest Range (year)				Coefficient of Variation (= Std. Deviation/Mean)			
	1960–72		1974–92		1960–72		1974–92	
UK	0.06	('67)	0.2	('85)	5.9	('67)	10.4	('85)
France	0.6	('69)	2.6	('85)	5.9	('69)	9.9	('85)
Germany	0.4	('71)	0.9	('85)	4.1	('71)	9.8	('85)
Sweden	0.3	('71)	1.8	('82)	2.01	('71)	10.6	('82)
Canada	0.06	('70)	0.1	('82)	2.6	('70)	2.4	('77)
Japan	42.8	('71)	65.4	('78)	4.5	('71)	10.3	('78)
Finland	1.0	('67)	1.5	('85)	12.8	('67)	8.0	('85)

Range: Difference between the highest and the lowest end-of-month currency value (measured as currency/U.S.$) during the period.

Coefficient of variation: Defined as the standard deviation/mean; both measured over the entire period for end-of-month values of each currency in U.S.$.

Source: International Monetary Fund, *International Financial Statistics*, various issues.

Exhibit 9.4
Movements in Exchange Rates Over Selected Periods

	Range for the Period			Coefficient of Variation (= Std. Deviation/Mean)		
	1960–72	1974–92	1980–92	1960–92	1974–92	1980–92
UK	0.1	0.5	0.5	7.4	17.8	16.5
France	0.7	6.2	6.1	4.7	24.6	21.2
Germany	1.02	1.8	1.8	6.9	19.4	21.8
Sweden	0.5	5.5	5.2	2.3	24.4	18.8
Canada	0.1	0.5	0.3	3.7	9.8	6.4
Japan	61.5	183.4	155.6	4.6	27.7	26.4
Finland	1.0	3.4	3.3	13.3	17.5	17.3

Range: Difference between the highest and the lowest end–of–month currency value (measured as currency/U.S.$) during the period.

Coefficient of variation: Defined as the standard deviation/mean; both measured over the entire period for end–of–month values of each currency in U.S.$.

Source: International Monetary Fund, *International Financial Statistics*, various issues.

Exhibit 9.5
Movements of Short–Term Interest Rates Within a Year

	Highest Range (year)				Coefficient of Variation (= Std. Deviation/Mean)			
	1960–72		1974–92		1960–72		1974–92	
US	3.1	('70)	8.7	('80)	14.7	('72)	24.8	('80)
UK	3.6	('72)	10.7	('78)	22.5	('72)	38.0	('78)
France	3.6	('68)	9.2	('81)	21.9	('72)	25.0	('79)
Germany	—		4.1	('81)	—		24.3	('79)
Sweden	4.5	('67)	7.1	('81)	28.6	('62)	41.6	('74)
Canada	3.4	('70)	7.0	('80)	27.3	('60)	17.6	('80)
Japan	9.5	('61)	5.4	('75)	24.3	('61)	21.9	('79)
Finland	—		14.03	('78)	—		39.8	('78)

Range: Difference between the highest and the lowest end–of–month currency value (measured as currency/U.S.$) during the period.

Coefficient of variation: Defined as the standard deviation/mean; both measured over the entire period for end–of–month values of each currency in U.S.$.

Source: International Monetary Fund, *International Financial Statistics*, various issues.

Exhibit 9.6
Movements of Short–Term Interest Rates Over Selected Periods

	Range for the Period			Coefficient of Variation (= Std. Deviation/Mean)		
	1960–72	1974–92	1980–92	1960–92	1974–92	1980–92
US	4.7	12.6	12.6	23.7	34.3	34.8
UK	4.2	15.3	8.7	17.9	21.8	19.1
France	6.7	13.6	12.9	30.8	25.6	25.1
Germany	—	9.5	9.5	—	35.5	35.0
Sweden	6.5	14.9	8.4	29.2	27.8	16.1
Canada	6.1	15.2	15.2	31.5	28.1	27.3
Japan	13.9	10.3	9.5	26.2	37.4	32.4
Finland	—	14.7	6.9	—	19.2	14.0

Range: Difference between the highest and the lowest end–of–month currency value (measured as currency/U.S.$) during the period.

Coefficient of variation: Defined as the standard deviation/mean; both measured over the entire period for end–of–month values of each currency in U.S.$.

Source: International Monetary Fund, *International Financial Statistics*, various issues.

as well as floating rate periods. For most of the currencies shown, the volatility of the exchange rate is higher in the floating exchange rate period than in the fixed rate period. Moreover, the high volatility does not seem to be a characteristic of the period immediately following the generalized floating of exchange rates in 1973. Exhibit 9.4, for instance, summarizes the same information for entire periods. For periods of almost equal lengths, the increase in the range over which exchange rates can move as well as average fluctuations (as reflected by the coefficient of variation) indicate that exchange rates have become more volatile in the last decade than in earlier periods.

Likewise, the evidence for increased volatility of interest rates is presented in Exhibits 9.5 and 9.6. For most countries, interest rates have fluctuated over larger ranges in recent years than was the case before.

Increased volatility increases financial risk for participants in the markets. Asset holders face the risk that the value of their assets will change when either exchange rates or interest rates or both change. As we saw in Chapter 4, the value of a bond drops when interest rates rise and the value of a share denominated in a foreign currency rises when the exchange rate for that currency appreciates. We will discuss other more complex situations later, but what is important for us to note at this stage is that, as volatility increases, the risk associated with holding financial assets also increases. Greater uncertainty about what the interest rates or the exchange rates will be also creates uncertainty about the value of an asset.

The new developments in the financial markets reflects the need of asset holders to manage and minimize the risk associated with changes in interest rates and exchange rates. With an increase in volatility in the 1980s, there was a greater demand for ways to manage the volatility risk, and financial markets responded to this need by introducing a number of instruments that manage, or transfer, the risk. Our challenge is to understand how the most important of these financial innovations work and how they help us manage the risks in international financial markets.

Identifying and Measuring Financial Risk

Before we can understand how recent financial innovations can help manage risk, it will be useful to understand how changes in interest rates and exchange rates create risks for different types of assets. For analytical purposes, we will separate the risks arising due to interest rate changes from the risks arising due to exchange rate changes. We will also look at different types of assets and examine the risks for individual assets as well as for a portfolio of financial assets. Although changes in interest rates and exchange rates also create risks for real assets, the study of such risks is left to others who are more concerned about the management of real assets. Note that we always make references to assets, not to liabilities. This is because a liability is just a negative asset. What is true for an asset can be easily applied to a liability also. We will therefore not make any references to liabilities in our discussion.

Exhibit 9.7 summarizes the most important situations under which various types of assets are subject to interest rate or exchange rate risks. In this section, we will discuss examples for each of these situations in order to define how financial risk is related to the change in any of these variables. The exhibit separates interest rate risk from exchange rate risk for three types of assets. We first look at the risk factor of isolated assets where we can ignore the interaction between different assets and liabilities. Then we examine the risk for a portfolio of assets and liabilities, most of which are financial assets or liabilities. Finally, we show how a portfolio of real assets and liabilities could also be subject to financial risk.

Interest Rate Risk

Specific or Isolated Assets

Consider the situation of an investor who holds a five–year Eurobond with an fixed coupon of 8 percent. The investor does not expect to hold the bond to maturity because he plans to sell it when a good opportunity for investment in stocks comes along. Thus he is sensitive to changes in bond prices. Why should bond prices change?

We will use one of the concepts developed in a previous chapter—yield of a bond—to answer this question. In Chapter 4 we saw that the price of a bond equals the cash flows of the bond discounted at the yield to maturity. Investors demand a certain yield on a bond, given its risk and the term structure of interest rates in the market. Based on the cash flows of the bond, they determine the price they are willing to pay. What if the

Exhibit 9.7
Interest Rate and Exchange Rate Risks

Type of Assets	Type of Risk	
	Interest Rate Risk	Foreign Exchange Risk
Specific or individual assets.	Changes in the value of an existing asset due to changes in the level of interest rates.	Changes in domestic currency value of an existing foreign currency asset.
	Change in the expected cost of an asset to be acquired, contingent or definite, due to changes in interest rates.	Changes in domestic currency value of a contingent foreign currency asset.
Portfolio of financial assets.	Gap analysis.	Balance sheet exposure.
Portfolio of real assets.	Interest rate sensitivity of assets.	Economic exposure of a company.

market interest rate changes? The change in the market interest rate will change the required yield on the bond. Given that the cash flows of the bond remain the same, if the market interest rate changes, so will the expected yield to maturity from the bond and, consequently, the price of the bond. The investor faces the risk that when he is ready to sell the bond, the interest rates would have changed in the direction that the price of the bond would have fallen. Hence, the financial risk of holding such a bond is the change in price that would result from a certain change in the interest rates.

To clarify further, the current market price of a five–year maturity, 8 percent annual coupon bond depends upon the expected yield to maturity. Suppose that the expected yield to maturity is also 8 percent. The price of the bond will be given by the following equation where 80 is the annual cash flow for the first four years and 1,080 is the cash flow for the fifth year:

$$P = \frac{80}{(1 + .08)} + \frac{80}{(1 + .08)^2} + \frac{80}{(1 + .08)^3}$$

$$+ \frac{80}{(1 + .08)^4} + \frac{1,080}{(1 + .08)^5} = \$1,000$$

(9.1)

What if the interest rates change and the expected yield to maturity becomes 9 percent? The price of the bond now will be:

$$P = \frac{80}{(1 + .09)} + \frac{80}{(1 + .09)^2} + \frac{80}{(1 + .09)^3} +$$

$$\frac{80}{(1 + .09)^4} + \frac{1,080}{(1 + .09)^5} = \$961.10$$

The price of *this* bond has fallen by about 3.89 percent for 100 basis points (= 1 percent) increase in the yield to maturity. The investor can thus calculate his gain or loss for any change in the market interest rates. Exhibit 9.8 shows the price of the bond for selected yields.

The exhibit indicates how the value of this bond, that is, its price, changes with changes in the interest rates. It provides a risk profile of the bond for interest rate changes.[1] Given the nature of the asset, that is, a bond, the value of the asset declines if the interest rate rises, and vice versa. The investor loses money if the interest rates rise and gains if they fall. Although the relationship between the price of the bond and the interest rates appears to be linear, it is not. A 1 percent decline in interest rates from 8 percent to 7 percent raises the value of the bond by $41.00, but a further 1 percent drop in the rates will raise the value by $43.25.

Before we can understand how the investor can eliminate his risk, we will develop a measure to calculate the approximate amount by which the price will change for a given change in interest rates. This measure is called **modified duration** and is calculated from the **Macaulay duration**.[2] Macaulay's duration, D, is defined as:

Exhibit 9.8
Interest Rate Changes and Bond Value

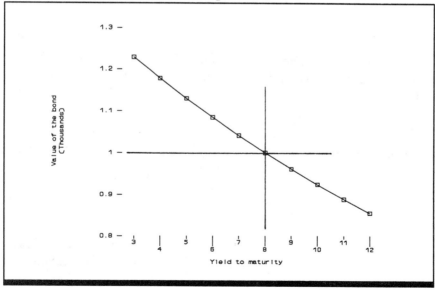

$$D = \frac{\sum \text{time-weighted present values of cash flows}}{\text{Total present value of cash flows}} \quad (9.2)$$

and can be calculated as follows:

$$D = \frac{\sum \dfrac{(i) \times (C_i)}{(1 + y)^i}}{P} \quad (9.3)$$

where C_i is the cash flow of the bond for i^{th} period, y is the yield to maturity, and P is the current price of the bond. The modified duration is calculated as follows:

$$\text{Modified duration} = \frac{\text{Macaulay duration}}{(1 + y)} \quad (9.4)$$

The modified duration can be used to calculate the approximate change in the price of the bond for a certain change in the yield:

Percentage price change = −Modified duration × Change in the yield

To verify, we can calculate the modified duration of our investor's bond and check if it provides an indication of the change in price. For a yield to maturity of 8 percent, the Macaulay duration turns out to be 4.312 from the following formula:

$$D = \frac{\dfrac{80 \times 1}{1.08} + \dfrac{80 \times 2}{1.08^2} + \dfrac{80 \times 3}{1.08^3} + \dfrac{80 \times 4}{1.08^4} + \dfrac{1{,}080 \times 5}{1.08^5}}{1{,}000}$$

which gives a value of 4.312/1.08 = 3.9927 for modified duration. If we expected the interest rate or the yield to maturity to drop to 7.8 percent, the modified duration would predict a price change of the following amount:

Percentage price change = –3.9927 × (8.00 – 7.80) = .79854 percent, or a new price of $1,007.99

If we calculate the price directly from Equation 9.1, we obtain a value of $1,008.03, a difference of four cents. The advantage of calculating the modified duration is that once we have the number, we can obtain the approximate price change for any value of the change in the interest rates. The following table provides the price of the bond and the modified duration for a number of yields.

Yield (YTM)	Price at YTM	Macaulay Duration at YTM	Modified Duration at YTM
4.0	1178.07	4.3717	4.2035
5.0	1129.88	4.3570	4.1496
6.0	1084.25	4.3422	4.0964
7.0	1041.00	4.3273	4.0442
8.0	1000.00	4.3121	3.9927
9.0	961.10	4.2968	3.9421
10.0	924.18	4.2814	3.8922

Notice that the expected change in the price of the bond depends upon the current yield. When the current yield is 10 percent, a change in the interest rates by 1 percent will change the price by about 3.89 percent whereas the change in price would be about 4.20 percent for the same amount of change in interest rates if the current yield were 4 percent.

The example given above applies to the interest rate risk for a bond, but the analysis would be equally valid for other types of assets. Consider for instance a short–term deposit which pays the principal and interest in one lump sum payment. The risk of this asset can be calculated by treating it as a bond with only one payment left. On the other hand, what about a mortgage which is repaid in part every year? This mortgage can also be treated in the same fashion as a bond except that instead of cash flows being determined by a coupon rate, they are fixed using some other formula. It is possible to calculate the duration of a mortgage by identifying the cash flows at various times and by recognizing that the discount rate for cash flows at different times must be equal to the yield to maturity for that length of time.

In summary, the interest rate risk profile of an asset shows how the price of the asset will change if the market interest rates were to change. The profile depends upon the nature of the cash flows associated with the asset as well as the current interest rates. Although we have illustrated the basic principle for a bond, it is equally valid for any other asset whose cash flows are known.

A Portfolio of Financial Assets

The best example of a portfolio of financial assets is a bank or a savings and loan association. Most of the assets and liabilities these organizations possess are financial in nature. Each of these assets by itself is subject to an interest rate risk. Some of the assets may increase in value when the interest rates fall while the value of others decrease. The risk of the portfolio is the net effect of interest rate changes on the individual assets that make up the portfolio.

The interest rate risk of a portfolio of financial assets can be calculated by using a concept known as GAP analysis. GAP analysis is based on the idea that various assets and liabilities within a portfolio have different interest rate "maturities." Interest rate maturity refers to the time for which the interest rate of an asset (or liability) is fixed. A variable rate mortgage, for example, may have the interest rate adjusted every three months even though the interest rates may change every day. The interest rate maturity of this mortgage will be said to be three months since that is the time for which the interest rate will not change. GAP analysis measures the interest rate risk of a portfolio of financial assets by quantifying the gap between interest rate sensitive assets, or RSA, and interest rate sensitive liabilities, or RSL. The interest rate in question here may be any interest rate, or we may calculate the gap only for short–term interest rates or only for long–term interest rates. To clarify further, consider the balance sheet of a hypothetical bank:

Bank Nicobar
Balance Sheet, December 31, 1993

Assets ($ millions*)		Liabilities ($ millions*)	
Short–term (3 month) revolving loans	500	CDs due in 3 months	400
Trade credit, in yen, at 3–month rate	600	Euro CP, in DM, due in 1 month	650
Project finance, in DM, at fixed rate	700	Long–term bonds (in pounds)	750
Real estate	300	Shareholder's equity	300
Total assets	$2,100	Total liabilities	$2,100
*Foreign currencies converted into dollars at current spot rate.			

The assets as well as the liabilities of the bank have mixed maturities. To simplify the calculations, we assume in this section that all the principal of any asset or liability is paid at maturity; in other words we assume that prepayments are not possible and none of the assets or liabilities are amortized. We will relax this assumption later when we examine the proposed methodology of the Federal Reserve Board in the United States. To determine the risk that the bank faces due to changes in short–term interest rates, we can calculate the corresponding gap as follows.

$$RSA_{short-term} = Loan + Trade\ credit = 500 + 600 = 1,100$$

$$RSL_{short-term} = CDs + CPs = 400 + 650 = 1,050$$

Hence,

$$GAP_{short-term} = RSA_{short-term} - RSL_{short-term} = 1,100 - 1,050 = 50$$

A positive gap of 50 indicates that if the short–term interest rate were to increase, the income of Bank Nicobar would also increase. The increase in interest income from the assets will more than offset the increase in interest expense of the liabilities. In fact, we can calculate the exact impact of the increase in the interest rates on the income of the bank. The increase in income will be a multiple of the gap and the increase in the interest rates. Thus, if the rates were to increase by 1 percent, the income of the bank would also increase by $50 \times .01$ or .5.

For long–term interest rates, on the other hand, the bank has a gap of -50 since its $RSL_{long-term}$ of 750 exceeds its $RSA_{long-term}$ of 700 by 50. If the long–term interest rate were to increase by 1 percent, the bank's income would fall by $50 \times .01 = .50$.

GAP analysis helps identify the interest rate sensitivity of a portfolio of assets and points to the actions that must be taken to prevent a change in the value of the portfolio when the interest rates change.

Application of GAP Analysis: Interest Rate Risks at U.S. Commercial Banks

The Federal Reserve Board has proposed that beginning in early 1994, U.S. commercial banks provide detailed data that will allow their interest rate risk to be calculated using the principles of GAP analysis. The Fed's methodology would, however, extend the GAP analysis to account for amortization and pre–payment of some assets or liabilities. The proposal would divide assets and liabilities into seven maturity categories. Risk factors would be assigned to each category with assets being divided into three: amortizing, non–amortizing, and deep discount. There will be only one category of liabilities. Further, any bank's holdings in each category will be multiplied by the risk factor assigned to that category. Netting out the calculations for assets and liabilities will thus provide a measure of net exposure or how much the banks' net worth would change as a result of interest rate changes. The Fed will then require banks to increase their capital base if the net exposure is found to be excessive.

Using the Fed's proposed methodology, and making some assumptions about data that were not available, one researcher has estimated that the U.S. commercial banking system as a whole had a net exposure of 0.85. This means that if the interest rates were to increase across the board by 200 basis points (that is, an interest rate that was 8 percent would become 10 percent), the net worth of the banks would decrease by 0.85 percent of their assets. However, the range of exposure between 1989 and 1992 was found to be between 0.70 percent to 1 percent, with a slight downward trend since early 1990. The Fed believes that this value is not excessive, and an interest rate risk below 1 percent of assets is within industry norms.[3]

A Portfolio of Real Assets

Firms that invest in real assets like plant and equipment can be said to have a portfolio of **real assets**. The real value of these assets (not their book values as in the case of financial assets) depends upon how efficiently and effectively they can be used to produce goods and services that can be sold in the marketplace. These assets are sensitive to interest rate changes only insofar as the sales of goods and services that are produced with the help of these assets are sensitive to interest rates. The estimation of interest rate risk in this case is very complex because the link between interest rates and sales of many goods is very difficult to establish. In other cases, however, it is easy to see the connection. Sales of consumer durables like white goods and cars are known to be sensitive to interest rate changes because consumers often borrow money to finance their purchase of these goods. It would be difficult, however, to establish the link between the sales of cosmetics and interest rates.

Since the management of real assets is beyond the scope of this book, we will not deal with the measurement of interest rate risk of real assets in any detail. A good methodology for estimating this risk is based upon regression analysis. Regression analysis between interest rates on the one hand and either the sales or the stock returns on the other could provide a good estimate of the relationship between the two.[4]

Exchange Rate Risks

Specific or Isolated Assets

The exchange rate risk of an asset is merely the amount by which the value of the asset can change if the exchange rates change. This risk can be measured as "exposure," which indicates the potential loss that an investor can suffer:

Exchange rate exposure = Value of the asset × Change in exchange rate

Consider a short–term asset like a bank certificate of deposit (CD) denominated in a foreign currency, say, Canadian dollars (C$). Assume that the nominal value of the CD is C$1.0 million and the exchange rate is US$0.80/C$. For the investor, the value of this asset is $1.0 \times 0.80 =$ US$0.8 million. If there is a chance that the Canadian dollar will depreciate in the future, the investor faces a risk that the value of her investment will decrease. Suppose that the Canadian dollar is expected to drop to US$.77/C$. To calculate the exposure of the asset, we must determine the percentage change in the exchange rate. This change is $(0.77 - 0.80)/(0.80) \times 100 = -3.75$ percent. Thus we are expecting the Canadian dollar to drop by 3.75 percent. The exposure of the asset will therefore be:

$$\text{Exposure} = 0.8 \times .0375 = \text{US } \$0.03 \text{ million}$$

The challenge for the investor is to then find the means to manage this risk using the available financial derivatives. We will discuss these derivatives in Chapter 10 and their use for managing risk in Chapter 12.

Another common example of a specific asset that is subject to exchange rate risk is an account receivable that is denominated in a foreign currency. A company that expects to be paid by its buyer located in, say, London has a foreign currency account receivable if the buyer has committed himself to pay a fixed number of pounds in 30 days. The U.S. company faces the risk that within these 30 days, the pound may fall by a large amount and the number of dollars that the firm will receive will be less than what is expected at the present time. The exposure of this asset is calculated in exactly the same manner as described here.

Besides the existing assets, the exchange rate risk can also arise for assets that an investor expects to acquire. Suppose our investor was planning to buy deutschemark bonds in 15 days. She may have set aside the amount of dollars required for the investment. But what if the deutschemark rises in value during the next 15 days? The investor will not have sufficient funds to purchase the bond, or will have to come up with more dollars from somewhere else to make the purchase.

In subsequent chapters, we will learn ways to protect against all these risks.

Portfolio of Financial Assets

The exchange rate risk for an investor or a firm with a number of financial assets is the sum total of the risks of the various individual assets. As in the case of interest rate risk, the risks of some of the assets will cancel each other. The estimation of exchange rate risk for a portfolio of financial assets can be illustrated with the help of the same example that we used for understanding the interest rate risk.

Consider the balance sheet of Bank Nicobar once again. Some of the assets are denominated in foreign currencies, others in dollars. Moreover, the bank seems to have assets or liabilities denominated in more than one foreign currency. We will measure the exchange rate risk in two stages: we first define the bank's exposure separately in each currency and then take into consideration the interaction between various currencies in which the bank faces exchange risk.

For each currency, we will measure the exposure of the bank as follows:

Exposure in a currency = Exposed assets − Exposed liabilities

Assets or liabilities are considered exposed if they are denominated in a foreign currency and their nominal values in dollars can change if the value of the currency of their denomination changes. Take, for example, the trade credit on the asset side denominated in yens that has a value of $600m on the date of the balance sheet. Suppose the exchange rate on December 31, 1993, was 110 yen/dollar. The nominal value of this asset, therefore, was $600 \times 110 = 660$ billion yen. If the yen/dollar exchange rate changes, the nominal value of the asset will remain the same in yens and the bank will have to show a different amount on the balance sheet. Suppose that the yen appreciates to 100 yen/dollar. The value of this asset on the bank's book will now be $660,000/100 = \$660$ million. The depreciation of the dollar against the yen has increased the yen denominated assets on the bank's balance sheet. The difference between $660 million and $600 million represents a gain for the bank. The bank has gained because it had an asset in an appreciating currency. Since the bank has no yen liabilities, its net exposure in yens will be:

Exposure in yen = 600 − 0 = $600 million

The exchange risk in yens will be given by the exposure multiplied by the change in the exchange rate.

Exchange rate risk = Exposure × Change in exchange rate

In this case, however, we need to ascertain the change in the value of the dollar. You may recall from Chapter 2 that we will need to obtain direct quotes on the yen.

Old rate = 1/110 = $.0090909/yen
New rate = 1/100 = $.01/yen
Change = (.01 − .0090909)/(.0090909) × 100 = 10 percent

Therefore, exchange risk = $600 × .10 = $60 million. This is the same answer we received without using the exposure formulae.

The exposure in other currencies can be calculated in the same manner:

Exposure in DM = Exposed assets in DM
    − Exposed liabilities in DM
    = 700 − 650 = $50 million

Exposure in pounds = Exposed assets in pounds
    − Exposed liabilities in pounds
    = 0 − 750 = − $750 million

This indicates that the bank has positive, or long, exposure in yen and deutschemarks and negative, or short, exposure in pounds. We could say that the bank is long in yen and deutschemarks, and short in pounds. It will therefore face losses if the yen or the deutschemark depreciate or if the pound appreciates. On the other hand, it will gain if the yen or the deutschemark appreciates or if the pound depreciates.

The second stage of assessing the exchange rate risk of a portfolio of assets is to recognize that movements of various currencies may be correlated. It is possible that if one currency goes up, some other currencies may also go up simultaneously and yet others may go down at the same time. When the United Kingdom was a member of the European monetary system (discussed in Chapter 2), both pounds and deutschemarks tended to move together. Both increased or decreased against the dollar more or less in tandem. There was only a small scope —4.5 percent all together, to be precise—for them to move against each other. Thus, the positive exposure of the bank in deutschemarks was more than offset by its negative exposure in pounds. In general, an investor must calculate the exposure in each currency and then assess if some of this exposure offsets the other due to correlated movements of the currencies involved.

Portfolio of Real Assets

The most complex, and also the most important, exchange risk is for a portfolio of real assets, that is, for a firm that is engaged in the production of goods and services for international markets. It is the most important aspect in the estimation of risk because exchange rate changes can dramatically alter the competitiveness of firms in international markets. A 10 percent decline in the value of the currency of the market where a firm exports has the same effect on the firm's customer as a 10 percent price increase by the firm itself. As we have seen, the volatility in foreign exchange markets makes it possible for currencies to change by amounts reaching 10 percent within a few months. Thus, a firm that has worked hard to reduce its costs, and its selling prices, by 10 percent may find that exchange rate changes can cancel the effects of those efforts within months.

Estimation of exchange risk for a firm is also very complex because it is rare that firms find themselves in the simple situation that we used to illustrate the importance of this type of risk. Firms often import from countries where they export. Thus, if the depreciation of a currency makes exports to the market more expensive, it also makes imports cheaper. We really need to estimate the net effect of the changes in exchange rates. The situation is made more complex because the actions and choices faced by competitors must also be taken into consideration. Our firm that exports its products to a market will not have to worry about a depreciation of that market's currency if its competitors also produce outside the market and will also have to raise their prices following a currency depreciation. The situation becomes complex if some competitors are located within the market and others outside of it.

The exchange risk for a firm's operations is generally known as the economic exposure of a company. It can either be estimated by a detailed analysis of the costs of the firm along with an analysis of the competitive situation, or by an analysis of the past data using the same methodology as used for the estimation of interest rate risk. Smith et. al. illustrate the application of this methodology for three different types of firms.[5]

Why Manage Risk?

Before launching into our next subject, which is the management of interest rate and exchange rate risks, it may be worthwhile to examine if economic theory justifies all the attention that is paid to risk management. Theory would seem to indicate that we should not worry about all these risks. Risk management involves expenses, and the risks should cancel out in the long run anyway. According to diversification theory presented in the previous chapter, investors should be concerned only about the systematic risk of their investments since the unsystematic risks can be diversified away. But are the financial risks discussed here systematic or unsystematic risks?

Unsystematic risks are those risks which can be easily neutralized or canceled by combining a few assets. By the same token, any risk which can be defined as a zero–sum game (that is, a game in which one party's gain exactly equals another party's loss) is a diversifiable risk because it can be diversified away by holding the opposite of a risky asset—a risky liability with exactly the opposite risk profile than that of the asset. It follows that most of the interest rate and exchange rate risks we identified are unsystematic risks because in most cases, these risks arose in zero–sum game situations. As we will soon see, they can also be easily hedged.

If these risks are diversifiable risks, why should corporate managers and investors spend money to eliminate them from their portfolios? It would be irrational to spend money to eliminate a risk by hedging when the same risk could be removed costlessly by portfolio diversification.

There are three reasons why managers or investors spend considerable resources to manage these risks. These reasons have to do with convex tax schedules faced by many corporations or investors, costs of financial distress, and what is known as agency cost associated with corporate management.[6]

A convex tax schedule means that the marginal tax rate is increasing. When corporations face convex tax schedules, they can reduce their total tax burden by smoothing their income with hedging. Consider a company whose income can fluctuate between two points over a region in which the tax rate increases with the level of income. Income smoothing will allow the corporation to pay taxes at a halfway level between the two extremes. Given the rising tax schedule, the increase in the tax burden in the period which would have had a lower income without hedging would be less than the decrease in the tax burden during the period which would see a smaller income due to hedging.

Firms may also indulge in hedging costs when there is a chance that losses may cause a firm to enter bankruptcy and the reorganization costs that will be incurred in the case of a bankruptcy are very high. These costs are borne by the stockholders and they have an incentive to avoid bankruptcy. Without hedging, the firm can expect that it will lose money in some years and gain in others. The problem here is that if the firm has limited resources, it may be forced into bankruptcy by bad luck in the form of a long losing streak which may exhaust the resources of the firm before its luck turns around. To avoid facing that situation, it is in the firm's interest to hedge its returns and prevent the consequences of the possibility of a long streak of losses.

The third reason for undertaking hedging is complex and offers a more sophisticated explanation for the firms' behavior. It is based on the potential of a conflict between the interests of stockholders and bondholders. Under some situations, stockholders have incentives to take actions that may cause the firm's bondholders to lose money. Bondholders would anticipate such actions and would therefore charge the firm a price for taking that risk. Since the firm does not really want to pay that price, it will find ways to demonstrate to bondholders that it will not take actions in the future which could hurt bondholders. One such action is hedging: hedging smooths the earnings of the firm and obviates the situations in which actions that hurt bondholders become desirable. Thus, by incurring expenses associated with hedging, the firm may save itself some of the expenses associated with issuing bonds, even though the smoothing of revenues or income, *per se*, is of no value to the firm.

Another reason why managers undertake hedging may have to do with their own self interests. Without hedging, firms may have to enter bankruptcy, thus disrupting the careers of managers. Managers may also want to avoid publicity associated with large reported losses.

In practice, all these reasons contribute to the popularity of risk management.

Summary

Financial markets were profoundly affected by three developments in the 1980s. Advances in technologies for telecommunications and computers, a trend toward deregulation of economic activities, and globalization of economic activities including those of financial markets led to increased uncertainty. In the financial markets this increased uncertainty reflected itself in the form of increased volatility of exchange rates and interest rates. Increased volatility in turn led to increased financial risk for investors.

The financial risk for investors can be measured by separating investors into those who own a single asset or a liability, those who own a portfolio of assets or liabilities, and those who own real assets. The risk for an investor is that the value of the asset or the portfolio will change to the detriment of the investor. In the three chapters that follow, we will examine the instruments and techniques that help corporations and investors manage risk.

Notes

1. The term "risk profile" is used by Clifford Smith, Charles Smithson, and D. Sykes Wilford in *Managing Financial Risk*, HarperCollins, 1990, in relation to the financial risk. Readers should refer to that book for a more detailed treatment of the subject of this chapter.

2. Readers interested in more details should see any standard textbook dealing with bonds. Frank J. Fabozzi and Franco Modigliani provide an excellent treatment in Chapters 11 and 12 of their book *Capital Markets: Institutions and Instruments*, Englewood Cliffs, NJ: Prentice Hall, 1992.

3. Jonathan A. Neuberger, "Interest Rate Risk at U.S. Commercial Banks," FRBSF *Weekly Letter*, no. 93-26, July 23, 1993. The details of the Fed proposal are summarized from this article.

4. For one such application, see Smith et. al., op. cit. pp. 35-42.

5. See, once again, Smith et. al., op. cit. pp. 35-42.

6. For a more detailed discussion of these issues, and for an empirical proof that these reasons indeed make sense in the business world, see Deana R. Nance, Clifford W. Smith, and Charles W. Smithson, "On the Determinants of Corporate Hedging," *The Journal of Finance,* March 1993, pp. 267-284.

Chapter 10
Financial Derivatives

One of the most remarkable developments in the financial markets during the 1980s has been the introduction and growth of what have come to be known as **financial derivative products**. Although some derivative products such as futures and options have existed for a very long time, the changes in the financial environment over the last two decades created demand for techniques for managing financial risk. The response of financial institutions was to offer an ever–increasing choice of complex combinations and extensions of existing and new assets to investors.

Derivative products are offered through two channels. Organized exchanges like the Chicago Mercantile Exchange and similar exchanges around the world have expanded their menu of products. Banks and some other financial institutions also offer, and are willing to tailor make, these products for their customers. This segment of the market is known as the over–the–counter market. Due to the flexibility of this market, it is much bigger than the exchange trade segment of the derivative market. Some data on the volume of transactions in the two segments of the market were presented earlier in Exhibit 1.6.

Although the pace of innovations has slowed down in terms of new products and extensions being offered, innovations continue. The innovations now aim to satisfy the needs of more sophisticated users of financial markets. An example of such an innovation, introduced in June 1993, is a rolling spot contract. Details of this innovation are discussed in the box at the end of this chapter.

In this chapter, our aim is to understand what these innovations are and how they work. We will look at futures, options, swaps, and some combinations of these basic instruments like options on futures and swaptions. In the following two chapters, we will learn how to use these derivatives to manage risks. We begin, however, with a brief glossary of some terminology that will be used throughout the chapter and the remainder of the book.

▼ ▼ ▼
Some Terminology of Derivatives

Basis and basis risk.   Most derivative or risk management products are based on the spot price of an asset or a liability. The difference between the prices of the spot and the future contracts of that asset is known as **the basis**. The difference between the spot and the future prices is governed by some economic fundamentals as well as supply and demand of these contracts. Basis risk refers to the risk that the basis for a contract may change in an unpredictable manner, thus changing the value of a derivative product.

Exercise price.   Exercise price refers to the contracted price of the underlying asset at which the particular derivative has a special value. It may be the price at which the contract is negotiated or it may be the price at which certain actions are triggered. We will define the exercise price more precisely for each derivative separately.

Margin.   Quite often an investor may purchase a derivative product with the intention of using it or canceling it in the future. In the meantime, however, the value of the contract may decline due to price changes, resulting in a loss for the investor. The seller of the contract may insist that the investor place a margin with a financial institution to minimize the credit risk associated with the contract. The margin can often be placed in the form of interest–bearing securities.

Payoff profile.   To understand the usefulness of a derivative product for managing financial risk, we need to understand how the value of the derivative changes as the market variables, especially the price of the asset underlying the contract, changes. We are interested in developing a "payoff profile" that shows what the value of the derivative would be for different values of the price of the asset on which the derivative is based. Since the most important derivatives available in the market are based upon the price of one particular asset, we will develop the payoff profile for each asset in terms of the price of the asset upon which the derivative is based. The payoff profile depends upon the cash flows associated with the derivative and the relationship between each cash flow and the price of the asset. It shows the value of the derivative for each value of the price of the asset.

Underlying asset.   As the name implies, most derivative products are derived from some asset, financial or real. The derivative product offers some variation of what is known as the underlying asset.

▲ ▲ ▲

Forward and Futures Contracts

A forward contract is one of the oldest derivative products on the financial markets. We have already discussed some basic features of a forward contract for foreign exchange in Chapter 2. In this chapter, we will expand on this, and a related contract, the futures contract, in more detail.

In its simplest form, a forward contract is merely a contract that will be fulfilled at some future date, unlike the spot contract which is fulfilled immediately. Thus, in relation to foreign currencies, a forward contract calls for an exchange of two currencies at a designated point in time in the future. Everything about this exchange is known when the contract is made: the two currencies that will be exchanged, the exchange rate at which the conversion will take place, the amounts of the two currencies, and the date at which the exchange will take place. The only difference between a forward contract and a spot contract is the time at which the transaction takes place: a spot contract is fulfilled immediately, whereas the time for the forward contract has to be agreed upon.

Although a forward contract can be created for any asset that can be traded in the spot market, such contracts are widely available only for interest rates and foreign currencies. Forward contracts are usually offered by banks whose customers have specific needs in terms of quantities and dates. Exhibit 10.1 provides an example of the range of currencies for which forward contracts are offered by one of the leading banks in the area of foreign exchange—Citibank of New York. In addition to industrialized countries, currency forwards are also available for a wide range of developing countries.

Exhibit 10.1
Range of Forward Contracts Offered by a Bank

CURRENCIES WHERE CITIBANK SELLS THE LOCAL CURRENCY SPOT + FWD (CASE BY CASE)

AFGHANISTAN – AFGHANI	GHANA – CEDI	PARAGUAY – GUARANI
ALBANIA – LEK	GUINEA – FRANC	POLAND – ZLOTY
ALGERIA – DINAR	GUINEA-BISSAU – PESO	ROMANIA – LEU
ANGOLA – KWANZA	GUYANA – DOLLAR	RWANDA – FRANC
ARUBA – FLORIN	HAITI – GOURDE	SAO TOME – DOBRA
BAHAMAS – DOLLAR	HUNGARY – FORINT	SEYCHELLES – RUPEE
BANGLADESH – TAKA	ISRAEL – SHEKEL	SIERRE LEONE – LEONE
BARBADOS – DOLLAR	JORDAN – DINAR	SOLOMON ISLAND – DOLLAR
BELIZE – DOLLAR	LEBANON – POUND	SOMALIA – SHILLING
BERMUDA – DOLLAR	LESOTHO – MALOTI	SUDAN – DINAR
BULGARIA – LEV	LIBERIA – DOLLAR	SURINAM – GUILDER
BURUNDI – FRANC	MALAGASY – FRANC	SWAZILAND – LILANGENI
CAPE VERDE – ESCUDO	MALAWI – KWACHA	SYRIA – POUND
CAYMAN ISLAND – DOLLAR	MALDIVES – RUFIYAA	TANZANIA – SHILLING
CFP – FRANC	MAURITANIA – OUGUIYA	TONGA – PA ANGA
CHINA – RENMINBI	MAURITIUS – RUPEE	UGANDA – SHILLING
CZECHOSLOVAKIA – KORUNA	MONGOLIA – TUGRIK	VANUATU – VATU
DJIBOUTI – FRANC	MOZAMBIQUE – METICAL	VIETNAM – DONG
DOMINICAN – PESO	NAMIBIA – RAND	WESTERN SAMOA – TALA
EAST CARIBBEAN – DOLLAR	NEPAL – RUPEE	YEMEN – RIAL
ETHIOPIA – BIRR	NETH. ANTILLES – GUILDER	ZAMBIA – KWACHA
GAMBIA – DALASI	NICARAGUA – CORDOBA	ZAIRE – ZAIRE

CURRENCIES WHERE CITIBANK BUYS AND SELLS LOCAL CURRENCY ON A SPOT BASIS
(SOME ONLY WITH COMMERCIAL DETAILS)

BOLIVIA – BOLIVIANO	FIJI – DOLLAR	MEXICO – PESO
BOTSWANA – PULA	GUATEMALA – QUETZAL	NIGERIA – NAIRA
BRAZIL – CRUZEIRO	HONDURAS – LEMPIRA	PAKISTAN – RUPEE
CFA – FRANC	ICELAND – KRONA	PAPUA NEW GUINEA – KINA
COLOMBIA – PESO	INDIA – RUPEE	PERU – NEW SOL
COSTA RICA – COLON	JAMAICA – DOLLAR	SRI LANKA – RUPEE
ECUADOR – SUCRE	KENYA – SHILLING	TRINIDAD & TOBAGO – DOLLAR
EL SALVADOR – COLON	MACAO – PATACA	ZIMBABWE – DOLLAR

CURRENCIES WHERE CITIBANK QUOTES SPOT AND FWD (SOME ONLY WITH COMMERCIAL DETAILS)

ARGENTINA – PESO	MALAYSIA – RINGGIT	SINGAPORE – DOLLAR
BAHRAIN – DINAR	MALTA – POUND	SOUTH KOREA – WON
BRUNEI – DOLLAR	MOROCCO – DIRHAM	TAIWAN – DOLLAR
CHILE – PESO	OMANI – RIAL	THAILAND – BAHT
CYPRUS – POUND	PHILIPPINES – PESO	TUNISIA – DINAR
EGYPT – POUND	QATAR – RIYAL	TURKEY – LIRA
HONG KONG – DOLLAR	SOUTH AFRICA – COMM. RAND	UAE – DIRHAM
INDONESIA – RUPIAH	SOUTH AFRICA – FIN. RAND	URUGUAY – NEW PESO
KUWAIT – DINAR	SAUDI ARABIA – RIYAL	VENEZUELA – BOLIVAR

Source: Citibank, New York, September 1992.

A forward contract is created by two parties who agree to the details of the contract according to their needs. As such, a forward contract is not a standardized contract. If one party to the forward contract were to realize that it did not need the contract anymore, it would either have to find another party that is willing to take over its side of the contract or pay a fee for the cancellation of the contract.

The forward contract seems to offer the flexibility of determining the size and the maturity date of the contract. This flexibility, however, comes at a cost. Each forward contract must be negotiated and can, therefore, be costly. Once a contract has been entered into, it is costly to change or cancel. Some of the shortcomings of the forward contract can be avoided by the use of futures contracts.

One way to look at a futures contract is to see it as a standardized forward contract. A futures contract is offered by an organized exchange which agrees to buy or sell a fixed amount of the underlying asset at the market price at fixed maturities known as delivery dates. For example, the International Money Market of the Chicago Mercantile Exchange, one of the first exchanges to offer futures contracts in foreign currencies in 1972, offers a futures contract in deutschemarks. Each contract is worth 125,000 marks and the exchange is ready to buy or sell any number of contracts to an investor. An investor can choose to purchase a contract that matures in any of the eight of the 12 months of the year which have been chosen by the exchange as maturity months. In each of these months, the contract expires on the third Wednesday of the month. Suppose that on March 10, 1993, an investor buys one deutschemark contract which matures in December of the same year. The investor is said to be taking a long position in deutschemarks which, in this case, is a short position in dollars. Suppose the investor buys the contract at a time when its price is $.62/DM. This means that the investor has purchased a right to acquire 125,000 deutschemarks at a price of 125000 × 0.62 or $ 77,500 on December 15, 1993. This right is promised by the exchange and the investor does not have to worry about who will provide the deutschemarks.

On the day the contract is purchased, its value is zero. This is because the investor has a contract for an exchange of two currencies at a rate at which anyone else would agree to exchange those currencies. On the day the contract is acquired, the contracted rate, $0.62/DM, is the same as the rate in the marketplace. Hence the value of the contract is zero. The next day when the market price of the futures contract for December changes, the value of the contract held by our investor will also change. If the market price goes up to, say, $0.63/DM, the contract will be worth (0.63 − 0.62) × 125000, or $1,250. The practice of the exchange, however, ensures that at the end of every trading day, the value of the contract is brought back to zero. Every day between March and December 15, the exchange will mark the contract to the market. This means that every day, the exchange will look at the new price and either require the investor to pay the amount by which the value would have gone down, or pay the investor the amount by which the value would have increased. Thus, on the day the price closes at $0.63/DM, the exchange will pay the investor $1,250, and it will be understood that at maturity on December 15, the investor will acquire the 125,000 deutschemarks at a price of $0.63/DM. The investor now has $1,250 in cash and a futures contract whose value, after being marked to market, is zero. The exchange follows this practice of marking to market to minimize the credit risk; in case the investor fails to fulfill the contract, the maximum loss that the exchange can suffer is due to the price movement during the day. Even that loss is limited because the investor has to keep a margin, usually about 10 percent of the value of the contract, with the exchange. When the contract is marked to market, it is really the margin that is made current, that is, brought back to its original level.

A futures contract for interest rates works in a similar manner except that the underlying asset in this case is a deposit. An investor buying an interest rate futures contract in Eurodollars will be making a commitment to acquire a deposit for a period of three months of $1.0 million at an agreed upon interest rate at a specified time. It is as if the investor is being told that if he were to bring a deposit of $1.0 million on the maturity date, he will be guaranteed the contracted interest rate for a period of three months. The deposit has to be accepted at the time the contract matures. The agreed upon price is the interest rate that will be paid on the deposit. The Chicago Mercantile Exchange offers Eurodollar futures that mature in March, June, September, and December of every year. The value of an interest rate futures contract goes down if the interest rates go up. This is only logical because an interest rate futures contract at a committed rate becomes less attractive when the market interest rate becomes higher.

Stock index futures are the most recent futures contracts to be introduced. The underlying asset in this case is a group of stocks that make up an index. The Chicago Mercantile Exchange, for example, offers "Nikkei 225 stock average" as one of the stock market indexes. An investor purchasing a futures contract on this index is contracting to buy a portfolio that consists of 225 stocks on the Tokyo stock exchange. The investor purchases the contract at a price that reflects the market's expectation of what the value of this index will be on the maturity date. If the Tokyo stock market begins to rise between the time of the purchase and the maturity date, the investor gains by an amount equal to the amount of the price increase times the value of the initial investment. Most industrialized countries have an index for some stocks of the country.

Differences Between Forwards and Futures

Exhibit 10.2 compares various characteristics of forward and futures contracts. The differences arise on the one hand from the standardized nature of futures contracts versus the adaptability of forward contracts, and on the other hand from differences in trading practices. The amounts and dates for the forward contracts are tailor made, whereas those for the futures contracts are standardized. Standardization and the limits on the credit risk make it easier to trade the futures. The main difference between the two contracts, however, is in the nature of cash flows and the values of the contracts. Futures contracts have a cash flow every day whereas forward contracts have one cash flow at maturity.

Payoff Profile of Futures and Forward Contracts

The most important aspect of a futures or a forward contract and, for that matter, of any derivative, is its payoff profile. How does the value of a futures or a forward contract change after it has been initiated?

The payoff of a futures or a forward contract depends upon the future price of the underlying asset. Consider first the investor who had purchased the deutschemarks future. The contract was purchased at an exchange rate of $0.62/DM. Since the investor has fixed the price at which she will purchase the foreign currency at a future date, her contract becomes valuable if the foreign currency rises in value immediately after

Exhibit 10.2
Comparison of Futures and Forward Contracts

Attribute	Forward Contract	Future Contract
The contract itself		
Size	Determined by the needs of the party.	Standardized, known in advance.
Maturity	Agreed upon by the parties.	Dates fixed by the exchange.
Settlement	Most contracts are settled by actual delivery.	99% of the contracts settled without actual delivery.
Transaction costs	Negotiated; reflected in the bid–ask spreads.	Standardized; fees payable for every trade.
Purpose	Mostly hedging.	Speculation and hedging.
Trading of the contracts		
Location	Negotiated over the counter, that is, over the telephone.	Traded on the exchange, in pits or electronically.
Price quotes	Traders free to make their own quotes.	Prices quoted on the exchange.
Minimum price movement	No limit.	Usually 1 basis point per unit of foreign currency.
Daily limit for price change	No limit.	No limit.
Cancellation of the contract	Must be negotiated between the parties.	Done easily by purchasing an opposite contract.
Market liquidity	Not a very liquid market; banks can settle with each other.	Liquid market for the major currencies.
Regulation	Self–regulated.	Regulated by the government of the country.
Risk of the contract		
Credit risk	Each party bears the risk of the other party.	The exchange bears the risk of the two parties.
Margins/deposit requirements	Banks may ask for a deposit or set credit limits for customers.	Buyer of every contract required to place a margin.
Value of the contract		
Frequency of cash flows	Only at maturity (other than initial deposit).	Daily cash flows may result when contract is marked to market.
Value of the contract after initiation	Value equals the cumulative changes in the price of the asset from the day of the inception of the contract.	Value is zero at the end of each day after the contract has been marked to market and margin has been settled.

the purchase of the futures contract. The higher the foreign currency rises in value, the higher will be the value of the contract. The relationship is shown in Exhibit 10.3. The exhibit shows the value of the contract for different values of the $/DM exchange rate. The contract becomes expensive if the deutschemark depreciates against the dollar. The relationship between the exchange rate and the value of the contract or the payoff of the futures contract is linear.

A forward contract has the same payoff profile as the futures contract.

Exhibit 10.3
Payoffs from Forwards and Futures

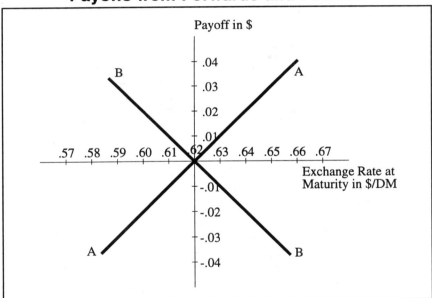

Payoff from forward or futures contracts:
  AA: Forward or futures contract to purchase deutschemarks
       @$.62/DM at a future date.
  BB: Forward or futures contract to sell deutschemarks
       @$.62/DM at a future date.

Exhibit 10.4
Quotations of Future Contracts

CURRENCY

JAPAN YEN (CME)–12.5 million yen; $ per yen (.00)

	Open	High	Low	Settle	Change	Lifetime High	Lifetime Low	Open Interest
Sept	.9211	.9251	.9182	.9243	+ .0032	.9540	.7945	69,087
Dec	.9249	.9260	.9195	.9251	+ .0033	.9529	.7970	2,968

Est vol 26,090; vol Mon 19,249; open int 72,158, +181.

DEUTSCHEMARK (CME)–125,000 marks; $ per mark

	Open	High	Low	Settle	Change	Lifetime High	Lifetime Low	Open Interest
Sept	.5824	.5855	.5805	.5851	+ .0026	.6720	.5720	162,460
Dec	.5775	.5806	.5758	.5802	+ .0026	.6650	.5677	5,121

Est vol 52,120; vol Mon 43,200; open int 167,647, –5,905.

CANADIAN DOLLAR (CME)–100,000 dlrs.; $ per Can $

	Open	High	Low	Settle	Change	Lifetime High	Lifetime Low	Open Interest
Sept	.7807	.7813	.7791	.7805	– .0003	.8335	.7515	25,320
Dec	.7790	.7792	.7780	.7783	– .0003	.8310	.7470	1,388
Mr94	.7760	.7768	.7760	.7761	– .0003	.7860	.7550	1,040
June	....	....	....	.7737	– .0003	.7805	.7515	306
Sept	....	....	....	.7713	– .0003	.7710	.7555	137

Est vol 3,464; vol Mon 2,838; open int 28,191, +81.

BRITISH POUND (CME)–62,500 pds.; $ per pound

	Open	High	Low	Settle	Change	Lifetime High	Lifetime Low	Open Interest
Sept	1.4926	1.5070	1.4900	1.5060	+ .0142	1.5800	1.3980	26,125
Dec	1.4898	1.4970	1.4840	1.4970	+ .0140	1.5670	1.3930	670

Est vol 16,266; vol Mon 10,533; open int 26,873, –1,065.

SWISS FRANC (CME)–125,000 francs; $ per franc

	Open	High	Low	Settle	Change	Lifetime High	Lifetime Low	Open Interest
Sept	.6650	.6677	.6616	.6670	+ .0019	.7100	.6380	38,658
Dec	.6642	.6660	.6590	.6652	+ .0019	.7050	.6400	1,811

Est vol 25,852; vol Mon 23,182; open int 40,555, –2,043.

AUSTRALIAN DOLLAR (CME)–100,000 dlrs.; $ per A.$

	Open	High	Low	Settle	Change	Lifetime High	Lifetime Low	Open Interest
Sept	.6754	.6765	.6750	.6759	+ .0007	.7202	.6595	3,890

Est vol 167; vol Mon 112; open int 3,905, –9.

U.S. DOLLAR INDEX (FINEX)–1,000 times USDX

	Open	High	Low	Settle	Change	Lifetime High	Lifetime Low	Open Interest
Sept	94.82	95.29	94.53	94.64	– .26	97.10	89.96	8,127
Dec	95.68	95.97	95.52	95.51	– .25	97.17	91.34	1,013

Est vol 2,350; vol Mon 1,508; open int 9,151, –297.
The index: High 94.54; Low 93.97; Close 94.02 –.20

INTEREST RATE

TREASURY BONDS (CBT)–$100,000; pts. 32nds of 100%

	Open	High	Low	Settle	Chg	Yield Settle	Yield Chg	Open Interest
Sept	115-31	116-01	115-06	115-26	– 5	6.568	+ .012	334,516
Dec	114-25	114-27	113-31	114-19	– 6	6.668	+ .015	24,073
Mr94	113-05	113-19	113-03	113-15	– 5	6.762	+ .013	10,890
June	112-06	112-15	111-29	112-13	– 4	6.851	+ .010	2,052
Sept	111-07	111-15	110-29	111-14	– 3	6.934	+ .008	2,459
Dec	110-11	110-19	110-11	110-18	– 3	7.010	+ .008	1,965
Mr95	....	....	....	109-25	– 3	7.078	+ .008	125

Est vol 345,000; vol Mon 226,255; op int 376,133, +3,005.

TREASURY BONDS (MCE)–$50,000; pts. 32nds of 100%

	Open	High	Low	Settle	Chg	Yield Settle	Yield Chg	Open Interest
Sept	115-23	116-01	115-06	115-26	– 5	6.568	+ .012	12,781

Est vol 3,000; vol Mon 2,657; open int 12,889, +168.

TREASURY NOTES (CBT)–$100,000; pts. 32nds of 100%

	Open	High	Low	Settle	Chg	Yield Settle	Yield Chg	Open Interest
Sept	114-05	114-05	113-20	113-26	– 12	6.132	+ .047	219,391
Dec	112-30	112-31	112-21	112-25	– 12	6.261	+ .047	16,728
Mr94	....	....	....	111-24	– 12	6.392	+ .048	204

Est vol 50,000; vol Mon 24,017; open int 236,351, –3,023.

5 YR TREAS NOTES (CBT)–$100,000; pts. 32nds of 100%

	Open	High	Low	Settle	Chg	Yield Settle	Yield Chg	Open Interest
Sept	11-285	111-29	111-16	111-19	– 10.5	5.328	+ .070	150,375
Dec	111-01	111-01	110-23	110-25	– 10.5	5.504	+ .071	5,371

Est vol 28,500; vol Mon 12,414; open int 153,746, –249.

2 YR TREAS NOTES (CBT)–$200,000, pts. 32nds of 100%

	Open	High	Low	Settle	Chg	Yield Settle	Yield Chg	Open Interest
Sept	106-22	106-22	06-165	06-175	– 5¼	4.539	+ .083	14,616

Est vol 2,000; vol Mon 398; open int 14,616, +52.

30-DAY FEDERAL FUNDS (CBT)-$5 million; pts. of 100%

	Open	High	Low	Settle	Chg	Yield Settle	Yield Chg	Open Interest
July	96.96	96.96	96.95	96.95	– .01	3.05	+ .01	2,176
Aug	96.93	96.93	96.92	96.92	– .01	3.08	+ .01	2,430
Sept	96.88	96.88	96.86	96.87	– .02	3.13	+ .02	2,446
Oct	96.85	96.85	96.83	96.84	– .03	3.16	+ .03	1,401
Nov	96.79	96.79	96.78	96.78	– .03	3.22	+ .03	1,370
Dec	96.61	96.61	96.60	96.60	– .03	3.40	+ .03	111

Est vol 444; vol Mon 161; open int 10,067, –1.

TREASURY BILLS (CME)–$1 mil.; pts. of 100%

	Open	High	Low	Settle	Chg	Discount Settle	Discount Chg	Open Interest
Sept	96.88	96.88	96.84	96.85	– .03	3.15	+ .03	23,372
Dec	96.68	96.68	96.60	96.61	– .09	3.39	+ .09	6,606
Mr94	96.54	96.54	96.45	96.48	– .08	3.52	+ .08	1,775

Est vol 2,674; vol Mon 1,559; open int 31,763, +105.

LIBOR-1 MO. (CME)–$3,000,000; points of 100%

	Open	High	Low	Settle	Chg	Settle	Chg	Open Interest
Aug	96.80	96.80	96.76	96.78	– .02	3.22	+ .02	16,244
Sep	96.72	96.72	96.70	96.71	– .03	3.29	+ .03	4,271
Oct	96.68	96.68	96.64	96.65	– .03	3.35	+ .03	1,172
Nov	96.59	96.59	96.59	96.59	– .03	3.41	+ .03	1,055
Dec	96.04	96.04	95.94	95.96	– .10	4.04	+ .10	1,900
Mr94	....	....	....	96.23	– .09	3.77	+ .09	393

Est vol 3,670; vol Mon 2,968; open int 35,436, +402.

MUNI BOND INDEX (CBT)-$1,000; times Bond Buyer MBI

	Open	High	Low	Settle	Chg	High	Low	Open Interest
Sept	101-26	101-28	101-11	101-13	– 18	102-28	96-00	11,655
Dec	100-17	100-28	100-15	100-15	– 18	101-25	97-18	185

Est vol 5,000; vol Mon 3,453; open int 22,022, +171.
The index: Close 102-13; Yield 5.78.

EURODOLLAR (CME)–$1 million; pts of 100%

	Open	High	Low	Settle	Chg	Yield Settle	Yield Chg	Open Interest
Sept	96.64	96.64	96.59	96.61	– .03	3.39	+ .03	299,334
Dec	96.28	96.28	96.15	96.18	– .10	3.82	+ .10	309,165
Mr94	96.20	96.20	96.07	96.10	– .10	3.90	+ .10	230,292
June	95.90	95.91	95.78	95.82	– .10	4.18	+ .10	163,398
Sept	95.60	95.61	95.49	95.53	– .10	4.47	+ .10	141,457
Dec	95.20	95.20	95.09	95.11	– .10	4.89	+ .10	99,753
Mr95	95.11	95.11	95.00	95.02	– .10	4.98	+ .10	103,521
June	94.90	94.90	94.81	94.82	– .09	5.18	+ .09	71,034
Sept	94.74	94.74	94.65	94.66	– .09	5.34	+ .09	57,266
Dec	94.45	94.45	94.37	94.37	– .09	5.63	+ .09	56,272
Mr96	94.43	94.43	94.35	94.35	– .09	5.65	+ .09	50,542
June	94.27	94.27	94.19	94.20	– .08	5.80	+ .08	34,736
Sept	94.14	94.15	94.08	94.09	– .08	5.91	+ .08	30,734
Dec	93.92	93.92	93.86	93.87	– .08	6.13	+ .08	27,732
Mr97	93.95	93.95	93.88	93.89	– .08	6.11	+ .08	22,285
June	93.83	93.83	93.77	93.78	– .08	6.22	+ .08	19,208
Sept	93.72	93.73	93.67	93.69	– .07	6.31	+ .07	16,236
Dec	93.52	93.52	93.47	93.49	– .07	6.51	+ .07	12,409
Mr98	93.55	93.55	93.51	93.52	– .07	6.48	+ .07	11,571
June	93.47	93.47	93.44	93.44	– .07	6.56	+ .07	5,616

Est vol 312,724; vol Mon 109,342; open int 1,762,561, –3,710.

EURODOLLAR (LIFFE)–$1 million; pts of 100%

	Open	High	Low	Settle	Change	Lifetime High	Lifetime Low	Open Interest
Sept	96.63	96.64	96.59	96.62	– .02	96.76	92.50	6,233
Dec	96.27	96.27	96.26	96.19	– .08	96.70	92.24	4,608
Mr94	96.19	96.19	96.19	96.12	– .08	96.30	92.20	1,944
June	95.88	95.88	95.88	95.84	– .08	95.98	93.36	590
Sept	....	....	....	95.54	– .09	95.62	93.76	171

Est vol 1,113; vol Mon 404; open int 13,674, –70.

STERLING (LIFFE)–£500,000; pts of 100%

	Open	High	Low	Settle	Change	Lifetime High	Lifetime Low	Open Interest
Sept	94.10	94.15	94.10	94.12	+ .01	94.94	87.20	96,971
Dec	94.28	94.33	94.27	94.30	+ .01	94.81	88.95	80,082
Mr94	94.28	94.33	94.27	94.30	+ .01	94.53	89.87	53,060
June	94.16	94.20	94.15	94.17	....	94.28	89.78	41,138
Sept	93.92	93.92	93.89	93.89	– .03	94.01	90.10	23,727
Dec	93.65	93.65	93.59	93.59	– .06	93.74	90.10	15,885
Mr95	93.38	93.38	93.31	93.32	– .06	93.48	90.70	11,493
June	93.16	93.16	93.07	93.11	– .05	93.23	91.73	5,863
Sept	92.90	92.90	92.85	92.88	– .04	92.96	91.65	6,307
Dec	92.62	92.70	92.62	92.68	– .04	92.73	92.25	4,034

Est vol 28,160; vol Mon 41,156; open int 338,560, +643.

LONG GILT (LIFFE)–£50,000; 32nds of 100%

	Open	High	Low	Settle	Change	Lifetime High	Lifetime Low	Open Interest
Sept	108-23	108-30	108-18	108-23	....	109-03	102-16	90,279
Dec	108-09	108-09	108-09	108-03	....	108-09	103-30	443

Est vol 27,018; vol Mon 17,543; open int 90,722, –2,388.

EUROMARK (LIFFE)–DM 1,000,000; pts of 100%

	Open	High	Low	Settle	Change	Lifetime High	Lifetime Low	Open Interest
Sept	93.30	93.32	93.26	93.27	– .05	94.35	91.12	212,873
Dec	93.98	94.00	93.92	93.93	– .07	94.62	91.31	151,275
Mr94	94.46	94.47	94.40	94.40	– .07	94.77	91.53	91,382
June	94.67	94.68	94.61	94.61	– .07	94.80	91.71	64,457
Sept	94.70	94.70	94.63	94.63	– .07	94.80	91.81	52,364
Dec	94.58	94.58	94.55	94.53	– .05	94.62	91.83	42,719
Mr95	94.45	94.46	94.42	94.42	– .04	94.60	92.45	24,315
June	94.32	94.33	94.32	94.32	– .01	94.52	93.15	13,382
Sept	....	....	....	94.20	– .01	94.26	93.62	4,366
Dec	94.04	94.04	94.04	94.03	– .01	94.11	93.72	2,617

Est vol 55,820; vol Mon 37,774; open int 659,750, +2,347.

EUROSWISS (LIFFE)–SFr 1,000,000; pts of 100%

	Open	High	Low	Settle	Change	Lifetime High	Lifetime Low	Open Interest
Sept	95.54	95.54	95.50	95.51	– .05	96.11	93.35	25,011
Dec	95.77	95.79	95.77	95.77	– .04	96.11	94.83	11,661
Mr94	95.96	95.96	95.93	95.91	– .05	96.16	95.49	5,184
June	95.96	95.96	95.96	95.94	– .05	96.02	95.79	2,411

Est vol 6,002; vol Mon 2,664; open int 44,267, +182.

GERMAN GOV'T. BOND (LIFFE)
250,000 marks; pts of 100%

	Open	High	Low	Settle	Change	Lifetime High	Lifetime Low	Open Interest
Sept	96.24	96.30	96.05	96.12	– .14	104.15	91.65	166,168
Dec	96.41	96.44	96.32	96.28	– .14	103.75	94.93	15,641

Est vol 40,550; vol Mon 34,390; open int 181,809, +1,149.

ITALIAN GOVT. BOND (LIFFE)
ITL 200,000,000; pts of 100%

	Open	High	Low	Settle	Change	Lifetime High	Lifetime Low	Open Interest
Sept	104.65	104.86	104.45	104.51	– .23	104.90	95.45	15,528
Dec	104.40	104.40	104.05	104.09	– .25	104.45	102.05	1,269

Est vol 16,797; vol Mon 14,851; open int 53,696, +399.

FT–SE 100 INDEX (LIFFE)–£25 per index point

	Open	High	Low	Settle	Change	Lifetime High	Lifetime Low	Open Interest
Sept	2858.0	2863.0	2820.0	2824.0	– 30.0	3001.5	2634.	44,051
Dec	2872.0	2872.0	2841.0	2841.5	– 30.0	2987.	2804.	630
Mr94	....	....	....	2857.0	– 30.0	2873.	2873.	221

Est vol 15,077; vol Mon 8,075; open int 44,902, +1,728.

Source: *The Wall Street Journal*, July 21, 1993, p. C14.

Quotations for Futures Contracts

Whereas the prices of forward contracts have to be obtained from the issuer of the contract, usually a bank, prices of futures contracts are widely reported in the financial press. Exhibit 10.4 shows the quotations of currency and interest rates futures for July 20, 1993, reported in *The Wall Street Journal*.

The first set of figures in the exhibit are the currency futures. The deutschemark quotes, for example, show that the size of the futures contract on the Chicago Mercantile Exchange (CME), is 125,000 DM and that the prices are quoted as dollars per mark. On July 20, quotes for only two DM contracts, those maturing in September and those maturing in December, were available. Since the year of the contract is not mentioned, it is understood that the two contracts expire in 1993. The first column against "Sept" shows the opening price of $0.5824/DM on that day followed by the highest and the lowest prices during the day. The last quote for the day was $0.5851/DM, an increase of .0026 from the previous day.

Interest rate futures are quoted in a manner that is unlike other futures contracts. Recall that an investor who has a long position in an interest rate futures contract will lose if the interest rates rise. This is the opposite of the futures contract for all other assets. The holder of a long foreign currency futures contract gains if the foreign currency rises in value. Similarly, the holder of a long position in a stock market index futures contract gains if the stock market index rises in value. To make the situation parallel for interest rate futures contracts, prices of these contracts are quoted not as interest rates but as 100 minus the annual interest rate. Thus, if the Eurodollar futures contract was being offered at an interest rate of 6.34 percent, the price of the contract would be quoted as $100 - 6.34 = 93.56$. In Exhibit 10.4, for example, the September Eurodollar futures contract on the CME closed on July 20 at 96.61. This implies that near the closing time of the market on that day, a three month deposit starting in September would be guaranteed an interest rate of $100 - 96.61$ or 3.39 percent per annum. Notice what happens when the market interest rate goes up, say, from 3.39 percent to 3.75 percent. Logically, an investor who had purchased the interest rate futures contract at 96.61 should lose money. In terms of the market quotation, the new quote will be $100 - 3.75$ or 96.25. Thus, the quoted price of the futures contract changes from 96.61 to 96.25. With this method of quotation, the investor in long contracts loses when the quote becomes lower and gains when the quote rises—just like all the other futures contracts.

The quotations for stock market futures contracts have only one other complication. The size of the contract is indicated as a multiple of the value of the index itself. Thus, the size of the CME's Nikkei index is given as $5 times the index. On July 20 when this index closed at 19615, one futures contract on the Nikkei index would have represented an investment of 5 × 19615 or $98,075. In all other respects, the quotations for stock market index futures contracts work like other futures contracts.

Forward Rate Agreement

Forward contracts on interest rates are known as FRAs, or forward rate agreements. An FRA is an agreement to fix the interest rate on a deposit at some point in the future. The main characteristic of an FRA is that it is almost never used to obtain an actual deposit; it is settled in the same manner as a futures contract. At maturity, the parties settle the difference between the contracted price and the spot price at the time of maturity. FRAs are available in a number of currencies.

Suppose that Firm F decides on August 17 that it is going to have to borrow $10 million for three months on October 16. Not wanting to take a risk with interest rates, it enters into an FRA with a bank at 7.5 percent. How will the agreement be settled if on October 16 the rate is 8.2 percent? First we see that the bank will have to pay Firm F since the rates have gone up and the firm has an agreement to borrow at lower rates. The bank owes the firm the difference between the contract rate and the actual rate. Since the funds would have been borrowed for 90 days, the interest saved is $17,500 = { 10,000,000 × (0.082 − 0.075) × 90/360}. This amount, however, would have been paid in 90 days from October 16. The bank, therefore, will pay the present value of these funds by discounting them at the current interbank rate. Assuming that the interbank rate is also 8.2 percent, the bank will have to pay $17,148.46 = { 17500 / [1 + .082 × (90/360)]}. The settlement of an FRA has to take into account not only the interest earned or lost, but also the present value of the interest payment. The settlement amount can be calculated from the following formula standardized by the British Banker's Association:

$$\text{Settlement} = \frac{(L - R) \times D \times A}{(B \times 100) + (L \times D)} \qquad (10.1)$$

where:

L = Interest rate at the time of settlement, expressed as a number
R = Contracted interest rate expressed as a number
D = Number of days in the contract
A = Contract amount
B = 360, except 365 for the pound

Substituting the numbers in the formula should verify previous calculations.

Practices for quoting FRA's vary from currency to currency, but the most common practice is to quote the interest rate along with the beginning period and its maturity. Thus a quote of "3 against 6 at 3.54–3.48" means that the bank making the quote is willing to lend funds in three months for a maturity of six months at a rate of 3.54 percent. It is willing to accept a deposit for the same time span at 3.48 percent.

Options Contracts

Perhaps the most useful concept in developing derivative products is the idea of an option. Unlike a spot, forward, or futures contract, an option does not *require* an investor to go through with a transaction. An option contract really provides an option: the investor can choose to undertake the transaction, or if she or he wishes, can ignore the contract. In reality, it is assumed that the investor will go through with the transaction if the events turn out to be in his or her favor, and will ignore the transaction otherwise. The concept of an option is useful not only in risk management but also in evaluating many other choices we may face in financial markets.

To understand how an option works, consider the same investor who had purchased a deutschemark futures contract at $0.62/DM for 125,000 DM. This investor would lose money if the deutschemark were to depreciate, say, to a value of $0.60/DM. What the investor would really like to have is the possibility to just forget about the contract if the exchange rate for deutschemarks moves in a direction that would cause her to lose money. An option offers such a contract, but, of course, for a price.

A foreign currency option provides the buyer of what is called a **call option** the choice of being able to buy the foreign currency at a fixed price, if he or she so desires. The option obviously has a maturity after which the investor no longer has this choice. With an American option, the investor can purchase the foreign currency any time before the expiry of the option; with a European option, the purchase can only be made on the maturity date. The contract price at which the investor can purchase the foreign currency is called the **exercise price**. The investor who has this choice is called the **holder of the option**. The choice is provided by someone who is called the **writer of the option**. Note that the choice exists only for the holder of the option; the writer of the option is required to fulfill the contract if the holder exercises the option.

Let us follow up on our investor to understand how a foreign currency option works. Suppose that instead of buying the futures contract, she had purchased a call option to buy 125,000 DM at $0.62/DM. What is she expecting to do in the future for different values of the deutschemark exchange rate? If the mark were to depreciate below $0.62/DM, say, to a level of $0.59/DM, she would be better off ignoring the option contract and buying the deutschemarks in the open market. She would be paying only 125000×0.59 or $73,750 in the open market instead of $77,500 to acquire the same number of deutschemarks through the option contract. If, however, the deutschemark were to appreciate, she would be better off exercising the option. If the mark were to rise to $0.66/DM, she would have to pay $ 82,500 in the open market and only $77,500 through the option contract. For all values of the mark above $0.62/DM, she will exercise the option. To compare the option contract to other alternatives, the following table gives the cost of acquiring DM 125,000 under three alternatives for different values of the future exchange rate of the mark. The three alternatives are: (1) do nothing now and purchase marks in three months at the then spot rate, (2) purchase a futures contract at $0.62/DM, and (3) purchase an option contract at $0.62/DM.

Cost of acquiring DM 125,000 in three months

DM exchange rates in three months	1 Do nothing now	2 Buy a futures contract at $0.62/DM	3 Buy an option at $0.62/DM (with zero premium)
$0.56/DM	$70,000	$77,500	$70,000
$0.58/DM	$72,500	$77,500	$72,500
$0.60/DM	$75,000	$77,500	$75,000
$0.62/DM	$77,500	$77,500	$77,500
$0.64/DM	$80,000	$77,500	$77,500
$0.66/DM	$82,500	$77,500	$77,500

Notice the advantage of the option contract. The price of acquiring the deutschemarks with an option is always the lesser of the other two options. Before we look at how this is possible, let us recognize that the option holder's gain comes at the cost of the option writer; in this case the option writer always receives the worst price. Why would a writer agree to do that?

The answer to that is that the writer of the option charges the holder a fixed fee, or a premium, for offering the choice. In exchange for the promise that the holder of the option will never have to pay more than $77,500 for the required number of deutschemarks, she will have to pay the writer a nonrefundable fee when the contract is made. Since we assume that the writer of the option is rational, we expect that the fee is equal to the expected value of the loss that the writer will suffer when the deutschemark appreciates above $0.62/DM.

In addition to the call option that gave the holder of the option the right to purchase a foreign currency, a put option gives the holder a right to sell the foreign currency at a fixed price. Thus, if an investor had wanted to sell deutschemarks at a future date, he could purchase a put option, say at $0.62/DM. If marks appreciate in the market and the investor would receive more dollars for a given number of deutschemarks in the open market, he can ignore the put option. If, however, the deutschemark depreciates, he can exercise the option and receive $77,500. Once again any fee that he had to pay in the beginning would have to be deducted from this amount. The following box summarizes some terms commonly used with option.

▼ ▼ ▼
Terminology of Options

American option. An option that can be exercised any time before the maturity date.

At–the–money option. For a call option, the exercise price equals the current forward rate. For a put option, the exercise price equals the current spot rate.

Call option. An option to purchase the underlying asset at the exercise price.

European option. An option that can only be exercised on the maturity date.

Exercise price. The price at which the option can be exercised. Also called strike price.

Fee. See premium.

Holder of an option. The party that has purchased either a call or a put option.

In–the–money option. The current price of the underlying asset is such that if the option were exercised, the holder would earn a profit.

Out–of–the–money option. The current price of the underlying asset is such that the option would not be exercised.

Premium. The amount paid by the holder of an option to the writer of the option.

Put option. An option to sell the underlying asset at the exercise price.

Strike price. See exercise price.

Writer of an option. The party that has sold either a call or a put option.
▲ ▲ ▲

Interest rate and stock options work in the same fashion as the currency options described here. The only difference for interest rate options is that there are two types of interest rate options available: organized exchanges trade options on the prices of underlying debt instruments—bonds or bills—and the over–the–counter market deals in options on interest rates.

Exhibit 10.5
Payoffs from Call Options

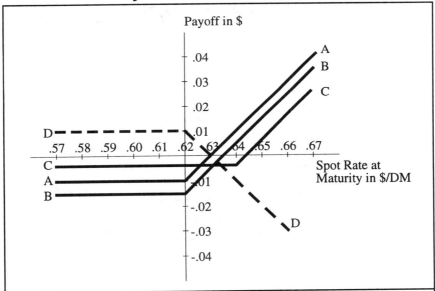

Payoff from call options:
  AA: Option to purchase deutschemarks @$.62/DM; option valid for three months; fee for option is $.01/DM.
  BB: Option to purchase deutschemarks @$.62/DM; option valid for six months; fee for option is $.015/DM.
  CC: Option to purchase deutschemarks @$.63/DM; option valid for three months; fee for option is $.004/DM.
  DD: Writer of Option A above.

Payoff Profile of an Option

We need to understand the values or payoff profiles for the holders of a call or a put option, as well as the payoff profiles for the writers of these options. For simplicity, Exhibit 10.5 shows the payoff for the two sides of a call option, and Exhibit 10.6 does the same for the put option. An important characteristic of an option is that it is a zero–sum game

Exhibit 10.6
Payoffs from Put Options

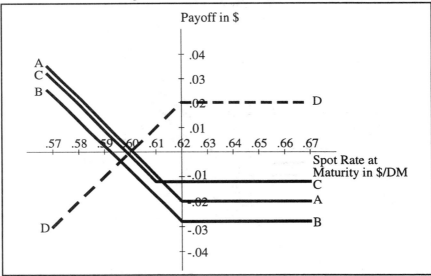

Payoff from put options:
    AA: Option to sell deutschemarks @$.62/DM; option valid for three months; fee for option is $.02/DM.

    BB: Option to sell deutschemarks @$.62/DM; option valid for six months; fee for option is $.028/DM.

    CC: Option to purchase deutschemarks @$.61/DM; option valid for three months; fee for option is $.012/DM.

    DD: Writer of Option A above.

between the writer and holder of the option. Moreover, holding one position does not preclude an investor from holding some other option contract to create any payoff profile. We will discuss the importance of these characteristics shortly.

Pricing of Option Contracts

It would not be possible to discuss risk management strategies using options without some understanding of how the premium or the fee for an option is determined. To understand option pricing, we begin with a brief review of what a holder of a call option on a foreign currency receives under various outcomes of the future exchange rate, or various states of nature, and assume that the option is held by a speculator. The following table summarizes various outcomes.

Outcome of the Exchange Rate	Payoff for the Speculator
exchange rate ≤ exercise price	Speculator loses all the premium
exchange rate just greater than exercise price	Speculator loses some of the premium
exchange rate >> exercise price	Speculator gains

The fundamentals of option pricing were first developed by Black and Scholes in 1973, and their pricing formula now forms the basis of all option pricing. The main points of their analysis are as follows. Assuming that both the holder and writer are rational investors, the premium will be set such that the expected gain from holding the option is comparable to that from holding other assets in the economy, after adjustments for risk. What determines an option holder's gains or losses?

Volatility of the exchange rate. The holder gains only if the exchange rate moves to the right of the exercise price in Exhibit 10.5. The more volatile the exchange rates, the higher the chance that the exchange rate for the foreign currency will move into the zone where the option will have to be exercised. The writer of the option will take this into account and, hence, options for currencies with high volatility will require high premiums.

Time. The longer that an option holder has to exercise the option, the higher the chance that the exchange rate will have the time to move into the profitable zone. Thus, options with long maturities will cost more than options with short maturities, *ceteris paribus*.

Exercise price relative to the spot price. How far the exchange rate has to move before an option enters the "in–the–money" zone will also influence the premium or the price of the option.

Risk free interest rate. Option price will also depend upon other investments available in the economy; the risk free interest rate is really a proxy for the other investments.

Exhibit 10.7 summarizes the effects of these variables on the price of an option. The price, or the premium, consists of two components: the intrinsic value and the time value. Intrinsic value is the part of the premium which can be obtained immediately if the option were exercised. Clearly, there is no intrinsic value for a call option below its exercise price. The time value accounts for the possibility that, given time and volatile exchange rates, the foreign currency may move into the region where the option is "in–the–money."

Understanding option pricing allows us to create combinations of options that allow for a positive payoff from the portfolio in accordance with our beliefs about the future events. Consider, for example, an investor who believes that the volatility of a certain currency is going to be lower than what the market believes it to be. Since the market has priced the options for this currency based on a belief of high volatility, the investor would gain by creating a portfolio which provides a high payoff when the exchange rates do not move much. In exchange, the investor would give up potential gains from situations where the exchange rate has to move a lot. (For comparison, recall from Exhibit 10.5 that the gains of the holder of a call option increase as the exchange rate moves farther away from the exercise price.) The ideal portfolio of options for this investor would be a combination of writing a call and

Exhibit 10.7
Price of a Call Options

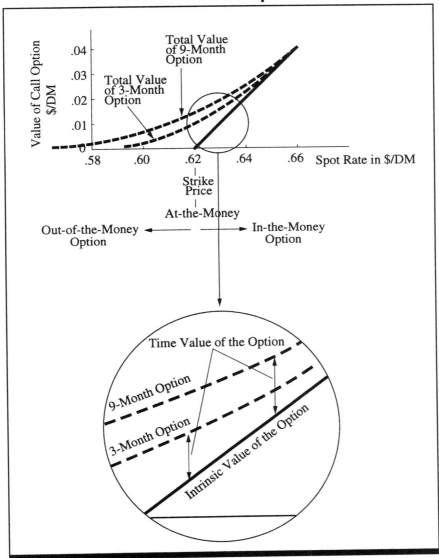

Exhibit 10.8
Low Volatility and Options

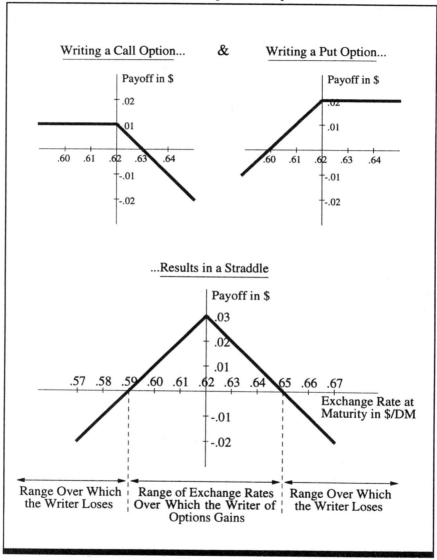

Writing a Call Option...　&　Writing a Put Option...

...Results in a Straddle

Range Over Which the Writer Loses ┆ Range of Exchange Rates Over Which the Writer of Options Gains ┆ Range Over Which the Writer Loses

writing a put at the same exercise price which would be the same as the current spot rate.

This combination is shown in Exhibit 10.8. Since the investor does not expect the exchange rate to move very much, she expects not to have to pay anything to the holder of the call or the holder of the put. If her expectations come true, she would have received premiums from both. On the other hand, the risk of this strategy is very high. If the exchange rate moves more than just a little in either direction, she could lose a lot of money.

Quotations of Option Contracts

Exhibit 10.9 shows the quotations for foreign currency options as reported in *The Wall Street Journal*. Quotations from the Philadelphia Exchange for American and European options are also shown in the exhibit. The largest choice of contracts is for the deutschemark and for the yen. The first column under German marks lists the strike or exercise price for a contract. The second column shows the maturity date. The premium for the call option is shown in the fourth column and the third column gives us an idea of the liquidity of the contract. The most liquid call option is for the strike price of 59-1/2, that is, $0.595/DM, for maturity in August. With about 1,060 contracts outstanding, this contract would be considered very liquid. Since the premium for this contract is 0.26 cents/mark, the purchase of a 59.5 cents call option on deutschemarks, expiring in August, would cost 0.0026 × 62500 or $162.50. It may be worthwhile to remember that the spot rate on that date was $0.5886/DM and that the September future closed at $0.5851/DM. Interpolation between the July 20 and September prices would indicate an expected rate of $0.5881/DM. Investors, it seems, were concerned that the deutschemark might rise above $0.60/DM and were protecting themselves by buying call options. The large number of puts outstanding at 58.5 (that is, $0.585/DM) indicates that other investors were concerned about the deutschemark falling much below that level. It seems that the put holders were right for being concerned; the deutschemark had fallen to $0.58/DM by the time the August contract matured.

Exhibit 10.9
Quotations of Option Contracts

CURRENCY TRADING

OPTIONS
PHILADELPHIA EXCHANGE

DMark — 58.87

62,500 German Mark EOM-European style.

	Call Vol.	Call Last	Put Vol.	Put Last
57 Jul	...	...	50	0.04
58 Jul	...	...	100	0.13
59 Jul	...	...	500	0.54

62,500 German Marks EOM-European style.

	Call Vol.	Call Last	Put Vol.	Put Last
58½ Jul	...	...	400	0.31
60½ Jul	50	0.04	...	...

Australian Dollar — 67.80

50,000 Australian Dollar EOM-cents per unit.

	Call Vol.	Call Last	Put Vol.	Put Last
66 Aug	...	...	200	0.35
68 Jul	20	0.33	...	...
69 Aug	200	0.41	...	...

50,000 Australian Dollars-European Style.

	Call Vol.	Call Last	Put Vol.	Put Last
68 Aug	20	0.56	...	...

50,000 Australian Dollars-cents per unit.

	Call Vol.	Call Last	Put Vol.	Put Last
67 Sep	...	...	20	0.80
68 Aug	10	0.55	20	0.93
68 Sep	7	0.83	...	...
69 Sep	...	...	10	1.99

British Pound — 151.09

31,250 British Pound EOM-cents per unit.

	Call Vol.	Call Last	Put Vol.	Put Last
150 Jul	292	1.68	10	0.90

31,250 British Pounds-European Style.

	Call Vol.	Call Last	Put Vol.	Put Last
150 Aug	1	2.30	...	...
155 Aug	32	0.45	...	...

31,250 British Pounds-cents per unit.

	Call Vol.	Call Last	Put Vol.	Put Last
142½ Sep	...	...	70	0.65
145 Sep	...	...	130	1.10
145 Dec	...	...	32	2.93
147½ Aug	8	3.70	150	0.82
147½ Sep	...	...	1	1.82
150 Aug	59	2.00	41	1.50
150 Dec	80	4.50	...	...
152½ Aug	206	1.10	12	3.10
152½ Sep	...	...	6	4.38
152½ Dec	4	3.35	...	...
155 Sep	32	0.90	...	...
157½ Dec	198	1.80	...	...
160 Dec	5	1.27	...	...

British Pound-GMark — 256.68

31,250 British Pound-German Mark cross.

	Call Vol.	Call Last	Put Vol.	Put Last
252 Aug	...	...	128	0.48
252 Sep	...	...	3000	0.96
254 Aug	...	...	64	0.94
262 Sep	3000	1.28	...	...

Canadian Dollar — 78.17

50,000 Canadian Dollars EOM-cents per unit.

	Call Vol.	Call Last	Put Vol.	Put Last
78 Jul	...	...	200	0.18
78½ Jul	...	...	500	0.46

50,000 Canadian Dollars-European Style.

	Call Vol.	Call Last	Put Vol.	Put Last
79 Sep	5	0.23	...	...

50,000 Canadian Dollars-cents per unit.

	Call Vol.	Call Last	Put Vol.	Put Last
77 Dec	...	...	600	0.80
78 Sep	...	...	950	0.63
79 Aug	...	...	20	1.00

French Franc — 172.32

250,000 French Francs EOM-10ths of a unit per unit.

	Call Vol.	Call Last	Put Vol.	Put Last
18 Jul	...	...	15	0.06

250,000 French Francs-European Style.

	Call Vol.	Call Last	Put Vol.	Put Last
16 Dec	...	...	500	1.68

GMark-JYen — 63.69

62,500 German Mark-Japanese Yen cross EOM.

	Call Vol.	Call Last	Put Vol.	Put Last
63 Jul	...	...	10	0.37

62,500 German Mark-Japanese Yen cross.

	Call Vol.	Call Last	Put Vol.	Put Last
61 Sep	...	...	100	0.44
61 Dec	...	...	10	1.19
62 Aug	...	...	45	0.30
63 Dec	15	1.73	...	...

German Mark — 58.87

62,500 German Marks EOM-cents per unit.

	Call Vol.	Call Last	Put Vol.	Put Last
53 Sep	...	...	400	0.04
54 Sep	...	...	800	0.08
55 Sep	...	...	400	0.18
57 Jul	...	...	150	0.04
57½ Jul	...	...	4010	0.08
58 Jul	...	...	20	0.22
58 Sep	...	...	1500	1.05
58½ Jul	21	0.44	...	...
58½ Sep	...	...	2	1.42
59 Jul	265	0.19	...	...
60 Jul	125	0.08	...	...

62,500 German Marks-European Style.

	Call Vol.	Call Last	Put Vol.	Put Last
56 Aug	...	...	50	0.07
57½ Sep	...	...	3	0.68
58 Aug	...	...	3	0.50
58 Sep	...	...	5	0.84
58 Dec	...	...	5	1.85
59 Aug	...	...	75	2.49
61 Aug	50	0.06	...	...

62,500 German Marks-cents per unit.

	Call Vol.	Call Last	Put Vol.	Put Last
55 Dec	40	3.63	5	0.64
55½ Sep	...	...	1	0.20
56 Aug	...	...	200	0.06
56 Sep	...	...	60	0.28
56 Dec	...	...	30	0.95
56½ Sep	...	...	100	0.14
56½ Sep	...	...	100	0.33
57 Aug	...	...	205	0.19
57 Sep	...	...	270	0.46
57 Dec	...	...	10	1.28
57½ Sep	...	...	1250	0.34
57½ Sep	...	...	5	0.73
58 Aug	...	...	330	0.36
58 Sep	301	1.30	...	...
58 Dec	...	...	50	1.71
58½ Sep	5	0.75	200	0.56
58½ Sep	...	...	5	1.23
59 Aug	226	0.42	10	0.86
59 Sep	200	0.71	102	1.42
59½ Aug	1060	0.26	400	1.47
59½ Sep	4	0.50	...	...
60 Aug	500	0.15	5	1.60
60 Sep	120	0.41	...	...
61 Aug	10	0.07	...	...
61 Sep	...	...	1	2.95
62 Sep	...	...	3	3.86

Japanese Yen — 92.37

6,250,000 Japanese Yen EOM-100ths of a cent per unit.

	Call Vol.	Call Last	Put Vol.	Put Last
90 Jul	...	...	36	0.23
91 Jul	...	...	80	0.40
93 Jul	18	0.50	...	...

6,250,000 Japanese Yen EOM.

	Call Vol.	Call Last	Put Vol.	Put Last
90½ Jul	...	...	160	0.72
92½ Jul	80	0.67	...	...
94½ Jul	5	0.20	...	...

6,250,000 Japanese Yen-100ths of a cent per unit.

	Call Vol.	Call Last	Put Vol.	Put Last
86 Sep	...	...	200	0.05
88 Sep	...	...	320	0.40
89½ Aug	...	...	338	0.38
90 Aug	...	...	50	0.37
90 Sep	...	...	1	0.63
90½ Jul	...	...	1	0.53
91 Aug	4	1.76	198	0.66
91 Sep	...	...	10	1.03
91½ Jul	...	...	70	0.85
92 Aug	4	1.41	...	...
92 Sep	1	1.63	1	1.85
92½ Sep	300	1.60	300	1.74
93 Aug	30	0.90	30	1.53
93 Sep	4	1.36	...	...
93 Dec	...	...	1	2.94
93½ Aug	15	0.67	...	...
94 Aug	6	0.54	...	...
94 Sep	21	0.88	...	...
95 Aug	1750	0.31	...	...
95 Sep	11	0.75	...	...
97 Sep	10	0.36	...	...

Swiss Franc — 66.87

62,500 Swiss Franc EOM-cents per unit.

	Call Vol.	Call Last	Put Vol.	Put Last
64 Jul	...	...	10	0.04
68 Jul	8	0.11	...	...

62,500 Swiss Francs EOM.

	Call Vol.	Call Last	Put Vol.	Put Last
66½ Jul	50	0.69	...	...
67½ Jul	50	0.58	...	...

62,500 Swiss Francs-European Style.

	Call Vol.	Call Last	Put Vol.	Put Last
67 Aug	...	...	5	1.19
69 Aug	...	...	5	2.65

62,500 Swiss Francs-cents per unit.

	Call Vol.	Call Last	Put Vol.	Put Last
65 Sep	...	...	3	0.71
65½ Aug	...	...	40	0.23
66 Sep	...	...	21	0.95
66½ Sep	33	1.20	...	...
67 Aug	...	...	40	0.91

Call Vol ...... 11,272 Open Int ... 621,262
Put Vol .... 23,740 Open Int ... 528,538

Source: *The Wall Street Journal*, July 21, 1993, p. C15.

Options on Futures

An extension of an option contract on a spot contract is an option on a futures contract. A futures contract can be the underlying asset for an

Exhibit 10.10
Quotations of Futures Options

CURRENCY

JAPANESE YEN (CME)
12,500,000 yen; cents per 100 yen

Strike	Calls—Settle			Puts—Settle		
Price	Aug	Sep	Oct	Aug	Sep	Oct
9150	1.61	2.11	....	0.68	1.18	....
9200	1.30	1.82	2.28	0.87	1.39	1.77
9250	1.03	1.56	....	1.10	1.63	....
9300	0.82	1.34	1.80	1.39	1.91	2.29
9350	0.63	1.14	1.59	1.70	2.20	....
9400	0.49	0.97	1.40	2.06	2.53	2.88

Est vol 6,678   Mon 2,788 calls 4,488 puts
Op int Mon   39,130 calls 51,754 puts

DEUTSCHEMARK (CME)
125,000 marks; cents per mark

Strike	Calls—Settle			Puts—Settle		
Price	Aug	Sep	Oct	Aug	Sep	Oct
5750	1.20	1.50	....	0.19	0.50	....
5800	0.84	1.19	1.27	0.33	0.68	1.25
5850	0.55	0.92	1.04	0.54	0.91	....
5900	0.35	0.71	0.84	0.84	1.20	....
5950	0.21	0.53	....	1.20	1.51	....
6000	0.12	0.39	0.53	1.61	1.88	....

Est vol 17,287   Mon 6,058 calls 3,262 puts
Op int Mon   156,631 calls 129,137 puts

CANADIAN DOLLAR (CME)
100,000 Can.$, cents per Can.$

Strike	Calls—Settle			Puts—Settle		
Price	Aug	Sep	Oct	Aug	Sep	Oct
7700	....	1.23	....	0.05	0.19	....
7750	0.68	0.89	0.99	0.13	0.34	0.66
7800	0.35	0.59	0.73	0.30	0.54	0.90
7850	0.15	0.37	0.52	0.60	0.82	....
7900	0.05	0.21	....	....	1.16	....
7950	0.01	0.12	....	....	1.56	....

Est vol 1,267   Mon 81 calls 89 puts
Op int Mon   3,232 calls 3,974 puts

BRITISH POUND (CME)
62,500 pounds; cents per pound

Strike	Calls—Settle			Puts—Settle		
Price	Aug	Sep	Oct	Aug	Sep	Oct
1450	5.76	6.24	....	0.18	0.66	....
1475	3.58	4.36	4.62	0.48	1.28	....
1500	1.90	2.86	3.30	1.30	2.26	....
1525	0.82	1.72	....	2.72	3.62	....
1550	0.30	0.98	1.50	4.70	5.36	....
1575	0.10	0.48	....	....	....	....

Est vol 1,551   Mon 1,259 calls 1,114 puts
Op int Mon   10,608 calls 9,610 puts

SWISS FRANC (CME)
125,000 francs; cents per franc

Strike	Calls—Settle			Puts—Settle		
Price	Aug	Sep	Oct	Sep	Sep	Oct
6550	1.43	1.81	....	0.23	0.62	....
6600	1.07	1.49	....	0.37	0.79	....
6650	0.76	1.21	1.52	0.56	1.01	....
6700	0.52	0.97	....	0.82	1.27	....
6750	0.34	0.78	....	1.14	1.58	....
6800	0.21	0.60	0.91	1.51	1.89	....

Est vol 2,079   Mon 594 calls 453 puts
Op int Mon   17,124 calls 11,180 puts

U.S. DOLLAR INDEX (FINEX)
1,000 times index

Strike	Calls—Settle			Puts—Settle		
Price	Aug	Sep	Oct	Aug	Sep	Oct
93	....	2.28	....	0.24	0.65	....
94	....	1.66	....	0.53	1.02	....
95	0.64	1.15	....	1.00	1.51	....
96	0.31	0.76	....	1.67	2.11	....
97	0.13	0.48	....	2.48	....	....
98	0.05	0.28	....	....	....	....

Est vol 228   Mon 130 calls 100 puts
Op int Mon   2,168 calls 929 puts

INTEREST RATE

T-BONDS (CBT)
$100,000; points and 64ths of 100%

Strike	Calls—Settle			Puts—Settle		
Price	Aug	Sep	Dec	Aug	Sep	Dec
112	3-53	3-58	3-44	0-01	0-07	1-11
114	1-54	2-12	2-32	0-02	0-24	1-57
116	0-12	0-58	1-34	0-23	1-07	2-60
118	0-01	0-16	0-57	....	2-28	4-17
120	0-01	0-02	0-29	....	....	5-52
122	....	0-01	0-15	....	....	....

Est. vol. 100,000;
Mon vol. 38,818 calls; 34,080 puts
Op. int. Mon 292,972 calls; 273,589 puts

T-NOTES (CBT)
$100,000; points and 64ths of 100%

Strike	Calls—Settle			Puts—Settle		
Price	Aug	Sep	Dec	Aug	Sep	Dec
111	2-53	2-54	2-34	0-01	0-03	0-49
112	1-53	1-61	1-57	0-01	0-09	1-07
113	0-54	1-11	1-21	0-02	0-23	1-35
114	0-08	0-37	0-59	0-20	0-49	....
115	0-01	0-15	0-39	....	1-27	....
116	....	0-05	0-25	....	....	....

Est vol 15,126   Mon 6,984 calls 7,223 puts
Op int Mon   74,282 calls 114,744 puts

MUNICIPAL BOND INDEX (CBT)
$100,000; pts. & 64ths of 100%

Strike	Calls—Settle			Puts—Settle		
Price	Sep	Dec	Mar	Sep	Dec	Mar
99	....	....	....	....	0-52	....
100	....	1-40	....	0-22	1-11	....
101	1-03	1-08	....	0-41	1-40	....
102	0-36	0-48	....	1-10	2-17	....
103	0-17	0-31	....	....	2-63	....
104	0-08	....	....	....	....	....

Est vol 127   Mon 50 calls 2 puts
Op int Mon   4,686 calls 4,622 puts

5 YR TREAS NOTES (CBT)
$100,000; points and 64ths of 100%

Strike	Calls—Settle			Puts—Settle		
Price	Aug	Sep	Dec	Aug	Sep	Dec
11000	1-38	1-42	1-26	0-01	0-04	0-42
11050	1-06	1-14	....	0-01	0-08	0-54
11100	0-40	0-52	0-55	0-02	0-14	1-05
11150	0-14	0-32	0-41	0-08	0-26	....
11200	0-02	0-16	....	0-28	0-42	1-43
11250	0-01	0-07	0-21	....	....	....

Est vol 10,000   Mon 665 calls 4,999 puts
Op int Mon   45,612 calls 65,975 puts

EURODOLLAR (CME)
$ million; pts. of 100%

Strike	Calls—Settle			Puts—Settle		
Price	Sep	Dec	Mar	Sep	Dec	Mar
9600	0.61	0.32	0.34	.0004	0.14	0.24
9625	0.37	0.16	0.19	0.01	0.23	0.34
9650	0.15	0.07	0.10	0.04	0.39	0.49
9675	0.02	0.02	0.04	0.16	0.58	0.68
9700	.0004	0.01	0.02	0.39	0.82	0.91
9725	.0004	.0004	0.01	0.64	1.07	....

Est. vol. 64,435;
Mon vol. 111,254 calls; 24,297 puts
Op. int. Mon 586,391 calls; 696,818 puts

LIBOR — 1 Mo. (CME)
$3 million; pts. of 100%

Strike	Calls—Settle			Puts—Settle		
Price	Aug	Sep	Oct	Aug	Sep	Oct
9625	0.53	0.47	....	.0004	0.01	....
9650	0.29	0.23	0.21	0.01	0.02	0.06
9675	0.06	0.06	0.06	0.03	0.10	0.16
9700	0.01	0.02	0.02	0.23	0.31	0.37
9725	....	.0004	0.01	....	....	0.61
9750	....	....	....	....	....	....

Est vol 200   Mon 0 calls 0 puts
Op int Mon   2,626 calls 1,224 puts

TREASURY BILLS (CME)
$1 million; pts. of 100%

Strike	Calls—Settle			Puts—Settle		
Price	Aug	Sep	Mar	Sep	Dec	Mar
9625	0.60	0.43	....	.0004	0.08	....
9650	0.35	0.25	....	.0004	0.14	....
9675	0.12	0.13	....	0.02	0.27	....
9700	0.04	....	....	0.16	....	....
9725	.0004	....	....	0.40	....	....
9750	....	....	....	....	....	....

Est vol 0   Mon 0 calls 0 puts
Op int Mon   152 calls 1,561 puts

EURODOLLAR (LIFFE)
$1 million; pts. of 100%

Strike	Calls—Settle			Puts—Settle		
Price	Sep	Dec	Mar	Sep	Dec	Mar
9600	0.62	0.32	0.34	....	0.13	0.22
9625	0.39	0.17	0.20	0.02	0.23	0.33
9650	0.16	0.08	0.10	0.04	0.39	0.48
9675	0.03	0.03	0.05	0.16	0.59	0.68
9700	0.01	0.01	0.02	0.39	0.82	0.90
9725	....	0.01	0.63	1.06	1.14	....

Est vol   Tues 0 calls 0 puts
   3,840 calls 1,335 puts

LONG GILT (LIFFE)
£50,000; 64ths of 100%

Strike	Calls—Settle			Puts—Settle		
Price	Sep	Dec		Sep	Dec	
106	2-56	3-04	....	0-10	0-62	....
107	2-03	2-27	....	0-21	1-21	....
108	1-21	1-55	....	0-39	1-49	....
109	0-50	1-25	....	1-04	2-19	....
110	0-26	1-01	....	1-44	2-59	....
111	0-12	0-46	....	2-30	3-40	....

Est vol   Tues 1,575 calls 1,073 puts
Op int Mon   64,444 calls 50,968 puts

Source: *The Wall Street Journal*, July 21, 1993, p. C15.

option just as a spot contract can be. An option on a future, however, has a unique purpose that we will examine in the subsequent two chapters.

A call option on a futures contract gives the holder of the call the right to acquire a long position on a specific futures contract. Consider the quotation for options on yen futures in Exhibit 10.10. A call option to acquire an August futures contract at a price of 0.92 cent/yen can be purchased for a fee of 1.30 cents/100 yen of the contract. Since the contract size is 12.5 million yen, the total premium will be (12500000 × .0130/100) or $1,625. It may seem like a high price, but the spot price on the day was $.009242/yen and the forward (Exhibit 2.6) and the future (Exhibit 10.4) prices showed that the market was expecting the yen to appreciate sightly over the next few months. Even if the yen did not move at all, exercising the option and then settling the futures contract would have returned about half of the premium to the investor. At a spot rate of $.009242/yen, the option at a strike price of $.0092/yen was "in–the–money" by $.000042/yen, or about a third of the premium of $.000130/yen. As it happens, the yen appreciated more than was expected, ending at about $.00925/yen by the time the contract reached its maturity in August.

We will discuss the usefulness of the futures options in the following chapter.

Swaps

Perhaps the fastest growing derivative products in the financial markets are the swaps. From a modest beginning in 1981 when the World Bank made a swap deal with IBM, the total volume of swaps outstanding had grown to about $4,500 billion by the end of 1992. Exhibit 10.11 provides some idea of their growth and the relative importance of two basic categories of swaps: interest rate and currency swaps. Interest rate swaps are far more frequent than currency swaps and the largest volume of swaps are done in U.S. dollar–denominated assets. For the currency swaps, the most common currency is the U.S. dollar and the largest volume of currency swaps is between yens and dollars.

In its simplest form, a swap is an exchange of two very similar assets which differ along some important dimension. By swapping these assets, two parties that originally owned these assets are changing the characteristic of the asset they own along that dimension. By swapping

Exhibit 10.11
Volume of Interest Rate and Currency Swaps

| Instrument | New Contracts Arranged | | | | | Amounts Outstanding Dec. 1991 |
| | 1988 | 1989 | 1990 | 1991 | 1992[1] | |
	(billions of U.S. $)					
Interest rate swaps	586	833	1264	1622	1318	3065
Of which:						
US dollar					682	1506
Yen					191	479
Deutchemarks					103	263
Currency swaps	124	178	213	328	156	807
Of which:						
Against US dollar					107	
Yen against dollar					26	
Swap related derivatives	—	335	292	383	296	577
Total		1347	1769	2333	1768	4450

[1]Data for the first half of the year.

Source: Bank for International Settlements, *63rd Annual Report*, 1993, pp. 126–126.

the assets, each party takes over the rights and the obligations associated with the asset previously owned by the counterparty and in exchange gives up those associated with the asset it had owned.

Interest Rate Swaps

Let us first look at an interest rate swap. In an interest rate swap, two parties, each of whom owns a debt instrument of certain maturity, would take over the payment obligations of the debt instrument that is owned by the counterparty. The motivation for this transaction is that each party may find the other party's debt instrument more desirable for some reason, let's say, future interest rate changes. The main question is, "If they find the other party's debt instrument desirable, then why don't they borrow debt in the form in which the counterparty has it?" This would be a valid question and the answer lies in market imperfections. To illustrate that, consider a typical interest rate swap. The following example shows the conditions that give rise to such a swap.

Plain Vanilla Swaps: Exploiting Market Imperfections. Two companies, A and B, need different types of funds. Company A needs floating rate funds, and Company B needs fixed rate funds. The "need" for floating or fixed rate funds is a function of the nature of other assets and liabilities and we do not question why the companies require those particular types of debt. Let us examine what the companies need and what they will have to pay for the funds they need. For convenience, let us assume that the principal amounts needed by the two companies are the same.

1. What the two firms need for their operations:

    Company A ——— Needs floating rate funds;
    would probably obtain the funds from banks

    Company B ——— Needs fixed rate funds;
    would probably issue a bond

2. What each company would pay for the funds if it raised funds either in the floating rate or in the fixed rate market:

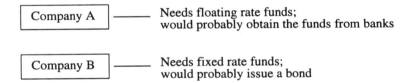

	Company A	Company B	Quality Spread or Differential B – A
Floating rate loan	LIBOR + 3/8%	LIBOR + 1-1/8%	3/4%
Fixed rate bond %	10-1/2%	12%	1-1/2%

3. What obligation each would have on its own:

    Company A would take the loan at LIBOR + 3/8%.

Company B would issue the bonds at 12%.

4. Now suppose we can arrange a swap such that Company A actually issues the bonds and B borrows the funds from a bank. They then swap their obligations, that is, they agree that each will make the payments associated with the debt raised by the other company except that Company B pays a small compensation to A by paying 1-1/8 percent above A's borrowing rate. Each company now has two payments—one to its creditors and other to the counterparty to the swap, and one receipt from the counterparty. Each company's net payments can then be easily calculated:

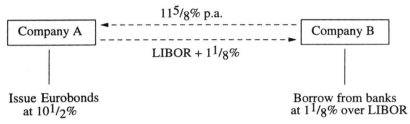

$11^5/_8\%$ p.a.

| Company A | | Company B |

LIBOR + $1^1/_8\%$

Issue Eurobonds
at $10^1/_2\%$

Borrow from banks
at $1^1/_8\%$ over LIBOR

5. Net costs to each company with the swap:

	Company A	Company B
Fixed rate payments	10-1/2%	11-5/8%
Fixed rate receipts	(11-5/8%)	—
Floating rate payments	LIBOR + 1-1/8%	LIBOR + 1-1/8%
Floating rate receipts	—	(LIBOR + 1-1/8%)
Net Cost	LIBOR	11-5/8%
Alternative cost, that is, cost of borrowing on its own	LIBOR + 3/8%	12%
Savings	3/8%	3/8%

The swap has saved money for both the companies. The source of savings in this case is a market imperfection. The imperfection arises from the different price of risk that is charged to Company B by lenders in the two markets—the fixed rate and the floating rate markets. Whereas the floating rate lenders put a premium or differential of 3/4 percent on

Company B over Company A, the fixed rate lenders want to charge Company B 1-1/2 percent more than what they want to charge Company A. The two companies can exploit this differential and in this case they have decided to split the excess profits, 1-1/2 − 3/4 equally between them. In a real transaction, the split will depend upon the bargaining power of the two companies and upon the fee that the financial institution that helps put this swap together is likely to charge. The intermediary provides two services: it helps a company find a counterparty, and it bears the risk of the transaction. With a financial intermediary, both companies are guaranteed their cash inflows by the intermediary. Even if one of the companies were to default on its payments, the other company would receive its inflow from the intermediary. With an intermediary, the swap transaction would look as follows:

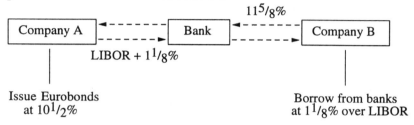

The cash flows of the swap at the initiation of the swap, during the year the swap is in effect, and at maturity, are shown below.

Initiation of the swap: There are no cash flows at this time because the principal or notional amounts are the same and in the same currency.

Cash flows every year, including the final year: The floating rate interest is calculated and the difference between the amounts of the fixed rate interest and the floating rate interest is paid by one party to another. At maturity, there is no need to settle any principal repayments.

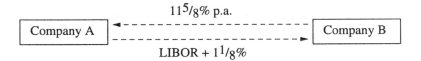

$11^5/8\%$ p.a.

| Company A | | Company B |

LIBOR + $1^1/8\%$

Note that the cash flows from Company B to Company A are fixed; those from A to B will change with LIBOR.

Credit Risk of a Plain Vanilla Swap. The credit risk of the swap explained here is that one party will not be able to make its payments *and* that inability will result in a loss for the counterparty. Inability of one party to make its payments does not necessarily result in a loss for the counterparty because non–payment by one party automatically releases the counterparty from its obligations too. The risk arises from the equivalence between fixed rates and the floating rates in the long run. Recall from Chapter 4 that, according to the expectations theory of interest rates, an investment in a fixed rate instrument over a certain period provides the same return as an investment in a floating rate instrument which is rolled over at every maturity. Thus, when a swap agreement is made, each party views the two streams—one from the fixed rate and the other from floating rate—as equivalent. Suppose that the term structure of interest rates is declining. In our example, Company A, which is making the floating rate payments, knows that the payments in the first few years are higher than they would be for a fixed rate debt, but it expects that lower payments in the later years will make up for the heavier burden in the initial years. What happens if Company B becomes bankrupt in the middle of the swap contract? Company A is now stuck with the bond payments. Since the years when floating rate payments expected to be lower than fixed rate payments were about to begin, Company A will suffer a loss. Having made the higher payments in the first half of the swap's life, default by B will require it to do the same in the second half also. Of course, if the term structure had been a normal one, A would have gained if B defaulted in the middle of the swap. The credit risk, of course, does not exist if an intermediary arranges the swap and agrees to bear the credit risk.

Swaps to Change the Interest Rate Profile. The existence of swaps between companies does not depend upon the existence of market imperfection. Interest rate swaps can also help a borrower change the profile of its debt instrument from a floating rate debt to fixed rate debt or vice versa.

In our example, assume that both the companies have issued the type of debt they would like to carry: A has issued bonds and B has raised funds from a bank loan. Due to changes in their circumstances, they may decide that they should switch the profiles of their respective debts: A should have a floating rate debt and B should have a fixed rate one. They could then enter into the same swaps as above except that their motivation would be different. A typical interest rate swap that helps firms change their interest rate profiles looks something like this:

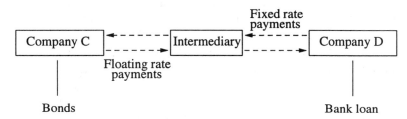

In addition, swaps exist that allow a borrower to swap one floating rate index, say the Federal Funds rate based loan, to another floating rate index, say LIBOR.

Currency Swaps

In a currency swap, assets in two different currencies are swapped. Each party to the swap takes on all the responsibilities of the debt issued by the counterparty, including the exchange risk. A typical currency swap may have the following structure and cash flows:

Position before the swap:

Cash flows at initiation of the swap:

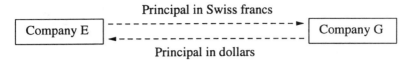

Principal in Swiss francs

Principal in dollars

Annual cash flows:

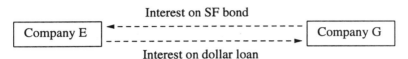

Interest on SF bond

Interest on dollar loan

Cash flow at termination of swap:

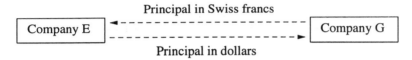

Principal in Swiss francs

Principal in dollars

Currency swaps, just like interest rate swaps, can become more complex with the involvement of three or more counterparties. Exhibit 10.12 shows the example of a deal involving two currency swaps and one interest rate swap. Company L swaps fixed rate Swiss franc funds for a LIBOR–based floating rate loan in dollars, Company M swaps prime–based floating rate dollar funds for fixed rate Swiss franc funds, and the mortgage company, which has ended up with prime–based floating rate assets, makes a basis swap to change the floating rate index of its debt from LIBOR to prime.

Payoff Profile and Cash Flows of a Swap. A swap is not a speculative instrument in the same way as a futures contract or an option. The value of a swap contract does not depend upon the value of an underlying asset as in the case of those two instruments. The value of a currency swap will change with exchange rates, but those changes alone do make a swap a desirable speculative vehicle. The value of an interest rate swap that has a floating rate contract on at least one side will change with changes in the interest rates. If the term structure of interest rates changes, the value of the swap will also change. As we discussed, the main risk associated with a swap is credit risk.

Exhibit 10.12
A Swap Deal with Three Counterparties

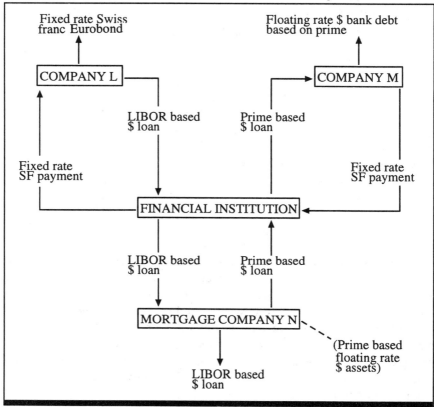

Swaptions or Options on Swaps. Like other options, a swaption is an option to enter into a swap transaction. The counterparties may design a swap agreement, say, to swap fixed rate debt into floating rate debt, but then one of the parties may merely acquire the option to enter into the swap at a future date. Clearly, the option will be entered into if the interest rates move in a direction that makes the swap attractive for the party holding the swaption. The most common use of swaptions is to take advantage of call provisions of bonds. An issuer of callable bonds has the right to call the bonds at some future date. Bonds will be called if the interest rates fall. The issuer may create a swap to convert the fixed payments of the bond into floating payments and sell the right to the swap as a swaption.

In market terminology, a swaption is generally defined in terms of the obligation of the holder of the swaption. If the holder acquires the option to pay a fixed rate in the option, and hence receive the floating rate payment, it is called a payer swaption or a call swaption. A payer swaption would be exercised if the market interest rates rise above the swaption strike rates. If the holder were to acquire the right to receive fixed rate payments, it would have been called a receiver swaption or a put swaption.

Basket Currencies and ECU. In Chapter 2, we had introduced the concept of a basket currency and had explained the composition of one

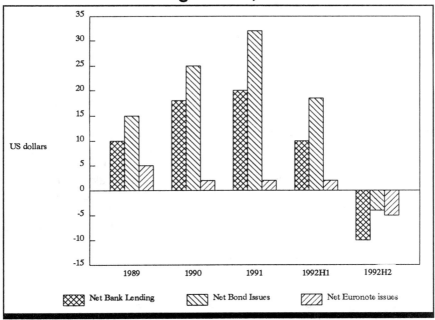

Exhibit 10.13
Financing in ECU, 1989–92

such currency—the European Currency Unit. Strictly speaking, a basket currency is not a derivative product, but we include a brief discussion of this concept because one of its uses is the same as that of derivatives: management of financial risk. A currency like the ECU that is composed of a number of other currencies can provide a diversification benefit to investors because it internalizes the relative changes between the values of the currencies that constitute the basket currency. As such, it provides a mechanism for risk management. The ECU had been used increasingly for international transactions in financial markets in the first half of 1992 until the Danish rejection of the Maastricht Treaty on June 2, 1993, caused a reappraisal by the market of the potential of adaptation of the ECU. Exhibit 10.13 shows the use of the ECU for private transactions over the last few years. It is expected that private transactors will return to the use of the ECU once the uncertainty about the Maastricht Treaty is settled.

▼ ▼ ▼

Spot–Rolling Contract: The Most Recent Derivative

By some count, the pace of innovations on the financial markets may have decreased from its hey days in the 1980s, but the process has by no means come to a halt. Innovations have become more sophisticated and directed to specialists in financial markets. One of the most recent innovations in foreign currency markets is the "rolling spot" contract introduced by the Chicago Mercantile Exchange in June 1993.

A rolling spot contract offers the holder, say a foreign currency trader at a bank, the benefit of maintaining a spot position in a currency without tying up the bank's credit lines. With a rolling spot contract at the Merc (as the Chicago Mercantile Exchange is often called), the trader can purchase, say, Canadian dollars. An ordinary spot contract would have required the trader to settle the contract on the subsequent day. In other words, with the ordinary spot contract, the trader would have had to deliver U.S. dollars and receive Canadian dollars the day after the contract was made. With a rolling spot contract, however, the trader can simply "roll over" the spot position by doing *nothing*. The rolling spot contract keeps the long Canadian dollar position of the trader until the time the trader wants to settle, or cancel, the rolling spot contract.

This contract offers some technical and some substantive benefits to the trader. Since an exchange–traded contract is called an **off–balance–sheet** item, it does not affect the total credit or the equity capital base of the bank. (According to the rules of international banking set by the Bank for International Settlements, banks must have equity capital equal to a certain proportion of their assets. Off–balance–sheet assets require less capital than on–balance–sheet assets.) The other substantive advantage for the trader is that, if the bank had wanted to keep the long Canadian dollar position for another day, it would have to settle the spot contract purchased the previous day and then purchase another Canadian dollar contract. The cost of such a transaction would be the difference between the bid and asked prices. With a rolling spot contract, however, there is no cost beyond the first day.

A technical advantage of the rolling spot contract is that the bank's credit risk has been reduced from the risk of the counterparty to that of the exchange when the contract is traded. In addition, since the bid and asked prices for a traded contract are publicly announced, the trader obtains the best price.

The Merc had initially planned to offer rolling spot contracts for sterling, Canadian dollars, deutschemarks, yen, and Swiss francs. Future and option contracts on rolling spot contracts will also be offered.

Summarized from "Merc Takes Aim at the Forex Markets," *Euromoney*, June 1993, p. 100.

▲ ▲ ▲

Summary

In response to the increased volatility of financial variables, financial markets have developed a large number of new instruments generally known as financial derivatives. These derivatives are based upon an existing financial or real asset and offer a series of cash flows depending upon the movements in prices of the underlying asset.

These derivatives differ from each other in terms of the payoff they offer in relation to the price of the asset. Contracts like forwards and futures offer the asset in the future at a fixed price, while the cash flows of derivatives, like options, depend upon the future movements of the price of the underlying asset. All derivatives can be analyzed by breaking them down into the cash flows that will result from the derivative.

The next two chapters examine how these derivatives can be used for the purpose of managing exchange rate and interest rate risks.

Chapter 11
Managing Foreign Exchange Risk

In Chapter 9, we identified the exchange risk for three types of assets or liabilities: an isolated or individual asset (or liability), a portfolio of financial assets, and a portfolio of real assets. By the term "portfolio of real assets" we mean a manufacturing company that has assets in the form of machinery, plant, and other capital goods which it uses to produce goods and services which are then sold to generate cash flows for the company. Since this book is mostly concerned with financial markets, we will not discuss the exchange risk of real assets any further. We will focus our attention on managing the exchange risk of isolated assets and liabilities, that is, risks of assets or liabilities considered in isolation of other assets or liabilities owned by an investor or a firm, and the exchange risk of financial firms which may be defined as holding a portfolio of financial assets. For the ease of exposition, we will continue to use the term "assets" to refer to assets and liabilities since a liability is merely a negative asset. We will also use the term "investor" to refer to an individual investor as well as to a firm, financial or otherwise.

Exhibit 11.1 provides an overview of the different types of exchange risk situations. The exhibit separates the exchange risk for an isolated asset from the exchange risk of a portfolio of assets. For each of these, the exhibit shows how the risk can arise and lists the most common techniques that can be used to manage the risk. Our task in this chapter

Exhibit 11.1
Techniques for Managing Foreign Exchange Risks

Type of Assets	Nature of Foreign Exchange Risk	Techniques for Managing Risk
	Existing Assets	
	Domestic currency value of a foreign currency asset may change with the value of the currency.	Futures or forwards Options Money market hedge
	Domestic currency cost of a foreign currency liability may increase by more than an acceptable level.	FX collars, cylinders or range forwards
Individual Assets	Cost of debt may increase if the currency of denomination of debt appreciates.	Currency swap
	Assets to Be Acquired	
	Domestic currency value of a contingent asset may change due to future exchange rate changes.	Option on futures
	Cost of future debt in a foreign currency may increase.	Swaption
	Foreign currency value of asset is a random variable.	Futures on the asset + futures on the currency
Portfolio of Financial Assets	Domestic currency value of portfolio of foreign currency assets and liabilities may change with changes in exchange rates. Values of assets in various currencies may change in unpredictable manner.	Balance sheet hedge Currency diversification Netting Use of basket currencies for denomination of assets

is to understand how each of these techniques can be applied and used to manage the risk.

Let us first understand how the exchange risk arises for isolated assets. For ease of understanding, these assets have been divided into two groups: those already owned by an investor and those that the investor plans to acquire in the future. There are at least three situations for assets that are already owned by an investor. For an asset that has only one cash flow, there is a risk that if the exchange rate for the currency in which the asset is denominated changes, the value of the asset for the investor will change. Take, for example, a foreign currency account receivable. A U.S. exporter may sell goods to a British importer who agrees to pay the agreed amount for the goods, £625,000, in two months. Let us assume that for competitive reasons, the exporter has to agree to quote the prices in pounds, not in dollars. Let us also assume that the importer is a well-established British company and there is no risk of default. The exporter's risk is that the pound will devalue and he will not receive the revenues that he expected at the time the sale was made. How he manages the risk will depend upon whether he wants to eliminate the risk completely, or whether he wants to avoid the effects of only very large devaluations. The first two rows under the existing assets in Exhibit 11.1 show the two situations and some of the techniques available to manage the risks arising in these two situations. The third situation arises when the existing asset is a debt instrument. A debt instrument like a bond usually has a number of cash flows associated with it—periodic interest payments and the principal repayment—either at maturity or according to an amortizing schedule. If the debt instrument is denominated in a currency that is expected to devalue, the value the cash flows of the debt in another currency—the reference currency of the investor—may change. This kind of risk can be hedged by swapping the debt from one currency into another.

An investor may also want to manage the risk of an asset that will be acquired in the future. Three distinct situations for such an asset are identified in Exhibit 11.1. A fourth situation, in which an asset will definitely be acquired, is analogous to the situation of an existing asset; since there is no doubt about the foreign currency value of the asset and about the fact that the asset will be acquired, it will be handled in the same fashion as an existing foreign currency asset. The three distinct situations when the asset to be acquired is subject to exchange risk are as follows. First, it may be a contingent asset. The acquisition may depend upon some other event taking place. Consider the case of a U.S. construction company that makes a bid to build one of the bridges in South Korea. The Korean government required the bids to be in Korean wons. The U.S. company has to bid very aggressively and keep the profit margin to the minimum. It is not sure that it will receive the contract and there is some risk that the won will be devalued between the time the bid is submitted and the decision is made. The asset in this case, the account receivable from the Korean government, is a contingent asset since it depends upon the decision of the government. Hedging of such an asset requires more planning than that of an existing asset. The same is true for a debt instrument that may be acquired in the future. The hedging of a future debt may require an option on a swap. Finally, an investor may have a foreign currency asset whose value in the foreign currency itself is unknown. An investor who buys foreign stocks faces such a situation. This investor cannot really hedge the investment in foreign stocks because the amount to be hedged will only be known at the time the funds have to be converted back into the domestic currency.

We will examine two types of portfolios of assets that face exchange risk. An investor may have foreign currency assets in a number of currencies. The exchange risks of these assets may show some correlations. There may be a pattern between the changes in the exchange rates in which these assets are denominated. Managing the exchange risk of these assets may require using a basket currency for denominating the assets or using a netting system. An investor, especially financial firms like banks or mortgage companies, may have a portfolio of assets and liabilities denominated in foreign currencies. To manage the exchange risk of such a portfolio may require balance sheet hedging and currency diversification.

Risks of Existing Assets

Let us look at the example of the U.S. exporter Azimin Softwares, or AZS for short, to understand how the risks of an existing foreign currency asset can be managed. AZS had an account receivable in pounds. At maturity, that is, in two months, the importer will deliver a check in pounds to the exporter. Therefore, if the pound goes up before the payment is made, the value of the account receivable in dollars will go up. If the pound goes down, the value of the account goes down. On the day the contract is made, the exporter checks the recent history of the pound. The spot rate was $1.5110/£. The dollar had risen 26.25 percent against the pound over the previous 12 months but had fallen by 2.22 percent against it over the previous four weeks. The pound had fluctuated between $2.004/£ and $1.4185/£ over the previous 12 months. The 90–day forward rate was $1.5003/£, indicating that the market expected the pound to depreciate slightly.

AZS has three alternatives. First, it can decide to take no action, in which case the account is subject to the full exchange risk. Its value will go up or down by the full amount of change in the value of the pound. Second, AZS can hedge the account completely and eliminate all the risk. In this case the value of the account in dollars will be the same regardless of the dollar–pound exchange rate. We will discuss three techniques for a full hedge: a forward or a futures contract, an option contract, and a money market hedge. Third, AZS can decide to hedge the account only partially. It can choose a derivative product that will protect the dollar value of the account only under certain conditions, and will let the account be subject to the exchange risk under other conditions. AZS may decide, for example, that it can afford changes in the dollar value of the account if exchange rates move by small amounts, but cannot afford the effects of large changes in exchange rates. Although a large number of combinations of options will allow the firm to do that, we will only discuss the following: FX collars, cylinders, and range forwards.

Full Hedge with Forward or Futures Contract

The principle of hedging the exchange risk of an asset with a forward or a futures contract is that we hold two assets whose payoff profiles with respect to exchange rates are opposite to each other. If the value of one asset increases with an increasing exchange rate, the value of the second decreases with an increasing exchange rate. Exhibit 11.2 illustrates this principle graphically. The first graph shows how the dollar value of the account receivable changes with the value of the pound. The right half of the graph represents the situations that are desirable for the exporter; it is the consequence of the exchange rate being in the left half that AZS would like to avoid. The graph in the middle shows the payoff profile of a short sale of pounds through a forward or a futures contract. AZS can

Exhibit 11.2
Hedging with Forward or Futures Contracts

1. Exchange rate profile of the pound account receivable.

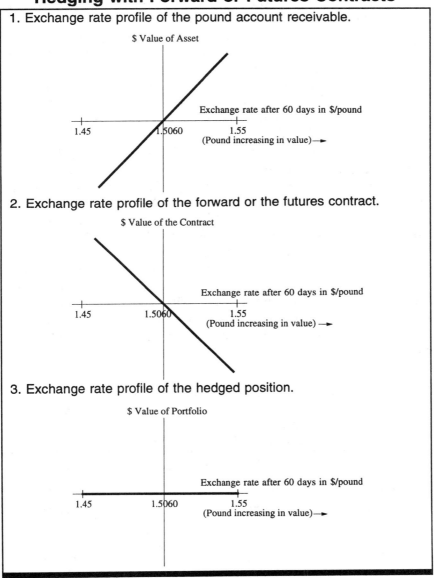

$ Value of Asset

Exchange rate after 60 days in $/pound

1.45   1.5060   1.55
(Pound increasing in value)→

2. Exchange rate profile of the forward or the futures contract.

$ Value of the Contract

Exchange rate after 60 days in $/pound

1.45   1.5060   1.55
(Pound increasing in value) →

3. Exchange rate profile of the hedged position.

$ Value of Portfolio

Exchange rate after 60 days in $/pound

1.45   1.5060   1.55
(Pound increasing in value)→

sell pounds forward either through a forward contract with a bank or by selling futures contracts on pounds on an exchange. To keep the example simple, let us assume that AZS decides to deal with futures contracts. In the afternoon of the day the decision is being made (July 20, 1993), the futures contract for about 60 days later, that is, the September contract, is trading at $1.5060/£. Since each futures contract is for £62,500 and the amount of the account receivable is £625,000, AZS will have to sell 625000/62500 or 10 future contracts to cover the full amount of the exposure. AZS will therefore contract to sell 10 futures contracts for pounds for September maturity that will commit it to sell £625,000 at $1.5060/£ for a total of $941,250.

The net position of AZS is shown in the third graph in Exhibit 11.2. With the futures contract, the company has no exposure and the dollar value of the account remains the same regardless of the exchange rate. That value is 625000 × 1.5060 or $941,250. We can verify numerically that this value will not change. Suppose the exchange rate after two months is $1.5560/£. AZS will receive 1.5560 × 625000 or $972,500 from converting the check of the exporter in the spot market. At the same time, it would have paid 1.5560 – 1.5060 or $.05/£ to settle its futures contract over the previous two months as the contract was marked–to–market every day. The total payment will be .05 × 62500 × 10 or $31,250. The net revenue of AZS, therefore, will be 972500 – 31250, or $941,250. The table below shows the revenues from the two contracts for different exchange rates.

Exchange Rates $/£	Cash Flow from the Account Receivable, $	Cash Flow from the Futures Contract, $	Total Cash Flow of AZS $
1.45	906,250	35,000	941,250
1.48	925,000	16,250	941,250
1.5060	941,250	0	941,250
1.55	968,750	– 27,500	941,250
1.60	1,000,000	– 58,750	941,250
1.65	1,031,250	– 90,000	941,250

Complexities of Hedging with Futures Contracts

The example we have given is quite simple and straightforward. The maturities of the asset to be hedged and the futures contract match almost exactly, and the amount to be hedged was a multiple of the size of one futures contract. What if the nearest futures contract expired, say, a month later than the maturity of the asset? In the example, this would happen if on July 20, the nearest futures contract was for October. How would AZS hedge its exchange risk?

One answer is that AZS could buy the October futures contract and in September, cancel it when the check from the importer is received. This strategy should work because the price of the October futures contract should move with the spot rate: if the spot rate increases from $1.51/£ to $1.52/£, the price of the October futures should also increase by $0.01/£. Thus, it should not matter as long as the futures contract matures within a short time of the maturity of the underlying asset. This is, however, not always true, and a **basis risk** exists in such a transaction. It is not necessary that the spot and the future exchange rates always move by the same amount. If the interest rates for the two currencies change during the time the futures contract is held, then the premium or discount between the spot and the forward rates will also change in accordance with the interest rate parity theorem (see Chapter 3). As the premium or discount changes, the price of the futures contract will also change relative to the spot price. The possibility that the spot and futures prices may not move by exactly the same amount is called the basis risk. When a forward or a futures contract with the same maturity as the underlying asset is not available, the investor is forced to take this basis risk. Due to this basis risk, it is possible that the cash flow of the asset may be slightly different from the hedged amount shown in the table.

The second complication associated with hedging futures contracts is that these contracts are not available in all currencies. What if the account receivable had been in Dutch guilders? There are no futures contracts for guilders. The investor in this case will have to use a **cross hedge**. A cross hedge, in this case, refers to the use of a futures contract for a currency that has the highest correlation with the currency that we are trying to hedge. In the case of the guilder, we will use a deutschemark futures contract to hedge a guilder exposure. These currencies move together most of the time, and it is the best way to hedge a guilder exposure, unless we negotiate a forward contract in that currency. With a deutschemark futures contract, the hedge will have a residual risk arising from less than perfect correlation between the changes in the spot guilder and the future deutschemark prices.

Finally, when the amount to be hedged is not a multiple of the size of one futures contract, the investor will have to decide if the hedge should be slightly less or slightly more than the value of the underlying asset. In the case of AZS, for example, we would have this problem if the value of the account receivable was £662,500. This would have required 662,500/62500 or 10.6 futures contracts. Since a fraction of one contract cannot be purchased, AZS would have had to decide to purchase either 10 contracts, in which £37500 would be subject to exchange risk, or 11 contracts, in which case it would have to risk £25000 on the futures market.

Partial Hedges with Forward or Futures Contracts

It is possible that an investor who has a foreign currency asset is in a position to take some but not all of the risk associated with changes in exchange rates. AZS may decide, for example, that it would not suffer badly if the exchange rate for the pound changes by about 2 percent from its present value. If the rate were to fall by 2 percent, the loss in the dollar value of the account would not put the company in a very difficult situation. But losses bigger than that would affect the income statement to a significant extent. AZS, of course, would like the pound to appreciate as much as possible. To protect itself against a large devaluation of the pound, the company can make an agreement with a bank that AZS would be able to convert the pounds into dollars at a minimum rate, say 2 percent below the current spot, if the rate were to fall more than that. The bank would agree to such a deal only at a price. One way in which AZS can compensate the bank is to also agree that if the exchange rate were to increase by more than 2 percent above the current spot, it would then let the bank keep the difference above 2 percent by agreeing to convert the pounds at 2 percent above the current spot. In effect, AZS is agreeing with the bank that the money will be converted at the future spot rate if that rate is within 2 percent of today's spot, or at exactly 2 percent from today's spot if the rate moves by more than 2 percent. If the rate falls by more than 2 percent, the bank suffers a loss; if the rate increases by more

Exhibit 11.3
Hedging with a Foreign Exchange Collar

1. Exchange rate profile of the pound account receivable.

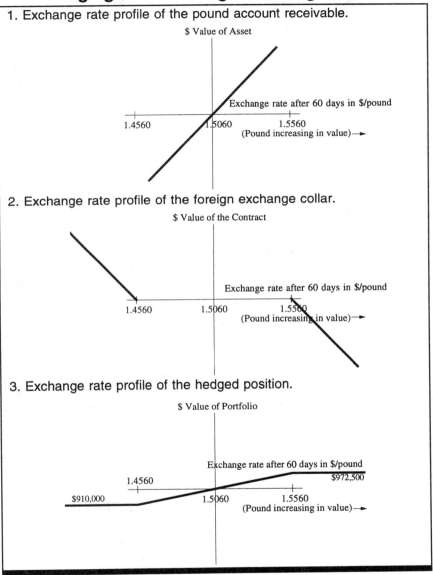

2. Exchange rate profile of the foreign exchange collar.

3. Exchange rate profile of the hedged position.

than 2 percent, the bank earns a profit. Effectively, the bank has provided a collar for the exchange rate within which AZS is subject to the exchange risk. It has no risk for exchange rates beyond this collar.

Exhibit 11.3 shows how a foreign exchange collar works. For the exhibit, it is assumed that the company wants a collar at $.05/£ above and below the current futures contract rate, that is, at $1.556/£ and $1.456/£, given the current future rate is $1.506/£. With these limits to the collar, the collar is effectively a futures contract as shown in the second graph in that exhibit. The first graph in the exhibit shows the profile of the account receivable. The final graph shows what the profile of AZS will be with the account receivable hedged with the collar. The company is guaranteed a minimum cash flow of 625000 × 1.456 or $910,000 and its cash flow could be as high as 625000 × 1.556 or $972,500. It will receive the minimum amount if the exchange rate is $1.456/£ or less. For exchange rates between $1.456/£ and $1.556/£, it will receive an amount equal to 625000 × (actual exchange rate), and for exchange rates above $1.556/£, it will receive $972,500.

These contracts that provide protection against exchange rate changes within a range are known as **foreign exchange collars**, or **range forwards**. They have the same effect as a combination of two options known as a **cylinder**.

Hedge with an Option Contract

The exchange risk of the pound account receivable can be fully hedged with an option instead of a forward or a futures contract. AZS can purchase an option to sell pounds at some price. Then if the pound rises, the company can let the option expire; if the pound drops, the option can be exercised. The cost that AZS has to pay for being able to gain from an appreciation of the pound is a front end fee which lowers the income from the asset in case the pound does not rise and the option is not exercised.

With the options, AZS has a choice of the exercise or strike price. Given the future price of $1.5060/£, let us assume that AZS wants a strike price close to that quote. The quotes for options in Exhibit 10.9 indicate that the nearest strike price for an American style option is 150, that is, $1.50/£. AZS can purchase options to sell pounds at this price up to August since a September quote is not available. December options at

Exhibit 11.4
Hedging with Option Contracts

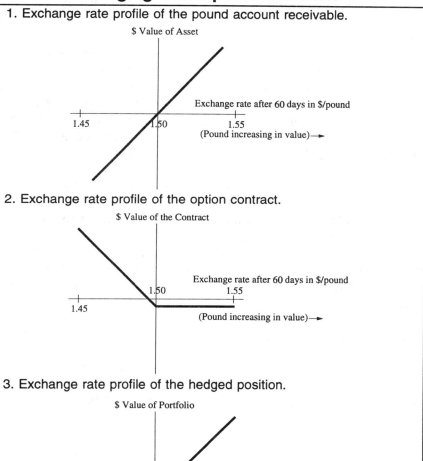

1. Exchange rate profile of the pound account receivable.

$ Value of Asset

Exchange rate after 60 days in $/pound

1.45   1.50   1.55
(Pound increasing in value)⟶

2. Exchange rate profile of the option contract.

$ Value of the Contract

Exchange rate after 60 days in $/pound

1.50   1.55
1.45
(Pound increasing in value)⟶

3. Exchange rate profile of the hedged position.

$ Value of Portfolio

1.45   1.50   Exchange rate after 60 days in $/pound
1.55
(Pound increasing in value)⟶

this strike price are available, but since the asset being hedged matures in September, purchasing an option beyond that date would be pure speculation in foreign currency markets. According to the exhibit, AZS will pay a fee of ¢1.5/£. Since the size of each contract is £31,500, it will have to buy 625,000/31250 or 20 option contracts.

Exhibit 11.4 shows the payoff profile of this option contract. The first graph repeats the payoff for the account receivable from Exhibit 11.2. The second graph shows the payoff for the option contract. It is allowed to expire unexercised for all exchange rates above $1.5/£ and the only cash flow associated with this option is the fee that was paid for the option. For all exchange rates below $1.5/£, the option is exercised. The payoff from exercising the option will be given by:

Payoff = 31250 × 20 × (actual exchange rate − $1.5/£) − Fee

The third graph in the exhibit shows the total payoff for AZS. For all exchange rates below $1.5/£, the payoff for AZS will consist of the profit from the option (= revenues from exercising the option less the fee, ignoring any transaction costs) plus the cash flow from converting the check from the importer. These will amount to $928,125 for all exchange rates below and including $1.5/£. Suppose the rate is $1.46/£:

Revenue from exercising the option = 31250 × 20 × (1.5 − 1.46) = 25000

Cash flow from account receivable = 625000 × 1.46 = $912,500

Fee for the option contracts = 625000 × 0.015 = $9,375

Net revenue = 25,000 + 912,500 − 9,375 = $928,125

For all exchange rates above $1.5/£, the cash flow for AZS will consist of the conversion of the amount in the account receivable less the fee. At an exchange rate of $1.53/£:

Revenue from exercising the option = 0

Cash flow from account receivable = 625000 × 1.53 = $956,250

Fee for the option contracts = 625000 × 0.015 = $9,375

Net revenue = 956,250 – 9,375 = 946,875

The table below shows the payoff for selected exchange rates.

Exchange Rates $/£	Cash Flow from the Account Receivable, $	Fee for the Option Contract, $	Total Cash Flow of AZS $
1.45	937,500	9,375	928,125
1.48	937,000	9,375	928,125
1.5060	941,250	9,375	931,875
1.55	968,750	9,375	959,375
1.60	1,000,000	9,375	990,625
1.65	1,031,250	9,375	1,021,875

The exporter may wish to consider option contracts at different strike prices to obtain different combinations of minimum receipt and gain from an appreciation of the pound. Exhibit 11.5 shows the payoffs for put options at different strike prices and AZS's payoff from hedging the account receivable with these put options. At lower strike prices, the hedger receives a lower minimum amount but higher profits when exchange rates rise above the strike price.

The option contract results in lower cash flow or payoff compared to the future contract under some states of nature, and in higher cash flows in others. The choice between the two depends upon the preferences of the decisionmakers in AZS. We will compare the payoff from using an option to that of using other techniques very shortly.

Partial Hedge with Options: FX Cylinders

One of the most interesting features of options contracts is their flexibility; various option contracts can be combined to obtain whatever payoff profile an investor may desire. One such combination, called a

Exhibit 11.5
Hedging with Options at Different Strike Prices

Total cash flows for AZS with the account receivable and put options at different strike prices.

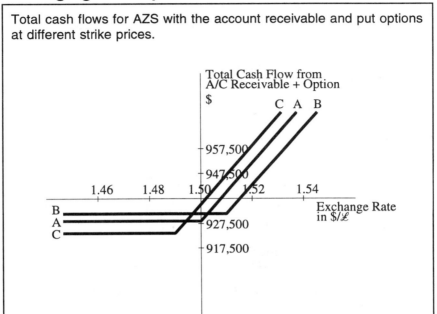

a. Account receivable + put option at $1.5/£ with a fee of $.015/£.
b. Account receivable + put option at $1.51/£ with a fee of $.0088/£.
c. Account receivable + put option at $1.49/£ with a fee of $.022/£.

foreign exchange cylinder, allows hedging foreign exchange risk in a manner very similar to a foreign exchange collar.

For the problem facing AZS, consider that the company acquires two options: it buys a put at the strike price of $1.475/£ and it sells a call at the strike price of $1.525/£. The payoff for each of these two options and the net payoff from the two options is shown in the middle panel in Exhibit 11.6. The payoff of the hedged position is shown in the third

Exhibit 11.6
Hedging with Foreign Exchange Cylinders

1. Exchange rate profile of the pound account receivable.

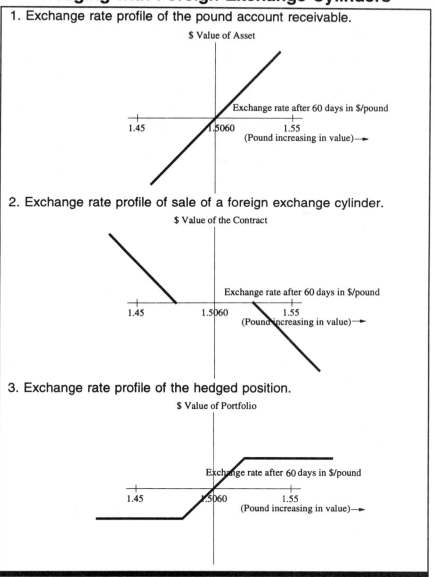

$ Value of Asset

Exchange rate after 60 days in $/pound

1.45   1.5060   1.55
                          (Pound increasing in value)→

2. Exchange rate profile of sale of a foreign exchange cylinder.

$ Value of the Contract

Exchange rate after 60 days in $/pound

1.45   1.5060   1.55
                          (Pound increasing in value)→

3. Exchange rate profile of the hedged position.

$ Value of Portfolio

Exchange rate after 60 days in $/pound

1.45   1.5060   1.55
                          (Pound increasing in value)→

panel in the exhibit. The payoff is very similar to that of a foreign exchange collar or a range forward.

Full Hedge with a Money Market Hedge

Financial derivatives like futures and options are not always available in all currencies. In some cases where the firm has access to financial institutions, it can use a money market hedge. A money market hedge involves borrowing money and relies on the principles of interest rate parity. It is based on the idea that interest rate differentials between two countries should equal the forward rate premium or discount. If the forward rate is not quoted in the marketplace, the differential between the interest rates should be an indicator of how much the exchange rate is expected to change. In a money market hedge, the investor borrows funds in one market and "invests" them in the other. Of course, the "investment" in the second market may take the form of reduced borrowing in that market; the investor may either repay an existing loan or not borrow the funds that he was planning to.

Suppose AZS did not have access to forwards, futures, or options. It could still hedge the exchange risk of its account receivable by borrowing money in one country instead of another. The following steps will be involved in a money market hedge:

1. AZS will negotiate a pound loan with a bank in England for a period of two months using the account receivable as a collateral. Given the nature of the collateral, it should not have any trouble receiving the loan. Assume it will have to pay about 300 basis points above the Eurocurrency market rate for this loan. With the sterling interest rate at 6 percent, AZS will pay an annual interest rate of 9 percent. The bank will lend a maximum of 625000/(1 + .09/6) or £615,764 given the size of the collateral.

2. It will convert this amount into dollars at the current spot rate. It will receive 615764 × 1.5110 or $930,419.

3. It has two choices for using these funds:

   a. AZS can invest the funds in the Eurodollar market. It will receive about 3.5 percent per annum. It will thus have $930419 × (1 + 0.035/6) or $935,846 at the time it would have been paid by the importer. When the importer sends the check, it is used to repay the loan.

   b. AZS can prepay one of its loans in the United States. If it were paying the premium of 300 basis points above the Eurocurrency rate, it would have been paying an interest of 3.4 + 3.0 or 6.4 percent per annum. By prepaying the loan, it would avoid having to pay 930419 × (1 + .065/6) or $940,498 at the end of two months. As in the previous case, the importer's check will be used to repay the loan.

The cash flows of AZS for the two alternatives of the money market hedge can now be compared to the cash flows from the other forms of hedging:

Hedging Action	Cash Flow in Two Months
Money market hedge: 1 + 2 + 3a: Borrow in U.K., convert into dollars, invest in U.S.	$935,846
Money market hedge: 1 + 2 + 3b: Borrow in U.K., convert into dollars, repay U.S. $loan	$940,498
Purchase forward or futures contract	$941,250
Purchase put option at $1.5/£	Minimum $928,125 Unlimited maximum
Foreign exchange collar (or range forward or cylinder)	Minimum $910,000 Maximum $972,500

The table highlights the differences between the various hedging techniques. The money market hedge and forward or futures hedge eliminate all risks from the transaction. The cash flow is known with certainty. The money market hedge provides slightly lower cash flow compared to the futures contract, but that may be due to the assumptions of the interest rates. In general, though, it is likely that the cash flow from a money market hedge is slightly lower than that from a forward or futures hedge. The option contract, on the other hand, provides protection only on one side of the possible changes in the exchange rates. The cash flow in the case of adverse movements in exchange rates is lower than it would be for future or money market hedges, but the maximum in the case of favorable movements is much higher. The option hedge, therefore, allows some speculation, obviously at a price. The foreign exchange collars or range forwards provide a cash flow similar to an option, except that there is an upper limit to potential profits.

Managing Exchange Risk Using Swaps

Up to now, we have dealt only with foreign currency assets that have one cash flow. There are many assets, especially debt related instruments, that have a number of cash flows. One way to hedge such assets would be to treat each cash flow as one asset and use one of the techniques described above to hedge it. For debt instruments like a bond, a variable rate loan (or a deposit that is continuously rolled over) can be used, although more efficient hedging techniques are available. A currency swap is ideally suited for managing the exchange risk of a loan. Let us illustrate how a currency swap will eliminate the exchange risk of a bond for a corporation.

Suppose a U.S. manufacturing company, Eastern Telecom, Inc., or ETI for short, had issued a 12–year deutschemark bond two years ago. ETI had decided to purchase some obsolete facilities in the former East Germany with the idea of modernizing them. It had planned to manufacture telecommunication equipment for sales in Germany and had decided that, since the revenues would be in deutschemarks, the debt ought to be in the same currency to balance any exchange risk. The modernized plant, however, was so successful that ETI has begun to sell almost the entire output in Japan, a market it had long wanted to break open. The only problem now was the deutschemark bond; since the revenues were now in yens, it was felt that the debt should also be in yens lest the exchange rates move in such a way that deutschemarks appreciated with respect to yen. The firm would then have a double whammy; its sales in Japan would become difficult because the cost of the products would rise in terms of yens, and the debt would become harder to service because deutschemarks would have become more expensive to obtain. This was only a "what if" analysis, however. There was no indication that this would happen.

The ideal solution to this problem would be to issue the debt in yens. The deutschemark bond, however, has no call provisions; the company would have to keep them for now. Issuing new bonds at this stage is not possible because no new investments are being planned and lenders will not look kindly at the firm increasing its debt/equity ratio too much.

The financial derivative that can help the firm in this situation is a cross currency swap. Through its financial intermediary, a commercial or investment bank, it can find a counterparty that has yen debt and wants to change the currency profile of that debt to deutschemarks. If a counterparty with exactly the opposite needs is not available, the job of the financial intermediary is to break up the debt of ETI into smaller pieces and find takers for each part of the debt. In any case, the swap would look something like this:

Before swap:

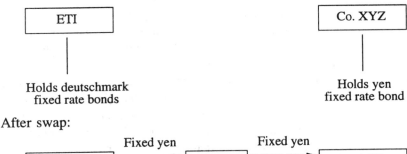

After swap:

Cash flows at initiation of the swap:

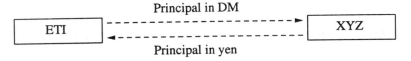

Annual cash flows:

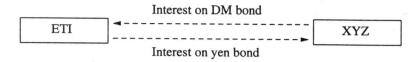

Cash flow at termination of the swap:

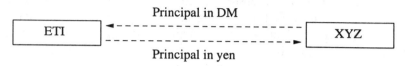

With this swap, ETI has changed the profile of its debt from deutschemarks to yens. The debt payments that ETI has to make are now independent of the value of the deutschemark. An increase or decrease in its value will not affect the cash flows of ETI. The cost of this hedging is the fee, usually less than 1/2 percent, that has to be paid to the financial intermediary. It is also noteworthy that ETI takes practically no credit risk in this transaction because the swap is guaranteed by the financial intermediary. Thus, even if company XYZ were to go into bankruptcy, it is the financial intermediary and not ETI that will have to worry about recovering funds from XYZ. Also, even if both the financial intermediary and XYZ were to go into bankruptcy, the risk for ETI is limited to change in the value of yen payments due to any exchange rate changes that may have taken place between the time of the swap agreement and the filing of the bankruptcy. This is because if XYZ fails to make payments on its deutschemark obligations, ETI will immediately stop making payments on its yen obligations. If the yen falls with respect to the deutschemark during this time, then ETI will suffer a loss. The probability of all three events, both XYZ and the financial intermediary declaring bankruptcy and the yen falling in value, however, are quite remote.

Risks of Assets to Be Acquired

We identified three situations in Exhibit 11.1 in which an investor faces exchange risk for an asset that he or she is planning to acquire. The three situations are as follows: the investor may acquire an asset where the chance of acquiring the asset depends upon some future event whose outcome is not known to the investor at this point; the asset to be acquired may be a debt instrument; and, the investor may have an asset whose foreign currency value, let alone its value in the investor's currency, is not known at the present time. We will look at the techniques for managing risks in each of these situations.

Contingent Asset

The first of these three assets is better known as a contingent asset. An asset is called a contingent asset when its acquisition is contingent upon some other event taking place. The most common example for a contingent asset is when a firm submits a bid to carry out a certain task at a quoted price. The firm is required to give the price which may depend upon the future price of a number of other assets without knowing what the prices of these other assets will be in the future. The firm that quotes a price, of course, takes the risk of an unfavorable price change. Foreign exchange rates are one of the assets that create risks for contingent assets. Such a risk arises when a firm quotes a price in one currency when the costs of the operation depend upon another currency. Even if the prices of inputs and raw materials being purchased in different currencies do not change in their respective currencies, exchange rate changes may create risks for the firm committing itself to prices in foreign currencies.

Management of such a contingent asset requires the investor to acquire an opposite contingent asset, for example, an option contract. As we have seen before, an option is a contingent asset because it has a value only if some other events take place, namely, that the underlying asset has a value in a certain range. Consider the case of a U.S. construction company that has submitted a bid to construct a bridge for a foreign government and assume that the bid has to be in the currency of the foreign country. As rational investors, the company would include into its bid any expected changes in the exchange rates, but due to the competitive nature of the construction industry, it cannot increase its price any more than that. The risk for this company is that it has committed itself to carrying out a task for a fixed amount of a foreign currency, a task that includes some expenses in dollars, and it is possible that the foreign currency will devalue before the funds are received. Such a devaluation would decrease the company's profits. It cannot go out and buy a hedge, say a forward contract, because if it did not receive the contract and the foreign currency revalued in the meantime, the company would end up suffering a loss without ever having done anything incompetently. It therefore needs a mechanism for hedging that will not involve large and unpredictable costs.

One approach for managing this type of risk would be to purchase an option to sell the foreign currency. If the contract is received, and if the foreign currency devalues, the option can be exercised. If the contract is not received, or if the contract is received and the currency does not devalue, the option can be allowed to expire. The cost of this contingent hedge is the fee that has to be paid for the option. This cost, though not trivial, is known as *ex ante* and is predictable. Such costs are the normal costs of doing business.

Another approach in this case will be to purchase an option to buy a futures contract or a futures option. This option gives the company a right to purchase a futures contract, instead of purchasing a spot contract. Thus, on the day that the company submits its bid, it can purchase an option to buy a futures contract that matures on the date that the payment will be received, if the contract is awarded to the company. On the day the decision is made, the company can cancel its option. If it receives the contract, it will sell the option and purchase a futures contract. By selling the option, it will earn back a portion of the fee that represented the time value of the option. The intrinsic value of the option will have changed by exactly the same amount as the actual futures contract; hence, the company will effectively receive the same future price as the day the bid was submitted. If it does not receive the contract, it can sell the futures option contract and receive back some of the time value of the option. The following box outlines the decisions and actions the company has to take to hedge its contingent asset.

▼ ▼ ▼

Hedging a Contingent Asset with a Futures Option

Bidding date   Purchase a futures option. Futures contract expires on the day the payment is to be received.

Decision date	Contract is awarded.	Contract is not awarded.
	Sell the option. Purchase a future.	Sell the option.
Cost	Change in the time value of the option.	Change in the time value and the intrinsic value of the option.
Payment date	Convert funds at the price of futures contract.	(No action)

▲ ▲ ▲

Future Debt

In addition to future assets with single cash flows, a firm may have plans to borrow money in the future. It is common for financial institutions to commit themselves to funds without guaranteeing the interest rate that would be charged on those funds. Once the currency and the amount of funds are locked in but the interest rate is not fixed, the borrowing company faces two risks. First, if the interest rates increase after the commitment is made but before the funds are received, the firm may end up having to pay more money for the funds than it had anticipated. Second, by the time the firm needs to receive the funds, it may realize that it should have chosen another currency for the funds than the one stipulated in the contract. It is also possible that at the time the commitment for the funds is made, the borrowing company feels that the exchange rate for the currency of the loan will devalue and that it would be profitable to lock into the rates that will be offered at the time the funds are drawn by the company.

In both these cases, the firm could use a swaption to protect itself or to take advantage of its expectations. As described in the previous chapter, a swaption gives the holder an option to enter into a swap. This company may, therefore, purchase a swaption that will allow it to change the currency profile of the debt if it chooses to do so. The swaption will work exactly like the swap described for the hedging of debt, except that with a swaption, the company will have the choice of either entering into the swap or ignoring the possibility altogether.

Future Asset with a Random Value

The most complex assets to hedge may be those whose values depend upon two variables: the value in the foreign currency and the exchange rate for the foreign currency. The most obvious example of such an asset is an investment in a foreign stock. Suppose an investor buys a stock of a foreign company in the country where the company operates. Suppose also that the planning horizon of the investor is one year. This investor is interested in measuring the value of investment in terms of dollars at the end of one year. The value in dollars, however, depends upon (1) the value of the stock in the foreign country in the foreign currency, and (2) that currency's exchange rate in terms of dollars at the end of one year. Both of these variables are random variables.

The investor's choices for hedging the exchange risk of this asset depend critically upon the nature of the foreign currency asset. It may help to view the risk of the asset as consisting of two components:

Risk of the asset = Price risk of the foreign stock

+ Exchange rate risk

If it is possible to manage the two risks separately, the investor's problem is easier. The risks can be managed separately when a hedging instrument (such as a future, an option, or some other derivative) to remove the price risk of the stock is available. By selling a futures contract on the asset, for example, the investor could lock into a future value of stock, which can then be hedged in the foreign exchange market to eliminate the exchange risk. The hedging strategy, therefore, would consist of the following:

Hedge of foreign currency stock =

Hedge of the value of the stock in the foreign currency +

Hedge the foreign currency value in the foreign exchange market

In the absence of a derivative on the asset itself, the investor has to try to minimize the risk of holding the foreign currency asset. He can try one of three approaches.

1. Hedge the foreign currency value of the asset with the help of a derivative on a close substitute of the asset. As we had mentioned earlier in relation to currencies for which derivatives are not available, an investor may be able to find a derivative for an asset whose values are correlated with the stock held by the investor. Hedging with this substitute will eliminate most of the risk, but some risk will remain.

2. The investor can leave the foreign currency asset unhedged and purchase foreign currency derivatives to hedge an expected amount of the foreign asset's value. The actual return of the investor will then be given by:

$$V_{\$,t} = E[V_{f,t}] \times F_{o,t} + (V_{f,t} - E[V_{f,t}]) \times S_t$$

where $V_{f,t}$ is the random value of the foreign currency asset at time t, $F_{o,t}$ is the forward rate for the currency at time 0 for maturity at time t, S_t is the spot rate at time t, and $E[V_{f,t}]$ is the expected value of the asset at time 0. The equation indicates that the investor buys foreign currency hedges for an amount of $E[V_{f,t}]$. The actual return consists of dollars obtained from converting that amount plus the dollars obtained from converting the difference between the actual value of the asset at time t and the hedged amount. The risk of this asset is given by the variance of $V_{\$,t}$ which depends upon the following:

$$\text{VAR } V_{\$,t} =$$

$$f[\text{Var}(S_t), \text{Var } V_{f,t}, \text{Corr}(S_t, V_{f,t}), \text{Volume of currency hedged}]$$

The important parameter in this equation is the correlation between the exchange rate and asset prices. It recognizes that the value of the asset in the foreign currency itself may depend upon exchange rate changes to some extent. It seems a realistic formulation of the actual world in that stock market prices can be expected to be correlated with exchange rates. The contribution of the above equation is in recognizing that even though the dollar value of the foreign currency asset cannot be fully hedged, a minimum variance asset can be created by hedging the appropriate volume of foreign currency. If the past values of variances and correlations are known, the investor can calculate the amount to be hedged that will minimize the variance of the return of the asset.

3. The investor can diversify into a large number of currencies to obtain some diversification benefits. We will defer the discussion of this technique to the next section.

All the techniques for managing exchange risk for assets with a single cash flow are summarized in Exhibit 11.7. Continuing with the separation of assets into existing assets and those to be acquired, the exhibit shows the technique that best helps manage the exchange risk given the market situation regarding the availability of derivatives and the risk strategy being pursued by the investor.

Risks of Portfolio of Assets

Although manufacturing companies may hold a portfolio of financial assets, we typically think of financial institutions as representing such a portfolio. In fact most of the assets and liabilities of these institutions are financial in nature. The most important risk for these assets and liabilities is either the credit risk or the interest rate risk. When some of these assets are denominated in foreign currencies, the institution will also face an exchange risk.

In Chapter 9, we had measured the risk of a portfolio of financial assets by calculating a net exposure in each currency in which any of the assets or liabilities owned by the institution were denominated. Let us return to the example of Bank Nicobar in that chapter. For convenience, the balance sheet of the bank is reproduced in the following box.

Exhibit 11.7
Summary of Hedging Techniques for Single Cash Flow Assets

Type of Asset	Market Conditions	Risk Strategy	Technique or Instrument	Trade-offs
Existing assets	Derivative on the asset not available.	Fullest possible hedge; minimize risk.	Cross hedge.	Basis risk from lack of perfect correlation between currencies. Basis risk remains if maturities do not match.
	Derivatives not available.	Full hedge; take no risk.	Money market hedge.	No opportunity gain or loss.
	Derivatives available.	No downside risk; take upside risk; full hedge; take no risk.	Option.	Give up some income for speculative gains.
			Forward or future contract.	No opportunity gain or loss. Basis risk remains if maturities do not match.
		Hedge only against large changes in exchange rates.	Collars, range forwards, or cylinders.	No opportunity gain or loss beyond small changes in rates.
	Derivatives available.	Hedge against possible changes in the value of contingent assets.	Option or futures option.	Avoid large losses at the cost of time value of the option contract.
Assets to be acquired		Hedge against unexpected changes in asset prices or exchange rate.	Futures or option for the value of asset as well as for exchange rate.	Give up opportunity gains or losses.
	Derivatives not available.	Minimize risk.	Hedge currency to minimize risk. Diversify into currencies.	Strategy depends upon availability and reliability of past data. Benefits of currency diversification may be limited.

Managing Foreign Exchange Risk   333

Bank Nicobar
Balance Sheet, December 31, 1993

Assets ($ millions)*		Liabilities ($ millions)*	
Short–term (3 month) revolving loans	500	CDs due in 3 months	400
Trade credit, in yen, at 3–month rate	600	Euro–CP, in DM, due in 1 month	650
Project finance, in DM, at fixed rate	700	Long–term bonds (in pounds)	750
		Shareholder's equity	300
Real estate	300		
Total assets	$2,100	Total liabilities	$2,100

*Foreign currencies converted into dollars at current spot rate.

We had measured the exchange risk of the bank in each currency in which it had either an asset or a liability. The risk was measured by identifying an exposure as the net of the values of assets and liabilities in each currency. Bank Nicobar had a net exposure of $600 million in yen, $50 million in deutschemarks, and a negative exposure of $750 million in pounds.

We will examine two methods of managing the exchange risk of a financial institution: a balance sheet hedge and currency diversification.

Balance Sheet Hedge

The first of the two methods for managing exchange risk of a portfolio is a direct outgrowth of the method of measuring the risk. Since the risk arises from the net exposure in a currency, the most obvious way to manage the risk should be to eliminate the exposure. Exposure can be eliminated by balancing the amounts of assets and liabilities in each currency. If the dollar value of assets in a currency is exactly equal to the dollar value of the liabilities in that currency, a change in that exchange rate cannot affect the value of the portfolio. If the exchange rate appreciates, the value of assets will rise by the same amount by which the value of liabilities will decrease, and vice–versa. The firm will, however, have to eliminate its exposure in every currency to eliminate all the risk from the portfolio.

Eliminating exposure will require the investor to change the currency of denomination of some of the assets or the liabilities. In the example of Bank Nicobar, for example, the yen assets can be changed to pound assets. If the bank were to swap the currency of its trade credit from yens to pounds, its yen exposure will be completely eliminated and its negative exposure of $750 million in pounds will be reduced by $600 million to an exposure of only $150 million. To eliminate all exposure in pounds, the bank will have to convert some of its dollar assets into pound assets.

Such hedging is, of course, not costless. It may seem that changing a yen asset to a pound asset would not involve any costs, but we must bear in mind that the bank's balance sheet, before balance sheet hedging is undertaken, reflects the optimal combination of assets and liabilities that a bank can hold. Any changes in that combination will require the bank to give up a higher earning asset or the lower cost liability and replace it with a less desirable one. If the asset or liability being acquired were more desirable than the one the bank has now, it would have been acquired without the need for a balance sheet hedge.

In the balance sheet hedge outlined above, we ignored the maturities of assets and liabilities. When assets and liabilities in one currency do not have the same maturity, the investor will have to enter into hedging repeatedly as the asset with shorter maturity matures and is replaced with a new asset.

Hedging with Derivatives

It is also possible to hedge a portfolio with derivatives like futures and options and other combinations of these contracts. To hedge the long yen exposure, Bank Nicobar can sell futures contracts on yen for the amount of the exposure. Then if the yen depreciates, it will suffer a loss on its assets but will gain an equal amount on the futures contracts. Such hedging is also costly because of the transaction costs of dealing in futures contracts. The investor must therefore balance the cost of hedging with derivatives with the potential benefits of hedging using other techniques.

Diversification into Currencies

An investor with exposure in many currencies can reduce the exchange risk of the portfolio by taking advantage of the principle of diversification. The diversification in this case would be in many currencies, not just in many assets. The investor can try and take advantage of the possibility that if some currencies appreciate during a particular time period, others depreciate at the same time. Assume an investor had a portfolio with exposure in many currencies, and the currencies were fluctuating freely. The portfolio would lose some value because some the currencies in which the investor had positive or long exposure will decline. However, the portfolio would gain some value because other currencies in which the investor had long exposure would rise in value. In the long run, if the fluctuations in the currencies' values are random, the risk of the portfolio will be minimized.

To test whether or not such diversification would have been possible during the last two decades, we examined exchange rate movements to determine how an investor would have fared if he had managed the risk of his portfolio solely through currency diversification. Suppose that an investor had decided to hold a portfolio consisting only of foreign currencies. Suppose also that the portfolio was first constructed by purchasing equal amounts of these currencies, the amounts being equal in the reference currency of the investor to, say, the U.S. dollar. The value of the portfolio at any future date would be measured by converting the amounts of each currency into dollars at the exchange rates on the day of the evaluation. If the principle of currency diversification were indeed valid in the real world, we should find that values of portfolios with a larger number of currencies will show smaller variations than the portfolios with fewer currencies. Portfolios with a larger number of currencies will be more stable because the fluctuations in larger numbers of currencies will tend to cancel themselves out.

Exhibits 11.8 to 11.10 show the results of simulating these portfolios. The results are based on portfolios with a maximum of 12 currencies: British pound, French franc, German mark, Italian lira, Dutch guilder, Swedish krona, Spanish peseta, Australian dollar, Finnish markka, Swiss

Exhibit 11.8

Performance of Diversified Currency Portfolios, 1970–92

(276 observations)

Minimum	Maximum	Range	Mean	Std. Dev.	CV
		Portfolios of 3 Currencies			
703.50	1533.21	829.71	1164.12	175.96	15.12
604.98	1330.90	725.92	1044.96	165.23	15.81
543.34	1238.45	695.11	900.31	187.62	20.84
998.10	2457.76	1459.67	1606.55	393.62	24.50
379.16	1119.96	740.80	758.37	213.22	28.12
715.38	1463.96	748.58	1143.64	163.16	14.27
757.28	1567.14	809.86	1207.38	181.62	15.04
799.48	1449.28	649.80	1153.63	152.75	13.24
				Average	18.37
		Portfolios of 6 Currencies			
654.24	1410.65	756.41	1104.54	165.99	15.03
884.96	1620.51	735.55	1253.43	174.58	13.93
715.61	1411.37	695.77	1119.14	147.28	13.16
823.59	1633.84	810.25	1238.84	181.31	14.64
774.70	1629.45	854.75	1235.15	189.93	15.38
764.50	1401.71	637.21	1122.82	138.35	12.32
				Average	14.08
		Portfolios of 12 Currencies			
769.60	1515.58	745.98	1178.99	160.06	13.58

Managing Foreign Exchange Risk   337

Exhibit 11.9
Performance of Diversified Currency Portfolios, 1970–79
(120 observations)

Minimum	Maximum	Range	Mean	Std. Dev.	CV
		Portfolios of 3 Currencies			
1001.27	1480.03	478.76	1178.86	124.28	10.54
993.89	1330.90	337.00	1136.35	87.09	7.66
942.98	1238.45	295.48	1075.14	86.38	8.03
998.10	1960.92	962.82	1319.21	236.60	17.94
752.72	1119.96	367.25	962.44	110.39	11.47
999.80	1463.96	464.16	1208.65	126.39	10.46
997.60	1503.22	505.61	1219.26	139.69	11.46
998.86	1377.92	379.06	1149.83	96.99	8.44
				Average	
					10.75
		Portfolios of 6 Currencies			
997.80	1396.98	399.18	1157.61	104.41	9.02
999.91	1516.62	516.70	1197.17	121.89	10.18
999.78	1344.77	344.99	1150.05	90.12	7.84
998.66	1579.88	581.22	1204.73	136.77	11.35
999.38	1585.25	585.87	1214.84	152.26	12.53
999.20	1328.34	329.14	1139.94	80.91	7.10
				Average	
					9.67
		Portfolios of 12 Currencies			
999.60	1456.80	457.19	1177.39	111.53	9.47

Exhibit 11.10
Performance of Diversified Currency Portfolios, 1980–92
(156 observations)

Minimum	Maximum	Range	Mean	Std. Dev.	CV
Portfolios of 3 Currencies					
703.50	1533.21	829.71	1152.78	206.83	17.94
604.98	1300.44	695.46	974.67	176.57	18.12
543.34	1064.13	520.79	765.82	121.89	15.92
1226.59	2457.76	1231.17	1827.58	344.71	18.86
379.16	925.53	546.37	601.40	119.44	19.86
715.38	1425.19	709.81	1093.63	170.81	15.62
757.28	1567.14	809.86	1198.24	208.20	17.38
799.48	1449.28	649.80	1156.54	184.81	15.98
				Average	17.46
Portfolios of 6 Currencies					
654.24	1410.65	756.41	1063.73	191.45	18.00
884.96	1620.51	735.55	1296.70	195.80	15.10
715.61	1411.37	695.77	1095.35	175.89	16.06
823.59	1633.84	810.25	1265.07	205.84	16.27
774.70	1629.45	854.75	1250.77	213.63	17.08
764.50	1401.71	637.21	1109.65	168.91	15.22
				Average	16.29
Portfolios of 12 Currencies					
769.60	1515.58	745.98	1180.21	189.47	16.05

franc, Canadian dollar, and Japanese yen. The U.S. dollar was not used as a currency because it is the reference currency and hence it will not fluctuate with respect to itself. Portfolios of three, six, and all 12 currencies were made. Although a total of 1,320 portfolios with three currencies can be created, we tested the principle with only eight portfolios of three currencies and six portfolios of six currencies. The portfolios were created on January 1, 1971, and changes in the values of the portfolios were measured over the two following decades as well as over the entire 22–year period up to the end of 1992 for which the data were available. The exhibits provide analysis of values of the portfolios at the end of each month during the period of analysis.

Each of the three exhibits, 11.8 to 11.10, shows the range over which the values of the portfolios moved over the period, the mean value over the period, the standard deviation of the value and its coefficient of variation (CV). The coefficient of variation is the standard deviation divided by the mean, expressed as a percentage. The three exhibits present results for the entire period (Exhibit 11.8), and for the two decades, 1971–79 (Exhibit 11.9) and 1981–92 ((Exhibit 11.10). Each exhibit summarizes the returns of the portfolios with three, six, or 12 currencies.

The results provide only a weak support for the proposition that diversification into many currencies will remove most of the exchange risk of a portfolio. For the entire period of 1971–92, holding a portfolio of 12 currencies reduces the coefficient of variation by about one fourth over what it would be with a portfolio of only three currencies. It is an important reduction, but hardly of the kind we had seen for diversification into stocks in Chapter 8. Moreover, the cost of diversification into 12 currencies for an investor whose main objective is to hold earning assets could become excessive. The benefits of diversification into 12 or six currencies over holding only three currencies is even smaller when smaller holding periods, that is 1971–79 and 1980–92 in Exhibits 11.9 and 11.10, are considered.

In conclusion, while the diversification into many currencies seems to offer some reduction in exchange risk, the benefits of this risk reduction must be compared to the cost of this strategy. For an investor with a portfolio of assets and liabilities in many currencies, the cost of adjusting the currencies of these assets or liabilities may become significant.

Summary

Foreign exchange risk for assets or liabilities, or for portfolios of assets and liabilities, depends upon the nature of the asset—whether it is a definite asset or a contingent asset, and upon the time frame over which the asset is owned—whether it is already owned by the investor or if it is to be acquired in the future. Strategy to manage the exchange risk depends upon the availability of derivative products in the market, and upon the risk strategy of the investor—whether the investor wishes to hedge the risk fully or only partially.

The simplest situations are those for existing assets which are to be fully hedged. Forwards and futures offer suitable mechanisms for managing risks of these assets. When the investor wishes only a partial hedge, option, range forwards, and collars become more desirable. A money market hedge may be the only choice for an investor who has assets in currencies in which a derivative market is not fully developed. Risk management becomes more complex for assets that are either contingent in nature or that will be acquired in the future. Techniques for managing those risks include options on futures and swaptions. The most complex situations arise for assets whose values in foreign currencies are themselves unknown at the time hedging decisions have to be made.

Chapter 12
Managing Interest Rate Risk

Interest rate risk arises when the value of an asset or a liability, or a portfolio of assets or liabilities, can change due to changes in interest rates. In Chapter 9 we examined a number of situations in which this is possible. We also developed measures to estimate how big the risk will be in these situations. In this chapter, we will look at ways to manage interest rate risk. As in the previous chapter, we will use the term assets to refer to assets or liabilities, since liabilities can be seen as negative assets, and we will continue to refer to all participants, whether individuals or corporations, and whether lenders of funds or borrowers, as investors. We will separate the risks for existing assets from those for assets to be acquired in the future, and we will examine the risks for individual assets separately from the risks for portfolios of assets and liabilities.

Exhibit 12.1 summarizes the main categories of assets and types of situations in which interest rate risk can arise. It also indicates the best risk management technique for each situation. Assets are separated into single assets and portfolios and into existing and future assets. We will first examine the management of risk for existing assets and then for the portfolios of assets.

Exhibit 12.1
Sources and Management of Interest Rate Risk

Type of Assets	Source and Nature of Interest Rate Risk	Technique for Managing Risk
	Existing Assets	
	Change in value of an asset if interest rates change before the maturity of the asset.	Zero–coupon bond. Immunization.
	Potential loss due to large fluctuations in interest rates for variable rate instruments.	Interest rate caps or collars.
Individual Assets	Changes in the term structure of interest rate can change relative attractiveness of variable rate versus fixed rate instruments.	Interest rate swap.
	Differential risk that two floating rate indexes will not change by equal amounts.	Interest rate swap.
	Assets to Be Acquired	
	Fix the future cost of an asset.	Interest rate futures. Forward rate agreement.
Portfolio of Financial Assets	Changes in interest rates can lower the value of a portfolio.	Match maturities of assets and liabilities. Change the interest profile of selected asset or liabilities from variable rate to fixed or vice versa.

Managing Interest Rate Risk   343

Existing Assets or Liabilities

Assets with Fixed Cash Flows

An investor who holds an interest–bearing instrument faces the risk that the value of the instrument will decrease if the interest rates change. The risk arises from the possibility that the investor may wish to sell the instrument before its maturity. Risk exists even if the interest rate of the instrument is fixed. Consider the fixed rate five–year maturity Eurodollar bond with 8 percent coupon for which we had calculated interest rate risk in Chapter 9. The value of this bond consists of two cash flows associated with the bond: the annual cash flows from coupon payments and the principal repayment at maturity. The value, or the current price, is calculated by discounting the future cash flows at the current or market interest rate. An implicit assumption in this calculation is that as each coupon payment is received, it will be reinvested at the discount or the current market rate. Thus, the current price of the bond depends upon market interest rates.

The interest rate risks for this bond arise from two sources. First, if the interest rates change, the reinvestment rate for the annual interest payments changes; if the rates go up, the coupon payments will be reinvested at a higher rate. The opposite is true if the rates fall. Thus, an increase in interest rate has a favorable impact for the investor. Second, the present value of future cash flows, which is calculated by discounting the flows at the current interest rate, will change with changes in interest rates. If the interest rates increase, the price or the value of the bond decreases because the cash flows will now be discounted at a higher rate. The opposite is true if the rates fall. The effect on the present value of future cash flows is opposite of the effect on the reinvestment of annual coupon payments. Exhibit 12.2 shows the values of the 8 percent five–year maturity Eurobond for various rates of market interest rates. The exhibit shows how the value of the bond will change at each year–end from the date of issue of the bond to its maturity if the market interest rate changes to a value at the top of one of the columns in the exhibit. The assumption of these calculations is that the interest rate changes the instant after the bond has been issued and then remains unchanged for the duration of the bond. The value shown in the exhibit

Exhibit 12.2
Interest Rate Changes and Bond Value
at Each Year–End

| | Value of Bond at End of Each Year[*] | | | | |
| | Market Interest Rate After Issue of the Bond | | | | |
Year:	4.0%	6.0%	8.0%	10.0%	12.0%
Year 0	1178	1084	1000	924	856
Year 1	1225	1149	1080	1017	959
Year 2	1274	1218	1166	1118	1074
Year 3	1325	1291	1260	1230	1202
Year 4	1378	1369	1361	1353	1347
Year 5	1433	1451	1469	1488	1508

[*] The value of the bond at any time is the sum of coupon payments received and reinvested at the market interest rate plus the present value of future cash flows.

for any interest rate in any year is the sum of the two cash flows—one from the reinvested past coupon payments and the other from the discounted value of future cash flows.

The exhibit shows that the value of the bond can fluctuate over a wide range. If the investor wanted to have a choice of being able to sell the bond at the end of the first year, she could expect to get anywhere from $1,178 to $856, provided the interest rates fluctuate between 4 and 12 percent. The range is narrower for the subsequent years.

The challenge of managing this kind of risk is to ensure that regardless of the direction of change in interest rates, the investor will not lose. The risk, however, cannot be managed for all future dates. The investor needs to fix the future date, that is, the investment horizon, at which she may want to sell the asset. Once the date can be fixed, the investor has two alternatives for holding an asset which will not have an interest rate risk.

Zero coupon bond. A zero coupon bond whose maturity coincides with the investment horizon of the investor eliminates the interest rate risk. This is so because a zero coupon bond has only two cash flows associated with it: one at the time of initial investment and the other at maturity. If the maturity of the bond coincides with the investment horizon of the investor, there is no risk that the value of any cash flows will change with the interest rates in the marketplace. Thus, a zero coupon bond eliminates interest rate risk for the investor for a given investment horizon.

Immunization. An investor can use the strategy of immunization to manage the risk of a bond. To understand immunization, consider the Eurodollar bond once again. We had seen how the value of the bond changes in response to changes in the interest rates. Exhibit 12.3 shows a plot of the data in Exhibit 12.2. It shows how the value of the bond changes over its life in response to a one time interest rate change.

Of the five curves in the exhibit, the one in the middle shows the value of the bond if the market interest rate remains unchanged at 8 percent. We will refer to this curve as the base case. The two curves above this curve in the left–hand part of the graphs show that if the interest rate falls, the value of the bond actually increases above the base case in the first few years but then falls below it during the later years. The lower value in the later years is due to lower cash flows from the reinvestment of coupon payments. The opposite happens when the interest rate rises and is shown by the two curves below the base case curve in the left–hand part of the graph. All the curves, however, meet at one point—about 4.3 years on the horizontal axis.

This point of intersection is not coincidental. You will recall from Chapter 9 that we had calculated Macaulay's duration for this bond and the number had come out to 4.312. At this point, the value of the bond becomes the same regardless of the interest rate in the market. The implication for the investor who wants to manage the interest rate risk of her assets is that she should choose an asset with a duration equaling her investment horizon. Thus, if the investment horizon of an investor were 4.3 years, she could buy the fixed rate, 8 percent coupon, five–year Eurobond. Then, whatever the market interest rate, she would receive the same amount of money in 4.3 years. Her asset, in other words, is hedged

Exhibit 12.3
Interest Rate Changes and Bond Values

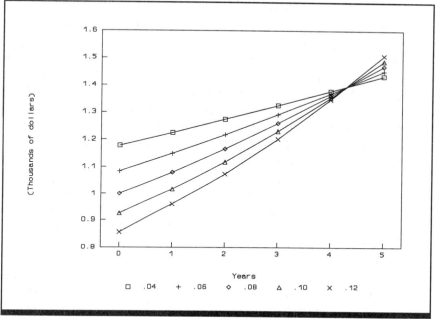

against interest rate changes. The asset is hedged only for a certain investment horizon.

Assets with Variable Cash Flows

Consider an asset (or a liability) with variable rate interest payments. In most cases, the interest rate for the asset or the liability is reset periodically according to a market index or a market interest rate. This market index may be an average of a number of other interest rates or may be a rate like LIBOR or Federal funds rates or T–bill rate. This asset faces three types of risks.

1. First, there is a risk that the variable interest rate may fall to a level below which the asset becomes very unattractive for the investor. For a liability such as a loan, the risk is that the interest rate will increase above a level where the cost of the liability becomes unacceptably high. If the variable rate falls below a certain level, the investor may not be able to meet certain financial obligations that she had planned to fulfill with the cash flows from the asset. Similarly, if the variable rate on a loan becomes too high, a company may find that the investment that was funded with the proceeds of the loan is not able to generate enough funds to pay for the loan. An individual who takes a variable rate mortgage on her house takes the risk that the rates in the future will increase so much that she will not be able to make the mortgage payments.

2. Second, an investor holding a variable rate asset may face an interest rate risk if the liability which is the counterpart of the asset is not a variable rate instrument. The risk here is that the actual fluctuations in the interest rate will not have the same relationship with the fixed interest rates as was expected when the asset or the liability was acquired. Consider the example of a bank that provides trade credit for short maturities. The bank really has variable rate assets. This is because the interest rate for each credit depends upon the market interest rate at the time credit is granted, and since the life of each credit is quite small, the assets of the bank earn interest very close to the short–term market interest rates. If the liabilities that constitute the source of funds for the bank are fixed rate liabilities, the bank faces the risk that, due to actual fluctuations in the interest rates, the average interest rate that the bank earns on the assets will turn out to be lower than the fixed rate it pays on its liabilities. Given a term structure of the interest rates, the bank expects that when the liability is issued, the future short–term interest rates will move such that the expected return from variable rate investments will equal the cost of fixed rate liability. A change in the term structure, however, may change the picture.

3. Third, there is a risk that even if both an asset and its liability counterpart are variable rate instruments, the indexes on which the two variable rates are based may not move equally. Consider a bank

that issues a variable rate Eurodollar loan whose rate is tied to LIBOR and that funds this loan with a certificate of deposit tied to the U.S. T–bill rate. The bank is subject to a risk if future movements in the T–bill rate are not exactly parallel to the movements in LIBOR. If the T–bill rate rises by 10 basis points on any day and the LIBOR by only 6 basis points, the bank's profit margin will shrink by 4 basis points.

Management of the various risks described here requires different techniques. The problem of an asset holder who does not want to face interest rates beyond a certain level is to obtain some type of a floor, or a ceiling in the case of a liability, for the interest rates. In response to market demand, instruments called caps, floors, and collars have been developed by financial institutions. As their name implies, these instruments either provide a "cap" or a "floor" for the interest rates above or below which the rates cannot move, or provide a "collar" beyond which the interest rate of an asset or a liability may not fluctuate. These instruments are extensions of options on interest rates and provide protection against the first of the three risks described earlier.

The second and third risks mentioned can be managed with swaps. The second type of risk requires a fixed to variable rate swap and the third requires a variable–variable swap.

Caps and Collars

To understand how instruments like caps, floors, and collars work, let us first understand clearly how an interest rate option works. Options on interest rates are slightly different from other options because the option in this case is really not on the underlying asset, which is a debt instrument, but on the cash flow associated with the asset, which is the interest rate.

A call option in this case is an option to obtain a certain interest rate and has a value when the market interest rates have risen above the contracted rate. When the interest rate increases, the price of the underlying asset, the debt instrument, decreases. The holder of a call option is expecting the interest rate to increase and the price of the debt instrument to decrease. Thus, a call option on interest rates is equivalent to a put option on a debt instrument. For interest rate options, we refer to the strike level, not a strike price. A call option at 6 percent means that the holder of the option has a right to obtain funds at a 6 percent interest rate. The amount of funds is fixed by the size of the option contract.

A cap on a variable rate instrument is nothing more than a call option on interest rates at the cap rate. Likewise, a floor is a put option on interest rates at the floor rate. If an investor wants to cap the interest rate on a variable rate at 10 percent, she will buy an interest rate call option with a strike level of 10 percent. Thus, if the market interest rates go above 10 percent, the investor will exercise the option. The writer of the call option will have to pay the investor the difference between the actual interest payments and those that would be required at an interest rate of 10 percent. This payment will compensate the investor for the extra payments she has to make for the loan, thus capping the interest payments on the loan at 10 percent. The cost of this insurance is, of course, the fee for the option. The market for exchange traded interest rate options, however, is very small. Exhibit 1.6 in Chapter 1 showed that these options account for only a small proportion of the total volume of derivatives outstanding. A large majority of interest rate options are offered over–the–counter by banks. A bank will provide a cap or a ceiling on a loan at, say, 10 percent by agreeing with the borrower that if the rates were to rise above 10 percent, the bank will charge only 10 percent on a variable rate loan. The bank agrees to absorb the difference over the capped rate. If the rates fall, the borrower benefits from the drop in interest rates. The bank receives a fixed fee in exchange for this agreement. Caps, floors, and collars can usually be arranged for any principal amount in over–the–counter markets, although amounts in multiples of $5 million are the easiest to arrange. Maturities for these instruments range from one to five years, and reset dates for interest payments can range from one to six months.

It is worthwhile to note that a futures contract on the interest rates would not have had the effect of providing a cap. The futures contract will fix the interest rate at the futures rate, rather than provide a cap. With a futures contract, the borrower will have to pay the contracted rate and will not benefit from a drop in the rates. With a cap or an option, however, the borrower pays the lower of the actual market interest rate or the cap rate, which was 10 percent in our example above.

A floor on interest rates is the opposite of a cap. It fixes the rate below which the interest rate on a variable rate asset cannot fall. A floor can be created by purchasing a put option which gives the holder a right to "lend" funds at the strike level. Let us assume that our investor wants to fix a floor of 4 percent on a floating rate note. She will buy put options at 4 percent for a fee for the principal amount of the notes. If the market interest rate stays above 4 percent, the option will expire worthless. If the rate falls to, say, 3 percent, she will exercise the option. The writer of the option, who in effect has agreed to borrow funds at 4 percent, will have to settle the option by paying the difference of 1 percent (4 percent – 3 percent) to the investor. The investor will thus receive 3 percent—the market rate on the floating rate notes—from the issuer of the notes and 1 percent from the writer of the put option for a total return of 4 percent. This is the level at which she would want to fix the floor on her return.

A collar combines the concepts of a cap and a floor. To understand how a collar works, consider a corporation that has negotiated a two–year $1 million Eurodollar loan at floating interest rates, with the interest rate to be reset every three months at LIBOR + 1/2 percent. The LIBOR is currently at 8.5 percent. The borrower is concerned about the loan becoming too expensive if the interest rates rise more than a little. The manager approaches a bank for the price of a cap at 10 percent, knowing that with a cap at 10 percent, the cost of funds, including the spread over LIBOR, will not rise above 10–1/2 percent. The bank advises the manager that to obtain a cap for the entire duration of the loan, the company will have to buy seven call options each with a strike level of the desired cap. The first option will expire in three months, that is, at the first interest reset date, the second in six months, and so on. The seventh option will expire on the last reset date of the loan, which is 21 months from the date of the loan. The bank quotes for the fee for these options is shown in Exhibit 12.4. The exhibit shows the fee for each of the seven call options at strike prices of 10 and 11 percents as well as for put options at strike prices of 7 and 7.5 percent.

If the company wants to cap the interest rate for the loan at 10 percent, it can purchase the seven options with the strike price of 10 percent. The total price of these seven options will be 147 basis points, or $3,675 (= 147 × $25). Thus for a price of $3,675, or about 0.18375 percent per annum of the value of the loan, the company can ensure that it will never have to pay more than a 10 percent interest rate. Its other choice is to accept a slightly higher cap. At a cap of 11 percent, the total

Exhibit 12.4
Price of Caps, Floors, and a Collar

	Option Prices – in Basis Points*						
	Maturity of Option – in Months						
	3	6	9	12	15	18	21
Call option at 10%	5.3	10.3	12.9	19.9	26.5	34.1	38.1
Call option at 11%	0.4	2.2	3.8	7.6	11.8	16.9	20.3
Put option at 7.5%	0.6	4.7	11.8	15.4	18.6	20.6	24.2
Put option at 7%	0.1	1.3	4.7	7.2	9.5	11.2	13.9

*The price of an interest rate option is quoted in basis points. Thus, for an instrument of $1.0 million of three months duration, a price of 1.0 amounts to a fee of $25 (= $1.0 million × .01 percent × 90/360).

Source: Option prices are from Peter A. Abken, "Interest Rate Caps, Collars and Floors," Federal Reserve Bank of Atlanta, *Economic Review,* November/December 1989, pp. 2–24.

cost of the cap amounts to only $1,575, based on the total fees of 63 basis points. The cost may seem high, but there is a way to reduce this cost. Just as the firm can buy an option contract for a fee, it can also write a put contract at some interest rate and receive fees for that. Exhibit 12.4 shows the cost of put contracts at 7.5 and 7 percents. If the firm were to write a put contract at 7 percent, it would be obliged to accept the interest rate of 7 percent even if the market interest rate were to fall below that. If the rates fall below 7 percent, the holder of the put contract will exercise the contract and will want compensation for the difference between the actual rate and 7 percent. The firm's cost of loan will therefore become 7 percent because it will pay the market rate to the bank and the difference to the holder of the put contract. The firm will, however, receive a fee of $1,200 because the total fee for the seven put options at 7 percent is 48 basis points.

What if the firm were to buy the call option at 10 percent and write the put option at 7 percent? Its net cost of this operation would be $3,675 − $1,200 = $2,475. Its cost of funds would then fluctuate only between 7 and 10 percent, as shown in Exhibit 12.5. The dark line in the exhibit shows the interest rate paid by the firm and the thin continuous line shows the market interest rate. If the market rate rises above 10 percent, it will not have to pay any more that 10 percent; if the rate falls below 7 percent, it will still have to pay 7 percent. In effect, the firm has created a collar such that its interest rate is free to fluctuate only inside that collar.

Exhibit 12.5
Interest Rate Changes and Bond Values

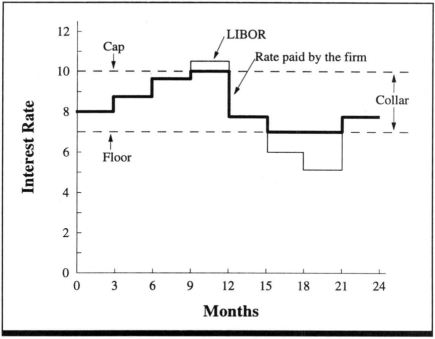

It is possible for the firm to design a number of strategies with different combinations of caps and floors. One strategy would be to develop a zero cost collar. Since the cost of caps decreases as the cap rate is increased, and the revenue of the floor decreases as the floor rate is lowered, the firm can find a cap and a floor rate such that the fee for one side is exactly equal to the fee for the other side. For a cap of 10 percent, for example, the firm could have created a zero cost collar by writing the put at 7.85 percent.[1] At this floor, the revenue from the seven put options is exactly equal to the cost of the seven call options. Thus, the firm can agree to limit its interest rate payments between 7.85 and 10 percent and not have to pay anything for this insurance. Another strategy that the firm can follow is to decide the maximum fee it is willing to pay and then choose the best caps and floors for its interest payments. Exhibit 12.4, for example, shows the premiums for 7 as well as 7.5 percent puts. The cumulative fee income from 7.5 percent puts compensates for more of the fee of the cap than does the fee for 7 percent puts.

A firm that needs to borrow funds for its operations is thus able to control the cost of those funds with the help of caps, floors, and collars. It can choose to limit the upper range of the cost for a fee or lower the fee by combining the limit on the upper range with a limit on the gains on the lower end. Similarly, in response to the risk faced by individual home owners who like variable rate mortgages, many banks now offer a cap on interest rates. Thus, an individual who takes a variable rate mortgage will find her mortgage payments increasing if the rates increase, but only up to a predetermined cap.

Swaps

The second and third risks described for variable rate instruments can be managed with the help of interest rate swaps explained in Chapter 10. It is important, however, to recognize when a swap is more useful than some other obvious technique for managing the risk of a variable rate instrument.

Assume that a bank has decided to raise money through long–term fixed rate bonds to fund its trade credits. As we saw earlier, this amounts to funding variable rate assets with fixed rate liabilities. Why would the bank raise money through fixed rate bonds when its assets are variable rate instruments? Would it not be safer to raise funds through variable rate liabilities so that future changes in interest rates would not create a risky situation for the bank? The answer to these questions lies in two concepts that we have discussed earlier in this book. First, based on the expectations theory of interest rates, the fixed rate would be set in such a way by the market that the total cost of a fixed rate liability over its life is expected to be the same as that of a variable rate one. In other words, current expectations are that short–term interest rates will change in such a way that the cumulative cost of a variable rate liability will be the same as that of a fixed rate liability for the same maturity. Thus, based on expectations, the choice between a fixed rate and a variable rate liability is irrelevant. Second, given the expectations about interest rates, there is probably a small imperfection in the market that makes the fixed rate liability more desirable at the time the bank wants to raise its funds. We will assume that the imperfection is small, but enough to motivate the bank to choose the fixed rate liability.

What happens if there is a shock and all the interest rates change? Assume that all the rates fall. The interest rates have changed in such a way that the fixed rate that the bank has committed to pay is no longer the average of future short–term rates. The new fixed rate is now the average of future short–term rates. The bank cannot hedge itself against the risk once the rates have already changed. But before the shock hits the markets and the rates change, and if the bank managers have anticipated such a shock may come, the bank can hedge the risk with the help of a swap. Before the market interest rates change, the bank can swap the fixed rate payments for a variable rate one as shown below.

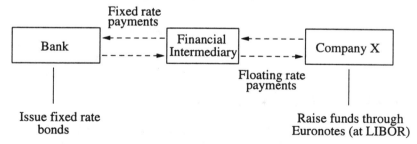

By swapping the fixed rate funds into floating rate funds, the bank eliminates its risk from future shocks that can change the expectations of short–term interest rates. The bank will make the fixed rate coupon payments to the bond holders and floating rate payments to the swap counterparty. It will receive fixed rate payments from the counterparty. Its net obligations, therefore, will be floating rate payments. The bank is able to take advantage of the imperfection in the market that made the fixed rate funds more attractive, and is still able to have floating rate obligations. This method of financing will be preferred to raising funds from the market in the form of a floating rate loan in the first place when the cost of entering the swap is less than the benefit derived from the market imperfection.

The third type of risk identified above in which the investor faces a basis risk that two indexes of market interest rates will not move together can also be managed with the help of a swap. The swap will be similar to the one above, except that in this case one floating rate payment based on, say, LIBOR will be swapped into another floating rate payment based on, say, the Federal funds rate. These swaps are generally known as differential swaps and can even be used to change the currency profile of assets or liabilities. Take the example of an investor who holds a dollar–denominated floating rate note whose interest rate is tied to LIBOR. Suppose that the investor believes that the dollar will depreciate with respect to the deutschemark, but he does not want to speculate in currencies. The investor can swap the dollar–LIBOR based floating rate payments for deutschemark–LIBOR based floating rate payments with the help of the following swap:

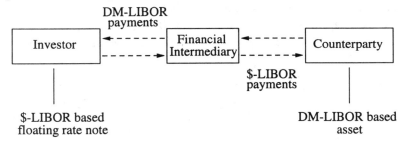

Assets to Be Acquired

In addition to existing assets, an investor may wish to manage the interest rate risk of assets or liabilities that may be acquired in the future. A corporation that plans to borrow funds in one year has to plan now for the type of funds to be borrowed, but it may not be able to fix the cost of these funds until the time the funds are actually raised. If the interest rates increase between planning and implementation, the corporation may find itself in an unpleasant situation. The most suitable way to manage this risk is with the help of interest rate futures or with forward rate agreements, or FRAs.

Recall from Chapter 10 that an interest rate future is a contract to borrow or lend funds at some future date at a predetermined interest rate. Similarly, an FRA fixes the interest rate for an asset of short maturity whose life begins at some point in the future. It is therefore useful for anyone who is either going to receive funds in the future or is planning to borrow funds in the future. Some examples of such investors include the following.

1. A corporation is planning a long–term bond issue in a few months. The finance manager feels that the long–term interest rates at this time are reasonable, but fears that they may go up before the bonds are issued. The firm can lock into the present long–term rates by using the long–term bond futures market.

2. A construction firm bid for a job and it had to include the cost of borrowed funds in the calculation of its price. If the firm believes that the interest rate may increase, and if such an increase could adversely affect profits from the project, it may want to purchase an FRA to lock into the cost of funds it will have to borrow. Insofar as the firm is not sure of receiving the contract, it may want to purchase only an option on an FRA. The option can be exercised if the contract is received and can be sold back if the contract is not received.

3. A manufacturer of Christmas ornaments in Taipei knows that it will be paid for the season's purchases by a store chain in Texas in early October, but the firm's own suppliers expect to be paid only in January. Since the funds are not needed for about three months, they can be deposited during that time. If the manufacturer fears that deposit rates may go down, it can purchase an FRA to lock into the interest rate.

Interest Rate Futures

Assume that a Canadian firm is planning a long–term bond issue in three months and knows that it will have to pay a premium of 100 basis point over the long–term Government of Canada bond yield. If the bonds were issued right now, the firm would have to pay 8.63 percent, including the 100 basis point premium. The opinion within the firm, however, is that the interest rate will increase very shortly and the bond issue is likely to become very expensive. The investment bankers advising on the issue have recommended that the firm hedge its future costs with the help of long–term government bond futures, in this case the Government of Canada Bond Futures (CGB) traded on the Montreal Exchange.

CGBs are traded on the exchange in units of Canadian $100,000 and consist of a 9 percent coupon government bond. There are four delivery months, March, June, September, and December. Government bonds with maturities between 6–1/2 and 10 years and with a specified minimum amount of bonds outstanding in the market can be delivered against the futures contract. A seller of one CGB futures contract promises to deliver a government bond with a face value of C$100,000 and a coupon of 9 percent at the futures price on the day the futures contract is made. Bonds with other coupon rates can be delivered, but then some adjustments have to be made in the prices. We will look at these adjustments shortly. If the interest rates increase between the contract and the delivery date, the bond which is to be delivered loses value and the seller of the futures contract makes a profit because she can now obtain the required bond from the market at a lower price than anticipated. This profit or loss from the futures position is what allows a corporation to hedge future issues of bonds.

Let us now return to the Canadian firm that is planning the bond issue in three months. To protect itself against a possible increase in interest rates, the treasurer of the firm will sell CGB futures. Suppose the size of the planned bond issue is C$10,000,000. Given the nominal size of the futures contract, it would seem that the treasurer should sell 100 contracts (= 10,000,000/100,000). Some adjustments, however, have to be made.

First there is a conversion factor. Since there is no guarantee that a 9 percent coupon bond will be available on the delivery date, the exchange regulations allow government bonds with other coupons to be delivered. Due to the differences between the coupon rates, however, prices have to be adjusted by a factor called the conversion factor. These conversion factors are calculated and published by the exchange for every eligible bond. The conversion factor is "the price per $1 nominal value at which a specific Government of Canada bond will yield 9 percent."[2] Thus, if the coupon of a specific bond that the seller wants to deliver is higher than 9 percent, its conversion factor will be greater than 1.0, and if the coupon is lower than 9 percent, the factor will be less than 1.0.

Second, there is an adjustment due to the volatility of bonds. Since different bonds will have different durations, their prices will change by unequal amounts in response to the same interest rate changes. To account for this, the number of contracts must be modified by an amount given by the following formula:

$$\text{No. Contracts} = \frac{\text{NVBH}}{\text{V-CGB}} \times \text{Conversion Factor}$$

$$\times \frac{\text{MD-NB}}{\text{MD-DB}} \times \frac{\text{PNB}}{\text{PDB}}$$

(12.1)

where:

NVBH	=	nominal value of the bonds that is to be hedged
V–CGB	=	value of one futures contract of CGB
MD–NB	=	modified duration of the bond to be issued
MD–DB	=	modified duration of the bond that is to be delivered
PNB	=	price of the bond to be issued
PDB	=	price of the deliverable bond

In the case of the Canadian firm, we can obtain the information from the Montreal Exchange. Since the bond to be issued is not yet quoted on the market, we will use the information on a Canadian government bond of equal maturity.

The exchange provides us with the following information in March 1993:[3]

Bond	Price	Conversion Factor	Modified Duration
Deliverable Bond (9.75%, June 2001)	111.35	1.0421	5.74%
Bond to be Hedged: (Nearest Canadian Government Bond: 7.25%, June 2003)	97.36	0.8862	7.07%

Substituting the values in Equation 12.1, we get:

$$\text{Number of Contracts} = \frac{10.0}{0.1} \times 1.0421 \times \frac{7.07}{5.74} \times \frac{97.36}{111.35}$$

$$= 122 \text{ contracts}$$

The treasurer will therefore sell 122 contracts on the exchange for three months later, that is, for June maturity. Suppose that the interest rate for long–term bonds increases by 100 basis points by June. The price of the deliverable bond will now drop. Given its modified duration of 5.74, its price should drop by about 5.74 percent. This will be the approximate gain on the futures contract. But now when the treasurer issues the bonds that she was planning to do, she will have to pay a higher interest rate on those bonds. The interest rate will be higher by 100 basis points. The loss on the new bonds to be issued, however, will be offset by the gain on the futures contract. When the markets are moving smoothly, the loss on the new bonds will be exactly equal to the gain on the futures contracts. The two may not equal when there are some shifts in basis and a small basis risk remains in the transaction. The net cost of the bonds will be very close to the one that was available at the time the treasurer entered the hedge.

The futures market in this case was able to help a firm fix the cost of future financing, even though the lenders themselves did not make any such commitment to the borrowing firm.

Forward Rate Agreements

In principle, forward rate agreements, or FRAs, work just like interest rate futures. The main difference between the two is that FRAs are not traded on the exchanges and they provide interest rate protection for one period. The period may be three, six, or 12 months and may begin up to 18 months from the time of the contract.

The period for which the FRA provides protection is called the contract period. Market participants may refer to an FRA as the "three against six," implying that the contract period begins in three months and ends in six. Thus, the Christmas ornament manufacturer in Taipei who will receive extra funds in three months for a period of three months will sell a "three against six" FRA to a bank. Three months later, the manufacturer will receive the funds and will invest them in the market-place. The interest received from the market plus or minus the profit or loss from the FRA will ensure that the net return to the manufacturer is exactly what she had contracted at the time she entered into the FRA. The exact settlement procedures for an FRA were explained in Chapter 10.

Portfolio of Assets

In Chapter 10, we had measured the risk of a portfolio of assets and liabilities using a technique called GAP analysis. GAP analysis separated assets into those that are sensitive to changes in interest rates and those that are not. It then measured the risk as the net of risk–sensitive assets and liabilities.

The management of interest rate risk of a portfolio of financial assets follows the same pattern as for the management of foreign exchange risk. The first approach to managing interest rate risk is to match the profiles of exposed assets and exposed liabilities. The second approach is to change the risk profile of some of the assets or liabilities using swaps or other techniques.

The first approach of matching the risk profiles of assets and liabilities requires that the dollar amount of assets whose value can change in response to a certain interest rate should equal the dollar amount of liabilities whose values will change with the same interest rate.

Thus, if a bank has 10 percent of its assets whose values can change with a three–month interest rate, then to hedge against a short–term interest rate risk, the bank will have to have 10 percent of its liabilities also change in value with the short–term interest rate. If the interest rate goes down, the assets of the bank will earn less, but an equal amount of the bank's liabilities will also cost less with the decline in interest rates.

If the portfolio being managed contains assets and liabilities in many currencies, one of the following two approaches will have to be adopted. The investor could match assets and liabilities in each currency by different maturities. For instance, if 5 percent of the portfolio consists of trade credits denominated in Swiss francs, then 5 percent of the liabilities will also have to be short–term instruments denominated in Swiss francs. This, however, is a very passive approach that may allow many opportunities in the market to be left unexploited. Alternatively, the investor could match the maturities of assets and liabilities in related currencies. We have seen in the previous chapters that many currencies move more or less in unison. When one of these currencies appreciates or depreciates, others follow in the same direction very soon. An investor could manage the interest rate risk by matching the maturity of assets in one currency with the maturity of liabilities in one of the related currencies. The hedging in this case may not be perfect, but would significantly reduce the interest rate risk of unmatched assets and liabilities.

The second approach to managing the interest rate risk of a portfolio is to change the risk profiles of selected assets and liabilities. If the portfolio has more risk sensitive assets than risk sensitive liabilities, the risk sensitivity of some of the assets can be reduced by changing the risk profile of an appropriate quantity of assets. The risk profile can be changed with the help of swaps. If there are too many risk sensitive assets because the portfolio has too many floating rate assets, some of the floating rate assets can be swapped into fixed rate assets. The same objective can be achieved by swapping some of the fixed rate liabilities into floating rate liabilities. The challenge is to identify a few critical interest rates and then identify the assets and liabilities that are sensitive to those interest rates.

Summary

Interest rate risk for assets or liabilities, or for a portfolio of assets or liabilities, depends upon the nature of the asset—whether it is an existing asset or an asset to be acquired—and upon the nature of interest payments—whether they are fixed or variable rate options.

Interest rate risk for assets with fixed payments for investors with known investment horizons can be managed by using the technique of immunization or by using zero coupon bonds. Partial hedges against interest rate changes can be obtained by using caps, floors, and collars, which are merely complex derivatives based on interest rate options. Interest rate risk for assets to be acquired in the future can be managed with the help of swaps, interest rate futures, forward rate agreements, and bond futures.

Notes

1. The calculations are shown by Peter A. Abken, "Interest Rate Caps, Collars, and Floors," Federal Reserve Bank of Atlanta, *Economic Review,* November/December 1989, pp. 2-24.

2. Defined in *Reference Manual, CGB Government of Canada Bond Futures,* Montreal Exchange, 1991, p. 30.

3. Price information is from *Futures and Options News*, March 1993, Montreal Exchange, p. 2.

Part IV

Financial Institutions in International Markets

This part of the book introduces the privately owned financial institutions that make the operations of financial markets possible. The one chapter in this section tries to provide a flavor both for the various types of activities that commercial or investment banks have to manage and for the type of competition that exists between these institutions.

Chapter 13
International Banking

Our focus so far in this book has been on the users of financial markets, individual investors and corporations, who borrow or lend and transfer money in a variety of forms to increase their wealth. These activities would not take place without the institutions that make the functioning of financial markets possible. Although international banks have existed since the Middle Ages, these institutions have acquired greater importance in the last three decades because of the rising importance of international activities in financial markets. In this chapter, we turn our attention to these private institutions—international banks. We want to understand who these institutions are, what they do, and what challenges they may face in the future. Throughout this book we have looked at public or supra–national institutions that play an important role in international financial markets wherever their activities have been most relevant.

Banks engage in four types of international activities. These activities cover commercial banking as well as investment banking services. Distinction between these two types of banking activities, which had traditionally been the hallmark of the banking system in the United States, is not recognized in international markets. Banks are free to provide all types of services in these markets. We will, therefore, discuss four activities of banks without attempting to distinguish as to which type of banks carry out those activities. First, banks provide operational services like foreign payments and collection, trade financing including letters of credit, foreign exchange, international treasury management, correspondent banking, private banking, etc. Second, they intermediate funds between savers and borrowers across national boundaries. Third, banks help their clients manage risk in financial markets by providing derivative products and advice on how to use them. Fourth, banks advise their clients on how to use international financial markets. They help borrowers who want to raise funds in international markets in the form of Euroloans, Eurocommerical paper, Eurobonds, and international equities, and clients who want advice and financing for mergers and acquisitions and leverage buyouts. They also help investors who want to earn the maximum returns on their savings. As part of all these banking activities, banks may issue depository receipts (American or global) and "make" markets and trade in a variety of financial assets, including foreign currencies, equities, bonds, Euronotes, and commercial paper.

We will examine the first three of these activities in some detail. These three international activities, although extensions of what banks do in their domestic markets, have some unique features that clearly distinguish the international from domestic activities. Some aspects of the last activity—advising clients on borrowing in international markets—have already been discussed in Chapters 5-7. In some other aspects of this activity—advising on mergers and acquisitions, for example—the international dimension is very similar to what banks do in their domestic markets and, hence, a separate discussion is not warranted. The third aspect of this activity—advising on privatization—will be discussed later. We begin this chapter with a discussion of who the main international banks are and then discuss the three international activities of the banks.

Main International Banks

We begin our study of international banking by looking at who the big institutions are and which countries provide the environment for the largest institutions to grow. Exhibit 13.1 provides a list of countries that were the headquarters of the 100 largest commercial banks in 1992. Japanese banks dominate the list with six out of the top 10 positions. Two factors have contributed to the rise of these banks in the 1980s. First, the large balance of payments surpluses of the Japanese economy placed large volumes of funds in the hands of these banks. Second, the appreciation of the yen raised the value of the assets and equities of these banks relative to non–Japanese banks. Most of the other countries that are home to the largest banks in the world are the industrialized countries.

Exhibit 13.1
National Origins of Leading Commercial Banks in the World, 1992[*]

Country	Number of Banks from the Country		
	Top 100	Top 50	Top 10
Japan	22	14	6
US	18	7	1
France	8	6	1
Germany	8	3	
Italy	8	1	
UK	7	3	1
Canada	5	2	
Spain	5	2	
Australia	4	1	
China	4	4	
Netherlands	3	2	
Switzerland	3	3	1
Brazil	2	2	
Belgium	1		
Denmark	1		
Iraq	1		

[*]Rankings of banks are based on value of shareholder's equity for the most recent fiscal year of the bank.

Source: "The Euromoney Five Hundred," *Euromoney*, June 1993, pp. 113–134.

The rankings reflect the banks' ability to attract and intermediate capital. Size, however, is only a limited signal of the power of the banks in international markets.

Perhaps a more appropriate signal of who has the power to influence the direction of events in international markets is the opinion of managers

Exhibit 13.2
National Origins of Leading Investment Banks[1]

Country of Origin of the Banking Institution	Performance of banks from the country in the first column		
	Number of Industries Which Gave Top Rankings[2]	Total Number of Rankings Obtained[3]	Total Score for All Rankings[4]
US	10	50	153
Switzerland	2	4	14
Germany	1	3	9
Japan		2	6
UK		2	5
Canada		1	2
France		1	1

[1] For the purpose of this exhibit, leading investment banks are defined as those who were ranked among the top five (three for insurance and airlines) investment banking advisors for 13 industries. The rankings are based upon the opinions of the managers in the top 500 industrial firms around the world. Inclusion in the top five banks is an indication of the quality of the professional staff of the bank. The 13 industries are: aerospace, beverages, building materials, chemicals, computers, forest products, industrial and farm equipment, insurance, mining and crude oil, motor vehicles, pharmaceutical, airlines, and metal products.

[2] This column indicates the number of industries out of 13 for which the banks from the country in the first column were considered to be the best advisor.

[3] This column indicates the total number of times that the banks originating in the country in the first column were included among the top five advisors for a particular industry.

[4] Total score was calculated by awarding 5 points to the first rank, 4 to the second, etc.

Source: "The Best Industry–Specialist Banks," *Euromoney,* June 1993, p. 83.

who use banking services. Although such a measurement is very subjective by nature, Exhibit 13.2 attempts to determine which countries produce the most competitive banks. The exhibit summarizes the opinions of managers in 13 industries as to the best investment banks for their industries. Banks are included in the exhibit if they were ranked among the top five (only three for two of these industries) for one of the 13 industries. It is clear from the exhibit that banks from the United States dominate the picture. A U.S. bank was ranked as the best bank for 10 out of the 13 industries, and U.S. banks obtained 50 out of the 63 mentions for the top five spots. Japanese banks, by contrast, received only a limited mention in this opinion poll.

The two exhibits show that it is very difficult to identify the most powerful banks in international markets. Banks from some countries seem to be very large, but they do not necessarily have the best services for their clients. Their large size seems to be a function of the size and characteristics of their economies, not necessarily a function of their ability to offer competitive services in financial markets. The information in the two exhibits is also an indication of how the international banking industry may be changing and what the future may hold for this industry. It would seem that the ability to offer products and services is becoming more important than managing a large volume of funds.

International Activities of Banks

International Payment Services

One area in which banks provide a unique service for the economy is that of international payments. Since at the present time there is no truly international currency, all economic transactions between entities in different countries require the transfer of funds from one currency to another and from one country to another. Although some currencies such as the U.S. dollar, the deutschemark, the yen, French or Swiss francs, and the pound are used in many transactions, they are almost always a foreign currency to one of the participants. This requires that at least one of the participants in an international transaction go through a foreign exchange transaction. Banks provide at least two services in this process that we should understand: foreign currency trading and trade financing.

Foreign Exchange Trading

As we had seen in Chapter 2, banks form the most important segment of the currency markets known as the interbank market. From their central position in the market, they buy and sell foreign currencies on behalf of their corporate clients and investors, and create a market in selected currencies for other banks, brokers, and dealers. The foreign currency operations of banks, however, often come under criticism because they seem to feed speculation in foreign currencies.

Given the size of this market, foreign exchange trading appears to be a very lucrative activity. Since customers would like to deal with institutions that can offer the most services for the best price, there is fierce competition among banks, brokers, and traders to be known as the leading trader of foreign currencies. This competition and the resulting rivalry has led *Euromoney* magazine to conduct an annual survey of users of the foreign exchange market to ascertain who is seen as the best foreign exchange dealer in the marketplace. The first accompanying box provides a summary of the latest such poll. Citibank, a bank based in New York, has headed these rankings over the last decade, and U.S. banks dominate the top ten list.

The profitability of banks' trading activities are very hard to assess. It is known, however, that trading activities (including those involving developing country debt, commodities, market making in securities and derivatives) are the only source of increasing profits for the banks. In 1991, the leading foreign exchange trader—Citibank—earned $705 million from trading currencies around the world. The second box provides some estimates of the trading revenues for commercial banks in the United States.

▼ ▼ ▼

Euromoney's Foreign Exchange Review, 1992

As it had done in the previous years, *Euromoney* asked about 1,000 "core users" of foreign exchange markets—users whose annual turnover exceeded $500 million—to identify the banks with which they did most of their foreign exchange business. The results of this survey put the New York–based Citibank at the top of the list by a wide margin. Citibank has occupied that position for the last 15 years in Euromoney's polls. The following are the others who made it into the top 10:

Rank in 1992	Rank in 1991	Bank	Country of Bank
1	1	Citibank	USA
2	7	Chemical	USA
3	2	Barclays	U.K.
4=	8	BankAmerica	USA
4=	9	Midland	U.K.
6	3	JP Morgan	USA
7	5	Union Bank of Switzerland	Switzerland
8	4	Natwest	U.K.
9	17	Bankers Trust	USA
10	12	Hongkong Bank	Hong Kong

The secret to success seems to have been a "combination of customer service and liquidity provision." Customers seem to want "good and timely advice, fast quotes, a dealer they like and error–free settlement and confirmation of trade" (page 63). As provider of liquidity, banks have to understand and communicate to their customers the "flow," that is, the general mood and direction, of the market. Citibank maintains market making facilities in a number of cities around the world. Moreover, Citibank also seems to have a strong position in derivatives and exotic currencies, that is, less frequently traded or otherwise called partially blocked currencies. (Some of these currencies were explained in Exhibit 2.7.)

Euromoney, May 1992, pp. 63–78.

▲ ▲ ▲

▼ ▼ ▼
Trading Revenues Increase, But Who Is Complaining?
The banking industry in the United States which had been battered by the third world debt crisis in the early 1980s and by the real estate crisis in the later 1980s, found something to cheer about in the development of derivative products. The large money center U.S. banks have seen their revenues from trading in derivatives and other products increase at double digit rates over the last decade.

Seven large money center banks reported trading revenues of $2.25 for the second quarter of 1993. These revenues have increased steadily over the last decade, as shown in the graph below. These revenues include all trading in foreign currencies, developing country debt instruments developed in the aftermath of the third world debt crisis of 1980s, commodities, securities and derivatives like swaps, and options.

Market observers raise two concerns about these activities. First, banks do not disclose if these activities are being undertaken on behalf of clients or on their own behalf. In other words, investors do not know what the extent of risk being taken by banks is. The second, and related issue, is that banks do not disclose any breakdown of what these trading activities are. Thus, it is not possible to see how a particular bank's performance is changing.

At the present time international bodies as well as U.S. authorities are discussing ways to improve reporting of these activities by banks so that the investors can better assess the risk of banks.

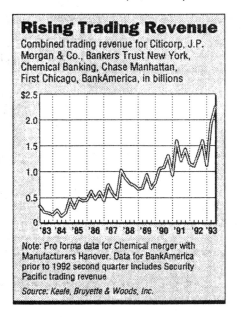

Rising Trading Revenue

Combined trading revenue for Citicorp, J.P. Morgan & Co., Bankers Trust New York, Chemical Banking, Chase Manhattan, First Chicago, BankAmerica, in billions

Note: Pro forma data for Chemical merger with Manufacturers Hanover. Data for BankAmerica prior to 1992 second quarter includes Security Pacific trading revenue

Source: Keefe, Bruyette & Woods, Inc.

Summarized from "Banks Rely More on Trading, But Say Little About It," *The Wall Street Journal*, July 30, 1993, p. B3.

▲ ▲ ▲

Trade Financing

The second unique and very important international service that banks provide is that of financing international trade. It is also one of the oldest international banking activities around.[1] Besides the need to transfer funds from one country to another, the need for trade financing arises for two reasons. First, since the trading parties are located in different countries, they need credit information on the party with whom they plan to trade. Different customs and market structures make it difficult for firms in one country to find out whether their counterparty in another country is worthy of their trust or not. Second, since international commerce takes much longer to complete than domestic commerce, importers and exporters need financing facilities from banks to minimize the inconveniences of dealing with foreign markets.

Banks have developed many instruments and techniques over the centuries to solve these two problems. The most common instrument in international trade is perhaps the letter of credit. With a letter of credit, banks solve the credit risk as well as the financing problem. It is perhaps the most efficient instrument for international trade, especially when importers and exporters are dealing with each other for the first time. In a typical letter of credit transaction, an importer asks its domestic bank to provide a guarantee to the exporter that if the exporter ships the goods described in the import–export contract, the bank will ensure that the payment is made. With the guarantee of a bank, both sides have transferred the credit risk of the transaction to the bank—a third party. The exporter is sure that if he ships the goods, he will receive the payment; the importer is sure that she will not have to pay unless the goods are shipped. Within this general structure, many variations of a letter of credit, or an L/C, have been developed. The L/C may be confirmed by the exporter's bank if the exporter feels that the importer's bank is not really independent of the importer, as might happen if the two had the same owner. The L/C may be revocable or irrevocable, it may be a revolving L/C, and it may have arrangements for one of the banks to lend funds for the transaction for a specified period of time.

Another very important instrument of international trade is a draft and the derivative of a draft, a banker's acceptance bill. A draft is simply an instrument for transfer of payments and appears and functions largely like a check that we use in our daily lives. The main difference is that drafts are usually written or guaranteed by corporations or banks with well- established credits. Unlike checks, drafts can have a maturity date that is some time after the date the draft is available to the beneficiary of the funds. When such a "time" draft has been either written or guaranteed by a firm of known standing in the marketplace, the draft becomes a trade or a banker's acceptance bill. An acceptance bill is a negotiable

Exhibit 13.3
International Assets of Commercial Banks
in BIS Countries*
(all numbers are billions of U.S. dollars)

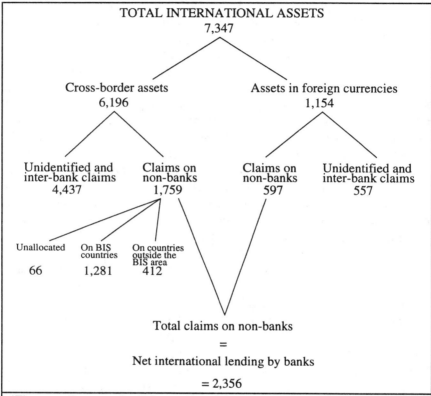

*The reporting area for BIS consists of Austria, Belgium, Canada, Denmark, Finland, France, West Germany, Ireland, Italy, Japan, Luxembourg, the Netherlands, Norway, Spain, Sweden, Switzerland, United Kingdom, the United States, and the Banking centers in the Bahamas, Bahrain, Cayman Islands, Hong Kong, Netherlands Antilles, Singapore, and Panama. Some of the data, however, may exclude some countries due to unavailability of information.

Source: Bank for International Settlements, *International Banking and Financial Market Developments*, May 1993, Table 1, p. 1, Statistical Annex.

instrument and can be easily traded in the open market. A banker's acceptance market can form an important segment of financial markets in some countries.

International Lending

At the end of 1992, commercial banks within the reporting area of the Bank for International Settlements (BIS) had international assets totalling $7,347 billion. Of these, only $2,356 billion could be identified as claims of commercial banks on non–banks and hence could be seen as total international lending by the banks. The remainder is either unidentifiable or represents interbank claims of banks. Since interbank claims represent transactions between banks, they cannot be included in the total amount representing the credit outstanding in the financial system. The amount of $2,356 billion represents the sum of three different types of lending activities of banks in various currencies and from various locations.

Exhibit 13.3 attempts to separate these amounts in as much as it can be done. Two of the three lending activities are shown in that exhibit. The first two activities are classified as cross–border lending. Cross–border assets represent the amount that banks lend to entities that are in a country other than the one in which the lending branch of the bank is located. For instance, this amount could include a loan in, say, Swiss francs by a branch of Citibank (a U.S. bank) located in Frankfurt, Germany, to a furniture company in Milan, Italy. If the same branch, however, had lent deutschemarks to a company in Hamburg, the transaction would come under the category of "assets in foreign countries," the third type of international lending. If the same deutschemark loan had been made by a German bank to a German company, it would not be included in our exhibit because then it would be a local currency loan from a German bank to a German company. Cross–border lending also includes funds lent by a bank in its own currency to a customer in a foreign country. A loan in U.S. dollars by Citibank from its New York branch to the same furniture company in Milan would also be classified as a cross–border lending activity. Exhibit 13.4 provides a schematic of various lending activities.

The amount of $2,356 billion is the sum of all three activities. Of this amount, $1,759 billion is cross–border lending, which represents loans to clients that are foreign to the lending bank. The currency of the

Exhibit 13.4
Schematic of International Loans

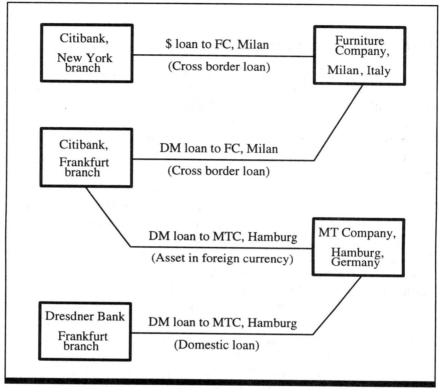

transaction is, for this kind of activity, irrelevant; it may be the domestic currency of the bank or a currency foreign to the bank. It is not possible, from the BIS data alone, to identify the proportions of these loans that banks made from their domestic offices and the proportions that they lent out of their external or Eurocurrency market locations. The difference between the two numbers, $597 billion, represents assets in a foreign country which are denominated in the currency of the country.

It appears from the data that the U.S. dollar is the dominant currency for international banking transactions. Of the total cross–border claims of $6,196 billion, about 46.5 percent are denominated in U.S. dollars. The next highest share of the market is for deutschemarks, which accounts for about 14.5 percent of the assets. About 12.3 percent of the assets are in yens and only about 3.5 percent in ECU.

The reasons why banks undertake these three types of lending, or intermediation, activities are very different. We will attempt to provide a very brief explanation of what motivates banks to undertake each of these activities.

Domestic intermediation, or lending in domestic markets, is carried out by domestic banks, between domestic savers and domestic borrowers. These activities are perhaps the *raison d'etre* of most banks today. In the domestic market, banks exist due to their ability to perform risk, liquidity, or maturity transformation functions or to provide a payments system. Explanation of why an intermediary will be necessary in competitive capital markets is provided by banking theory, coverage of which is beyond our scope at the present time.[2]

In **foreign intermediation**, banks from one country intermediate funds between borrowers and savers in a foreign country using the host country's currency under the host country's regulations. Banks enter a host country to serve customers in that country and compete with domestic banks of that country. A banks' first customers may be subsidiaries of multinational corporations from the home (or a third) country. The main difference between foreign and domestic activity is the nationality of the bank; the transaction remains the same. The distinction is important because we must explain a foreign banks' competitive advantage *vis–a–vis* a host country's domestic banks in undertaking intermediation in the host country. Why would a foreign bank be able to out–compete a host country's own banks, given that foreign banks have a competitive disadvantage of being unfamiliar with the market? Most explanations of "foreign" activities draw heavily upon the theory of foreign direct investment that explains foreign investments by non–financial corporations.[3] The foreign activities of commercial banks are the most easily identified. The total size of this activity depends upon the market share of foreign banks in each domestic market. Penetration of foreign banks in some industrialized countries is shown in Exhibit 13.5.

Cross–border intermediation occurs when the borrower and the saver fall under different jurisdictions and the transaction is carried out under the regulations of the authorities that issue the currency of the

Exhibit 13.5
Foreign Bank Assets in Selected Countries

Host Country	1960	1970	1980	June 1985
Belgium	8.2	22.5	41.5	51.0
Canada	–	–	–	6.3
France	7.2	12.3	15.0	18.2
Germany	0.5	1.4	1.9	2.4
Italy	–	–	0.9	2.4
Japan	–	1.3	3.4	3.6
Luxembourg	8.0	57.8	85.4	85.4
Netherlands	–	–	17.4	23.6
Switzerland	–	10.3	11.1	12.2
UK	6.7	37.5	55.6	62.6
US	–	5.8	8.7	12.0

Source: Bank for International Settlements, *Recent Innovations in International Banking*, Basle, 1986, Table 7.2, p. 152.

transaction. Banks may lend their domestic currency to foreign borrowers or may lend foreign currencies to their domestic, or other, customers. The difference in the residencies of borrowers and savers implies that the currency of the saver is different from the currency of the borrower as long as settlements of private transactions have to be in the currency of one country and there is no "international" currency. The cross–border intermediation is, therefore, accompanied by a currency or transfer risk. Transfer risk arises because intermediation is accompanied by a foreign exchange transaction and there is a possibility that the borrower (or the bank, if it takes the currency risk) may not have sufficient funds in the currency of transaction at the time of repayment even if it has sufficient funds in its own country. Economic theory for cross–border activity must explain the drive behind the intermediation of funds from one country to another and the competitive advantage of banks as intermediaries. Moreover, the theory must be able to explain why banks are able and willing to take foreign exchange risk in some cases. Relatively little attention has been paid in the international banking literature to explain such an intermediation activity.

External intermediation is of recent origin and exists because banks and at least one of the participants can exclude the activity from the regulatory restrictions and costs that control financial transactions in a domestic setting by carrying out the transaction in an "off–shore" or "external" location. We had discussed this activity earlier in Chapter 5. In most cases, both savers and borrowers escape restrictions of regulatory authorities and both sides of the intermediation take place in external markets. In Chapter 5, we also studied the advantages and costs of "external" activities over "domestic" activities.

Challenge of International Lending: Managing a Debt Crisis

One of the unique risks of some cross–border lending is what is termed as "country risk." This is the risk that a country that has borrowed funds from international banks is unable to repay its loans. As we had discussed in Chapter 5, the problem is somewhat different from a loan to a private entity because in most cases, assets of private borrowers are identifiable and can be liquidated by creditors in case of default. It is, however, not possible to imagine how creditors can take over the assets of a country. Moreover, an international court that could have jurisdiction and power to settle disputes between a sovereign country and a private bank does not exist at the present time. Managing defaults by countries requires a very different approach from international banks than that used for private debtors. Indeed, international banks had an opportunity to test their skills at managing such a crisis in the 1980s when a number of developing countries failed to make payments on their international debts.

The crisis, whose roots were laid in the 1970s when the oil–producing countries took control of oil prices, burst into public domain in August 1982. On August 12, Mexico's Finance Minister Silva Herzog called the U.S. Treasury Secretary Donald Regan, the Federal Reserve Chairman Paul Volker, and the IMF Managing Director Jacques de Larosiere, to tell them that Mexico had run out of reserves to pay its creditors. He was seeking help from the institutions these individuals represented and from other central banks. The events of that day sent tremors through the international financial system. Many other countries, most notable among which were Brazil and Argentina, were to follow the

Exhibit 13.6
Exposure of Large U.S. Banks to Selected Countries: End 1982

Bank	Bank's Exposure to the Country as a Percentage of Its Capital					Total Exposure to the 5	Bank's Capital $ mil.
	Argentina	Brazil	Mexico	Venezuela	Chile		
Citibank	18.2	73.5	54.6	18.2	10.0	174.5	5,989
Bank of America	10.2	47.9	52.1	41.7	6.3	158.2	4,799
Chase Manhattan	21.3	56.9	40.0	24.0	11.8	154.0	4,221
Morgan Guaranty	24.4	54.3	34.8	17.5	9.7	140.7	3,107
Manufacturer's Hanover	47.5	77.7	66.7	42.4	28.4	262.8	2,592
Chemical Bank	14.9	52.0	60.0	28.0	14.8	169.7	2,499
Continental Illinois	17.8	22.9	32.4	21.6	12.8	107.5	2,143
Bankers Trust	13.2	46.2	46.2	25.1	10.6	141.2	1,895
First National Chicago	14.5	40.6	50.1	17.4	11.6	134.2	1,725
Security Pacific	10.4	29.1	31.2	4.5	7.4	82.5	1,684
Wells Fargo	8.3	40.7	51.0	20.4	6.2	126.6	1,201
Crocker National	38.1	57.3	51.2	22.8	26.5	196.0	1,151
First Interstate	6.9	43.9	63.0	18.5	3.7	136.0	1,080
Interfirst Dallas	5.1	10.2	30.1	1.3	2.5	49.2	787

Source: William R. Cline, *International Debt and the Stability of the World Economy*, Institute of International Economics, Washington DC, 1983, p. 34.

example of Mexico in declaring their inability to pay their debts in the following weeks.

About 2,000 banks around the world had lent funds to developing countries during the decade from 1973–82. Of these, about 171 U.S. banks were known to have lent a total of about $127 billion to 46 developing and seven Eastern European countries. This exposure represented about 155 percent of the capital of these banks. Further, the large U.S. banks were even more heavily involved in these loans. Indeed, the top nine U.S. banks had lent amounts equal to about 90 percent of their of capital to Mexico and Brazil alone. Exhibit 13.6 shows how deeply some of the banks were committed to the five largest borrowers in Latin America. Banks from other countries, however, were not affected equally by the crises in different borrowing countries. German banks were the most affected during the Polish crisis of 1981 and U.S. banks during the Latin American crisis of 1982. German banks were responsible for about $6 billion of the $16 billion of bank loans that Poland owed in 1981, but for only about 15 percent of bank loans of Latin American countries. U.S. banks, which held only about 7 percent of the bank loans to all Eastern European countries, had a 60 percent share of the loans to Latin American countries. Clearly the failure of the indebted countries to repay their loans was a serious crisis from the point of view of the banks.

After an initial period of panic, commercial banks around the world were able join together and by the end of the decade were able to manage the crisis in such a way that their exposures to these countries were reduced. It is difficult to say that the banks "managed" the crisis; it is perhaps more accurate to say that they muddled through it. The following may be seen as the main elements of the strategies that allowed these banks to survive that crisis.

1. Banks made sure that they presented a common front to the debtors. The banks formed committees to deal with each country such that the solutions were applied equally to all creditors. Any incentive that some banks may have had to make side deals was preempted partly by the banks and their home country governments joining together and partly by cross default clauses in the loan agreements.

2. Banks managed to keep debtors from leaving the rescheduling and negotiation process by offering just enough concessions such that total default of the loan was always seen as less desirable than rescheduling the debt. Although some debtor countries thought about declaring outright default in which they would refuse to repay the loans, enough pressure in the form of threats of future retaliations from the governments kept debtors from taking such an action.

3. Banks were effectively able to obtain full cooperation from their respective governments. They fully exploited their importance for the survival of the economic system and were able to prevent governments from focusing too much on the folly of lending in the first place. In what must be seen as a coup, banks were even able to get the exporters in the United States to lobby the Congress to help both the banks and the debtor countries. The exporters had been convinced that a prevention of the loss of their export markets to debtor countries justified any degree of expenditure of the taxpayers' money.

4. Banks reduced their exposure to the debtors as a proportion of their capital, thus improving their bargaining position, by following three strategies. First, they did not increase the absolute dollar value of loans to these countries. Second, they increased their capital base. Third, banks began to accept that some of these loans would never be repaid and accepted the losses. Writing off the loans meant a one–time loss for the banks, but it freed them from threats of future losses. Along with the increase in the value of their other assets due to inflation, the relative importance of developing country debts decreased over the decade as a result of these actions.

5. Banks relied on financial innovations to reduce the volume of debts. First, the loans were securitized and a secondary market for third world debt was developed such that these loans could be sold off in the marketplace. The trade in Third World debt took place mostly between banks themselves, and by trading their debts, banks were able to balance their portfolios between different countries and reduce their exposures to a few specific countries. Second, a concept of debt–equity swaps was developed wherein the banks were able to

sell their debt to manufacturing corporations that wanted to make investments in these countries. Banks received part of their money, and the manufacturers received the equivalent of the full value of the debt in the local currencies from the governments. The government was able to cancel some its foreign currency debt by making payments in its own currency. Third, banks were able to convert some loans into bonds under what came to be known as the Brady plan. The scheme allowed banks to recognize some losses, but it guaranteed them the remainder of their capital.

6.   A very important part of the renegotiation and rescheduling process was the involvement of the International Monetary Fund in the process. The IMF effectively became the policeman for the bankers by setting up and monitoring adjustment and austerity programs in debtor countries. Beginning in 1983, banks realized that they had neither the capacity nor the credibility to decide the most effective economic policies for debtor countries. Effective economic management would, on the one hand, reduce the need for foreign loans and on the other, make foreign loans available when they could be used effectively. The economic management of the debtor countries could not be trusted since domestic policies had created the mess in the first place. The IMF filled the vacuum by first taking a leading role in devising macroeconomic plans for these countries and then setting up a monitoring mechanism. From the mid–1980s, bank negotiators insisted that debtor countries follow these policies if they expected to receive some relief on their debt problems, and especially if they wanted some new funds.

By the early part of the 1990s, most of the Latin American countries had returned to conditions where their economies began to grow once again. Many of the countries in Africa, however, had not yet managed to turn their economies around.

Risk Management Products

Throughout this book, we have talked about the rapid growth of financial derivatives over the last decade and how investors can use these derivatives to manage risks. We have also mentioned that banks have been in the forefront of developing these derivatives. The banks' involvement in the derivatives market, however, is very uneven. It is estimated that about 90 percent of the derivatives exposures are with seven banks. The extent to which these banks are exposed is shown in Exhibit 13.7. One of these banks, Bankers Trust, has exposure to

Exhibit 13.7
U.S. Banks in Derivatives Markets

Source: "Stop Swapping?" *The Economist*, March 13, 1993, p. 94.

derivatives that is about one–third of its total assets.[4] The following section assesses the implications of providing services for these banks.

Banks offering derivatives to their clients take many risks. The challenge for a bank is, of course, to assess these risks accurately and then make decisions accordingly. Due to the critical role that banks play in our economies, the regulators of financial institutions are legitimately concerned about the consequences of these risks for banks. They therefore want to control the consequences of these risks through bank regulation. In this section we will first study the risks associated with derivatives and then look at two regulatory responses to such risks: the bank capital standards imposed in 1988 and the recommendations of an important non–official but influential group released in 1993. The recommendations, though not official, are important indicators of the banks' intention to regulate themselves. These indicators are especially important given that a joint study of the Federal Reserve, Federal Deposit Insurance Corporation, and the Office of the Comptroller of the Currency reported to the U.S. Congress in March 1993 that new laws regulating derivatives were not needed at that time.

Risks of Derivatives[5]

Derivative products create the same risks for banks that arise from other—more traditional—activities of banks, such as borrowing and lending money and maintaining positions in securities. The main difference is in the management of these risks.

Market risk. Market risk arises from the change in the price of the underlying asset. The market risk of a bank loan, for example, is that the interest rates will increase after the bank has contracted the rate it will charge for a loan. The accompanying box identifies a number of ways in which a portfolio of derivatives can be subject to market risk.

▼ ▼ ▼
Fundamental Risks Associated with a Portfolio of Derivatives

Absolute price or rate (or delta) risk provides an indication of the change in the value of the portfolio for a given change in the price of the underlying asset.

Convexity (or gamma) risk depends upon the extent to which the value of a portfolio is a non–linear function of the price of the underlying asset.

Volatility (or vega) risk refers to the change in the value of a portfolio due to a change in the volatility of the price of the underlying asset. This risk arises for options. The value of a call option, for example, drops with a decline in the volatility.

Time decay (or theta) risk denotes the change in the value of a portfolio with the passage of time. An option, for example, loses value with time.

Basis or correlation risk arises when an asset is hedged with a derivative that is a close approximation of the asset being hedged. In Chapter 11, we had given the example of hedging a Dutch guilder exposure using a deutschemark futures contract. The portfolio consisting of these two assets would have a basis risk.

Discount rate (or rho) risk arises when the risk free rate used to discount all cash flows is changed.

▲ ▲ ▲

Market risk is best managed by using the portfolio approach. The risk of a portfolio can be much smaller than the risk of some individual contracts because a portfolio can contain many positions that offset each other. Thus, a bank that sells a forward rate agreement to one customer may find another that wants to sell one to the bank for the same dates. The bank's risk from interest rate changes will be canceled if its portfolio consists of these two contracts alone. In managing portfolio risk, banks must look to the fundamental market risks described in the accompanying box. Individual derivatives may have some or all of these risks. Futures and forwards, for example, have only the absolute price risk. An option contract, on the other hand, has all the risks described in the box except the basis risk. If a derivative has a complex risk structure, and especially if there is gamma, theta, or vega risk, the portfolio has to be **hedged dynamically**. Dynamic hedging requires that the exposure of an asset or a portfolio be constantly monitored and the hedge adjusted, if necessary, as market prices or expectations change in any way.

Credit risk.   Credit risk arises from the possibility that the counterparty in a contract may default on its obligations. If that were to happen, the bank would have to replace the cash flow of the defaulted party with a new contract. In the case of some derivatives, a swap for example, the counterparty pays as well as receives cash flows. The bank, of course, will not make any payments to the defaulted party. The risk of such a derivative is only the amount by which the cash outflow of the defaulted party may have increased in value over its cash inflow. In other cases, the amount of risk may be the amount given by the price risk. A party that defaults on its obligation to fulfill an option contract causes the holder of the option to lose the amount by which the value of the option may have increased from the time of the contract.

A bank trying to estimate the credit risk of individual derivatives must ask what the loss would be if the counterparty to a derivative were to default. While calculating the credit risk of a portfolio, the bank can take advantage of **netting** by offsetting risks of different derivatives held by the same counterparty. It is quite likely that a defaulting counterparty holds many derivatives contracts whose cash flows offset each other.

Banks manage their credit risk by assessing the credit risks of their clients before they enter into derivatives contracts and by placing limits on how much derivatives exposure each client will be allowed to have with each bank. These limits and risks are constantly monitored in response to changing market conditions.

Operational risk.   Operational risk arises from the possibility that human or systems errors or failures can cause a loss for the bank. This type of risk may arise due to an error in entering information or failure of a manager to be fully aware of what the other people in the department are doing. Although such a risk exists for all activities that banks undertake, it is more serious in the case of derivatives because these are very complex and sometimes very intricate instruments. This type of risk is managed by having a good control system with checks and balances built into it. It requires a well–informed senior management team that fully understands the risks of the operations. Documentation of policies and procedures as well as a clear understanding and documentation of the limits of clients and traders help manage this risk. Finally, banks should require independent audits and checks, both internal or external.

Legal risk.   Legal risk arises from problems of enforceability of derivatives contracts. Derivatives contracts may be more difficult to enforce than other contracts because these instruments are new and existing laws may not have covered the possibilities that can arise with derivatives. A serious issue with some derivatives has been **ultra virus**, in which a counterparty is found to lack the capacity or the authority to enter into derivatives contracts. In the 1980s, the local government in London entered into swap contracts to lower its cost of funding. When the swaps became expensive, the local authorities found themselves unable to make the required payments. The House of Lords in the United Kingdom ruled that the local authorities had lacked the capacity to enter into the contracts and, hence, were not liable for the payments. The loss to the swap dealers from these defaults supposedly accounts for about half of all the losses on swap activities since the inception of swaps.[6]

Recommendations of the Group of Thirty

In July 1993 the Group of Thirty, which is a non–official but influential body based in Washington, DC, released its report on the management of risk associated with derivatives. The study group consisted mainly of bankers and, hence, the recommendations must be seen as the banks' announcing the extent of self–regulation they will follow. The main recommendations regarding how banks should manage risks from their derivatives activities are summarized in Exhibit 13.8.

The main theme of these recommendations is for banks to first understand how risks of different derivatives contracts may cancel or enhance each other and then to take a portfolio approach for managing the risk. Each derivatives contract can be broken down into a stream of cash flows, and the risk of each cash flow can be assessed. Many of these cash flow streams will cancel each other. The study also provided a description of different types of risks that we summarized earlier.

Bank Capital Standards

Banks differ from manufacturing corporations in terms of the importance of stockholders' equity. Banks usually maintain a very small proportion of their assets in the form of equity; most of the funds they lend are raised either through deposits or other long–term liabilities. The small proportion of equity acts as a double–edged sword: it allows banks to

Exhibit 13.8
Recommendations for Management of Derivatives

Global Derivatives Study Group was created by the Group of Thirty to study, among other things, the practices followed by banks, referred to in the report as dealers, for managing the risk arising from their dealings in the derivative products. The Study Group issued 20 recommendations for how the banks should manage these activities. The following is reproduced from the Group's report in July 1993.

"... the recommendations suggest that each dealer and end–user of derivatives should:

- *Determine at the highest level* of policy and decision making the scope of its involvement in derivatives activities and policies to be applied.

- *Value derivatives positions at market*, at least for risk management purposes.

- *Quantify its market risk* under adverse market conditions against limits, perform stress simulations, and forecast cash investing and funding needs.

- *Assess the credit risk* arising from derivatives activities based on frequent measures of current and potential exposure credit limits.

- *Reduce credit risk by broadening* the use of multi–product master agreements with close–out netting provisions, and by working with other participants to ensure legal enforceability of derivatives transactions within and across jurisdictions.

- *Establish market and credit risk management functions* with clear authorities, independent of the dealing function.

- *Authorize only professionals* with the requisite skills and experience to transact and mange risks, as well as to process, report, control, and audit derivatives activities.

- *Establish management information systems* sophisticated enough to measure, manage, and report the risks of derivatives activities in a timely and precise manner.

- *Voluntarily adopt accounting and disclosure practices* for international harmonization and greater transparency, pending the arrival of international standards."

In addition, the group recommended that "(T)o help strengthen the financial infrastructure for derivatives activities, officials are called upon to:

- *Recognize close–put netting arrangements* and amend the Basle Accord to reflect their benefits in bank capital regulation.

- *Work with market participants to remove legal and regulatory uncertainties* regarding derivatives.

- *Amend tax regulations* that disadvantage the use of derivatives.

- *Provide comprehensive and consistent guidance* on accounting and reporting of derivatives and other financial instruments."

Source: Global Derivatives Study Group, *Derivatives: Practices and Principles*, The Group of Thirty, Washington DC, July 1993, pp. 7–8.

accumulate a large volume of assets based on a small equity, but at the same time it does not allow for a large margin of safety if some of the loans turn sour. We saw in the discussion of the third world debt crisis of the 1980s that the bargaining power of banks was affected by the fact that large proportions of their equity were lent to single borrowers and that the banks could not afford to let any of these countries be declared as a defaulted country. Banks, however, have incentives to maintain less equity than might be prudent just to acquire a competitive edge over other banks in the market. Due to the importance of equity, bank regulators impose requirements on their banks for maintaining a minimum amount of equity in relation to their assets.

National requirements for equity, however, can create inequality between banks from different countries. A bank from a country with low equity requirements will have to maintain less equity and, hence, will have a competitive advantage over banks from a country with more prudent regulators. To make the playing field level for all banks, bank regulators from major industrialized countries, under the auspices of the Bank for International Settlements in Basle, agreed to common equity or bank capital standards in 1988. These "Basle capital standards" took effect in 1992 and were supposed to be implemented by the end of that year.

The standards require banks to have equity capital, called "tier I" or "core" capital, equal to at least 4 percent of "risk–weighted" assets. Banks are required to have total capital, called tier I and tier II or "supplemental" capital, equal to at least 8 percent of these assets. Total capital is defined as common equity plus long–term funds raised as bonds, preferred stocks, and some reserves. The total value of risk–weighted assets is calculated by assigning different weights to different categories of assets. Corporate debt is given a weight of 100 percent, private mortgages of 50 percent, government agencies' mortgages of 20 percent, and treasury bills from OECD countries carry no weight at all. Thus, a bank having $1.0 million of each of these assets will have risk–weighted assets of 1.0 + 0.5 or $1.5 million. What is important is that for the first time, off–balance sheet items like contracts for derivatives also have to be included in the asset calculations. Thus, different derivatives contracts are assigned different weights.

Privatization

One of the changes that accompanied the opening up of Eastern European economies in the late 1980s was a general belief that the government was not really fit to run productive economic enterprises. This is not the place to discuss whether this belief caused the political changes that came about or if it was merely a consequence of those changes. The important point for our discussion is that a phenomenon called **privatization** that had begun in the United Kingdom in the 1970s became one of the corner stones of the economic reforms of former communist countries. Banks around the world became intimately involved with this process as advisors and financiers to potential buyers of state–owned enterprises.

Privatization refers here to the process by which the ownership and management of state–owned enterprises is transferred to individuals and private corporations. In terms of the underlying economic philosophy, this amounts to converting centrally planned economic activities to market-based economies. In centrally planned economies, and in some non-centrally planned economies, governments determine what some enterprises will produce and where and at what prices they will sell their output. These governments control the activities of state–owned enterprises through administrative mechanisms; they have the authority to appoint the management team, and the ability to legislate activities of these enterprises.

Although the purpose of such control is to mitigate the effects of market imperfections, governments, like most other large organizations, succumb to corruption and incompetence. In countries where either the public or the governments have realized that private ownership of economic enterprises with market–determined prices is a more suitable form of economic organization, they have embarked upon programs to transfer the control of state–owned enterprises to private entities. According to the estimate of one bank, about $120 billion will be raised in the form of equity for the purposes of privatization between 1993 and 1995. Of this, "$55 billion will be raised in Europe, $30 billion in Latin America, $20 billion in Asia, and the remainder in the rest of the world."[7]

Exhibit 13.9 provides a summary of the countries that are going through privatization programs. As this list indicates, the idea is not limited to centrally planned countries. Within these countries, a variety

Exhibit 13.9
Privatization Activities Around the World

Country	1988 ($ million)	1992 No. of Transactions	1992 Amount ($ million)
Industrialized Countries	36,773		24,398
Australia	1,450	2	1,297
Austria	569	1	162
Canada	1,962	5	1,217
Finland	303		
France	360	2	1,353
Germany	1,333		16,350
Italy	840	2	1,566
Japan	22,800		
Netherlands		1	100
New Zealand	1,846	5	1,052
Spain	810		
Sweden		1	263
UK	4,500	5	1,038
Developing Countries	2,457		23,260
Argentina		8	6,200
Brazil	250	8	2,150
Chile	170		
China		9	543
Czechoslovakia		7	361
Greece		2	648
Hungary			845
India			261
Israel	95	1	235
Jamaica	19	1	23
Kenya	8		
Malaysia		5	1,619
Mexico	1,915	10	6,374
Pakistan		1	82
Peru		1	120
Philippines		1	368
Poland			309
Portugal		4	1,023
Puerto Rico		1	142
Russia		1	50
Taiwan		2	1,363
Thailand		1	240
Turkey		2	304
Global Total	39,230		47,658

Source: Gerd Schwartz and Paulo Silva Lopes, "Privatization: Expectations, Trade-offs, and Results," *Finance and Development*, June 1993, pp. 14-17.

Exhibit 13.10
Privatization Program in Argentina

Company	Industry	Comments	Advisors	Date
Petroquimica Bahia Blanca	Defense			1993
Transener	Electricity	65% to be sold for $200 million.		1993
Hidronor Companies (Alicura, Cerros, Colorado, and Chocon)	Hydro generating			1993
Hidronor Companies (Oichi Picun and Peidra del Aguila)	Hydro generating		Banco General de Negocios, First Boston, Klienwort Benson	
Yaciemiento Petroliferos Fiscales	Oil	IPO of 35%, expected price of $17-20 a share for 100 million to 126 million shares - raising $2.5 billion.		
Yaciemiento Carboniferos Fiscales	Coal	20 year concession to be offered.		
Caja Nacional de Ahorro y Seguros	Banking	60% sale postponed.		
Encotel	Postal assets	Government retaining 51%.	Coopers and Lybrand, Ecolatina Asesors Economicos	
Caja de Ahorro Postal	Banking			
National Mint	Misc.			
National Grain Board	Misc.			
Elma	Shipping	Reorganization plan announced.		

Source: "Who's Selling What: The Global Picture," *Euromoney*, July 1993, pp. 114-125.

International Banking   395

of firms belonging to many industries are being privatized. Exhibit 13.10 provides an example of the scope of privatization in one country—Argentina. As the exhibit shows, firms in a number of diverse industries are being turned over to private investors. Over the last decade, banks have participated heavily in these activities as advisors.

Future of International Banking

What will banks have to do or offer to be successful in the future? It is a very difficult question to answer, especially in view of the rapid changes that have marked this industry in the last decade. We can at least look at what distinguishes the top–rated banks from ordinary banks at the present time.

Exhibit 13.11 summarizes some of the characteristics of banks that have been rated as the top banks in some areas of their activities. The ratings are based upon formal and informal opinions of market participants. The ratings included in the exhibit are divided into three banking activities: raising funds for clients and intermediation of funds, derivative products, and trading services. Banks have been rated on a product or service according to whatever was considered important for that service, and the characteristics of the best–rated bank are summarized in the exhibit.

Each area and product seems to have different requirements and banks within each activity seem to have different characteristics. It may be possible, however, to discern some patterns. Size seems to be important for the first of these three activities. All the banks rated as the leading bank for raising funds or for intermediation have been recognized for their size. Banks seem to get recognition for their ability to come up with new solutions in the areas of derivatives and trading. In all these three areas, however, a common thread is the focus on the client. In most of the activities or products, top–rated banks have been identified as being focused on the client's needs. As in non–financial, that is, manufacturing sectors, globalization of markets has made customer satisfaction the most important characteristic for the success of a business enterprise. It would seem that the financial services industry, which in the past has been able to exploit its unique position in the economic system to place customers in the back seat, may have to change also.

Exhibit 13.11
Requirements for Excellence in
International Banking

Activity	Leading Bank	Characteristics
To Raise and Intermediate Funds		
Best bank	Deutsche Bank (Germany)	Growing presence in international markets; prudent management.
Raising capital	Goldman Sachs (USA)	Strength in a number of markets; satisfaction of clients in equity issues.
Managing Eurobonds	Goldman Sachs (USA)	Focus on the client; distribution and trading.
Floating rate notes	Kidder Peabody (USA)	Large investor base; innovative; secondary market trading.
Euro–commercial paper	Lehman Brothers (USA)	Global distribution system.
Syndicated loans	JP Morgan (USA)	Ability to arrange large deals.
Privatization	Goldman Sachs (USA)	Distribution capabilities; experience with privatization; inventive with equity deals.
Derivatives		
Swaps	JP Morgan (USA)	Size of portfolio; bank's credit rating; client focus.
Derivatives	Bankers Trust (USA)	Innovativeness and creativity; pioneer in many products; ability to help client manage the risk they want to take; integrated services.
Futures & options	LIFFE (London)	Ability to handle crisis situations; rapid growth; ability to take risk; innovations.
Trading and other services		
Foreign exchange	Citicorp (USA)	Size of the operations; foreign exchange dealing all over the world; market making in 140 currencies; combination of product and client focus.
Trading Eurobonds	Deutsche Bank (Germany)	Integrated sales and trading with a client focus; making market in many currencies; primary dealership in many locations.
Global custody	Chase Manhattan (USA)	Problem solving in complex areas; sophisticated and differentiated services for clients.
Mergers & acquisitions	CS First Boston (USA & Switzerland)	Global reach; early start; ability to manage complex deals.

Source: "Euromoney Awards for Excellence, 1993" *Euromoney*, July 1993, pp. 91–133.

▼ ▼ ▼
What Kind of an Animal Can Do International Banking Without Being a Bank?

As if the banks were not having enough problems competing with each other? Now they have to deal with firms that don't even call themselves a bank! According to observers, GE Capital, which started about 60 years ago as the financing arm of consumer durable goods manufacturer General Electric, is a formidable competitor in the financial services industry. The company continues to finance the sales of its parent company in the areas of consumer durables, power plants, and jet engines. GE capital, moreover, is not alone in offering competition to the banks; all auto manufacturers in the United States have similar financing subsidiaries, and an oil company even makes market in foreign currencies rather than pay commission to banks for foreign exchange services.

None of the other captured finance companies, as they are known in the financial markets, have the assets or the market position of GE Capital. Its assets have reached $150 billion, and its profits after taxes amounted to $1.5 billion in 1992, about the same as for the most profitable commercial bank in the United States—Bank of America—and representing a return on equity of 19.2 percent. It boasts a credit rating of AAA, matched only by one commercial bank—JP Morgan.

GE Capital offers competition to banks not only for financing business of its parent's sales, but also for the sales of other manufacturers. It is among the largest firms in the areas of life reinsurance, insurance of mortgages, and issuance of private label credit cards. In addition, it has an investment banking subsidiary, a corporate financing arm, and a number of leasing activities. Although the company is active in international markets, those operations account for only about 10 percent of its profits. Given its strength derived from its management style and the breadth of the business, it is expected that the firm will continue to offer competition to the banks in the years to come.

Summarized from "Raw Money, Rich Pickings," *The Economist*, July 24, 1993, p. 73–74.

▲ ▲ ▲

The change in the focus seems to have come with an increased competition in this industry. The competition has increased not only because of the opening of capital markets which has allowed firms from one country to enter other countries, but also because of innovations and diffusion of technology which has allowed new forms of business to compete with existing banks. As shown in the accompanying box, even nonbanks can now offer a formidable challenge to banks in their own back yard. Banks from smaller economies that are able to follow well–planned strategies may also offer competition to established banks in the industrialized world. The accompanying story of a bank from Hong Kong shows how a good strategy helps capture new markets. As computing and telecommunications technologies develop and diffuse more, users of banking services will find that they can come up with innovative ways to satisfy their demands for funds and financial services. Banks will have to constantly update their skills and knowledge to remain competitive in global markets.

▼ ▼ ▼

Turning International Markets into Cash

Faced with the oncoming transfer of Hongkong to the Chinese government in 1997, Hongkong & Shanghai Bank has decided that it will not take the risk of being controlled by the ambitions of its future regulators. It has decided to build a global financial empire, but directed from the U.K., not Hongkong, where it started its operations 128 years ago.

From its headquarters in London, the bank has loosely controlled subsidiaries in 66 countries. These subsidiaries include commercial banking units, investment banking units, and leasing and insurance operations.

The strength of the bank is its well–capitalized subsidiaries that can take risks. Managers are given freedom to make their own decisions— which may lead to big losses in some cases. The group lent $758 million in loans to Olympia and York, of which $450 million has been declared as a loss. The bank, however, wants to establish a presence in the main markets around the world with well–funded and autonomous subsidiaries.

Perhaps the strategy of the bank is working. The bank is expected to earn $2.5 billion this year after having earned $1.85 billion in 1992. Next year's profits are expected to jump to a record $3.0 billion.

Summarized from "Hongkong & Shanghai Turns Bold Ambitions into Cash in the Till," *The Wall Street Journal*, July 27, 1993, pp. A1, A12.

▲ ▲ ▲

Summary

International markets present banks with some tasks and opportunities that do not exist in domestic markets. Banks provide the critical function of trade financing and international payments without which international commerce would be very difficult. Banks also extend some of their domestic activities to international markets. These activities include lending to clients across borders and helping them raise funds in international markets. The most important activity, however, would seem to be the banks' involvement in financial derivatives. It is difficult to over–emphasize the risks and opportunities created by these innovations. Banks cannot afford to ignore these products as their clients are becoming very knowledgeable about them. Offering these products, however, entails new risks for banks that they may not have faced in the past. The requirements of international markets will force banks to understand these products and the risks involved with them.

Notes

1. For some history, see Samuel Hayes and Philip Hubbard, *Investment Banking*, Harvard Business School, 1990, Chapter 1.

2. For a review of the banking theory, see Anthony M. Santomero, "Modeling the Banking Firm," *Journal of Money, Credit, and Banking*, 16:4, November 1984, Part 2.

3. See, for example, Robert Z. Aliber, "International Banking: A Survey," *Journal of Money, Credit, and Banking,* 16, November 1984, Part 2, pp. 661-95; Arvind K. Jain, "International Lending Patterns of U.S. Commercial Banks," *Journal of International Business Studies*, 17, Fall 1986, pp. 73-88; or Adrian E. Tschoegl, "International Retail Banking as a Strategy: An Assessment," *Journal of International Business Studies,* 19, 1987, pp. 67–88.

4. Bankers Trust is an unusual bank in that it does not like to keep loans on its books for very long. In mid–1992, loans accounted for only 19 percent of Bankers' assets, compared to an average of 57

percent for nine of its competitors. "Trading accounts," or derivatives, were 42 percent of its assets against an average of 6 percent for the other nine. Bankers, however, is supposed to have the best risk management system in the industry. See Carol J. Loomis, "A Whole New Way to Run a Bank," *Fortune*, September 7, 1992, pp. 76–85.

5. The section on risks of derivatives is summarized from Global Derivatives Study Group, *Derivatives: Practices and Principles*, The Group of Thirty, Washington, DC, July 1993, pp. 43–54.

6. Global Derivatives Study Group, *Derivatives: Practices and Principles*, The Group of Thirty, Washington, DC, July 1993, p. 51.

7. "Who's Selling What: The Global Picture," *Euromoney*, July 1993, pp. 114–125.

Bibliography

Bank for International Settlements, *Recent Innovations in International Banking*, Report of the Study Group established by the Central Banks of the Group of Ten Countries, Basle, Switzerland, 1986.

Campbell, T. S. and W. A. Kracaw, *Financial Risk Management*, New York: HarperCollins, 1993.

Copeland, L. S., *Exchange Rates and International Finance*, Boston: Addison–Wesley, 1989.

de Carmoy, H., *Global Banking Strategy: Financial Markets and Industrial Decay*, Cambridge, MA: Basil Blackwell, 1990.

Dufey, G. and I. Giddy, *International Money Market*, 2e, Englewood Cliffs, NJ: Prentice Hall, 1994.

Edwards, F. R. and H. T. Patrick, (eds.), *Regulating International Financial Markets: Issues and Policies*, Boston: Kluwer Academic Press, 1992.

Enderwick, P., *Multinational Service Firms*, London: Routledge, 1989.

Fabozzi, F. J. and F. Modigliani, *Capital Markets: Institutions and Instruments*, Englewood Cliffs, NJ: Prentice Hall, 1992.

Geanuracos, J. and B. Millar, *The Power of Financial Innovation*, New York: Business International Corporation, 1991.

Grabbe, J. O., *International Financial Markets*, 2e, New York: Elsevier, 1991.

Hayes, S. L., III and P. M. Hubbard, *Investment Banking: A Tale of Three Cities*, Boston: Harvard Business School, 1990.

Jones, G., *Banks as Multinationals*, London: Routledge, 1990.

Kapner, K. R. and J. F. Marshall, *The Swaps Handbook*, New York: Institute of Finance, 1990.

Kester, W. C. and T. A. Luehrman, *Case Problems in International Finance*, New York: McGraw–Hill, 1993.

Krugman, P. R., *Currencies and Crises*, Cambridge: MIT Press, 1992.

Meerschwam, D. M., *Breaking Financial Boundaries: Global Capital, National Deregulation and Financial Services Firms*, Boston: Harvard Business School, 1991.

Pauly, L. W., *Opening Financial Markets: Banking Politics on the Pacific Rim*, Ithaca, NY: Cornell University Press, 1988.

Sarver, E., *The Eurocurrency Market Handbook*, New York: Institute of Finance, 1988.

Smith, C. W., Jr., C. W. Smithson, and D. S. Wilford, *Managing Financial Risk*, New York: HarperCollins, 1990.

Solnik, B., *International Investments*, 2e, Boston: Addison–Wesley, 1991.

Stein, J. L., *International Financial Markets: Integration, Efficiency and Expectations*, Cambridge, MA: Basil Blackwell, 1991.

Tucker, A. L., J. Madura, and T. C. Chiang, *International Financial Markets*, St. Paul: West Publishing Company, 1991.

Volker, P. and T. Gyohten, *Changing Fortunes: The World's Money and the Threat to American Leadership*, New York: Times Books, 1992.

Walter, I. and R. C. Smith, *Investment Banking in Europe*, Cambridge, MA: Basil Blackwell, 1990.

Index

A

Absolute purchasing power parity, 69-72
African Development Bank, 207
American Depository Receipts, 168, 178, 194-96
American options, 282, 284
Appreciation, 36
Arbitrage, 58
    interest, 59-60
Asian Development Bank, 207
Ask quotation, 28
Assets
    choice between risky, 213
    contingent, 327-29
    with fixed cash flow, 344-45
    foreign, of pension funds, 203-4
    optimal allocation of, in international markets, 230-35
    portfolio of, 306, 361-62
        risks of, 332-40
    risks of acquired, 326-32
    risks of existing, 309-26
    with variable cash flows, 347-49
At-the-money option, 284

B

Balance of payments, 14
    accounts for, 13
    analysis of, 15
    crisis in, 44
    and exchange rates, 77-82
    and international capital flows, 13-16

I

K

Kennedy, John F., and imposition of interest equivalization tax, 156
Kyrgyzstan, foreign exchange in, 42

L

Lead banks, 135-36
Lead manager, 158, 159
    in bought deal, 161
Legal risk, 389-90
Letter of credit, 375
Liquidity preference theory, 102
London InterBank Offer Rate (LIBOR), 130

M

Maastricht Treaty, 46-47
Macaulay duration, 254, 346
Macroeconomics
    and exchange rates, 57-58, 82-83
    and external debt capacity, 138-39
    and international financial markets, 13-16
Malaysia, financial market in, 7
Margin, 270
Market risk, 387, 388
Marshall plan, 125
Members of the selling group, 158
Merrill Lynch, 201
Mexico
    Eurodollar debt of, 126
    exchange rates in, 75-76
Modified duration, 254
Monetary policy, influence on exchange rates, 79
Money market hedge, full hedge with, 322-24
Morgan, J. P., 201
Mutual funds, 178, 192-94

N

O

P

Risky assets, choice between, 213
Rolling spot contract, 269

S

Secondary markets, 166
    for Eurobonds, 159-60
Securities and Exchange Commission and American Depository
    Receipts, 194
Securities Trading Automatic Quotation System, 191
Segmentation theory, 103-4
Sharp performance measure (SHP), 232-34
Simple interest rate, 104
Singapore International Monetary Exchange (SIMEX), 37
South Korea, financial market in, 7
Special Drawing Rights (SDRs), 50-51, 55
Speculation, and exchange rates, 83-87
Spot contract, 33
Spot rates
    difference between forward rates and, 34
    movements in, over time, 35-36
Spot-rolling contract, 304-5
Spread, 136
Stanley, Morgan, 201
State Administration of Exchange Control (SAEC), in China, 40-41
Stock exchange, classification of, into developed markets and
    emerging markets, 179-89
Stock index futures, 275
Stock market indexes, major, 175
Stock markets
    around the world, 179-94
    capitalizations, 18, 21
        of the U.S., 179
    innovative bonds in managing volatility in, 154-55
    performance of world, 190
    shares of, 178
Strike price, 284
Structural Adjustment Facility (SAF), 52
Student Loan Marketing Association (SLMA; Sallie Mae), 113
Supplemental capital, 391
Surplus units, 4

U.S. interest rates, and convergence of Japanese interest rates, 109-12
U.S. multinationals, issuance of international equities by, 201

V

Variable rate instrument, cap on, 350
Vega risk, 388
Volatility
of exchange rates, 244-50
of interest rates, 250
Volatility risk, 388
Voluntary Credit Restraint Program, 125-26, 147*n*

W

Wall Street Journal
issuance of World Stock Index by, 176
quotations of exchange rates in, 38-40
Warburg, S. G., 161
World Bank, 206
and International Finance Corporation, 189
issuance of global bonds by, 162
sources of funds, 206
World Bank Group, 206-7
Writer of an option, 282, 284

Y

Yield of zero-coupon bond, 106
Yield to maturity, 104-6

Z

Zero cost collar, 354
Zero-coupon bond, 346
yield of, 106